Levinas *and the* Torah

SUNY SERIES IN CONTEMPORARY JEWISH THOUGHT
RICHARD A. COHEN, EDITOR

Levinas *and the* Torah

A Phenomenological Approach

RICHARD I. SUGARMAN

Cover image: Gustave Dore, Jacob Keeping Laban's Flock (1866).

Published by State University of New York Press, Albany

For information, contact State University of New York Press, Albany, NY
www.sunypress.edu

Library of Congress Cataloging-in-Publication Data

Names: Sugarman, Richard Ira, author.
Title: Levinas and the Torah : a phenomenological approach / Richard I. Sugarman.
Description: Albany : State University of New York, [2019] | Series: Suny series in contemporary Jewish thought | Includes bibliographical references and index.
Identifiers: LCCN 2018043671 | ISBN 9781438475738 (hardcover : alk. paper) | ISBN 9781438475745 (e-book) | ISBN 9781438475721 (pbk.: alk. paper)
Subjects: LCSH: Bible. Pentateuch—Criticism, interpretation, etc. | Levinas, Emmanuel. | Jewish philosophy—20th century.
Classification: LCC BS1225.52 .S84 2019 | DDC 222/.106092—dc23 LC record available at https://lccn.loc.gov/2018043671

10 9 8 7 6 5 4 3 2 1

The knowledge of God comes to us like a commandment, like a Mitzvah. To know God is to know what must be done.

—Emmanuel Levinas, *Difficult Freedom*

My spiritual needs are the other person's material needs.

—Attributed to Rabbi Israel Salanter

For the absolute hermeneutic of a verse, the entirety of the book is necessary! Now, in the entirety of the book there is always the priority of the other in relation to me. This is the Biblical contribution in its entirety.

—Emmanuel Levinas, *Of God Who Comes to Mind*

Our relation to time finds itself in crisis. It seems indispensable that we Westerners situate ourselves in the perspective of time bearing a promise.

—Emmanuel Levinas, *Is It Righteous to Be*

For Rabbi Rafoel Zalman Levine Ha Cohen (1900–1992)

Master Teacher, Talmud Chacham, Friend ZT"L

Contents

DEUTERONOMY: DEVARIM

Preface

My first encounter with the thought of Emmanuel Levinas occurred as a result of a paper that I had written for a graduate seminar at Yale in 1966 on Heidegger's *Being and Time.* The course was taught by John Wild who served as my mentor in philosophy and phenomenology for the better part of eight years. My essay was on "The Death of the Self and the Death of the Other in Heidegger and Tolstoy." Even though he appreciated my critique of Heidegger's devaluing of the death of the other and thought that it was suggestive, he did not think that I had demonstrated my case. I had argued that because Heidegger did not take the death of the other with any kind of moral seriousness, it was more difficult for him to take the lives of others as ultimate as well. I concluded that this gap of being with others (*Mitsein*) was at the heart of Heidegger's acquiescence to the Nazis and their murderous regime.

Later that year, Wild returned from a trip to Europe. I had not seen or spoken with him in some time. Still, as was so like him, he began with our last conversation and picked it up as though there had been no interval. He said, "There is a man in Paris who agrees with you about the death of the other in Heidegger. However, he proves it." When I asked him who this person was, he said prophetically, "You do not know his name and most Americans do not. But by the end of the twentieth century, every philosopher will." That person was Emmanuel Levinas.

In the spring of 1969, Wild's last year of teaching at Yale, he proposed to teach a seminar on Levinas's first major work, *Totality and Infinity.* The English edition, for which Wild had written an important and laudatory introduction, would not be available from Duquesne University Press until the semester was over. Wild changed the subject of the course to "A Phenomenology of the Other." For a significant period of time he taught from a manuscript that I later learned he had begun to write on *Totality and Infinity.* Later still, I found this manuscript among Wild's posthumous papers and edited the text with annotations and published it for the first time under the title "Speaking Philosophy," in an issue of *Phenomenological Inquiry,* volume 24, October 2000.

Wild spent his last year teaching, in 1969–1970, at the University of Florida and, not unexpectedly, he taught *Totality and Infinity* to what he believed was a receptive group of students. Wild argued that Levinas represented an original and positive turn in continental philosophy. After Sartre and Merleau-Ponty, Wild found Levinas to be the first thinker to confront Heidegger's fundamental ontology and to successfully challenge his notion that Being took precedence over the basic patterns and elements of the human life-world. By arguing that ethics was first philosophy and that the fundamental human task was responsibility for others, Levinas changed the trajectory of contemporary phenomenology. Wild was especially impressed with Levinas's contesting of Heidegger's notion that anxiety over one's own death was the only authentic human mood. Therefore, Wild felt that the major criticisms of contemporary phenomenology were on their way to being successfully addressed by Levinas. Phenomenology did not imply ethical relativism, a sealed anthropocentrism, and above all, there was a generative character to life and philosophy that had escaped Heidegger's vision. Nihilism was on its way to being overcome.

In the fall of 1973, while serving as a visiting professor at Johns Hopkins University, Levinas agreed to meet with me, undoubtedly because of my relationship with John Wild, who had passed away in October of 1972. Two colleagues, Helen Stephenson and Robert Anderson, came with me. Stephenson served at that time at the University of Vermont as an assistant to Professor Raul Hilberg, who inaugurated the academic study of the Holocaust in America. Robert Anderson was at the time an instructor in philosophy at St. John's College in Annapolis, Maryland. Wild had already told me about Levinas's very recognizable sense of humility. What he had not told me about was Levinas's keen sense of humor and irony. He and Madame Levinas were very gracious in welcoming us to their apartment at Johns Hopkins where we spent most of the afternoon in conversation. Much of the conversation was understandably in French. When we asked Levinas if we could tape record our session with him, he said to us in English, "Have you not heard of Watergate?" Levinas, when asked about the connection between his philosophical and his Jewish writings, responded that his Jewish writings were to be understood as his "avocation." My impression, then, was that Levinas wished to be recognized as a philosopher and not as a theologian. Still, I did not completely accept his claim that his Jewish writings, on which he was most focused at the time, were to be read as something separate or of lesser value. As his career reached the kind of success that Wild had predicted, the distance between his religious writings and his philosophical work grew smaller to the point where the continuities between both approaches seemed to form a single vision. In our book *Levinas and the Torah*, we draw on both the philosophical and Jewish writings of Emmanuel Levinas.

During our visit, Levinas asked us a surprising question in the midst of our speaking with him about Heidegger. He asked us if Madame Toni Cassirer was still living and if so, where was she living? He asked because he had promised himself that if he ever came to America, he would seek her out personally to ask her pardon for the humiliation he thought he had visited upon her late husband, Ernst Cassirer during a student performance that followed the famous debate at Davos between Cassirer and Heidegger in 1929. In the academic year 1928–1929, Levinas, having finished his doctoral studies at the University of Strasbourg in France, had traveled to Freiburg in Germany where he took Husserl's last course at the University of Freiburg and Heidegger's first course there. Levinas was invited to the debate by Heidegger. He told us how, for the student parody that followed the debate, he had been assigned the role of Cassirer, who had, as Levinas put it, "an abundance of white hair that looked a little like an ice cream cone." Levinas powdered his own curly hair, which was abundant at the time, and proceeded to impersonate Cassirer. By his own lights, Levinas was not only successful at this impersonation but rather much too successful. He looked up and said to us, "Who could have imagined in 1929 what would take place in 1933 in Freiburg when Heidegger gave his infamous speech as rector of the university enthusiastically endorsing Hitler and the Nazis." His regret was accompanied by a remorse that was all too genuine. Later we found out that Toni Cassirer had died in New Haven in 1961.

Levinas added with insistence that no serious philosopher in the twentieth century could bypass the work of Heidegger. He considered *Being and Time* one of the five greatest works of philosophy. He especially appreciated Heidegger's analysis of care, anxiety, and being-toward-death and above all the dynamic existence of the human being whose coming to terms with himself could be described in a disciplined manner. Then he said something in a way that I shall never forget. He looked directly at me and said, "No friend of ours." The meaning was not lost. Heidegger would not be exculpated from his Nazism by Levinas.[1]

---

1 Our colleague Professor Robert J. Anderson had been a student of Richard Kroner, the well-known Kant scholar who had taught in Germany prior to 1933. Anderson remembered the usually mild-mannered Kroner displaying the front page of the *New York Time Review of Books* that featured Heidegger in 1962. Kroner then added, in a thunderous voice, "They forgot something: this man is a monster. How can they forget that?"

The last part of our conversation turned toward the Bible and Levinas's Jewish writings. We asked Levinas what he thought was the best way to approach the Hebrew Bible. He said, "Learn to read it in its original language. Then you will understand how little you understand." He asked if we might be interested in translating his Jewish writings into English. Helen Stephenson and I succeeded in translating only one chapter of his book *Difficult Freedom: An Essay on Judaism*. We translated "To Love the Torah More than God," and it was published in *Judaism* in spring 1979 with a short commentary by me. I hasten to add that in our visit with Levinas we were treated with graciousness and warmth by both Levinas and his wife, Raissa, who was an established concert pianist. It had been an eventful encounter for us.

A BRIEF BIOGRAPHY OF EMMANUEL LEVINAS

The life and thought of Emmanuel Levinas was intimately intertwined with the history of the twentieth century. Levinas was born on January 12, 1906, or December 30, 1905, according to the calendar used in the Russian Empire. He preferred the former date. He was raised in a traditional Jewish family in the town of Kovno (now Kausnas), Lithuania, a town which was for centuries a citadel of Talmudic learning until it was utterly annihilated by the Nazis. His first historical memories were of the death of Tolstoy and his family's exile from Kovno and relocation to Kharkov, Ukraine, in 1916 for the duration of World War I. From afar he witnessed, in quick succession, the fall of the czar and the rise of the Soviet Union, and the February and October Revolutions respectively, before returning to Kovno to complete his studies in a Jewish gymnasium in 1920.

The Jewish education of Emmanuel Levinas was unusual and marked by interruptions. As a child in Kovno, he was tutored in Hebrew so that he was able to read the Jewish Bible with fluency in its original language. It was only much later in his life that he began to study in earnest the oral, or rabbinic, commentary tradition. His immediate family of origin was religiously traditional, unlike his paternal grandparents, who were strictly Orthodox. From his family and his schooling, Levinas absorbed the classics of Russian literature as well as the works of Shakespeare.

In 1923, he traveled to Strasbourg in France, the western European university nearest to Kovno. There he began the study of philosophy and proved to be a prodigy, completing his Doctorat d'Université in six years. In 1928–1929 he went for two semesters to the University of Freiburg in Germany to study with Edmund Husserl, the founder of phenomenology, and with Husserl's disciple and later critic, Martin Heidegger. Husserl retired from the University of Freiburg in 1928 and was later excluded from the university along with all Jewish faculty, while Heidegger was made the rector in 1933.

In 1934, Levinas authored an article on the menace of Nazism, which he called "On the Philosophy of Hitlerism" and later regretted using the exalted term "philosophy." In 1935, he was for the first time exposed to the original and compelling Jewish philosophical thought of Franz Rosenzweig. Rosenzweig had opened a new vein of inquiry with the publication of his work *The Star of Redemption*. In that work, Rosenzweig argued that Being was not all encompassing. In fact, there were three realms that stood independently in relation to one another: God, man, and world. For Rosenzweig, these three categories corresponded to creation, revelation, and redemption. More precisely, neither of these three realms were reducible to one another, or to being qua being. Rosenzweig's breakup of Hegel's notion of Totality would remain a primary influence on Levinas. Levinas later notes, in his book *Totality and Infinity*, that the book "owes more than it can say to the discoveries of Franz Rosenzweig" (TI 1969, 28).

Levinas writes on many levels. From among his vast philosophic *oeuvre* there are only a few texts devoted exclusively to the Holocaust. However, from the mid-thirties until his last works in the early nineties, the haunting challenge presented by the phenomenon of the *Shoah* is always a shadow on the margins of his philosophical and Talmudic reflections. Writing his own one-paragraph autobiography, in "Signature," appended to *Difficult Freedom*, Levinas states, regarding his life and works, "It is dominated by the presentiment and memory of the Nazi horror" (DF 1990, 291).

Despite his early academic recognition and philosophical accomplishments, Levinas remained an outsider in France, his adopted homeland. As an outsider, he was perhaps better able to view with skepticism as well as engagement trends in current continental philosophy, and to assume a keen awareness of the position of a Jew in Europe in the thirties and forties, during and after World War II. Naturalized as a French citizen in 1930, Levinas served as a teacher at the Alliance Israélite Universelle in Paris, and he later became director of *École Normale Israelite Orientale* (ENIO) in Paris from 1930 to 1961.[2]

---

2 The ENIO was a Jewish secondary school established by the Alliance to train teachers in Jewish thought and conduct in those countries bordering the Mediterranean that had been influenced by French culture.

In 1932, he married Raissa Levy, a childhood friend whom he met again in Paris. They had two children, Simone Hansel born 1936, later a physician, and after the war, Michael Levinas born in 1949, a composer and concert pianist.

After the war, Levinas made the acquaintance through a close friend of an itinerant Talmudic master known as Mordechai Shoshanni. Levinas was so taken with the vibrancy, originality, and importance of Shoshanni's approach to the Talmud, that his central preoccupation for four years, 1947–1951, consisted of studying under him.[3] For Levinas, there was an almost seamless movement between his philosophic and Jewish preoccupations in learning. It is clear that in Shoshanni he had found someone who, while not of the philosophic sophistication of Levinas, believed that philosophy, done properly, was the genuine companion of Talmudic inquiry, a view they shared with Maimonides and his contemporary American Talmudist, Rabbi Joseph Soloveitchik.

Levinas was known throughout his life and career as a generous and modest person. Professor Anna Krakowski and her husband, Bernard, were neighbors and friends of the Levinas family in Paris after the war. Bernard Krakowsi had been a friend and colleague of Levinas at the ENIO. His wife, Professor Anna Krakowski, later taught French studies and Tanakh at Yeshiva University in New York. Her husband had been consumed with the writing of a book entitled *Mediations Sur Le Pentateuch*. Shortly after her husband's passing, Professor Krakowski called Levinas. He came over to her home and after a time asked Madame Krakowski what the fate of her late husband's book would be since according to her, it was not finished. Levinas said, "It is so close to being finished, it should be regarded as virtually finished; if you permit me, I will help you edit the matters that need attention and see to it that it is published by a suitable press." I saw this book myself in Monsey, New York, when I paid a condolence call to Professor Krakowski's two sons upon the occasion of her own passing in the beginning of 1998. The sons confirmed that Levinas made himself invisible in the book, which was credited only to her husband. According to Madame Krakowski, this was the only condition that Levinas had attached to his contribution in completing the book.

---

3   However, the relationship with Shoshanni was not without domestic repercussions. Shoshanni was infamous for his dubious hygienic habits as well as his mysterious comings and goings. Levinas had been introduced to Shoshanni by a close friend, Dr. Henri Nerson. At that time, just after World War II, each apartment was quite small, though it had one extra room. For approximately four years, Shoshanni alternated between staying at the Levinas home or that of the Nersons.

Levinas continued his philosophic writing as principal of the ENIO. Most of his students were unaware of this activity. They tended to think of him as their teacher, the principal, and a kind but serious disciplinarian. It was not until 1961, with the publication of *Totalité et Infini*, that Levinas began to receive wider recognition as an original and important philosopher.

Levinas approached the Talmud from a phenomenological point of view, although against the background of traditional commentaries. His presentations at the colloquia of French Jewish Intellectuals, beginning in 1957, sponsored by The World Jewish Congress, were subsequently revised and published. Through these lectures and writings Levinas shows how the Talmud remains the most faithful guide to addressing the condition of the Jewish people in the context of humanity today.

Levinas received his Dotorat d'Etat when his magisterial work *Totalité et Infini* was accepted in lieu of other requirements. He began his university teaching career quite late, first at Poitiers, then at Nanterre, and finally, in Paris at the Sorbonne. Later, in 1973, he published *Otherwise than Being: Beyond Essence*. From a biographical standpoint, the dual dedications that Levinas makes to this book are worthy of the reader's attention. Translated into English by Alphonso Lingis, the dedications read: "To the memory of those who were closest among the six million assassinated by the National Socialists, and of the millions on millions of all confessions and all nations, victims of the same hatred of the other man, the same anti-Semitism."

Below this dedication, Levinas writes an epitaph in Hebrew on the frontispiece of *Otherwise than Being*. Here I translate it: "In memory of my father, my teacher, R' Yechiel, son of Avraham HaLevi; my mother, my teacher Devorah, daughter of R' Moshe; my brother, Dov, son of R' Yechiel HaLevi; and Aminadav, son of R' Yechiel HaLevi; my father-in-law, R' Shmuel, son of R' Gershon HaLevi; and my mother-in-law, Malka, daughter of R' Chaim. Their souls should be bound up in the bundle of life."[4]

All of the relatives named were murdered during the Shoah by the Nazis and their Lithuanian accomplices. Taken together, these two dedications awaken a clearer understanding of the lasting burden Levinas endured from the Holocaust, a point of tangency between the ethical-political destruction and his personal, religious identification.

---

4   The "R'" most likely represents the term "Reb," signifying the word "Mr.," a common, though formal designation.

This dual legacy of Levinas found its way into both his Talmudic reflections and his philosophical expositions. His Talmudic essays and reflections on Jewish life and thought are marked by a concern with the well-being of the people, Israel, and with the demands placed upon them by their new position in history after the Holocaust and with the establishment of the modern nation-state of Israel. In his Talmudic essays, he devotes himself to such topics as forgiveness, the rights of workers, the vital distinction between holiness that must pass through morality, and sacrality that can remain utterly indifferent to moral claims and ethical expectations.

From a philosophical point of view, Levinas appears to be advocating what we might call a "transcending humanism." For him, the central work of philosophy is to explore the various ways in which the human subject is constituted and challenged by commodification. The themes that the reader encounters in his Talmudic reflections are approached in a philosophical manner without appeals to theological authority. The fruits and accomplishments of the scientific enlightenment are not to be ignored. Like Rabbi J.B. Soloveitchik, he affirms that such achievements have shown the capacity to create a greater sense of human dignity. However, the globalizing humanism of the enlightenment increases the emphasis on a culture of immanence and loses sight of the yearning for transcendence. What first transcends the subjectivity of the subject is the other who is not reducible to my intentional grasp.

It is not a matter of reconciling the Bible and philosophy. As we shall see, the primary purpose of Levinas is to show how human decency can arise to awareness in the vicissitudes of the drama of everyday existence. He played a crucial role in responding to and shedding light on these times. Toward the end of his life, Levinas gave a number of important interviews in which he remained extremely alert to distilling his views without distorting their complexity. The reader is encouraged to take a look at a compilation of a number of these interviews in the book *Is It Righteous to Be,* edited by Professor Jill Robbins.

LEVINAS'S PHILOSOPHICAL WORKS

Levinas began the study of philosophy with a special emphasis on the approach of phenomenology. He explains his reason for this in an interview in *Ethics and Infinity: Conversations with Philippe Nemo* (translated by Richard A. Cohen, Duquesne, 1995). There Levinas is asked, "How does one begin thinking?" He answers: "It probably begins through traumatisms or gropings to which one does not even know how to give a verbal form: a separation, a violent scene, a sudden consciousness of the monotony of time" (EI 1985, 21). In 1930, Levinas published *Husserl's Theory of Intuition*, thereby helping to introduce phenomenology from Germany into France.[5] In 1931, Levinas further solidified his reputation for introducing phenomenology into France by co-translating from German into French Husserl's *Cartesian Meditations*. It was not until 1973 that this book on Husserl was translated into English by Northwestern University Press' Series in Continental Philosophy, whose founder and general editor was John Wild.

Even at this early stage, Levinas recognized that there were axiological or value dimensions to Husserl's thinking that remained to be explored. In 1935, he published his first original work, a monograph entitled *De L'évasion*. This work anticipates many of the prominent philosophical themes in Levinas's mature work. In it, he describes the human person as caught within his own self, besieged by the phenomena of fatigue, hunger, insomnia, and cut off like a "windowless monad" from others. The person is carried along by what he calls the *il y a* or the "there is," that is experienced as impersonal in terms of duration, monotony, and sheer existence. The *il y a* has neither direction nor purpose. He compares it frequently to the neutrality of the insomnia of the young child who hears murmuring outside of the door of his room that disturbs him but that he does not at all understand. This passive static version of the self wants to go out of himself, out of this suffocating sense of being. Only when he recognizes the claims and demands of others does he begin to appear to himself as a human subject possessed of subjective awareness and now burdened with a responsibility that will make him also a moral subject. In *De l'évasion*, the subject is always oscillating between his sense of being an ethically elected subject and falling back into his egological sense of self. Levinas does not present these descriptions as "ontological" but elaborates on these themes during the course of his long philosophical career.

Three of his books appeared in quick succession just after World War II: *Existence and Existents* (1947), *Time and the Other* (1947), and *Discovering Existence with Husserl and Heidegger* (1949). Levinas argues that the existent takes precedence over the category of existence. He is unconcerned with the charge that his new philosophic outlook is merely contingent or ontic. In fact, it becomes progressively clear that for Levinas the concrete phenomena of everyday ontic life, disparaged by Heidegger, is recognized by Levinas as the

---

5   It was Levinas's book on Husserl that Simone de Beauvoir recommended to Sartre and which introduced him to phenomenology. Levinas, with his usual modesty, remarked that Sartre found the approach sound but said he could do it much better (Ed. Richard Cohen, *Face to Face with Levinas,* State University of New York Press, 1986, 17).

primary domain of philosophical inquiry. As he says in *Time and the Other*: "Traditional philosophy, and Bergson and Heidegger too, remained within the conception of time taken to be either purely exterior to the subject or entirely contained in the subject" (TO 1987, 90). Time does not arise for Levinas in a solitary subject. As he says, "The dialectic of time is the very dialectic of the relationship of the other, that is, a dialogue which in turn has to be studied in terms other than those of the dialectic of the solitary subject" (Ibid., 93). This means that for Levinas, what he refers to now as "diachrony," time that originates from the other, makes time and alterity virtually synonymous.

Here we also see a searching critique of Plato that reaches all the way back to Parmenides: there is a multiplicity and transcendence in the verb to "exist"—"a transcendence that is lacking in even the boldest existentialist analysis" (Ibid., 91). It is no longer necessary for multiplicity to be subordinated to the one. Moreover, the role of the feminine does not have to be thought of in categories of passivity and activity and reduced to matter (cf. TO 1987, 93). Levinas then makes the first and only claim of originality for his own thinking. He reminds the reader that the phenomenon of fecundity has not previously been presented in a philosophic manner. Levinas presents paternity, and later maternity, fecundity, femininity, and love as generative patterns of human existence that are open to phenomenological investigation. It is no longer sufficient to merely explore the solitude of the human self in relation to his own finitude. For example, the child is a paradox that formal logic cannot explain. The child both is and is not the continuation of the parent. In this way, the child represents an irreducible existent not completely reducible to genetics or biology with an identity to claim as his or her own.

In the preface to his first independent philosophic work, *Existence and Existents*, published just after World War II, Levinas notes: "These studies, begun before the war, were continued and written down for the most part in captivity" (EE 2001, 15). This book challenges Heidegger's notion that ontology is fundamental and to be regarded as first philosophy. It is very clear at this moment in his philosophic itinerary that he is moving in a direction different from that of Heidegger:

"If in the beginning our considerations as far as the concept of ontology and the relation of man to being are concerned are inspired in high measure by Martin Heidegger, Heidegger's philosophy, they are (nevertheless) dominated by the deeply felt need to relinquish the climate of this philosophy" (EE 2001, 91). Levinas has now become more aware of the untoward consequences of Heidegger's insensibility toward the death of the other and therefore to the time and life of the other. He is also more aware of a totalitarian egocentrism inscribed in the arbitrariness of the resoluteness of the will. He prepares the reader for a new path in philosophy following upon the destruction of European Jewry. It is here that the phenomenon of the other in relation to time emerges with particular clarity and urgency.

In 1951 Levinas authors an article called *Is Ontology Fundamental?* By this time, he explicitly rejects Heidegger's formulation and can be seen to be on his way to arguing his original thesis that ethics, not ontology, is "first philosophy." The notion of ethics as primary is found in its first full exploration in Levinas's majestic work *Totality and Infinity: An Essay on Exteriority* published in French in 1961. This book represents an important new direction for phenomenology. It explores the relation of time and alterity, the other and the self, justice and freedom, as well as ethics and ontology. Levinas argues that morality is irreducible, despite war, which would vitiate its application. He begins his phenomenological exposition with a critique of the notion of "totality," setting it in opposition to infinity from which our sense of otherness rather than sameness derives. Furthermore, Levinas elevates the position of hospitality and welcome to a place of such prominence that it becomes easier to imagine how philosophy can proceed anew through time: "The welcoming of the other is ... the consciousness of my own injustice—the shame that freedom feels for itself. If philosophy consists in knowing critically, that is, in seeking a foundation for its freedom, in justifying it, it begins with conscience, to which the other is presented as the Other, and where the movement is inverted" (TI 1969, 86). Ethics arises as communication through discourse that defies the subject-object model. A much-contested position of Levinas argues that there is an asymmetry between the other and the self. He argues, not for reasons of altruism but of phenomenological evidence, that the other is always situated beyond the self. In fact, philosophic explanation begins in the self's ongoing response to the questioning glance of the expression of the other person. This is the common origin of both responsibility and rationality. As Levinas says, "The relation with the child—that is the relation with the other that is not a power, but fecundity—establishes a relationship with the absolute future, or infinite time" (Ibid., 268). Here we can see Levinas moving visibly in the direction of a phenomenology of transcendence where transcendence "is time and goes to the Other" (Ibid., 269). *Totality and Infinity* opens a new way of speaking philosophy with the conclusion that "morality is not a branch of philosophy but first philosophy" (TI 1969, 301).

Levinas's most original exploration is found in his most difficult and radical book, *Otherwise than Being or Beyond Essence*. This book does not dispute the tenets of *Totality and Infinity* but rather attempts to move beyond them. Levinas here makes an important distinction between the language of the *saying* (le dire) and the language of the *said* (le dit). He recognizes the importance of ordered propositional discourse and the declarative mode of speech—the said. Still more, he argues that such discourse depends on the prior assumption of responsibility, where the speaker signifies what he or she is intending in the saying. *Otherwise than Being* is an unprecedented, valiant exercise in discussing subjectivity in the language of the saying. New categories and new linguistic terms are needed to permit the expression of new phenomena.

Levinas acknowledges that *Otherwise than Being* was built around chapter 4 entitled "Substitution": "This chapter was the germ of the present work" (OBBE 1991, 193). "Substitution," as he calls it, is the "very subjectivity of a subject, interruption of the irreversible identity of essence" (Ibid., 9). The phenomenon of substitution thus inverts the ontological "essence" of being. By this Levinas means it inverts the *conatus essendi*. I am not only responsible for my own reasoning in relation to the other, but I am responsible for his or her responsibility toward the third party as well. This extravagant sense of responsibility can be challenged but in its simplest form we might say that the other knows before I speak whether I am for him. According to Levinas, no escape from this responsibility is possible. "Proximity" is another category associated with my responsibility for the other. Proximity is the category of moral nearness where I am vulnerable to "an obsession with the responsibility I have for others," even to the extent of permitting myself to become, in Levinas's language, a hostage to the other. Levinas is showing how the subject can move in a direction of the "each for each and all for all." This is opposed to the model of political philosophy established at the beginning of modernity by Machiavelli and Hobbes where the each against each and all against all appears as the first premise of all practical thinking.

THE IMPORTANCE OF LEVINAS TO CONTEMPORARY JEWISH THOUGHT

The intellectual heritage of the West derives from the encounter between Greek philosophic thought and that which is, as Levinas puts it, "Otherwise than Greek, the Bible." Levinas shows himself fully conversant with each of these traditions. However, he does not set out to conciliate or reconcile them even in the sense of Maimonides's *Guide for the Perplexed*. Levinas admired the rigor of the thought of Maimonides and valued him as a philosophic thinker who believed that "truth is universal like reason: its rule and moral institutions ... its genius is a practical one" (DF 1990, 274). At the same time, Levinas departs from the neo-Aristotelianism of Maimonides in search of a new metaphysics that derives from a *rationality of transcendence.*

He is not concerned with the great debate that flourished from medieval times to the present between faith and reason. Nor is he interested in reducing the study of Scripture to philosophy in its pre-established Greek forms and categories. His approach is both more traditional and more innovative. It is traditional in the sense that he believes that the Jewish relation to God is found primarily in the devotion to and learning of texts, as well as in the interpersonal sphere. For this reason, he does not directly ask the question: "Where was God?" during the time of the Shoah. He does ask the question of what became of *morality* during this terrible time. It is not for Levinas primarily a theological question; rather it is a philosophical question. Can we really do without morality? As he puts it in the opening of *Totality and Infinity*: "Is not the question whether (or not) we are duped by morality?" The brazen and unprecedented injustice of the Nazis does not overturn the aspirations for a just world. How one acts in relation to Jewish law during this time of greatest distress has already been prescribed by the tradition in general; as he states, "To know God is to know what must be done" (DF 1990, 17). This also implies what cannot be done.

What is most innovative in Levinas's reflections on Jewish texts and themes is the way he recovers the intentions of the *saying* before they settle into the language of the *said*. What this discloses perhaps above all else are the folds of diachronic time, where time emerges in my response to the exigent demands of the other. These phenomena include but are not limited to the human face, the irreducibility of the human subject: the meaning of generativity, fecundity, hospitality, the priority of the other over the self, hope, and promise. In this way, he explains how my sense of responsibility arises even prior to my sense of my own freedom thus tearing me out of a primal egocentrism. In *Levinas and the Torah: A Phenomenological Approach,* we show the thinking of Levinas in conversation at times with other great Jewish thinkers and commentators, a conversation which is infinite but not uni-directional. As Adam Z. Newton has shown in his important book *The Fence and the Neighbor*, Levinas can be meaningfully placed in conversation with the Rav, Rabbi J.B. Soloveitchik (1903–1993). Like the Rav, Levinas always searches for reasons, lessons, and meanings that seem to be on the verge of being expressed in various places.

From a phenomenological point of view, Levinas coaxes into explicit awareness a world of yearnings, intentions, aspirations, regrets, and hopes that have not yet risen to the conceptual level. In this way, Levinas regards the unfolding of meaning through expression as always provisional and in need of elaboration and sometimes, correction. At times, he deals with questions that remain to be articulated. In this way, he does not ignore the great thinkers in the history of philosophy but rather augments their categories and themes from biblical and rabbinic sources. The forced translation of the Pentateuch into Greek by command of Ptolemy was the first and, for a while, the only translation the rabbis permitted to be written and used. Levinas takes the phenomenon of Greek a step beyond the matter of language. By this he appears to signify the residue of Greek philosophic thought that still permeates Western culture. Levinas is fond of saying: "The Septuagint is not yet complete" (*Face to Face with Levinas*, ed. Cohen 1986, 19). I believe that Levinas is attempting to do more than he says while translating the "Bible into Greek." He is involved in a two-way translation that draws upon the saying or intention of the biblical text that alters our representation and understanding of Greek philosophy, where the self always comes first.

Otherwise, Levinas could be misunderstood as something that he is distinctly not—another Hellenizing Jewish philosopher who merely places the Bible before the court of established philosophical reason. For him in fact, his rendering of "to love your neighbor as yourself," helps us to begin again the task of transforming philosophy (the love of wisdom) into holiness (the wisdom of love). By placing the other before the self, Levinas makes explicit a theme that appears in Hebraic texts and is original to them as far as Greek philosophy is concerned.

"Responding" to the other is how all philosophy and right conduct begin. It is for this reason that he argues that justice is prior to freedom (cf. TI 1969, 45). Levinas describes the spontaneity of the ego as at the core of the Western notion of freedom. In this way, the freedom for the ethical subject both begins and goes toward my sense of responsibility to and for the other. For Levinas, as we shall see, the time of the other as measured by urgency is more precious than all eternity. What follows is a new direction in Western thought where the Hebraic tradition provides essential preconceptual contents, and some of the new categories of Greek and Western philosophy.

No less than Spinoza, Levinas was concerned with demythologizing Jewish thought from myth, irrationality, dogma, and superstition. However, unlike Spinoza, who did so much to naturalize Judaism in particular and religion in general, Levinas proceeded in an entirely different direction. Levinas recognized that Spinoza, a kindred spirit to Descartes, believed at rock bottom that valid philosophic conclusions could only be based on the findings of the natural sciences or geometrical exposition. For Spinoza, like Descartes, time on the mathematical-scientific model was reducible to space. This meant that the promise of time beginning with its phases past, present, and future, was no longer meaningful in a strict philosophic sense. Banished also from Spinoza's system was any sense of transcendence and along with it the idea of the Infinite. For Spinoza, only objective measurement counted. In order for something to be measureable, it had to be extended. If this extension could not be demonstrated, then the phenomenon was of no philosophic consequence. Therefore, the phenomenon of meaning and the human aspiration for meaningfulness were reduced to a subjective psychological, rather than a philosophic, category.

Spinoza advocated a kind of a rational humanism that depended solely on the dictates of reason, which in turn was governed by a mathematical-scientific model of rationality.[6] In this way, Spinoza anticipated and undergirded the modern naturalistic critics of religion and gave heft to their critiques with the powerful installation of mathematical reason as the arbiter.

Because he reconceives and searches for what he calls a "rationality of Transcendence," Levinas differs not only from Spinoza but from important contemporary Jewish thinkers. Before Levinas, no other thinker placed the other in a privileged position with respect to the self. This is a radically innovative notion advanced by Levinas in the history of philosophy. There are, of course, contemporary Jewish thinkers who have looked for and described mutuality, reciprocity, and dialogue. Martin Buber and Franz Rosenzweig fall into this

---

6   For Spinoza, the only important and true parts of the Hebrew Bible were those passages that concerned morality. However, for him, at least in the opening of the *Theological and Political Treatise*, these moral lessons were better expressed in the New Testament than the Old. It is not hard to see, even though the *Theological and Political Treatise* was published posthumously, why Spinoza was on his way to the rare accomplishment of being publicly excommunicated from Judaism in the most severe way. According to Maimonides, there is only one criterion for a *herem* or ban—that is, teaching falsely about the Torah and its tradition. The Burghers of Holland surely had reason to impose this ban upon Spinoza, a matter that has been fought over ever since but never reversed. One might think that Spinoza would be appealing to Christians. Not so. The central figure of the gospels was a spiritually elevated human being but really not necessary to communicate the importance of love for others and for God. It is still to this day not clear whether the Jews of Holland were yielding to Christian pressure or simply deciding on their own to place Spinoza outside the Jewish fold. Nonetheless, his influence cannot be denied. The reader, interested in exploring in a detailed manner, the importance of Levinas's critique of Spinoza is encouraged to read *Out of Control: Confrontations Between Spinoza and Levinas* (SUNY Press, 2017) by Richard A. Cohen.

category, and Levinas is often compared to them. But, while Buber and Levinas both emphasize the centrality of dialogue to philosophy, Buber's rejection and Levinas's acceptance of the integrity of both the written and the oral Torah, set them worlds apart both as religious thinkers and as philosophers. Contrary to Rosenzweig, whom Levinas read as early as 1934, and who so deeply influenced *Totality and Infinity*, Levinas neither employs nor appears to rely upon theological premises or arguments.

Like the philosopher Hermann Cohen, Levinas sees an intimate connection between reason and ethics. Like Cohen, he takes not only the words of the Hebrew prophets earnestly but also presents a philosophic reflection on the nature of "prophetism," which he believes finds its origins in daily inspiration and daily speech. However, unlike Cohen, he sees the spirit of the law reflected in the words, letters, and even "the Crowns of the letters of the Torah." I am not saying that Levinas has not been influenced by the prophetism of Cohen, the metaphysical pluralism of Rosenzweig, or the dialogical character of Buber; however, Levinas insists on the centrality of the oral tradition of the Talmud while arguing that genuine philosophy, especially in the aftermath of the utterly dehumanizing Holocaust, must begin with the face-to-face encounter with the other.

THE BURDEN OF POST-HOLOCAUST JEWISH THOUGHT: THE RADICALIZING OF LEVINAS'S PHILOSOPHICAL THINKING ON THE HOLOCAUST

Levinas was a victim as well as a witness and survivor of the Holocaust of European Jewry. In *Difficult Freedom,* he recalls a time when the German bystanders to their suffering "stripped us of our human skin," regarding the Jewish prisoners as subhuman. With his remaining sharp wit and sense of irony intact, he remembers his unit in captivity adopting a friendly dog, whom they called by "the exotic name of Bobby, who seemed to be the last creature in Germany still abiding by Kant's categorical imperative" (DF 1990, 153). Unlike the German soldiers or townspeople, Bobby recognized the prisoners as human beings.

In the essay "Nameless," found in *Proper Names* (1996), Levinas asks: "How does one deal with a people that had been abandoned to this fate? Without institutions of Justice, and yet unwilling to abandon the idea of their return" (PN 1996, 121). The expectation of justice appeared to have sunk below the horizon. The "death of God," for many, had moved from metaphysical speculation to virtual empirical fact at Auschwitz. It is the absence of God that concerns Levinas rather than God's nonexistence. The vital distinction between metaphysical absence and nonexistence had long been obscured in the history of philosophic thought. Tied intimately to the question of the absence of God was the disavowal of human responsibility for the Jews who were abandoned to their fate. In this order, Levinas appears to ask, Where were other people? and Where was God?

As noted, Levinas was introduced to one of the few remaining Talmudic masters in Europe, the enigmatic, peripatetic genius who went by the name, Mordechai Shoshanni. During evenings of the next four years Levinas learned how to learn Talmud with Shoshanni. We do not know precisely the nature of Shohanni's approach to Talmudic texts and thinking, but we do know that questioning and responding to each other in its presence demanded the highest order of attention. We also know that Shoshanni valued worldly knowledge of virtually every sort as important to understanding the workings of nature, science, and technology. And finally, we know that among his best-known students, Emmanuel Levinas and Elie Wiesel stand out. It was, in fact, the voice of Shoshanni that Elie Wiesel said he heard in his first encounter with Levinas in the early sixties, while the latter was giving a Talmudic reading. Wiesel said, "You were a student of Shoshanni's weren't you?" Levinas replied, "Yes, how did you know?" "I could tell by the manner of your speaking."[7] While there is no evidence that either Levinas or Wiesel studied together or knew of each other's existence prior to this meeting, it is important to point out that Levinas, like Wiesel, regarded himself as responsible for explaining some of the lessons from the Holocaust that could be known. For both Levinas and Wiesel, the more we learn about human suffering during this time, the more responsible we become for transmitting whatever lessons it might hold.

One of Levinas's best known reflections on the Holocaust, published in French in 1963, is called *To Love the Torah More than God*. This piece first appeared in the course of a radio broadcast from Paris in the early fifties, when Levinas was commenting on a manuscript called "Yosl Rakover Talks to God." At the time, this manuscript was thought to have been written by an unknown survivor of the Warsaw ghetto. Levinas was the first person to recognize that this piece was fiction, but as he says, "True only as fiction can be." Levinas asks how one can still affirm the existence of God in the aftermath of these horrors that divide Jewish history into two. In his response, he does not rush to defend Divinity. Rather, like Martin Buber before him, he likens the situation as an

---

7 Wiesel told this to me at a gathering honoring him, prior to giving an address at the University of Vermont in May of 2007.

eclipse of God. His analysis helps us to reformulate the attention he gives to Talmudic and biblical studies after the time of the Shoah.

His argument goes like this: What the Jewish people and God have in common is the Torah in its full sense. The central teachings of the Torah are the place we go to know how human beings should act. How does a human being act in the apparent absence of God? Again, as Levinas says, "To know God is to know what must be done" (DF 1990, 17). Levinas speaks about *Hester Panim*, or God concealing His Face, and when he does his thinking resembles a strain of earlier Jewish thought. This is why the veiling of the Face or the turning away of the divine presence is considered the worst and most ultimate source of human tribulation. As it says in Deuteronomy, after enumerating in ascending order the terrible sufferings that will befall Israel, the concealing of the divine face is listed as the last and worst of the sanctions: "My anger will flare up against it [Israel] on that day and I will forsake them; I will conceal my face from them and they will become prey, and many evils and distresses will encounter it" (Deut. 31:17). When God conceals his face, as it were, people are abandoned to the ferocious instincts of the animal within man. Nonetheless, this does not serve as the devaluing of the Torah, but rather intensifies its critical importance.

Yet, Levinas is concerned with what might be seen as a still more enduring question. God's presence is not always visible in the human intrigue. According to rabbinic tradition, prophecy in an open sense was closed at the time of the last of the biblical prophets, Malachi (Kaplan 1979, I, 169). How then, are we to know in our time what should and should not be done? We can better answer this question by recognizing the conduct of children when their parents are not present. They may either act in a manner that is consistent with the teachings of their parents or go in a different direction. One of the most visible expressions confirming the education of children is how they behave in the absence of a parent. Nevertheless, we can see the difference between someone who had a father who is no longer, and one who was unrelated to the father altogether. In both cases the father is absent; in the second case, however, the father is virtually nonexistent. From a logical and formalistic point of view, these two positions are equivalent in terms of their syntactical significance. In terms of meaning, however, the difference is far more.

In *To Love the Torah More than God*, Levinas, perhaps inspired by a midrash, analyzes God's response to the imprecations of the Children of Israel to their Creator. They reiterate how much they love God. The response given is most instructive. "It's good that you love Me but love My teachings even more."

In other words, keep learning and keep doing by studying and acting upon the teachings of the Torah.

If we look at some of the *responsa* literature given at the time of the Holocaust, we can see that the petitioners asked and answered questions regarding what kind of conduct is permissible and not permissible. While the answers are not always satisfying, the questions point to an elevated ethical conscience that moves beyond the mere desire to preserve one's own life.

There is a radicalizing of Levinas's thinking expressed most succinctly in his last formal lecture given at the Sorbonne in 1976, where he describes transcendence to the point of absence. What does he mean by this? He appears to mean that there is a kind of absence that pertains to all other human beings. He refers to this with a coinage of his own, *illeity*. The meaning of *illeity* becomes clearer when we contrast it with what he calls the *il y a*. The il y a, compared by some commentators on Levinas to the void that ruled before creation, the *tohu va'vohu* expresses the absence of purpose, direction, and oriented movement. It expresses a time that is totally folded in on itself without any sense of the other or otherness. Illeity, on the other hand, begins with an awareness that I live in a world with multiple others, near and far, present or absent. It is the absent others, the ones whom I cannot perceive, who make the possibility of human justice extend beyond the reaches of my family, my society, my nation. This involves a certain kind of self-transcendence, where I am constantly bidden to go out toward the other and others. For according to Levinas, I am responsible for each of them. Critically, this seems like an extravagant ethical position, where responsibility is itself founded upon an absence to which I may remain faithful. Perhaps this is why Levinas refers to his reflection as "A God 'Transcendence to the Point of Absence'" (GDT 2000, 219). From a phenomenological point of view, this formulation of Levinas might be reconfigured. This is why, perhaps, it may be referred to as "absence to the point of transcendence, absent or present." This way, one can continually and concretely experience the glimpse of transcendence in the face of the other person.

Such thinking appears to animate many of the crucial passages that will appear in Levinas's Talmudic reflections and in our commentary on the Hebrew Bible through the lens of Levinas. Following this logic, the transcendent would be responsible for grounding the possibility of my turning toward rather than away from the face of others. From an ethical/religious point of view, the key moment would occur in this incessant striving to bring about an order of meaning that begins with pacific and non-totalizing relations with others.

What is visible in the philosophy of Levinas, inspired by Rosenzweig, is the dynamism of human time in the realm of speaking, one comes upon one's own thoughts in the presence of other people.[8] Living speech will inform Levinas's study of the Talmud, Scripture, and philosophy. The model provided by Rosenzweig and modified by Levinas makes questioning not a prelude to learning but a recurring aspect to learning itself. The questioning is always in response to the face of another person who, by facing me, is the one to whom I initially explain and justify what I am saying. Unlike Buber's *I and Thou,* there is an asymmetry to such dialogue, at least for Levinas. I am always moving from the position of teacher to student. As teacher, I have a responsibility for the expression of astonishment or non-comprehension expressed by the face of the student. This is how lived pedagogy takes place.

Emmanuel Levinas recognized that the prescriptions and injunctions of the Torah and the Talmud were obligatory on the people, Israel. At the same time, there is a universality of principle that opens onto all other people. The emphasis on ethical-metaphysical phenomena is open if not always easily accessible to all. For Levinas, all precepts of normative Judaism arise from preconceptual experience. It is for this reason that for Levinas the Talmudic dictum, "All Israel is responsible for one another" (Shevuos 39a), is understood as an obligation incumbent upon the whole of humanity.

LEVINAS'S PHENOMENOLOGICAL APPROACH

The approach of Levinas to both Talmudic texts and philosophy is governed by the discipline of phenomenology. Levinas characterizes phenomenology in the following way: "Phenomenology is the recall of these forgotten thoughts, of these intentions; full consciousness, a return to the misunderstood implied intentions of thought in the world. This complete reflection is necessary to the Truth even if its effective exercise must in doing so make limits appear" (EI 1985, 30). What Levinas is implying is that we must seek to rediscover our original experience of the world as we live it through, prior to abstraction and conceptualizing. Most of the time our attention is absorbed in the objects that we find around us; however, when we pull back from these objects, we become aware of the fact that we ourselves are human subjects who are oriented in a temporal and spatial field with concerns and anxieties for one another and for ourselves.

But using the phenomenological approach keeps Levinas from falling into the fallacy of *naturalism.* Naturalism involves the reduction of phenomena to their mathematical/scientific description and analysis. In no way is Levinas to be understood as anti-scientific, or unlike Heidegger, as anti-technological.

---

8 See "The New Thinking" in N. Glatzer's *The Life and Thought of Franz Rosenzweig.*

Rather, he is concerned with the way that patterns of existence arise to human awareness and therefore are subsequently endowed with meaning. Naturalism by itself is, therefore, an abstraction or part of what the French phenomenologist Merleau-Ponty calls "secondary reflection." This is to say that it is derived from primary experience and cannot substitute for the original encounter between the subject and what it finds over against it. Perhaps this is why Levinas also does not substitute *supernatural* discourse for philosophic language. He is not excluding the realm of the supernatural but, for the most part, bracketing it or putting it in *epoché*.[9]

More often than not, we rediscover what we thought we meant and knew by reflecting upon the direction in which we are moving, towards a goal that may or may not be defined. This is the world of everyday life that is obscured by what Husserl calls the "natural attitude," the scientific and cultural abstractions that make up the categories of what we call "objectivity" and its companion notion, what we call "subjectivity." As we have already pointed out, philosophy according to Levinas is not so much awakened in "wonder" as Aristotle thought, but in thinking that begins in the "traumatisms" to which one does not even know how to give verbal form: a separation, a violent scene, a sudden consciousness of the monotony of time. It is also from the reading of books, not necessarily philosophical, that these questions become problems "giving one to think" (EN 1998, 109).

For example, there are phenomena that are expressed in the Bible that while pre-philosophic in character inform philosophic discourse. Such an example is the human face or countenance whose expression is, after all, the beginning and end of all signification. Put simply, we know if we have been understood only by looking towards the face of the other. This means that explanation already involves the act of justifying what it is that I am saying to another and that I am able and willing to withstand sustained interrogation by him/her. In other words, ethics for Levinas is already there at the beginning of philosophy, simply because truth is founded for him at the juncture of justice and peace. Peace is invoked at the outset because philosophy is not possible unless

---

9 The reader should pay close attention to what he says about revelation. As we shall see, he rethinks and reconfigures this. There is a precedent for this in the writings of Chaim of Volozhin. For example, the Alef of the first letter of the first word of the ten utterances at Sinai is silent. As Ira F. Stone observes, "[I]t is 'the saying' of the word unspoken. When God spoke only the Alef was heard" (*Reading Levinas/Reading Talmud*, 27). Here, too, Levinas is concerned with exploring the "supernatural" only to the extent that it arises within possible human experience. It can be asked whether or not supernaturalism presupposes naturalism for its vitality. This, however, is a question that exceeds the bounds of our book.

there is the assurance that we are not going to do battle with one another in a way that endangers the other's life. Furthermore, justification is the way that the ongoing action of reasoning expresses itself in human discourse.

A central element of the phenomenological method derives from "the new vigor given to the medieval idea of intentionality of consciousness: all consciousness is consciousness *of* something, it is not describable without reference to the object it 'claims'" (EI 1985, 31). In other words, there is no understanding without the understanding *of* something. This is why Levinas has spoken earlier of the "forgotten intentions" that we have invested in the meaning of our intentional acts of consciousness. Here Levinas argues an original point within the approach of phenomenology. The other person exceeds, in advance, my intentional grasp of him/her. The other person remains always in advance unknown to me. Levinas argues that the other person always comes to me from without. That means that I recognize him/her as beyond my intentional claims. The term "*non-intentional* consciousness" is often used to describe this phenomenon that Levinas has uncovered. In this sense, the absolutely other is completely transcendent to my consciousness and appears primarily as the trace of the infinite on the face of the other person.

For Levinas, if explanation is always for the sake of someone else, then the other is there for me at the outset of my justification and reasoning. This is why the original phenomenological doctrine of intentionality must be modified so that we can recognize that it will always be incomplete. Levinas does not abandon, but enlarges, the phenomenological approach or method to include a theory of explanation for which he is seldom credited. This theory does not end in an infinite or bad regress, as in Hegel. Rather, we may employ the coinage an "infinite *egress.*" The asymmetrical responsibility that the subject assumes for the other implies, therefore, that the discourse can be elevated and elaborated. In this way, justification and thereby ethics, is always present at the beginning of inquiry. The scope of phenomenology becomes, in this way, attentive to a plurality of others. It is more precisely the scope of the phenomenological approach, which is thereby enlarged and given greater urgency. By emphasizing those lessons of the Talmud that are applicable to all, the humanity of the human emerges with greater focus and clarity.

It is in much the same way that Levinas recovers the originary intentions and experience of the Bible. One of the purposes of our book is to demonstrate how this phenomenological approach opens up various portions of the Hebraic Bible. The basis of the Talmud is the Mishnah, whose six volumes taken together represent the first formally recorded conversations on matters primarily of Jewish law. Inserted within most of the discussions of the Mishnah is already an explicit reference to biblical verses. Levinas, in the title of one of his books on Talmudic reflections, accurately observes that it is necessary to go "Beyond the Verse"—namely, to recover the depth dimension of its multilayered meanings. This is the way for him that the ethical life is amplified through exegesis, or what we would today call "hermeneutics." In other words, what Levinas came to learn and to teach others is that commenting on the Bible is inseparably linked to the oral tradition that guides Jewish interpretation of Scripture from one generation to the next, including our own.

Acknowledgments

I have had the support and encouragement of many people in doing the research and writing of this book. Early influences include my mother who read to me from the biblical texts when I was convalescing as a young boy. It is to her that I am greatly in debt for teaching me to read and to write and to value the world of words. My father taught me the lesson that one can have "long days" even without long years—a life dedicated always first to other people.

To Paul Weiss, America's most original metaphysical thinker who secured for me the Carnegie Teaching Fellow in philosophy in Yale, in 1966. My mentor in philosophy at Yale University, John D. Wild, first introduced me to the thought of Emmanuel Levinas in the late sixties. Wild had written the introduction to the English edition of *Totality and Infinity*, and left an extraordinary manuscript on *Totality and Infinity*, Levinas's first great work, which I discovered after Wild's death, and which I annotated and edited under the title *Speaking Philosophy*. Wild was responsible for first bringing attention to English-speaking readers of Levinas in America.

Emmanuel Levinas was kind enough to speak with me about the relation of the Bible to philosophy at Johns Hopkins University, where he was a visiting professor in the fall of 1973. Subsequently, Levinas read *Speaking Philosophy*, and in a letter to me in August,1992, he characterized it as "an excellent piece." This provided encouragement to me to continue in my work.

I would like to thank Helen A. Stephenson, my early collaborator in reading and translating the works of Levinas from French. Richard A. Cohen, Professor of Philosophy and Chair of Jewish Studies at SUNY, Buffalo, has encouraged the writing of this text almost since its beginning. My two constant companions in philosophy, since graduate school days at Yale, Professor Roger B. Duncan and Professor Robert J. Anderson, have both encouraged me and discussed the project with me, providing valuable insights throughout. To my late lamented colleague, Alan Paskow, for his encouragement, especially to speak in my own voice.

Regarding the approach and understanding of the commentary tradition on the Bible, I was privileged to spend seven years studying with a Talmudic master,

Reb Rafoel Zalman Levine HaCohen. It was with Reb Zalman that my Jewish learning took on a new depth dimension and introduced me to the world of the Maharal of Prague and some of the great thinkers and commentators of both the Lithuanian and Hasidic traditions. I was his last student, but by no means his best. He affirmed this by referring to me as his "friend" rather than his student.

Before that time, I had first studied the oral tradition with Rabbi Murray Daitschman, beginning in the early seventies. A little later, I gained insight and experience from the Bostoner Rebbe, Levi Y. Horowitz, America's legendary Hasidic storyteller. Subsequently, I learned Torah from the discourses of the last Lubavitcher Rebbe, R' Menachem M. Schneerson, and from two of his Vermont emissaries, Rabbi Shmuel Hecht and Rabbi Yitzchak Raskin. In recent years, I have had the occasion to listen to the discourses of Rabbi David Lehrfield, of North Miami Beach, who, like Reb Zalman Levine, was trained in the Lithuanian Yeshiva tradition.

I would also like to thank Dr. Joelle Hansel, Dr. David Hansel, and his father, Dr. George Hansel, and Rabbi Shmuel Wygoda, for inviting me to attend major Levinas conferences connected with Hebrew University in Jerusalem. In this way, I had the chance to meet many other scholars and students of Levinas. Also, I have a special debt to colleagues of mine, Rabbi Shloimie Markstein, who introduced me to the teachings of his Rebbe, the Slonimer Rebbe, and Rabbi Dr. J. Luchins of Monsey, New York for impressing upon me the importance of the commentator Sforno. I also want to express my gratitude to Professor William Paden, Professor Emeritus of Religion at the University of Vermont for his constant encouragement and for showing me the importance of the field of the interpretation of religion. Among other colleagues and associates who have encouraged me have been Patrick Hutton and Frank Manchel, Professors Emeriti at the University of Vermont, who have made important suggestions and kept me from getting discouraged along the way. My thanks to Bill Dauster who is a scholar on the Pentateuch and who distributed early drafts of chapters of this book to a Congressional study group devoted to weekly portions of the Pentateuch.

This book has also been nourished by some excellent assistance and a superb reader and editor. Much of the legibility of the text owes a great deal to Elizabeth Wirls, MA, from Cornell, who spent countless hours trying to make the book more readable and less tendentious. The preparation for this book was aided by the work of Sivi Kreindler, whose alertness assisted in transliterations, grammar, and delicate sensibilities directed at helping me to respond to questions that are not often found in Jewish day schools or academies. In addition, my longtime assistant in Vermont, Lauren Kenney, spent many hours keeping track of the drafts of the texts and typing them meticulously. Several former students of mine at the University of Vermont also deserve special mention—Ian Nagel and Rabbi Binyamin Murray, who have been reading variants of the book for the last seven years. My special thanks to my teaching assistant and exemplary student, Rebecca Gollin, for helping me with the final draft of the book. Also, I would like to thank Celeste Morton for her careful reading of what I have written on the trace.

I also want to take this opportunity to thank SUNY Press, especially my editor Rafael Chaiken and his staff for their hard work, encouragement, and patience. This is a far better book than it might otherwise have been without their stalwart support. Special thanks are due to the meticulous reading, copy editing, and support of Jenn Bennett-Genthner of SUNY Press, who was vital in seeing this paperback edition of the book to publication.

I would like to thank the University of Vermont, especially the Department of Religion and its Chair, Professor Anne Clark, for granting me sabbaticals to help me research and write this book.

My youngest daughter, Chani Sugarman, early on said, "Dad, this book, unlike your others, might actually help people." My other children, Yehuda and Chaya, have always understood and tried to foster an environment for my writing. I'd like to thank Chaya Sugarman Milchman for her knowledge of biblical Hebrew, and my son Yehuda Sugarman for appreciating the saying beyond the said of Levinas. My gratitude also extends to my sister Judith Abramson who wanted the book to be readable for others, and to my sister Ellen Gayle who has always encouraged me.

Living with the Torah each week makes reading and writing about it more meaningful. My wife, Linda, has served as a continuing reminder to a way of life inscribed in the Torah. Without her the existential dimension of *Levinas and the Torah* would be absent. She has fostered the conditions for me to have the time, place, and spirit to accomplish this work. For her patience, support, and incredible resilience, I am most grateful. My family, especially my children and grandchildren, have helped to give life to the meaning of the phrase used by Levinas of "time bearing a promise."

Richard I. Sugarman
Burlington, Vermont
9 Iyar 1 5779
May 14, 2019

Note to the Reader

What follows is a modest and abbreviated readers' guide to *Levinas and the Torah: A Phenomenological Approach*. Its purpose is to give the reader more context and some indications of how this book might be meaningfully approached.

It should ideally be read in concert with the Bible itself in the original Hebrew if possible, or with an accurate translation and, at times, some annotated commentary material. Unless otherwise noted, we have used and cited the Stone edition of the *Chumash,* published by Mesorah Publications. The great advantage of the Stone edition is that it is accompanied by a compendium of distilled classic commentaries in English. The drawback is that it is not always the most poetic or elegant of translations. Also, the Stone edition at times may appear dogmatic in its theological assumptions and positions. It is surely open to the reader to choose whatever edition he/she prefers, and at times we do use, as is noted, other English editions of the text.

At times, I have chosen to put Levinas in conversation with some classic rabbinic commentators and texts. Levinas's relation to Rashi (1040–1105), the commentator par excellence, is a close one. Rashi is never far from Levinas's own understanding. Like Rashi, Levinas wants to understand the plain meaning of the text as it appears. For over thirty years, Levinas presented after the morning Sabbath service at the ENIO a discourse on Rashi's reading of the Torah portion of the week, welcoming the questions and contributions of others. This course was open to anyone who wished to attend.[10]

Though often unnamed, Maimonides (1135–1204) is another frequent touchstone for Levinas's thinking, especially concerning the phenomenon of revelation as it prescribes right conduct and rational laws. He does so without invoking Maimonides's neo-Aristotelian metaphysics. His project is not, as

---

10 There are no official transcripts of these sessions on Rashi, primarily because writing and recording are both prohibited on the Jewish Sabbath. At the same time, there are some glosses written down by non-Jews or not-yet-observant Jews. These notes are in the possession of an Israeli Levinas scholar at the present.

it was for Maimonides, to reconcile the understanding of the Torah with Greek philosophy.

While the term "midrash" is used in contemporary academic discourse in an elastic fashion, it originally referred to rabbinic commentaries on the non-legal portions of the Bible and Talmud. More precisely this is called "midrash aggadah" as opposed to commentaries on the legal portions of the Bible and Talmud, referred to as "midrash halakha." The midrash, as we are employing the term, refers to the expansive meaning of the passage or text. This most frequently signifies for Levinas the moral or philosophical dimension of the passage or text. The midrashic texts that Levinas cites include both classical and more modern material. While Levinas does not always cite this midrashic material explicitly, the material appears to be drawn from authoritative mid-rashic sources such as the Midrash Rabbah, especially those sections that deal explicitly with the ethical dimension of the Torah and the Midrash Tanchuma. Both of these texts have been or are being translated into and annotated in English and are quite accessible to the English-speaking reader. Levinas appears to have been especially fond of the Maharasha (Rav Shlomo Eidel's, 1555–1632), whose brilliant take on the aggadic, or nonlegal, portions of the Talmud he takes with great seriousness. Levinas has an acknowledged fondness for the lit-erature of what is called the "Musar movement," focusing on ethical teachings and moral conduct. The generally acknowledged leader of this movement, Rabbi Israel Salanter (1809–1883), is someone to whom Levinas refers peri-odically. Other commentators are brought into the conversation with Levinas where explicitly warranted.

Levinas shows the awareness of experience arising to meaning before it is conceptualized. For him, everyday experience appears to be consonant with this submerged dimension of the Bible. This confluence of everyday experience with the submerged dimension of the Bible constitutes the immediate con-temporary value of approaching the Bible through the phenomenological phi-losophy of Emmanuel Levinas.

THE JEWISH BIBLE

When is it appropriate to refer to the Bible as the "Jewish Bible"? Perhaps we might refer to the "Jewish reading" of the Bible. Christianity and Islam share with Judaism the written text (*Mikra*) of the Pentateuch, prophets, and writings. But the Jewish reading of the Bible is identified with a commentary tradition that is inseparable from the biblical text and held to be essential for its interpretation. This conjuncture is a matter of intelligibility for the reader, and of the humanizing of the written text. As Levinas puts it, "Exegesis would come to free, in these signs, a bewitched significance that smolders beneath the characters that coil up in all this literature of letters" (BTV 1994, 109).

Because of the special education required to study and practice matters of applied Jewish law (*halakah*), we follow Levinas in dealing primarily with the nonlegal (*aggadic*) dimensions of the biblical and rabbinic texts. Of course, there is at times an overlap between the descriptive or nonlegal and prescriptive or legal dimensions of the texts. Here we focus primarily on the moral and metaphysical aspects of the human condition highlighted in the Jewish Bible.

At times, we involve Levinas in a discussion with some important commentators of the past and present. At other times, we rely specifically on his own words. His words are not always self-evident and in what follows we try to make his distinctive vocabulary more accessible. Perhaps somewhat more controversially, we have chosen to reposition Levinas's distinctively Talmudic writings in relation to scriptural passages, something that he himself did only very sparingly. This juxtaposition should help to illuminate his thought as well as raise to awareness a vital preconceptual dimension of the biblical texts.

We have tried to include other major figures, in addition to Rashi and Maimonides who have inspired Levinas and upon whom he draws. One such figure is Abraham Ibn Ezra (1089–1164), an arch-rationalist grammarian of the eleventh century. Another continuing source of inspiration for Levinas, situated at the juncture of Judaism and philosophy, is Rabbi Chaim Volozhiner (1759–1821). The Volozhiner was the author of *The Soul of Life* (*Nefesh ha Hayyim*) and founder of the first modern traditional Yeshiva, or Rabbinical academy that bore the stamp of the Vilna Gaon, the doyen of Lithuanian Judaism. As Levinas puts it in his Introduction to a French edition of the book, for Chaim Volozhiner, "the act of study constituted in itself the most direct communication with a transcendent, nonobjectifiable God, whose word and will and commandments create an inexhaustible text which seems, with each new day, to present itself for the first time" (LR 1989, 228). Commenting on *The Soul of Life*, Levinas states that "it tells us that God's creative word was placed in the mouth of man: the being or non-being of the universe depends upon his adherence to the Torah" (LR 1989, 231). Reflecting on *The Soul of Life*, Levinas asks, in a philosophical vein, "[C]an we see, in this possibility given to humanity, that of historical being responsible for the other—the foremost meaning of Israel's existence? Does it lie in this possibility, where the ultimate stake is being itself? Or, should we understand this reversal of the self (*moi*) into the for-the-other as the Judaic endowment of all men?" (Ibid., 231). Levinas concludes that the teaching of Chaim Volozhiner's specific precepts does not rule out a universal application for all human beings.

The careful reader will not fail to see that Levinas's comments help to illuminate ethical and religious concerns and anxieties in the Talmudic humanizing of the biblical text. Levinas effects this illumination by retracing the concerns in the texts back to their originary existential questioning. The contemporary reader, who, like Levinas, living after the time of the Holocaust and the founding of the modern nation state of Israel, will at the same time be drawn into a conversation on issues of immediate concern.

Both Levinas's philosophical and Jewish writings, then, bear the stamp of modernity and the concerns of contemporary life. The opening of his first great work, *Totality and Infinity*, begins with a reflection on morality and its relation to politics. The preeminent question: How is it possible to affirm the irreducible character of moral life after the time of the prototype of all genocides and the other depredations of the blood-stained twentieth century? The subjects of war and peace, repentance and forgiveness, the work of contemporary Israel in the midst of the nations—these phenomena are dealt with in the foreground of his Talmudic readings and the background of his philosophic expositions.

TORAH AND INTERPRETATION

The "Torah," in its most restrictive sense, refers to the Pentateuch, or Five Books of Moses. According to the oral (interpretive) tradition, the five books have a foundational authority that continues with varying degrees of sanctity, in the remainder of the Hebrew Bible: the Prophets and the Writings. In no sense are the Prophets, beginning with Joshua and extending to Malachi, understood by the tradition as "improving" upon the Pentateuch. Rather, the Prophets, like the Writings that follow them, emphasize certain aspects of just human conduct that always presuppose an essential continuity across time and place. The entire Hebrew Bible is often referred to by the acronym *TaNaK,* standing for *Torah,* deriving from the same root words as: "teaching," *ha'orah*; or "way"; *Neviim,* meaning prophets; and *Kesuvim,* meaning "writings." The Writings include but are not limited to the Books of Psalms, Proverbs, Job, Jonah, and Ruth.

The oral or rabbinic interpretation of biblical laws is set out in the six volumes of the Mishnah that make up the core of Talmudic commentary on biblical laws. For the most part, the Mishnah, redacted by the second century of the Common Era (CE), deals with the practical application of laws (*halakah*). These laws are understood by the tradition as deriving from the *mitzvot* or commandments of the Torah. The seventy volumes of the Babylonian Talmud, preceding from the rabbinic equivalent of an ongoing constitutional convention over a period of approximately three hundred years, was compiled at the beginning of the sixth century CE (Kaplan 1979, I, 236).

This book can be read in the order of the fifty-four weekly portions of the Pentateuch that follow the sequence of the Jewish liturgical year, or it can be read in sections that the reader finds most compelling. The obsessed reader can of course read the entire work. The portions to which attention is paid in our book ask to be further interpreted by others.

Levinas binds himself explicitly to the Jewish reading of Scripture. He reminds the reader of the four dimensions of interpreting Scripture. These four levels in Hebrew are referred to as PaRDeS, or orchard. The plain meaning of the text, *P'shat*, not to be confused with what some call the "literal text," concerns what appears to be the evident meaning expressed. This first level of the text is most often associated with the explications of Rashi or Soforno. A second and allegorical dimension of the text or its allusive meaning is referred to as the *remez*. The third level, which concerns the moral lesson taught by the text is called the *d'rosh*. It is this third level, along with the plain meaning of the text that Levinas focuses upon. The fourth level, the mysterium of the text, is referred to by the Hebrew word *sod* meaning foundation and is reflected in the kabbalistic texts. These four levels are not insular but often interpenetrate. This interpretive tradition is always expressed in such a way that it conveys lessons for everyone, although in a plurality of ways.

THE ORDER OF THE BOOK

Our book follows the five books that make up the Pentateuch: Genesis, Exodus, Leviticus, Numbers, and Deuteronomy. These five books collectively follow the fifty-four subdivisions of the Masoretic version of the Pentateuch, redacted approximately 930 CE, which became the authoritative Hebrew text of the rabbinic tradition. Our commentaries on excerpts from each of these sections differ in length. Their length is primarily a function of the kind of insight that the phenomenological explorations of Levinas can bring to the themes, categories, and content of each section. The sections and subsections are meant to stand on their own, though they do have a reference to what comes before and prefigure what comes after. The biblical text should be consulted along with our reflections on it. Each subsection or Torah portion of the book has its own specific themes.

NEW WORD CONCEPTS ADVANCED BY LEVINAS

As Jacques Derrida makes clear in his book-long eulogy for Emmanuel Levinas, *Adieu to Emmanuel Levinas* (1997), the notion of hospitality and the welcome accorded to the other are raised by him to a level of philosophical categories. What originates in the Book of Genesis in the reception by Abraham and Sarah of the three men of God (or angels) is more than a matter of etiquette, for it is the welcoming of the other person that makes it possible for human discourse to proceed peaceably and agreeably. Hospitality occurs when Abraham welcomes his guests to his home to assuage their hunger, fatigue, and discomfort. This too is the prelude to responsible human interaction. Hospitality is the reception of that which is other, by my going out from the interiority of my home (*chez moi*).

Prior to this, the welcoming of the other is my awareness of his or her face, (hebr) *panim* deriving as Maimonides puts it from the Hebrew word *panah*, meaning "to turn." This turning toward the other or, in some cases, away from the other is the beginning of diachrony, which is a sense of time in the philosophic sense that begins with the other rather than the self. For example, I may choose to greet the other person or to ignore him. A revealing case that illustrates this point of facing or not facing the other is told by Martin Buber about his early mystical phase. An acquaintance came to see him. He did not explicitly ask anything of Buber who was busy meditating. To his horror, Buber soon learned that his acquaintance had taken his own life. Buber had not responded to what was later discovered to have been the urgency of the moment. According to Buber, this trauma was perhaps the genesis of his I-Thou philosophy (Buber, *Between Man and Man*, 13).

Levinas sharply distinguishes between the phenomena of progress and promise. Progress derives from the mathematical-scientific turn and implies that the future will *necessarily* be better than the present because of scientific discovery and technological application. The phenomenon of promise, as I have called it, binds the other to the self and the future to the present, which means that the future *can* be better than the present depending largely on the right conduct of human beings. This notion of promise arises from the other person and makes it possible for the "I" to hope that the future will be promising. Levinas does not so much take issue with the enlightenment notion of progress or its accompanying twin categories of objectivity and efficiency, but rather sees them as belonging within a realm that is defined by the relation of parts to whole—that is, of totality.

The alterity of the other, is not completely graspable by the subject. The other has a dimension of the infinite, which is there at the outset and bestirs the subject out of him-herself toward the other. Levinas resists a philosophical theology that would require a complete and synoptic view of history. Rather, he argues for an eschatology that means that human beings are not judged at the end of time as the bearers of some greater historical meaning. Rather they are judged at each of time's instants. He argues that what the other asks first of me is not that I love him but rather that I do not kill him. The movement toward working for what is best for the other is what he calls in *Otherwise Than Being*, the wisdom of love. In this way, there are two poles of humanity for Levinas: for-the-other, or the each-for-each as opposed to each-against-each or all-against-all. The covenantal relation then moves in the direction, by no means without detours, to a world where the future *can* be better for the others and for me.

In proximity, I recognize the nearness of the other and the closeness of others. We see this enacted when Joseph's brothers are willing to substitute themselves for Benjamin, or preform what Levinas calls substitution, and in so doing begin the process of reconciliation with Joseph in Egypt. This is already an affirmative answer to the question first asked by Cain in Genesis: "Am I my brother's keeper?" Genesis is not a book of laws, but a book of stances taken up in advance of the steps that must be taken for justice to be enacted. This sense of uprightness is a precondition for the receiving of the law at Sinai. It is as law that justice is expressed economically and socially at the first culmination of the outgoing from oppression to freedom. The exodus is in this sense a moral one before it is a political one. We shall see the development of these phenomena in Exodus just as we will have seen the successive moral stances taken up in Genesis.

There are elements that are and must be common to both Levinas's philosophical and distinctively Jewish reflections. Such elements arise out of the primary or preconceptual, prephilosophic patterns of every day human experience. It may even be the case that, for Levinas, what is most important about his Talmudic and biblical reflections, is the fact that life is lived with other people. It is here in relation to the beloved, the friend, the neighbor, and others that a life arises devoted to and for others. All of these kinds of relations with the other are subject to distortion, devaluing and disappointment. Not every person appears as a saint, nor is every action saintly.

In the Book of Genesis, for example, we see a series of stances that are taken toward others on the part of central biblical figures. While Genesis is not a book of laws, the application of Jewish law (*Halakah*) is derived from the root word *to go* (*halak*). Here we are introduced to the matriarchs of Judaism—Sarah, Rebecca, Leah, and Rachel—as well as the patriarchs—Abraham, Isaac, and Jacob. The descriptions are rich enough to appear accessible even through the mist that arises prior to political history. Still, the phenomenon of fraternity so vital to the ethics of Levinas persists throughout the Book of Genesis. Special emphasis on the complex patterns of fraternity, enmity, forgiveness, and reconciliation are found in abundance in the sagas of Jacob and amplified in the dealings of Joseph and his brothers. Responsibility is a meta category that is at the basis of much of Levinas's philosophical as well as religious thinking. There is, in fact, what we might call a pedagogy of responsibility in relation to others near and far. We find that some of the other classic commentators have much to say here and that Levinas brings the argumentative threads of many of these discourses into contemporary life.

With the opening of the book of the Exodus, the idea of political history is born in the biblical and Western imaginations. This means that the present *can* be better than the past, and the future different from and perhaps better than the present. The dialectic of liberation and even revolution is found here. The movement from oppression to freedom to justice, expressed as law, is well known. Less well known is the moral exodus leading from the self to the other for whom Moses and subsequently the people, Israel, become responsible. Patience, forbearance, angry impatience, and repentance are all found linked in the receiving of the laws. Here, the category of the trace advanced by Levinas is of great importance. What is it that passes Moses by and somehow remains with the giving of the Torah a second time? To speak simply of memory is not sufficient. Memory, from a phenomenological point of view, is always memory *of* something.

What remains is the trace of the past and the other. The trace, for Levinas, can be effaced but not eradicated. It is the trace of the Divine Other that remains after the theophany at Sinai. In this way, the trace, as he puts it, is the "insertion of space in time" (BPW 1996, 62). As such it grounds the relation of the past to the present, and thereby, makes memory philosophically intelligible.

The fireworks of revelation are ancillary to what is contained in the teachings of the Torah. The concern with economic, social, and moral justice is always closer to the figure than the ground of perception. A democracy is advocated in the realm of action, if not in the realm of understanding. According to Levinas, it is as action that the Torah is understood: "We shall do and we shall understand" (Exod. 24:7). There is then a pedagogy whereby every person is at once both a learner and a teacher, a tradition that continues through the Talmud with historical alterations to the present.

With the Book of Leviticus, the phenomenon of holiness becomes preeminent. Levinas distinguishes sharply between holiness and sacrality. While the sacred can manifest itself as a function of pure power, the holy begins with the other and ethics. Religion as such can be spoken of only as meaningful when it is emancipated from myth, magic, or enchantment.[11]

There is a rich description of times and places that are holy. More demanding is the insistence that there be a people that can act in a manner that is also holy. In everyday life it is not only what is done and what one refrains from doing, but *how* one acts. There is a way of speaking that is holy and a way that contests this holiness and moves away from it. There are rituals that break up the monotony of natural existence. Such rituals can be maintained, preserved, and enlivened by a concern for how to ameliorate life's sufferings and celebrate their happy occasions. It is more than simply a matter of punctuating the periodic phases of time and the designation of holy places. It includes our comportment with one another. With the emergence of holiness as a central category, responsibility for one another also is graduated. Levinas proves particularly instructive in analyzing the statement that Rabbi Akiva saw as the heart of the Torah: "to love thy neighbor as oneself." For Levinas this includes the accompaniment of his central idea that the other is always there before me, and I must practice kindness as well as justice toward him. In the latter part of Leviticus, we see a place reserved for what might be called an ecology of holiness. Before a field can be made my own, those portions that are given over to the most vulnerable must already in advance be designated and/or allocated. So too with the giving of the law that pertains to letting the land of Israel lie fallow during the seventh year.

The itinerary of the Book of Numbers recounts different kinds of journeys. Levinas is especially concerned with why the Israelites are not permitted to go into the land after explorers are sent into it. Did they commit a transgression comparable to the erection of the golden calf prior to Moses's first descent from Sinai? There it appeared to be a philosophic confusion between the categories of absence and nonexistence. Or do the people really not want to enter the land where the elevated spiritual life of their wanderings will give way to the everyday practices and burdens of agriculture? Has the absent past now been registered as nonexistent? Is this perhaps a case of angelism like the one presumably experienced at the beginning of Leviticus by the two sons of Aaron who, according to some commentators, wish to divest themselves of their own bodies?

Deuteronomy is often referred to as the repetition of the Torah (*Mishneh Torah*). Divinely inspired, the word would be understood as Moses's own in

---

11 A classic view contra Levinas that would absorb the "holy" into the "sacred" can be found in Mercea Eliade's *Sacred and the Profane* (Houghton Mifflin, 1959).

the thirty-seven days preceding his death. Rav S.R. Hirsch regards the Book of Deuteronomy as preparing the Israelites for their own imminent future and therefore their change of conditions to those more resembling our own. Hirsch, with his continuing moral emphasis on the text, often seems to prefigure this dimension of Levinas's reflections. The opening word in Hebrew, *Devar,* can mean either "word" or "thing." There are many new Mitzvot that are given in Deuteronomy. However, the repetition appears to draw speech ever more closely to the things that it names or to which it refers. This parallels the distinction Levinas makes between the saying *(le dire)* and the said *(le dit).* It elaborates specific conditions under which courts of justice shall judge. Some of the most enduring and primary rituals of daily Jewish life are introduced. Prayer, about which Levinas speaks in its nonegological form, is also introduced as a prescribed ritual. Echoing the last portion of Numbers, questions of inheritance are raised and to some extent decided. The last consideration deals with the fact that even Moses, who was called the Man of God, gets only to glimpse the land of promise from a distant hill but does not get to enter it, which leads to a reflection on the finite nature of human life and the broader question of generational responsibility.

ON TRANSLITERATION FROM HEBREW TO ENGLISH

Transliterations in general follow the Ashkenazic or Eastern European tradition. For the word "God," we follow the format of Eliyahu Munk: G'd. In places where it seems more appropriate, the word "God" is spelled out. Usually the difference is that the word "God" is spelled out when not taken specifically from the biblical, Talmudic, or midrashic sources.

Because our book is addressed to the English-speaking reader, we have used English translations of the Bible, biblical commentaries, and translations of texts of Levinas into English. These citations are most often accompanied by abbreviations, the full titles of which can be found in the short bibliography.

Biblical names are transliterated from Hebrew to English. On some occasions, we have simply used the translated names in English.

Each Torah portion is named by the tradition after what is regarded to be the first key Hebrew term in the text. Our subtitles of each Torah portion are taken from the content of the text, and otherwise have no special standing. The quotations at the beginning of most Torah portions highlight a single theme or themes from the Torah portion, and/or salient comments by Levinas. Interested readers are advised to start with whichever portion discussion they find most compelling. There are foreshadowings and reiterations throughout. Both the foreshadowings and reiterations are meant to help keep track of what has been studied.

Key to Abbreviations of Works by Levinas

(AT) *Alterity & Transcendence*
(BPW) *Basic Philosophical Writings*
(BTV) *Levinas: Beyond the Verse*
(CPP) *Collected Philosophical Papers*
(DF) *Difficult Freedom*
(EE) *Existence and Existents*
(EI) *Ethics and Infinity*
(EN) *Entre Nous*
(GDT) *God, Death, and Time*
(GWCM) *Of G'd Who Comes to Mind*
(IRB) *Is it Righteous to Be? Interviews with Emmanuel Levinas*
(ITN) *In the Time of the Nations*
(LR) *The Levinas Reader*
(NTR) *Nine Talmudic Readings*
(NwTR) *New Talmudic Readings*
(OBBE) *Otherwise than Being or Beyond Essence*
(OE) *On Escape*
(OTS) *Outside the Subject*
(PN) *Proper Names*
(TI) *Totality and Infinity*
(TO) *Time and the Other*
(UH) *Unforeseen History*

Genesis

BEREISHIS

ON GENESIS

Rashi (1040–1105), the commentator par excellence, opens his own reading of Genesis by posing a question. The question concerns the importance of the Book of Genesis itself. Rashi asks why the Torah begins with an account of creation. Implicitly, he appears to be asking about the placement and importance of the entire Book of Genesis. His reason for doing so is that it is not until the book of the Exodus that laws are given pertaining to human conduct. If conduct is the essential thing, as the Talmud holds, then why not begin with the first of those laws that belong to the whole of the newly emerging people of Israel, those that deal with the establishing of their own calendar (Exod. 12:2)? The applied law, or *halakhah*, tells us which steps to take at every stage on life's way. The Book of Genesis, or *Bereishis*, is "narrative" in character and offers the reader, for the most part, no immediate response to the questions of what, when, and how we should engage in practical action.

It is worth noting, however, that the word *halakah* derives from the word *halkh*, which means "go." Before a person begins to take steps in going somewhere, he or she is visited with a question of where he or she is going. Before going, before walking, one must stand upright and take a stance toward one's destination, even if that destination is open-ended. The taking of such a stance is also pure Torah, more than mere literary narrative. It is commonly referred to by the Hebrew word *hashkofa*, meaning "a specific perspective or outlook that is more or less global in character." In other words, before we are given commandments (*mitzvot*), we must gain some idea, however dim, of who we are and the direction in which we are going. This, in turn, involves understanding what it means for us to encounter the text with others as well as the tradition of interpretation and its contents.

As the philosopher-psychiatrist Erwin Straus points out, the upright posture permits a perspective that is distinctively human and permits us to look beyond the immediacy of our present preoccupations (Straus 1980, 137). Samson Raphael Hirsch, in his commentary on the Psalms, provides insight into the connection between moral and physical uprightness. An upright stance gives us a sense of poise or balance in the absence of which we find difficulty holding-ourselves-together. This does not mean that every figure, person, or action spoken of in Genesis is always morally upright. However, to go somewhere, someone must already be standing, and according to Hirsch, stride forward (Psalm 1).

The stances taken up by some of the key figures in Genesis help us to better understand how they become who they are. We begin with a reflection inspired by Levinas on Cain and Abel. This section describes some of the dynamics of fraternity, enmity, and responsibility of one for the other. Reading Genesis with Levinas, we dwell in an atmosphere of each against each and all against all. It is not, therefore, an accident that the first death we see in Genesis involves a fratricide. However, the pole of humanity that we can move toward is the each-for-each and all-for-all.

The stance of the biblical Abraham offers a new model for the human self in the West. Abraham is told originally to "Go for (from) yourself from your land, from your relatives, and from your father's house to the land that I will show you" (Gen. 12:1). Abraham's departure does not conclude as does the journey of Odysseus, with a return to home. It is an open-ended itinerary that he takes together with Sarah, where the turn toward the other will define his identity. This is not the heroic journey undertaken by the protagonists of Greek tragedy. It moves through themes quite familiar to us in most ways, and it deals with phenomena of hunger, hospitality, justice, covenant, and above all, relations with other people. In the journey of the biblical Abraham, we see what we might call an *Infinite e-gress*. This means we are constantly challenged with moving out of ourselves so that we may extend a welcome and do justice toward the other. The integrity and identity of the other helps to establish my own sense of unity. This phenomenon begins to be enacted by the infinite that bestirs our inertia by making possible for us to come out of the self and thereby establish an ethical subject.

From Rebecca, Sarah's daughter-in-law and Isaac's wife, we learn about the various modes of human responsibility. Unlike Cain and Abel who are distinctive in evading various forms of responsibility, Rebecca takes responsibility not only for her own conduct but for her sons, Jacob and Esau, and her husband, Isaac. While Cain and Abel are torn between the each-against-each and the all-for-all, Rebecca clearly moves toward the moment of each-for-each.

With the appearance of her son Jacob whom she elevated, we see a stance toward life that is involved in the constant overcoming of obstacles. Jacob suffers from oppression, exile, and deception, yet it is in exile that he and his wives rear their twelve children. He is a man who constantly wrestles with opposition and yet for the most part does not turn his eyes away from the challenges that confront him. It is Jacob who becomes Israel. It is he who wrestles with Divinity and prevails. With the appearance of Jacob's brother, Esau, we see someone who cannot accept the death of his righteous grandfather, Abraham, and thereby suffers from a life of errancy. Still it must be conceded that there is no greater discrepancy between the life of Esau depicted in the written text and the insistence on his sense falling short by the commentary tradition (Telushkin 1991, 38). How is there, then, an alternative to facing finitude that we can see in the life of Jacob and his descendants? In what way does this open a hope founded upon the promise of others beginning with my descendants?

Jacob, however, is not described as a perfect human being or parent. After the premature death of his beloved Rachel, he clings to her oldest son, Joseph, and does so by exhibiting favoritism that results in much suffering. Such favoritism incurs the enmity of his brothers. These troubling passages force us to reconsider, with Levinas, the meaning of justice, pardon, forgiveness, and fraternity. The ambiguity of the human situation is revealed in the repentance practiced by the brothers after they have been forced to come down to Egypt and encounter their brother Joseph. What is human fraternity? How can it be achieved, expressed, and stabilized in the midst of genuine conflict? In the person of Joseph, we see the world of the political arise explicitly in relation to the ethical, with regard to the inhabitants of Egypt and to his own brothers.

In the Book of Genesis, we encounter and see dramatically expressed some of these ultimate stances toward other people, toward the future, justice, and covenant. We do so primarily through the philosophic lens of Emmanuel Levinas. As G'd tells Abraham in the opening of chapter 12: "Go to the land that I will show you." In a similar way, we might describe the value of philosophy, as Levinas envisions it, as a "fine risk" where the end is not known in advance.

FACING RESPONSIBILITY

Beresheis: In the Beginning
(Genesis 4:9–4:16)

Am I my brother's keeper?

—Genesis 4:9

Emmanuel Levinas places great emphasis on the responsibility that each person has for the other. There is virtually no limit for such responsibility. He frequently cites an expression found in Dostoevsky: "[E]ach is responsible for each, and I more so than all the others." The contemporary popular Jewish writer Joseph Telushkin advances the notion that the whole of the Jewish Bible can be read as an elaboration of an affirmative response to Cain's original question, "Am I my brother's keeper?" (Gen. 4:9). In a way, we might reasonably argue that the religious philosophy of Emmanuel Levinas demonstrates why and how this is the case. By elevating responsibility to an ethical-metaphysical category, Levinas frames one of the key arguments of his philosophy reflected in biblical sources. At the heart of Levinas's transcending humanism is the governing idea of human fraternity. This involves no less than rethinking the kind of responsibility we have for the death and life of another person.

The first death recorded in the Bible is also a fratricide. When Cain responds by hiding from the divine question, "Where is Abel, your brother?" he answers evasively and with what Levinas calls the "stone coldness of indifference." Clearly, it is an affirmative answer that is called for. As Levinas puts it, "To be the guardian of others, contrary to the vision of the world according to Cain, defines fraternity" (BTV 1994, 104). Still, "the personal responsibility of man with regard to man is such that G'd cannot annul it" (DF 1990, 20). This is why, according to Levinas, "the rabbinical commentary tradition does not regard the question as a case of simple insolence. Instead, it comes from someone who has not yet experienced human solidarity and who thinks, like many modern philosophers, that each exists for oneself and that everything is permitted" (DF 1990, 20). The American Levinas scholar, Richard A. Cohen, speaks of the identity of the human person as the most basic expression of the "I" as the "for-the-other."[1] In other words, identity becomes distinctively human as "I exist for-the-other."

Abraham Ibn Ezra, the Jewish medieval commentator and grammarian asks, given the language and context of Scripture, whether Abel, the victim of the first homicide, also bears some responsibility toward his brother (Eisenmann 2002, 104–9). The repetition of the expression "his brother" (*achiev*) serves to alert us to the question of guardianship for another even when the other has expressed hostility toward me. Consider that when Cain is crestfallen because his sacrifice has been rejected by G'd that he is told that if he does *teshuva* ("turns himself around"), things will go well for him. It is at this moment that Cain is described as going out to the field to "speak with his brother." The text gives no expression for any kind of response on the part of Abel. Is it not possible, asks Ibn Ezra, that Cain wished to share with Abel G'd's encouraging response, as well as or more than the divine rebuke: "If you lift yourself up, will it not go better for you" (Eisenmann; Gen 4:6)? Is it not likely, Ibn Ezra continues, that Abel did not turn toward Cain to listen to him, let alone to speak with him (Eisenmann 2002, 104–9)? The "stone-cold indifference" would apply then, to Abel as well as Cain.

In no way does this collapse the distinction between victim and perpetrator. Cain emphatically and unequivocally is the perpetrator; Abel, the victim. Nonetheless, Abel, according to the reading of Ibn Ezra, followed in part by Nachmanides, bears a degree of responsibility toward his brother, in the moment preceding the fratricide by refusing to turn toward his brother. Responsibility is the personalizing of justice, where I become responsible before justice is installed and after it is created. It is justice, the stabilizing of responsibility, that makes fraternity and society possible. In this way, there must be room for me to have a place under the sun as well as the others.

With Cain condemned to be a fugitive and wanderer on the earth, the language of the "Face," so central to the thinking of Levinas, is introduced. The Hebrew for "face," *panim*, is given a three-fold expression in the exile of Cain. Maimonides explains that the word for "face" is derived from the biblical verb

---

1   Richard A. Cohen, *Ethics, Exegesis and Philosophy* (Cambridge University Press, 2001), 212.

panah meaning "to turn or to aim"[2] (GFP 1956, 15). We see this in everyday language when we speak of "facing" the future or "facing" one another. Regarding his punishment, Cain complains to God that "from Your Face I will be hidden." This is the ultimate punishment with which Israel is later threatened if it goes contrary to the morality inscribed in the divine law. *Hester panim* (the hiding or concealing of the expression of the divine face) is a worse punishment than all the illnesses, plagues, and persecutions: "[A]nd I will surely turn My Face for that day, and all the evil which they have wrought" (Deut. 13:18). This means that human beings will experience everything that happens as though with divine indifference, and therefore only according to the laws of nature.

The rabbinic tradition associates this kind of exile with the reversion of the interhuman order to the each-against-each and the all-against-all. This includes the natural realm as well, understood as brute force. The earth, its foliage and its fruit, will take on an indifferent, rather than benign, expression, and in this way, the earlier admonition, "You will eat your bread in the sweat of your face," becomes intensified.

Cain expresses what is perhaps his deepest existential fear. Other people, seeing that he has lost divine favor, will seek to kill him. He responds, "He who sees me will slay me." Cain is given a divine mark upon his forehead to protect him from exactly this kind of eventuality. To use the categories of Levinas, the infinite mark upon Cain's forehead is perhaps meant to make his own humanity visible once again, at least to other people. Cain will eventually succumb to the hands of a blind descendant, one who cannot recognize this mark and who mistakes Cain for an animal.

Levinas speaks at length of the face as an utterly irreducible category that serves as the beginning of all ethical relations. This sign of the Infinite marks every human being as "holy"—even Cain. Levinas observes that the face of the other person appeals to me, before all else: "Do not kill me!" Without this primary expression, we cannot begin to explain how morality registers within the subject's awareness. The human countenance is vulnerable beyond any other kind of nakedness. It is also the origin of all expression. The human face permits all human discourse to proceed, assuming that this first imperative is met. When only the animal is expressed in the human, the Infinite contracts immediately into the finite, where the interdiction of killing the other is no longer visible. Even knowledge is subordinate to responsibility. The more I learn, the more responsible toward others I become for what I have learned.

---

2   I first heard this at a public Saturday evening gathering at the Maimonides School from Rabbi Joseph B. Soloveitchik in Boston, MA, in the fall of 1972.

To explore this a little further, the scriptural text uses the plural of the Hebrew word for "blood," *demei*, in the statement usually translated as "your brother's blood cries from the ground to me." The Talmudic commentary tradition is virtually in agreement in arguing that this means that not only has Cain murdered his brother, but also all future progeny that could have come from him (BT, Sanhedrin 37a). In the language of Levinas, we can say that this raises the issue of generational responsibility. More precisely, are we responsible for the future of the other? We might similarly ask, could we possibly be considered responsible for the pasts of other people before we encounter them?

For Levinas, the past of the other, like my own, inheres in the present and therefore shapes our expectations for the future as well. It would be very odd to say to another person, "Yes, from the moment I met you, I became your friend. But, however you got to be who you presently are before our meeting, for that I am not responsible." This is not only to deny his or her past, but his or her present and, in a way, his or her near future as well. Embodied friendships and human relations of all kinds have an intersubjective dimension that is central to their description.

To amplify what this means for generational responsibility, "to be my brother's keeper," indicates the way that this pertains to the future as well as the present—that is, "I will remain my brother's keeper." Or, in a transposition to alterity, we might say that the other *IS* my future, just as his or her past has awaited my present. This argument needs to be formulated and explicated.

1. Levinas affirms, "I am responsible for the future of the other."

2. If 1, then my responsibilities continue in (or are implicated in) the future of the other.

3. If 1 and 2, therefore the other IS my future insofar as he or she is the subject of my continuing responsibilities.[3]

I cannot guarantee the hopefulness of a future that I cannot foresee. However, this "deep future," as we might call it, corresponds in Levinas, but is not identical to the immemorial past that I cannot remember. The deep future cannot be anticipated but is perhaps the promise of infinite time that is a necessary if not sufficient precondition for human hope. The full measure of the humanity of the human is to be measured in the ultimate "not-yet" that requires refinements in the realm of ethical elevation.

---

3 I am indebted to my colleague, Robert J. Anderson, Emeritus Professor of Philosophy at Washington College for the formulation of this argument.

THE LOVE OF WISDOM AND
THE WISDOM OF LOVE

Noach: Noah
(Genesis 6:9–9:32)

May G'd extend Japheth, and he will dwell in the tents of Shem.

—Genesis 9:27

According to rabbinic reckoning, Noah's son Japheth stands for the Greeks (MeL, 393–99). It is the "love of wisdom"—philosophy—that expresses the essence of Greek culture. Over against this, the rabbinic tradition values what Levinas calls the "wisdom of love." The Greek philosophic tradition begins with the Socratic-Platonic-Aristotelian tradition and continues through the medieval attempts to reconcile the Greek version of reason (*nous*) with what is understood to be a fidelity to the rabbinic tradition of transcendence, law, and holiness. This is the philosophic project of Maimonides in his *Guide for the Perplexed*. In the language of medieval theology, this involves a certain kind of convergence between the God of philosophy and the G-d of Abraham, Isaac, and Jacob. The aim, presumably, from a theological point of view, is to secure the findings of philosophy within the tradition of Revelation. However, it is not so clear why this is the case. A concern with knowledge and Being dominates this medieval paradigm. In "God and Philosophy," Levinas rejects this notion of God based upon the understanding of Being as "onto-theology" (GWCM 1998, 55–60). This, in fact, reflects a subtle destruction of transcendence. Only with the promotion of the Infinite to a pre-eminent philosophical category in Descartes and, religiously in the Zohar, is it possible to pierce the monism of Being so that the existent can emerge in its singularity, and therefore permit philosophy to expose its holiness (AT 1999, 54)?

The historical relation between Greek philosophy in its continuation in the modern world and the biblical/Talmudic tradition has been fraught with tension.

In philosophy, at least since the time of Philo Judeaus (20 BCE–50 CE), the main objection is that the tradition of the Torah is always interpreted in terms of philosophic reason. This means that the original imperative directed at Japheth reverses the relation between philosophy and Torah, according the priority to Torah. *May God extend Japheth, but he will dwell in the tents of Shem* (Gen. 9:27).

In the thinking of Emmanuel Levinas, the reader can see a revaluation of Torah and philosophy. Repeatedly he cautions the reader not to think that he is citing biblical verses as a kind of philosophic proof text. Levinas is embarking on a new project that does more than translate the language of the Bible into philosophy. Most emphatically, he cannot be considered another Hellenist.

It surely must be conceded that Levinas, drawing on pre-philosophic experiences, many of which appear for the first time in Genesis, has elevated to philosophy phenomena that have been merely understood from literary and psychological points of view. Some of these phenomena, such as the face, expression, the primacy of responsibility, we have already glimpsed. Others depend, in part, upon conceptual reversals. For example, Levinas argues against the priority of sameness, a position that has held sway since Plato's *Sophist*.

Levinas also takes human hunger with a philosophic seriousness seldom seen in the literature of western philosophy. For Levinas, justice, as we shall see, founds truth, and not the other way around. This is a way of reflecting upon the very conditions under which philosophic discourse takes place. Explanation is always an explanation to a *someone else*. This means that I am called upon to justify what it is I am saying or doing to or for an other. This is a necessary condition for philosophic discourse. The preeminent interrogative for Levinas becomes, *to whom* am I speaking? Does my explanation make sense to them in a timely way?

More importantly, for our purposes here, is Levinas's discovery of the two-fold aspect of human language—the *saying* (*le dire*) and the *said* (*le dit*). Almost all language focuses on "the said." These are variously and alternatively our 'conclusions,' words that we will be held to, words that more or less accurately depict the subject matter as named or described. However, there is also the intentionality to speak. This usually refers to what is meant, whether voiced or not. We are not saying that the biblical prophetic tradition is all saying and that the tragic, philosophic tradition all belongs to the said. Nonetheless, there is something irretrievably personal about the saying that is properly associated with proper names, times, and events. This is what makes the biblical tradition more refractory to conceptualization. It is governed by the realm of infinity rather than totality.

Levinas writes that this knowledge is the conjuncture, and not the merger, of the Bible into philosophy, in his words: "The Septuagint is not yet complete" (BTV 1994, 75). There is a sense in which the meaning of the said is transparent. However, what is decisive about the saying of the statement is its ambiguity and irony. It is not complete to begin with because it can never be complete. Every new reader, as Levinas generously acknowledges, is a new interpreter of Scripture (LR 1989, 190). When Levinas affirms and demonstrates that ethics rather than theory of knowledge is "first philosophy," this affects the way that knowledge is reintegrated into the human world of meaning.

To argue, as he does, that the other comes before the self, is a genuine novelty that spills over in multiple directions. He is not arguing this out of some romantic sensibility or aiming even at an existential empathy. Rather, he is arguing that the expression of the other person is what makes it possible for me to think self-critically. In this way, I am responsible for the other as he/she entrusts his words to me, including the questions announced by expression but not asked. Hence, we understand the biblical expression used later in the text: "[T]hat his face was not to him as before." A philosopher, for whom the love of wisdom follows upon the wisdom of love, concedes the priority of peace and thereby brings questioning, answering, and responding into the dynamics of human time. Philosophy then, for Levinas, begins not with wonder or curiosity, as it does for Aristotle, but rather with urgency—my awareness that I must make time for the other, because his or her time becomes a matter of my responsibility.

THE META-COVENANT

> And I will confirm my covenant with you.... This is the sign of my covenant between Me and you and every living being that is with you, to generations forever. I have set my rainbow (Hebrew, keshes) in the cloud, and it shall be a sign of the covenant between Me and the earth.
>
> —Genesis 9:11–12

What was decreed to be "good" in the beginning of the order of Creation, now is a plurality of "goods" to be achieved through time. The covenant is a promise that makes all purposive action possible. In this sense, it is the "Meta-Promise" or signature of what Levinas calls the "Otherwise than Being." *To be is to Promise.* This is especially important since this covenant is enacted just after the Deluge that is depicted as nearly resulting in the destruction of all terrestrial life.

One of the more overlooked aspects of the phenomenology of Emmanuel Levinas concerns the way that he approaches the creature and the Creator. He argues that theology based upon being, mostly fashioned by the medievals, is unhelpful: "Theology imprudently treats the idea of the relation between God and the creature in terms of ontology. It presupposes the logical privilege of totality, as a concept adequate to being" (TI 1969, 293). By substituting transcendence for totality, Levinas believes that a philosophic advance is possible. He argues that the notion of transcendence, whether it applies to the human other or the absolutely Other, makes it possible for the idea of Infinity to remain allergic to a complete absorption to conceptualization. Rather, what he is proposing is, as he notes, "in our own way, the Platonic idea of the Good beyond Being" (Ibid., 293). The "Good beyond Being" is drawn from passage 509b of Plato's *Republic*. This formula, in the hands of Levinas, takes on significance when it is thought together in proximity with the notions of time, otherness, absence, and in the biblical world, with the notion of creatureliness.

By no means is Levinas commenting on the theological affirmation of creation *ex nihlio*. Nonetheless, he shows how it makes sense to think of the creature as so severely conditioned as to indicate a kind of transcendence through which the notion of creation makes sense. This is what he says: "To affirm origin from nothing by creation is to contest the prior community of all things within eternity, from which philosophic thought, guided by ontology, makes things arise as from a common matrix" (TI 1969, 293). The Israeli Levinas scholar Shmuel Wygoda situates this within the context of the biblical notion of time in relation to the "days" of creation (Wygoda 2006, 296–99). Taking Levinas at his word that he is not trying to establish a congruence between philosophical understanding and biblical teaching, the reader can see that he advances a philosophic argument for creation.

The absolute gap of separation which transcendence implies, could not be better expressed than by the term creation, in which the kinship of beings, among themselves, is affirmed, but at the same time, their radical heterogeneity, also their reciprocal exteriority, coming from nothingness. One may speak of creation to characterize entities situated in the transcendence that does not close over into a totality. (TI 1969, 293)

The move that I would suggest Levinas is making is to advance the notion of what I would call a philosophical *"e-gress"* that is always moving from sameness toward otherness. For he relates this to the discourse of justification before the other.

The good, when thought together with human time, is now always on its way to being achieved. It is good therefore in prospect, not necessarily in an immediate self-evident way. In this sense, what is prospectively good can be glimpsed also in its absence. Here there would remain two kinds of absence.

First, the not-yet good of which we have spoken. This would be a moral or ethical kind of goodness consistent with the metaphysics that Levinas is delineating. The second would be an ontological absence that would belong to the created, or natural sphere by itself. The ravages of the natural world, the repeated disruptions of human creativity, the paths away from, rather than toward, good outcomes, would also be registered to human awareness.

Therefore, we can speak of "the Good beyond Being" as taking on the appearance or shape of the promise of time and of human experience. But we should recall that Levinas's magisterial work is not called Totality *or* Infinity, but Totality *and* Infinity. The *and* (et) therefore would become the promise of time. In this way, sameness would move toward otherness, the self toward the other, freedom toward responsibility, and totality toward infinity. This nonetheless is still distinguishable from the time of promise.

The covenant appears and reappears as the piercing of the neutrality of Being. This is the metaphysical critique of Nietzsche and Heidegger, launched by Levinas. What all human beings have in common, according to the view of fundamental ontology is *that they are*. What is most important for Heidegger is that each being then would share a commonality with every other being, the fact of its being, or having been. This is what Heidegger calls *ontological difference*—the relation between specific beings and Being in general. Levinas rejects this point of view and its fundamental philosophic project to uncover "the meaning of Being" as a deepening rather than a rectification of the night of European nihilism.

What Levinas resists is the notion of ontological imperialism. Neither Nietzsche's theory of eternal return nor Heidegger's monistic concept of being permits creatures to breathe, to hope, to live in a way that the future can be better than the past. There is neither direction nor purpose nor orientation to such positions. What is at stake here is nothing less than a prefiguring of what is promising for the human. By no means is the position of Levinas committing him to a view of undiminished progress or human enlightenment. Just as in our everyday experience, our itinerary can appear as unpromising. So too with the not yet historical future. Nonetheless, understanding the human being as a creature rather than simply an expression of the power of nature makes us think, act, and speak differently.

More precisely, for Levinas, to be is not simply to strive for power and the overcoming of all obstacles in the way; rather it is to be for another. Can this be demonstrated or described or is it merely a disguised theological assertion? Let us reflect again on the conditions necessary for a philosophical explanation. In rhetorical debate, an opponent often asks the other about his or her presumed "pre-mises" to which he or she is holding or from which he or she is departing. This suggests that the future *can be* other than the past and better than the present or the eternal recurrence of the present. The promise of the human remains to be achieved. The promise of every living being, including the human, is what all existents have in common—that is, *to be is to promise.* Concretely, what does this mean for me and for the others? It means that I can hope because the future of the other is promising throughout all of time.

More specifically, this does not mean that existence always appears promising, to others or to me. It can be most *unpromising.* Here it is necessary to clarify or perhaps even to concede two important philosophic matters. Levinas is highly suspicious of the notion that there is a unitary form of goodness that can be administered and applied. As he puts it, "But it is true that the moment this goodness organizes itself, it goes out. Despite the rottenness, the magnitude of evil wrought in the name of the good, the human subsists in that form of one for the other in the relation of one to the other" (AT 1999, 109). In this sense, there is a plurality of acts that are good. Levinas does hold that time bears a promise, and that this is a transcendent phenomenon that must be sustained to withstand the destruction of transcendence through totalization. Nonetheless, he states without sufficient elaboration, "The first and last manifestation of G'd would be to be without promises" (Ibid.). He does clarify this a bit, however, in praising the value of a kind of saintliness as "a time where the only right to a reward would be not to expect one" (Ibid.). It is therefore as he puts it a "faith without triumph," and then goes on to add, "perhaps this is the end of all preaching" (Ibid.). It is not possible, therefore, for me to rationalize the sufferings of others for themselves.

Human suffering, however, cannot be completely neutral—that is, being that is simply there. This would mean the reversion for Levinas to what he calls the *il y a*, the "there is." Or in the language of Genesis, it would mean the reappearance of void and chaos (*tohu v'vohu*). This state of being, of the il y a, can certainly be experienced by me personally. It would appear as the sheer overwhelming arbitrariness of that which is, at a given moment. The *il y a* unfolds as a separate instance temporally, without orientation, direction, or purpose. However, in relation to the other, I am always summoned out of myself into a world where the other can make demands upon me and therefore orient me toward a future measured by his or her urgencies.

The sign of the covenant is revealing, a rainbow that is one and many. This is the originary Trace, "The Between," where the Infinite is made partially visible. The covenant is prior to all contract where the face of every living being refracts the rays of the Infinite. The multiple colors of the rainbow between heaven and earth signify that each creature has a specific promise to be realized. This is also what creatures have in common. The situation of the human being is distinctive. His or her sense of promise is two-fold: there is the open-endedness of what he or she can become or make of him-herself. At the same time, he or she is the only creature that can make and keep a promise. In this sense, he or she establishes, in advance, an intended course of action by sending his or her word ahead of his or her deed. At its most sublime level, this can be employed to create what Levinas calls "time bearing a promise."

The prospect of good, otherness, a future—however radically contingent—still provides us with an oriented time. In other words, time "bearing a promise" is the very condition upon which hope depends. The fact that this promise extends not only to humankind but to every living creature bestows a central role to human beings, while avoiding the fallacy of anthropocentrism. Is it any wonder then that the Talmud derives the seven universal Noachide laws from this most primary of covenants?

HUMANISM WITHOUT TRANSCENDENCE

> The whole earth was of one language and of common purpose ... and they said "Come, let us build us a city and a tower with its top in the heavens and let us make a name for ourselves lest we be dispersed among the whole earth."
>
> —Genesis 11:1–4

"Biblical Humanism" is the term that Richard A. Cohen uses to describe the philosophy of Emmanuel Levinas. By this, Cohen suggests a humanism that is ordered and given meaning by its relation to the Infinite or the transcendent. This is not to be confused with the globalizing or totalizing humanism of the Enlightenment. In fact, the Generation of Dispersion is criticized precisely for its prefiguring of a kind of humanism that is associated only with an inevitable progress in which other people can be understood not only as ends in themselves but as means to an end. This would mean a progress for no one in particular and, therefore, would be self-defeating. According to the midrash, human beings were utterly replaceable because they were subsumed in the project of building a tower to the heavens at all costs.

In what way is the desire to build a tower to the heavens an error? We might also ask, why was the Generation of Dispersion spared the fate of the Generation of the Flood? Rashi remarks that the transgression of the Generation of the Flood, where each contended with each and all with all was here displaced by a kind of fraternal love toward one another. This spared the Generation of Dispersion from a similar fate to the one that had come before. The *Sefas Emes* advances the following original explanation: The Generation of Dispersion was on a higher level because they employed their intelligence as human beings, where the Generation of the Flood behaved in an animalistic fashion (Nachshoni, vol. 1, 45). Therefore, there was still hope for the former, even though, according to the sages, they were guilty of violating the prohibition of idolatry. However, what was lacking in the Generation of Dispersion was a recognition that people are unique and therefore different from one another. What must be kept in mind is that uniqueness founds difference rather than difference founding uniqueness. This is reflected in the inability to understand a divine sense that can only be expressed as transcendence. Notice that the punishment that is dealt out to the Generation of Dispersion is that "they should not understand one another's language" (Gen. 11:7). In a more contemporary idiom, the error of the Generation of Dispersion subsumed all particulars, including existing human beings, under a single concept that is the human species. Drawn to its extreme, this represents a kind of human self-adoration or, in biblical language, idolatry, and is, therefore, inconsistent with an metaphysics of pluralism.

Idolatry, understood as a moral rather than a theological concept, is prohibited by the first of what the Talmud characterizes as the Noachide laws. Levinas puts it this way: "Anyone who obeys these seven laws is a Noachide: six negative laws—abstain from: (1) idolatry, (2) blasphemy, (3) murder, (4) debauchery, (5) eating meat cut from a living animal, (6) iniquitous and violent appropriation—and one positive law—recognize the authority of a court" (UH 2004, 119). These laws are drawn from the Talmudic reading of the text (BT, Sandrehin 56a). What Levinas emphasizes in his comment on the Noachide laws is, as he puts it, "that the idea of human society, finally, encompasses all humanity" (UH 2004, 120). Stepping back from the immediacy of the biblical verses, he makes an observation about the method of Talmudic reasoning in relation to the Bible: "Talmudic deduction takes axioms of a natural moral conscience as its guide in Biblical interpretation, so from a Jewish point of view, attachment to the morals of the Torah can do without any dogmatic beliefs" (Ibid., 121).

In other words, what both the love of wisdom in Greek thought, philosophy, and the wisdom of love, drawn from the biblical/Talmudic tradition, is a reality founded upon the axioms that can be derived from morality. Levinas sees Greek thought as inherently valuable for the proper administration of the city, the beauty of the arts, and the mathematical precision of the sciences. Levinas is far removed in his reflections from any kind of religious triumphalism or theological posturing against secularism. There is a distinctively Jewish contribution to Greek wisdom. It is this: "The idea of possible concord among men obtained not through war *but through fraternity*" (UH 2004, 118). He characterizes this as the "planetary dimension of human society" (Ibid.). Why, more precisely, must the wisdom of Greece dwell within the atmosphere of the Hebraic outlook? "The idea of humanity suspends the threat of war that hands over a solely national justice. War makes all morality tentative; when a national society is in danger, it lives on a war footing and compromises moral imperatives. *It is the idea of the fatality of war on which the ancient world lives that keeps it from liberating its morality from politics*" (Ibid.).

It is in this way that Emmanuel Levinas has prepared the groundwork for a humanism with transcendence, unlike the Generation of Dispersion. It begins by acknowledging the asymmetrical relations between the Infinite and the finite and the other and the self. In this way, while it still privileges the human creature, it is not indifferent to other creatures. It sees human beings as irreplaceable, one for the other, and therefore, not merely as means to an end, but as capable of holiness. For the Jewish Bible and for Levinas, politics can be rendered just or authentic only if it is an expansion or application of morality. We are not duped by morality despite the fact that it can be turned on its head when the fatality of war takes precedence over the liberation of peace.

A NEW PARADIGM FOR THE HUMAN SUBJECT:
THE OTHER BEFORE THE SELF

Lech Lecha: Go Out of Yourself
(Genesis 12–17)

What we find announced in the opening of the sections dealing with Abraham and Sarah are more than simply individuals who have superlative characters. It is rather the announcing of the new type or paradigm of the human subject. Several points should be made here. What the life of Abraham signifies is the beginning of a way out of human egocentrism. This does not happen all at once. It is a long and demanding itinerary. From one of his earliest texts Levinas wrestles with this question in a strictly philosophic form. In his book, authored in 1935, *On Escape* (*De l'évasion*), Levinas describes and analyzes some of the ways in which it is made very difficult to exit (*sortir*) from the self. For example, we experience an overwhelming sense of inertia that corresponds to what he calls the *il y a*. The il y a, or the "there is," is the self before it becomes "elected"— that is, self-conscious of itself as a responsible subject. We are weighed down by fatigue, hunger, and the impossible claims put upon us by others. However, it is both morally possible and necessary to go out of or beyond ourselves. The inability to go out from ourselves is transformed clearly and poignantly in the Abraham saga.

The opening words in Hebrew contain an apparent redundancy. The text says *Lech Lecha*. Following Rashi, this is most widely understood as "go for yourself," as for your own benefit. However, this phrase can also be understood as "go *out* from yourself." This going out from the self does not annul the human self or personal identity. The human being as "subject" arises when it becomes aware of the fact that it is answerable to the claims of the other, whether human or divine. It is a constant struggle always threatened by returning to the position of the il y a. This means the collapsing back into one's self. The subject becomes fully human when it recognizes that its central purpose is a responsibility to and for others. As Levinas argues, Abraham as human subject signifies that the other comes *before* the self. We have reason to return to this theme.

It is in this way that Levinas rediscovers some of the existential questions that animate the human sojourn.

The biblical Abraham, according to Rashi and virtually all the commentators who follow, leaves the familiar markers of identity—personal, social, and familial—and is commanded to go to a place of which he will be told. This is not simply a journey mirroring the heroic model that we find in Greek epic or tragedy. Abraham's humanity is what is at stake, along with that of Sarah and the generations that would come from and after them. In other words, it is not simply the circuit from home and back with all of its eventual security and rootedness that is to be followed by adventures at every level and then completed with the return home, as with Odysseus who reclaimed sovereignty over Ithaca and himself. As Levinas puts it, "[F]or the transcendence of thought remains closed in itself despite all its adventures—which in the last analysis are purely imaginary, or are adventures traversed as by Ulysses: on the way home" (TI 1969, 27).

What summons Abraham forth is not yet disclosed or shown to him. This trauma of the movement out of the self that Levinas names expresses a kind of a transformation of the human subject. It is a kind of going out from the self that permits an awareness of the movement toward the Other. The subject discovers the self as overfull, lacking but wanting direction toward an elsewhere. Yet, the restlessness that accompanies this stirring from the self is lacking the specificity of the elsewhere. At this early stage, the first stirring is primarily an unknowing sense that the present situation is not yet what it could be. In this sense, it is primarily privative in its sensibility, aware only of its outgoing from the self and not yet for the other. This is seen in the movement of Terach, Abraham's father, from Ur of the Chaldees to Haran. According to the tradition Haran, approximately midway between Ur and the land of Promise was as far as Terach got before he died. In other words, Terach, unable to turn completely toward the other, did succeed in uprooting himself from the tyranny of sameness. To this extent, Terach partially succeeded in liberating himself from the idolatry with which the tradition associates him. The more positive later turn toward the land of Canaan first required movement out of virtually complete immanence. Only then would the pivot toward transcendence or holiness convey a sense of promise. It is from this sense of promise deriving from the Other that Abraham is readied to take up a series of stances toward other people. This change in Abraham and Sarah is more than an alteration in an essential or static identity. We see this transformational process come to a provisional conclusion when Avram and Sarai are renamed in the covenant that G'd subsequently enacts with them and their descendants after them (Gen. 17). Their own lives may be viewed as having the shape of a promise, announced and awaiting enactment.

What the text announces is a new model or paradigm of the human person. The biblical understanding of time and potentiality differs from the Greeks and, in particular, Aristotle, in an important way. While Aristotle sees an end or purpose (*telos*) to human striving through time, these ends are given by nature. In this sense, telos is associated with something quite definite and therefore closed and finite. Hence the Aristotelian notion of potentiality and *dynamis* is toward a pre-established limit. Human nature can achieve its full potential by the development of good habits, use of moderation, and the pursuit of living well. Nonetheless, "human nature" is not itself something that can be changed or modified or overcome.

The primacy of sameness, according to Levinas, was also the teaching of Socrates: "To receive nothing from the Other but what is in me, as though through all eternity I was in possession of what comes to me from the outside— to receive nothing, or to be free" (TI 1969, 43). Permanence and sameness are, for Socrates, the essence of reason: "Cognition is the deployment of this identity; it is freedom that reason in the last analysis would be the manifestation of a freedom, neutralizing the Other and encompassing him, can come as no surprise once it was laid down that sovereign reason knows only itself, that nothing other limits it" (Ibid., 42). The ultimate quest for Levinas is found in transposing the love of wisdom into "the wisdom of love." This is to say that other people cannot merely be the occasion for my reflected self-discovery, however lofty. From the very outset, I have a responsibility before the Other and to others.

Something new is taking place here. This something new originates with the Infinite that tears the human self out of its inertia. Only that which is transcendent to the world has the capacity to open up the elevation of the self in relation to others. The other comes before my own self. This is to say, in the language of Levinas, that ethical life arises in the for-the-other. This is the beginning of a new paradigm of the human person.

It should be conceded that according to the tradition, the Bible, especially the Book of Genesis, is so textured and so nuanced that every statement is open to seventy interpretations. It is out of this abundance that one treads with great apprehension at conceptualizing biblical phenomena by making them into themes for analysis. Nonetheless, the rabbinic tradition has its own hermeneutic. The Bible becomes the "Jewish Bible" by recognizing and affirming the priority of the oral tradition over the written one. One of the primary ways of seeing and assessing the life of Abraham is to recognize, as the Mishna does

(*Ethics of the Fathers, Pirke Avos*, 5:3), that Abraham was subjected to testing on ten occasions.[4]

There is a striking parallel between the first and the last of these ten tests. In the first test, Abraham is asked to "go to a land that I will show you." Upon arriving he finds the land of promise facing a famine. In the last of the tests he is told to go to the land "of Moriah" and to one of the mountains "that I will show you" (Gen. 22). With this begins the famous enactment of the binding of Isaac by Abraham. The last of these tests turns into what we might call an ordeal, or perhaps even a "trial." Levinas would suggest that while there is no single unifying theme or concept that can be used to describe the lives of Abraham or Sarah, the different turnings in their lives can be better understood in the language of promises. These are promises often associated with commands. The promises are extended before them as though neither the author of the command nor the subject appears to know the outcome. Only in this way can their lives be taken with full seriousness, facing each other and their own radically contingent futures.

Clearly, in this very same passage, it is evident that the promise announced to Abraham and Sarah is one of surpassing significance. While G'd is depicted as accompanying them, their future remains both unknown and to be determined by their own decisions and responses to other people and the Other. G'd says to Abraham, "[A]nd I will make you a great nation; I will bless you and make your name great, and you shall be a blessing" (Gen. 12:2). Yet the God of Abraham does not in this blessing immediately give a direct indication for what makes Abraham worthy of such distinction. Abraham and Sarah are childless and landless. It is at this early moment that G'd appears and says to Abraham that they should go to the land of Canaan, and once there, tells him "to your offspring I will give this land." The second trial of Abraham is the discovery of famine in that same land that has been promised to his offspring. He is depicted as journeying on and descending to Egypt as a way of escaping from the famine. Immediately, a third test presents itself, one that makes Abraham appear utterly

---

4   We follow Maimonides rather than Rashi in reference to these ten tests. It is not simply a matter of identifying the tests, but of assessing their meaning. However, there is basic agreement that what Maimonides regards as the first test and Rashi the third, is Abraham's departure from his family and homeland. The rest of the tests, for the most part according to Maimonides, are as follows: (2) the hunger in Canaan, (3) the abduction of Sarah in Egypt, (4) the war in which Abraham was forced to participate because of the abduction of his nephew Lot, (5) his marriage to Hagar at Sarah's request, (6) his command at a great age to circumcise himself and his son Ishmael, (7) Abimelech's abduction of Sarah, (8) the driving away of Hagar after she gives birth, (9) the sending away of Ishmael, (10) the binding of Isaac.

unheroic by Greek standards and that calls into question his relation to Sarah. The famous request: "Please say that you are my sister, that it may go well with me for your sake, and that I may live on, on account of you" (Gen. 12:13).

Sarah's compliance in this case testifies to a supreme regard for the life and well-being of Abraham. Abraham and Sarah are already outsiders in the land of Canaan, and now they are asked to become strangers to one another. In moving out of, or transcending itself, the human subject is at one and the same time singularized and set apart. Clearly, we are not dealing here with the virile virtues. Yet, in order to preserve the promise made by G'd to Abraham concerning his offspring, he must nonetheless preserve his life and that of Sarah. In other words, by restraining his sense of proper pride, he is forced to deal with and overcome his masculine ego.

What most emphatically distinguishes the biblical Abraham is that he manages to discover a humanism that derives from transcendence. In one of his very last Talmudic discourses entitled "Who Is One-Self?" Levinas comments upon a Talmudic passage that he sees as dealing with one of the ultimate questions of philosophy (BT, Chullin 88b–89a). He asks: "In human existence, is a person's 'as-for-oneself' preserved?" (NwTR 1999, 112). In what sense is the "as-for-oneself" consistent with the self for-the-other? These questions lead Levinas to explore the relation of the death and life of the other person to my own. In the spirit of the Talmudic passage under consideration (BT, Chulin 88b–89a), he reflects upon the subjects of purity and impurity. About impurity he says, "Impurity is the name of an always already sordid egoism, which death—my death—awakens like an ultimate wisdom" (NwTR 1999, 116). Levinas finds in the ritual concepts of purity (*Tahor*) and impurity (*Tumah*) an ethical dimension to ritual life. To be alive is to be open to and there *for* others. It is in fact only in death where there is the complete coincidence of the self with itself. Spiritual death signifies the inability to stand in relation to or act on behalf of others. To it belongs a total immobilization of the soul. This is the "sordid egoism" of which Levinas speaks. It is for this reason that what is radically new in the life of the biblical Abraham is that he and Sarah are fully awake and alive—for their lives are lived for the sake of other people.

Upon his return to the land of Canaan, Abraham continues "on his journeys," now the beneficiary of wealth acquired in Egypt through divine intrigue. His nephew Lot accompanies them. Abraham and Lot part ways when it becomes evident that Lot lacks the moral seriousness of Abraham.[5] Abraham is given the occasion to display both his love of peace and his generosity. In

---

5   This is Rashi's generally accepted opinion.

the separation from Lot, the as-for-me and the for-the-other are in tension but not in contradiction. The repetition and detailing of the divine promise to Abraham follows.

We cannot conclude that Abraham is unfamiliar with the virile virtues. After all, he goes to war to rescue his nephew Lot, from whom he has parted on generous, if not altogether amicable terms. We see that before Abraham goes out to war he is a man of peace (an *ish sholom*):

And there was quarreling between the herdsmen of Abram's livestock and the herdsmen of Lot's livestock. Abram then said to Lot "please let there be no strife between me and you, and between your herdsmen and my herdsmen, for we are kinsmen. Is not all the land before you? Please separate from me: if you go left, then I will go right, and if you go right, then I will go left." (Gen. 13:7–9)

According to Rashi, the herdsmen of Abram discovered that the herdsmen of Lot were grazing in pastures that were not their own. This is seen as a form of theft by Abram and, therefore, impermissible (Gen. 13: 7).

However, it is only when Lot is subsequently taken hostage, in the war of the four kings against the five kings, that Abram goes to war to rescue Lot. Upon his military success, the king of Sodom offers Abram the booty of war. Abram refuses and says in effect, I will not take anything of yours, not even a shoelace, so that you will not say, "It is I who made Abram rich." In other words, Abram is not a self-made man. Rather, he is defined in his relation to the transcendent Other. In this sense, we might call him an "Other made" man. A man who regards himself as self-made also, whether knowing or not, has committed himself to a subtle kind of idolatry where he becomes both the idol and the worshipper. While Abraham is granted moral autonomy, the purpose and direction of his life comes from the Most High.

"And he took him outside, and said, 'Gaze, now, toward the Heavens, and count the stars if you are able to count them!' and He said to him, 'So shall your offspring be!'" (Gen. 15:5). According to a midrash, G'd took Abraham beyond the realms of reason and nature. There is still a more concrete meaning to the sense of his being taken "outside." This refers to Abraham being taken "out of himself." His relations with other people, as is evident, shows the ethical priority that he places on the other person even before himself. In a way, what is suggested here is the dimension of moral "height" that Levinas associates with the Other. What remains an enigma is the relation between Abraham and the absolutely Other. Perhaps this is why when the king of Salem (Melchizedek) blesses Abraham he does so in the name of what is referred to as the "Most High" (*Elyon*). In other words, the trace of transcendence can be glimpsed in the everyday gestures of hospitality and appreciation shown toward an other.

Nonetheless, the Most High, a formulation that Levinas uses often, would seem to suggest a dimension of moral height that is ultimately associated with absolute transcendence.[6]

Both Sarah and Abraham are guided by their relation to the Most High. Sarah possesses a sense of selflessness that culminates in her giving her servant Hagar to Abraham for the purpose of having a child. In this way Sarah also becomes a paradigm of living for-the-other. Still, she is not someone with whom to be trifled. When Sarah sees that her esteem in the eyes of her servant has suffered, she treats Hagar sternly, even harshly. Abraham finds himself in the midst of a domestic conflict that he cannot control. The first time Abraham defers to Sarah after Sarah complains, "Let the Lord judge between me and you" (Gen. 16:5). Hagar flees to the wilderness, where she prays to G'd, and her prayer is answered with a child whom she is instructed to name Ishmael, meaning "consciousness of G'd." However, after Isaac is born and, according to the commentary tradition, Ishmael menaces Isaac, and Sarah forces both Hagar and Ishmael out of the house. G'd says to Abraham: "Whatever Sarah tells you, heed her voice, since through Isaac will offspring be considered yours." Moreover, it is a common theme in the commentary tradition that women in general are thought to enjoy a higher degree of inspiration than do men. The entire commentary tradition sees this as evidence that Sarah has a degree of inspiration that surpasses that of Abraham. According to S.R. Hirsch, a distinction is drawn between the voice of Sarah, or what Levinas later calls "the saying," and the content of the words used, or "the said." This is a vital distinction in that it reveals not simply a sensitivity to tone or inflection, but rather the intention that surpasses the words spoken. It is in this sense that Sarah remains an other to both Abraham and Isaac.

---

6 What has puzzled many commentators is why Abraham's question, "How shall I know?" is held to be not only inappropriate but according to some, a precipitating cause of the subsequent exile in Egypt and all the exiles that follow. Let us keep in mind that the language of Scripture is not only hard to penetrate, but also it purposefully uses hyperbole. Does the insistence on knowledge show an absence of trust? Or is this something quite different? There is a kind of love that is disturbed when one asks for the wrong kind of proof. Such proof is impossible given the limits of time and most especially the unpredictability of the future. In this sense, there is a kind of standing guard for the other like a sentinel not waiting to be relieved. Otherwise, one would get into what Hegel referred to as "the bad infinite." However, the very idea that this could serve as a rationalization for subsequent suffering at the hands of others on a mass scale in Egypt and in later exiles, over-determines and explains more than it possibly can about the exile in Egypt.

COVENANT

Only when Abram and Sarai have their names changed with the ratifying of the covenant do they rise to the sublime level of going out of themselves for the sake of the other. Their renaming occurs in the full announcing and partial enacting of the covenant. The covenant opens up a future for Abraham and Sarah as well as their offspring in perpetuity. This covenant represents the religious amplification of the ethical life that they have been living. The terms of the covenant are prefigured in G'd's telling Abraham to "Walk before Me and be perfect." In the realm of ethical life, Abraham has already achieved the stature of being morally upright. The autonomy granted to Abraham is inscribed in the phrase "Walk before me." Is this not to say, 'continue to walk by yourself in an upright manner?' This is to say without strings and that Abraham is not to think of himself as merely a marionette of the Divine. When God sees that Abraham is a whole-hearted or righteous person, we can begin to more readily respond to the question, why were Abraham, Sarah, and their descendants singled out for a blessing? In another way, this is to ask why Abraham was subject to, what in theological language is usually called "election" and/or "choseness." For Levinas, election signifies not privilege but responsibility. This sense of responsibility is ever increasing in scope and intensity. This elevation is accompanied by the following terms that the covenant announces: paternity and, by implication, maternity for Sarah; sovereignty, in a religious as well as a moral sense, meaning a sovereignty of the subject over himself. This expresses an asymmetry between the Infinite and the human, as well as the promise of land, "The land of Canaan—as an everlasting possession."

In the same breath as the promise of land, there is the enigmatic statement, "[A]nd I shall be a G'd to them" (Gen. 17:9). In searching the commentary tradition, this expression calls for but does not appear to receive adequate commentary. One opinion is that this means if you treat me as God, I will act as God toward you. Does it mean that if the descendants of Abraham act as they should then they will inhabit the land of Canaan in peace and plenty? Or does it signify something broader?[7] This would further amplify Rashi's first commentary in Genesis that serves as a reminder that all possessions, including that of land, depend upon an appreciation that "[t]he earth is the Lord's and the fullness thereof" (Psalm 24). This interpretation would embody Levinas's

---

7   In other words, perhaps as Martin Buber indicates, what is most important is the three-fold relation between the people, their God, and the land. This threefold relation is unique among the religions of the world.

idea that the signature of Abraham is the transposition from the for-one-self to the self-for-the-other. Does this not further imply that the covenant is to be reenacted by each generation to work out its own relation to the promissory future established for it?

The Abrahamic covenant is more limited in scope than the ontological covenant announced earlier in Genesis with Noach to the human being and every living being. What can then be said of the asymmetrical covenant between God and Abraham? Abraham is celebrated for his expressions of justice in the face of power, even, as we shall see, divine power, reasonableness, which makes it possible for him to almost always modulate his conduct, and generosity, which we have seen already in his willingness to let his nephew Lot take the first claims to the land. The decisions that are to be made by Abraham and Sarah are fraught with a certain degree of anxiety, especially when it comes to dealing with the domestic turmoil that rages within their own home. The promise held out to Abraham is very concrete and specific and intimately intertwined with the expectations of everyday life. It is not simply a matter of cause and effect that good behavior equals to a happy outcome. There is a heterogeneity to the goodness practiced by Abraham and Sarah. There is no question that the well-being of Ishmael is subordinated to that of Sarah's son, Isaac. At the very same moment when Abraham and Sarah are told that Sarah will bear a child of her own, Abraham says that it is enough that Ishmael lives. Very clearly, he anguishes over what happens to Ishmael prior to and during his banishment. But his worries appear to have been heeded, as Ishmael will also receive a blessing.

Abraham and Sarah are the harbingers of a world where the future will not necessarily be better than the past or present. Still, on this we must insist, the future *can* be better than the past and present. This is not understood to be inevitable *progress*, as it is during the Enlightenment, but rather it indicates a direction that can be meaningfully interpreted as virtually correlative with the stance and steps taken by the human subject. We say "virtually" advisedly, because time bearing a promise has an element of radical contingency where the deep future remains ultimately unknowable. What has become more clear is that human conduct will largely determine what becomes of the future. This emerges with greater clarity as we see the more nuanced, ethical implications of human conduct. This includes the way that we care for one another.

ON JUSTICE AND ITS SURPLUS

Vayeira: The Lord Appeared
(Genesis 18–22)

> Hashem appeared to him in the plains of Mamre while he was sitting at the entrance of the tent in the heat of the day. He lifted his eyes and saw: And behold! Three men were standing over him. He perceived, so he ran toward them from the entrance of the tent and bowed toward the ground. And he said, "My Lord, if I find favor in Your eyes, please pass not away from Your servant."
>
> —Genesis 18:1–3

According to a midrash, we learn three things from this passage: visiting the sick (*bikkur cholim*), hospitality to strangers (*hachnosass orchim*), and perhaps, for our purposes, most importantly, that the welcoming of others surpasses even the divine presence (*Shekinah*). What can be greater than being in the immediacy of the Shekinah, the indwelling presence of godliness? The welcoming of others and the attending to their material needs are expressions of an even more sublime spirituality. It is for this reason that Abraham runs toward the three strangers, imploring them not to pass him by.

Surely this is an ethical gesture that may include, but surpasses, the realm of etiquette. The movement out of the self toward the other, which begins with Abraham leaving his birthplace, is replicated here in a direct and immediate fashion. Let us remember that, according to the midrash, the three strangers appear to Abraham three days after the enacting of his circumcision in his old age. His actions are accompanied by a sense of urgency: "So he ran toward them from the entrance of the tent." In other words, according to Levinas, he left the security of home that makes interiority of the subject possible. It is in the realm of exteriority that the conduct of Abraham and his household is exemplary.

Hospitality, for Levinas, plays a central role in his philosophy. He writes in *Totality and Infinity*, "This book will present subjectivity as welcoming the Other, as hospitality; in it the idea of infinity is consummated. Hence intentionality, where thought remains an adequation with the object, does not define consciousness at its fundamental level. All knowing, qua intentionality, already presupposes the idea of infinity, which is preeminently non-adequation" (TI 1969, 27). Levinas is advancing the notion that the welcome, expressed through hospitality, is more than making the other feel comfortable or at home. The transitive character of subjectivity in fact arises when it goes out toward the other. The other bears within him a trace of the Infinite. "The idea of infinity, which is not in its turn, a representation of infinity, is the common source of activity and theory" (Ibid., 27). In this way, I cannot presume to completely understand the other even after I have welcomed him. However, I could not begin to truly speak with him without the first gesture of welcoming. Why? Because of the inherent systematic ambiguity of language. I can either receive the other amicably or turn away from him or her, pretending that I do not understand what he or she means to signify. It is through the welcome, by way of hospitality, that I engage the other's material needs so that his or her hunger can be assuaged, and he or she can be given a place to rest. The infinity of the other means that he always remains outside of my intentional consciousness. In this way, I help to create the conditions for his subjectivity by enacting my own.

In his mature philosophic writings, Levinas argues that we cannot even meaningfully speak with one another before the welcome that precedes the specific contents of what is said in specific language. This welcome shows itself in the expression of the human face. In the welcome, the human face initially turns toward the other rather than remaining indifferent. The receptivity of language is established through the welcome that is developed in material hospitality. It is Abraham, after all, who personally waits upon the Men of G'd, who washes their feet, feeds them, even in the midst of his recovery. Why does Levinas want to call this welcome "philosophy?"

Is this not because he sees that philosophy originates with what he calls "pre-philosophic experiences" that give a content to otherwise formalistic and abstract language? The most basic of these philosophical experiences is expressed in the statement that Levinas is fond of citing ascribed to Rabbi Israel Salanter: "[M]y spiritual needs are the other person's material needs." He expresses this maxim concretely in the forward to *Difficult Freedom*: "The Other's hunger—be it of the flesh, or of the bread—is sacred; only the hunger of the third party limits its rights; there is no bad materialism other than our own" (DF 1990, xiv). Abraham's hospitality not only involves turning his face toward the others in a gesture of welcome, but it involves the concrete, embodied actions of looking after their material well-being. This includes providing them with a place to rest, to recuperate and above all, with feeding them.[8]

In an episode that follows welcoming the three men of G'd, Abraham is solicited by G'd regarding His intention to destroy Sodom. In other words, G'd is inviting Abraham to speak up on behalf of even these unworthy souls. The commentary tradition regards the abject refusal of hospitality to strangers as the most severe of all the transgressions of the inhabitants of Sodom. Very precisely, the text says that in response to the invitation to speak directly to G'd, "He (Abraham) drew near (*v'yigash*)" (Gen. 18:23). His drawing near is an ethical matter before it is a spiritual one. What does he have in common with these base inhabitants who are about to face destruction, and for whom he pleads? But this drawing near is the first moral gesture characterized as "proximity" by Levinas. Before one can perform a moral action, one must be alert to one's desire to do so. Such awareness is provoked from outside the subject before it registers to conscience. In other words, the person must become aware of the claims of the absent others and assume his or her own sense of responsibility for them. This kind of proximity then, is an ethical rather than a spatial one. The others are not physically present but Abraham, as it were, "draws them close." Only when we act on behalf of the absent other, and ultimately all of the others, can we speak about acting in a manner that is just or ethical without being clouded by self-interest.

MORAL REASONING: EXPLANATION AND JUSTICE

The importance placed upon human discourse can be seen clearly in a passage that Levinas explores from one of his Talmudic readings. In a heated discussion recorded in the Talmud (BT, Baba Metzia 59b), Rabbi Eliezer is outvoted by his colleagues on a matter of law. After exhausting every imaginable argument, Rabbi Eliezer initiates several miracles in support of his position but is rebuked by Rabbi Joshua: "When scholars are engaged in legal (halachic) discussions,

---

8 The fact that the three strangers are understood by most texts in the commentary tradition as angels creates delicate problems regarding whether or not they actually ate the food prepared for them, personally, or only appeared to do so. For Levinas, it is important to note that human beings already are regarded as metaphysically more lofty than the angels, who are limited by their capacity to go on only one mission at a time and who are not tested by the ways of the world.

what right have you to interfere?" His esteemed colleagues point out to him that such matters are to be decided according to the principles of rabbinic hermeneutics and even a Heavenly Voice (*Bas Kol*), confirming one opinion or another is considered impermissible evidence in such a serious conversation. This apologue from the Talmud concludes by God laughing and saying, "My children have defeated Me" (Ibid.). Is this why Levinas upon occasion refers to the divine-human intrigue as "the Divine Comedy?" Were the sages of the Talmud also then unconcerned with matters of theology, let alone theodicy, as Levinas himself has been reproached? Despite this, the Talmud retains a trace of transcendence in both the rabbinic commentary tradition and the philosophy of Levinas. Yet what makes Levinas's phenomenological interpretation distinctive is the fact that he explores the core existential questions of our own time by focusing on the acutely moral dimension of the Talmudic tradition.

The biblical text says that Abraham appeals to G'd in the name of His own justice to weigh out the consequences of the announced destruction of Sodom. The demand for justice depends upon the human capacity for reckoning with the claims of all people, whether present or absent, near or far, worthy or not. In fact, the capacity to press the claims of all the absent others is a necessary, if not sufficient condition for the very appearance of ethical life. This is why even the unworthy inhabitants of Sodom are worthy of Abraham's appeal. In other words, justice always includes at least three parties: the other person, the person's neighbor, as well as me. "Shall not the Judge of all the Earth do justly?" (Gen. 18). This is Abraham's question, one that G'd solicits and for which He makes Himself answerable. Abraham follows by affirming: "Surely it would be far from You to slay the righteous with the wicked, for then the righteous would be as the wicked" (Gen. 18:25).

Abraham is appealing to G'd to put His power in the service of His justice. For if justice is merely an expression of power, then it may be experienced as arbitrary and understood as a mere social or political construct. This, for Abraham, would render reality chaotic, completely unpredictable, and utterly incomprehensible. If this were the case, we could not engage in the original task of philosophy—that is, the explanation to and for an other *ad infinitum*. We would simply exist in a world that is dominated by fiat, where explanation is neither desired nor given. In such a world, there is a separation between the divine and the human that is so complete that it would have little or no bearing on human experience. Abraham asks: "Shall the judge of all the earth not do justly?" (Gen. 18). The source of all explanation may be withheld from us. Nonetheless, we live in the expectation of justice, even when it does not appear. Abraham is distinguishing between the "justice of order," or arbitrary power coercively impressed upon a world of mere appearances and "the order of justice" of which we can be made aware, however dimly, of that which counts, and for that reason, makes the order of meaning more or less understandable. The extraordinary dialogue that Abraham has with G'd gives a new originality, generativity, and responsibility to the relation between G'd and human beings, however asymmetrical.

The reader will notice that Abraham's dialogue with G'd proceeds with what we might call "moral reasoning." Notice the way that Abraham's moral reasoning proceeds. It appears to presuppose that there is a mathematics of existence as well as a mathematics of things. The quantitative and the qualitative are found together before they are abstracted from one another. The question of whether or not there are fifty or forty-five or forty or fewer righteous ones in Sodom indicates that numbers can be understood as embodied. Furthermore, the process of subtraction also has a human dimension. The worth of human life may ultimately exceed our capacity for counting and calculation. However, this does not free us from the task of ordering that which is preeminently meaningful to us. We might profitably call this the "ordering of meaning." This is the preeminent task of education to which Levinas properly recalls us. In the language of Richard A. Cohen, Levinas is preoccupied with the "importance of importance" (Cohen 2000, 27).

The inhabitants of Sodom were considered the most inhospitable of all people. The stranger was to be preyed upon rather than welcomed. A person was valued only by his assets. Ultimately, this view is one that ends in turning one's face away from other people. It empties society of its very humanity. And is this not the reason that the remnant of Lot's family that survives is forbidden from facing backwards, to see the destruction visited upon the city?[9]

To reiterate, according to the rabbinic tradition, Abraham and Sarah were exemplars of hospitality, with the midrash stating that their home was open on all four sides. Abraham goes out of his way for others, even searching for people to practice kindness upon. This stands in dramatic opposition to the example set by Sodom—that is, of each-against-each and all-against-all. Of greatest importance perhaps, this contrast appears to indicate why it is that Abraham is worthy to plead on behalf of the unworthy inhabitants of the twin cities.

---

9   That is the very refusal to turn one's face in a gesture of welcome toward the stranger that is said by the commentary tradition to have affected Lot's household as well. One particularly suspicious exegete claims that Lot's wife went to her neighbors to ask them for salt, as a way of alerting them to the fact that her husband had violated the town's injunction against welcoming strangers. Hence, the precision of the punishment visited upon her.

The epochal dialogue between Abraham and God begins, "Perhaps there are fifty righteous in the city; surely You would not destroy it for the sake of the fifty?" (Gen. 18:26). The question is often asked why Abraham does not go down to a single righteous individual, rather than stopping at ten. This is usually linked to the question of why he is willing to appeal on behalf of Sodom, but not for his own son Isaac. Levinas, like Martin Buber before him, highlights what appears to be an insurmountable tension between the ethical and religious in the last test and crowning episode of Abraham's life.

THE BINDING OF ISAAC: THE YOURS

Akedah: Binding
(Genesis 22)

While the binding of Isaac remains the subject of many commentaries, it is vital that we keep in mind that we already know that Abraham is a just and righteous person. Otherwise the Binding of Isaac would not express the kind of tension between the ethical and religious realms that marks this episode so clearly. From the standpoint of the ethical alone, we already have the interceding by Abraham on behalf of Sodom. What is striking about the binding of Isaac is that the religious does not appear to be the expansion of the ethical, but its very contradiction. One way of overcoming this contradiction is to argue that it is apparent, rather than real. Rashi does this when he argues that the words for "bring him up" do not refer to actual slaughter: "This resolves the apparent contradiction between God's original command that Isaac be brought as though an offering and His later order that he remain unharmed" (Stone, 101n2). Levinas offers an important variation on Rashi. The voice of the angel calls out to Abraham not to sacrifice Isaac after every preparation has been made to do exactly that. He regards this "no" as a more ultimate achievement than Abraham's original "yes." Levinas's view makes this episode morally consistent. Furthermore, it appears to be consonant with both Rashi and Reb Chaim Soloveitchik. Reb Chaim Soloveitchik of Brisk points out that "only God could tell Abraham that Isaac was to be 'brought up,' but not slaughtered" (Stone, 101n2).

The position of Levinas puts the binding of Isaac in more stark relief. He acknowledges the ambiguity of the original command, though seeming to favor the view that this was not a misunderstanding of language on the part of Abraham, as Rashi would have it. Nonetheless, there is some support for his view in the midrash where it is asked whether it was harder for Abraham to bring him up, or having committed to this intended course of action, to bring him down. Levinas argues that the harder and more difficult course was to bring him down and therefore to affirm the "no" even more emphatically than the "yes."

In *Fear and Trembling* Kierkegaard asks, "Is there such a thing as a teleological suspension of the ethical?" Commenting on Kierkegaard's question, Levinas writes: "Thus he describes the encounter with God as a subjectivity rising to the religious level: God above the ethical order! His interpretation of this story doubtless can be given a different orientation. Perhaps, Abraham's ear for hearing the voice that brought him back to the ethical order was the highest moment in the drama" (PN 1996, 74).

In each of the other nine tests he faces, Abraham acts immediately or "that self-same day." His alacrity is a source of praiseworthiness. Still, clearly in the command regarding Isaac, he sleeps on it. It is hard to conceive that Abraham sleeps peacefully the night before his leaving with Isaac. Also, the journey with Isaac to the unspecified mountain takes three days when it should have taken only eight hours from Hebron to Jerusalem (Meam Loez on Genesis 22).

If Levinas is correct, then there is no suspension of the ethical involved in the binding of Isaac. Yet, to deny this tension is to conclude before the fact that Abraham knows for sure what its outcome would be. And he does not—otherwise it would not be a test, at least for him. Let us remember the fact that Abraham does not tell Sarah, and not even Isaac, of that which he is about to do.

On the way, Isaac asks him, "[W]here is the lamb for the burnt offering, my father?" With perfect systematic ambiguity Abraham replies, "God will provide Himself the lamb for the burnt offering, my son." It is more reasonable to understand this as a hope against hope than it is a statement of fact. Why hasn't Abraham said anything to Sarah of his intention? Or if a great miracle is to take place, why has he not told his friends, Aner, Mamre, and Eshkol?

How can Abraham speak of that which he is about to do in any public way, if speech itself has an inherently ethical configuration? In speaking we are always speaking to a *someone*. This means that we are called upon to justify what it is that we are saying or doing or explaining to someone else. What would have happened if he had told Sarah about that which he was intending to do with Isaac? Let us keep in mind that Scripture informs us that at the time of an earlier trial, Abraham was told that "in all that Sarah says unto you, harken unto her voice" (Gen. 21:14). If so why didn't he tell her in this case? In this silence, there is yet to unfold the purpose or intention attending most speech that gives it a moral dimension. Could it be that he does not tell her because he sees a direct contradiction between the action he has been commanded and ethical life?

More importantly, what does Isaac know, and when does he know it? If Isaac knows nothing at the outset of the journey, then surely his question indicates an apprehension that is more than mere curiosity. Still, the text states that "the two of them went together" (*Yachdav*). Since this Hebrew expression is used twice on the way to their destination, it would seem that they are of one purpose and of one mind. After all, Isaac could have stopped this event from taking place any step along the way. If Isaac does not know at the outset, or on the way, then surely, he must have known when his father binds him to the altar and how much more so when he raises his hand. Is there a way really to explain this as other than the impulse of a fanatic rather than a devotee? We can conclude simply that Isaac is never sacrificed.

Let us keep in mind that Abraham and Sarah have waited a lifetime for Isaac who bares the trace of the covenant within him. Can this be compared to Abraham's trying to argue with God when he intercedes on behalf of the doomed inhabitants of Sodom? Why doesn't he say anything to God? Why doesn't he raise his voice on behalf of his son to the God who follows him like the shadow on his right hand?

The test, from Abraham's point of view, is clear. Still, what does he see in the reflection of the gleaming knife that he lifts on the altar? Is it the face of a holy man or someone possessed by sacred violence? Or is it first one and then the other? It is this very moment of being possessed by the sacred that must be resisted. For possession by the sacred is, for Levinas, far different from the goodness that is associated with holiness, which is the surplus of all ethical life.

Nonetheless, clearly Abraham is listening to the voice of the angel to take Isaac down from the altar. Is his resistance to the violence of the sacred ethically on a higher plane than his apparent willingness to bind Isaac on the altar as Levinas implies? The distinction that Levinas introduces between the sacred and the holy is vital to understanding the growing importance in our own time between devotion and fanaticism. The sacred would relieve the subject of his or her autonomy and therefore divest the human subject of responsibility for his own conduct. It too easily lends itself to be understood as that which is beyond the realm of responsibility, justice, and morality. In this way, it leaves itself open to the dizzying dimension of a command that appears arbitrary. In all forms of fanaticism, the ego disappears for a moment before it finds its salvation in an egoism that is perhaps not so very pure. In this way, the subject would become linked to eternity, with all of its promised rewards and satisfactions. The fanatics find only egoistic salvation practiced at the expense of other people. Did Abraham then, make a move from the intended violence associated with the sacred to a less egocentric position that appears to us holy in its outcome?

We must keep in mind that holiness values the irreplaceable uniqueness of the face of the other person, his very singularity. To practice violence toward the other person while thinking one serves the Most High is absurd—not in Kierkegaard's sublime way, but in the plain sense of the term. Holiness, understood in the manner we are suggesting, is the "otherwise than arbitrary." Rather than being associated with power, totality, and ontology, holiness resists the will to power and belongs to a realm of the Infinite that I cannot absorb, but more importantly cannot absolve me of my ethical relations to others.

Devotion, as opposed to fanaticism, remains then attached to a path of holiness where the other cannot be made into the same or infinity into totality. The reason for this, according to Levinas, is that the infinite always escapes any act of seizure or grasping or even turning the other into a mere theme. Totality, on the other hand, which is thought to exhaust ontology, is concerned only with that which is common to all beings and thinkable by them. For these reasons, can we recognize the difference between the holiness of Abraham and the practitioner of sacred violence?

Still, we have not yet asked what this episode signifies to Isaac. From a purely existential point of view, Isaac is menaced in connection with his imminent death. Even in the last moment, before Abraham raises the knife, Isaac remains faithful to the command of his God, resolute, and unswerving. Levinas observes that death, all death, contrary to pious rationalization, "threatens me from beyond. Death … is a menace that approaches me as a mystery. Its secrecy determines it. It approaches without being able to be assumed, such that the time that separates me from my death dwindles and dwindles without end involving a sort of last interval, which my consciousness cannot traverse and where a leap will somehow be produced from death to me" (TI 1969, 234). He adds, "The last part of the route will be crossed without me; the time of death flows upstream; the I in its projection toward the future is overturned by a movement of imminence, pure menace, which comes to me from absolute alterity" (Ibid., 235). The existential position of every person is first expressed in the fear of Isaac. It is true that Isaac will be spared. We, of course, already know that God does not want human sacrifices, so this could not have been the reason for the test at all. While Isaac is spared and the role of the ethical remains preeminent, Isaac and every person will come to a time that brings with it an enigma that is not so terribly satisfying. Can the meaning of life still be affirmed when we are no longer there to witness it? This question is addressed straight away upon the sudden and quite shocking death of Sarah, which according to the commentary tradition, arises immediately from having been informed of the near-death of Isaac by the hand of her own beloved husband. Are we not always in the position of yielding, after the fact, to the afterthought, what then were my actions, my relations with others, my life, worth anyway?[10] How could Abraham not have suffered from ethical insomnia before leaving with Isaac to go to the land of Moriah?

In the binding of Isaac, the unusual language of *lech lecha* is repeated. Is this still a going out from the self or is it perhaps more the case of going for your own benefit while it seems to be otherwise? Let us remember that this trial begins with G'd using the language of request, not command. It says, "Take please your son" (Gen. 22:2). Or might it mean, as Isaac Abarbanel indicates, that this reiteration of the phrase *lech lecha* now refers to the future (Stone, 100). He and Sarah are commanded to go to a "land that I will show you." For Levinas, this means a redefining of human identity itself. It involves *sortir,* a "going out from the self to the other." The other remains the unknown, and in certain instances, the Unknowable. This is not a mystical transcendence that ends in a union of the self with the Other but rather a way that I go toward the other without violence. For these reasons, we can recognize the difference between the holiness of an Abraham and the practitioner of sacred violence.

From an existential perspective, however, it is Isaac whose very life is in danger. He is the one who is threatened with capital punishment, and without any visible reason. If we put ourselves in the position of Isaac, we are all of us aware, if only from time to time, that our stay in this world is a temporary one. How do we reconcile this with the fact that we still affirm that what we do and what we say, and even what we think, can make a difference to others if we are not there in the present to be aware of what is happening? In other words, how do we maintain a fidelity to a certain way of life when life itself is threatened in advance by annihilation? Is our response not the beginning of a gesture of what is usually called faith? In an active, transitive sense, such faith affirms that the promise set out in the covenant does not come to nothing.

It must be stressed that Isaac appears fully aware of what is going on and is in fact of the same mind and resolve as his father. Several times, as we have noted, the text says, "And the two of them went together (*yachdav*)." After all, Isaac's son Jacob subsequently refers to G-d himself as "the Fear of Isaac." This does not explain what is going on but makes it clear that Isaac is no less inspired by divine fear and faith than is his father Abraham. Why else would Scripture continually use what appears to be redundant language, "The G'd of Abraham,

---

10 I'm indebted to Rabbi Zev Dickstein of Monsey, New York, for pointing out to me the importance of what he referred to as the "*yetzer machrenu*" that comes alive to make one question if the good that one has done is worthwhile. In advance, of course, this inhibits or possibly undoes additional acts of goodness.

the G'd of Isaac, the G'd of Jacob." Does this not testify to the inescapability of each generation and each person developing his own relation to G'd? Is Isaac now ready to go on his own way? Unlike Abraham, Isaac would appear to have matured all at once. Isaac has taken the abyss into himself and affirmed none-theless that life, even when one cannot see with one's own eyes its visible purpose and end, is still promising.

According to most, but not all, commentators, the binding of Isaac is the ultimate test and it assumes the shape of a paradox. Abraham and Sarah have waited a lifetime for Isaac, and then Abraham is asked to offer him up as a sac-rifice. It is not sufficient simply to say that we learn from this that G'd does not desire human sacrifice; we already know this from the seven Noachide laws that prohibit the shedding of innocent blood (BT, Sanhedrin 56a). However, the seven Noachide laws are applicable to everyone. They belong squarely within the realm of the ethical—that is to say, the "ours."

In the binding of Isaac, we are speaking about what is most dear or most precious—that is to say, this test belongs to the realm of the "yours." Before and during the event of the binding, this must be regarded as terrifyingly real. The "yours" would normally pertain to the other person, in this case Isaac, and the absolutely other as well. Here, the collision between the ethical and the reli-gious is a virtual biblical anomaly.

It is after an event, whether it be a test, trial, or ordeal, or the self-sacri-fices of everyday life, that we are visited by the question: Was it really worth it after all? The death of Sarah follows immediately after, whether from shock or because all her days were immediately completed, or for reasons we cannot understand. The test, then, of moral life—that is the refusal to devalue morality itself—is the most subtle kind of test that shadows righteous conduct.

Given the fact that we come to be and pass away, what difference does it make what we do? If faith is something that I *have*, then it appears to me to be a diminished form of reason. More importantly, how does this help us to make a distinction between living well and living a meaningless life? But, if we render "faith" not as something we have, but as something toward which we are incessantly moving, then faith is intimately linked with transcendence. For this reason, we can speak of faithfulness or fidelity. This means affirming that life lived righteously is the most dynamic, active expression of faith. Now we are in a better position to begin to explore what this kind of fidelity might signify. We might gain a certain insight into the question of how we can affirm how life is promising, even when we are no longer here, by looking at the death of the other or more precisely, in the case before us, that of Sarah.

THE DEATH OF THE OTHER

Chayei Sarah: The Life of Sarah
(Genesis 23–25:18)

And Abraham came to eulogize Sarah and to bewail her.

—Genesis 23:2[11]

What we have learned from the binding of Isaac, among other things, is that the test for Isaac involves looking into the abyss while still affirming that life matters despite its death-bound subjectivity. For Isaac, the test is passed through a kind of pure passivity, not to be confused with Stoicism. Life comes to an end. The test for Isaac is to affirm that life remains meaningful and consequential. In this way, both Abraham and Isaac pass the test of remaining faithful to the covenant announced to Abraham and Sarah, which they must resume and take up. As we shall see, there is both a discontinuity between the lives of Isaac and Abraham, in which Isaac establishes his own identity, and a continuity where he adds to the life of Abraham.

Notwithstanding all the other opinions, there is an exception made by the great medieval Jewish moralist R. Yonah of Gerona (*Pirke Avos* 5), who regards the death and burial of Sarah as Abraham's tenth and perhaps ultimate test. Upon the death of Sarah, Abraham faces a dual test. On the one hand, Sarah's death must be a devastating event for him. The text states that, "Abraham came to eulogize Sarah and to bewail her" (Gen. 23:2). The commentary tradition makes it clear that he did not give full public expression to the depth of his grief. S.R. Hirsch notes that in the Hebrew word for weeping, one of the letters is written smaller than the others.

---

11 "His grief was infinite, but the full measure of his pain was concealed in his heart in the privacy of his home" (Gen. 23:2).

We have no specific idea of what thoughts are going through the mind of Abraham as Sarah lies before him unburied. According to the rabbinic tradition, before the time of burial, those who mourn for the deceased are exempt from all positive commandments, except attending to the burial itself. S.R. Hirsch points out that the mourner whose dead lies before him (the *onen*) does not participate in communal actions because the "feelings of the *onen* [the one whose dead lies unburied] violently oppose this communal sense ... his inner personality, mutilated by suffering, is so dominated that he has no room for any other feeling, let alone for a communal sense" (Horeb, 214). The other periods of his mourning will consist in the recuperation of his sense of alterity.

There is little question that the death of Sarah deeply affects and changes the life of Abraham. Hirsch comments, "His grief was infinite, but the full measure of his pain was concealed in his heart and the privacy of his home" (Stone, 107n2). It is true that the commentary tradition ascribes her death to the shock and trauma experienced by her learning of the near death of Isaac. Nonetheless, is it not supremely ironic that Abraham's first acquisition in the land of promise is for the purpose of burying his beloved wife? Do we really want to say that this is what the Promised Land is for—for burial and not for life? This appears to be the key reason why Rabbi Yonah considers the death and burial of Sarah to be Abraham's tenth and final trial. It can be said that Abraham passes this test with his taking responsibility for the future of the covenant. He does this by finding a righteous wife for Isaac, thus continuing the life of Sarah.

For Levinas, the death and life of the other have a dimension of moral height that places the other before me: "I do not define the other by the future, but the future by the other, for the very future of death consists in its total alterity" (TO 1987, 82). Death is based on time, not time on death as is true for the philosophers of finitude in the twentieth century. What does this mean? This means that it is the other person who makes it possible for me to measure time based on *urgency*. The other calls upon me to *make time for her*. Time becomes generative only in and through the other. She or he calls upon me to be straight with her or him, or more precisely, to be upright in responding.

Death based upon time is responsible for a new relation between time and infinity. Levinas puts it this way, "Time is not the limitation of being, but its relationship with infinity. Death is not annihilation, but the question that is necessary for this relationship with infinity, or time, to be *produced*" (GDT 2000, 19). Levinas holds this position despite the common view that for time to be recognizable as such, it would have to be finite. What a wonderfully simple and yet deep notion; time is something that I make ... make for the other person. This gives it an ethical meaning at the outset. Only when it is abstracted does human time become a neutered mathematical term or concept. Given the moral asymmetry between the other and the self, it is the 'I' that remains responsible for making time for the other, even when the other does not make time for me. For him or her however, time is going somewhere, toward a future. In the case of the death of the other, it is a future that remains a mystery. Nonetheless, I do not remain indifferent to the death of the other. It is authentic and meaningful to speak of the death of the other as a loss for me and a hole in the social fabric of life.

In this way, the death of the other marks the absolute limit that keeps me from making the other person an extension of myself or my possession. Unlike the great scandal of twentieth century philosophy, Martin Heidegger, Levinas argues that the death of the other is not merely a distraction that would divert me from an awareness of my own finite being. Quite the opposite is the case. It is with the other person that the promise of time opens for me: the other is my future. The very relationship with the other is the relationship with the future. With the anticipation of the death of the other, it is not simply that my projects are unsettled. What we come to realize is that, as Levinas puts it, "Death becomes the limit of the subject's virility" (TO 1987, 74). The approach of death remains a mystery, both for the other and for me. Death comes to us, as Levinas puts it, like a menacing violence from outside the subject. As he says, "[D]eath threatens my life from beyond. This unknown that frightens the silence of the infinite spaces that terrify, come from the other, and this alterity … as a kind of judgment of justice" (TI 1969, 234). Just as we have seen that explanation is always an explanation to a *someone*, so too does Levinas argue, "that death approaches in the fear of someone and hopes in someone" (Ibid., 234). In other words, "a social conjuncture is maintained in the menace … the violence of death threatens as a tyranny, as though proceeding from a foreign will" (Ibid.). In Talmudic thought it is the Angel of Death who comes for me. The death of the other is folded within a time that does not belong to me either. I wait upon the urgent requests, needs, and aspirations of the other person. She does not simply fit into my ongoing existential autobiography. I am also a part of her life, where my responsibility continues, even after the time of her death. Hope originates for me in the promise of time that bears a trace for me in the other.

Abraham appears to have been absent at the death of Sarah. While this surely must have been a matter of self-reproach for him, the bigger question is what the covenanted land is truly for. According to Jewish tradition and law, every descendant of Abraham and Sarah through Isaac is entitled to four cubits in the land of Canaan.[12] It does not state explicitly that this refers to a plot for a burial. But, can it be coincidence that it seems to correspond to a burial plot in size? This should not, however, make us think of time based on death, especially when it concerns the death of the other person, but rather it is, as Levinas argues, death based on time—the time of the other person. While I can hope for a promising future, the promise continues through the trace of the other where hope originates with me.[13] Is this also not another reason why this section of the Torah is called "The Life of Sarah" and not her death?[14]

According to Levinas, we are responsible for tending to the other person even before we care for ourselves. This includes both the death and life of the other. Therefore, Abraham fulfills his obligation to bury Sarah in the Cave of Machpelah. This, according to the tradition, is the ultimate expression of kindness, called "kindness-in-truth" (*chesed shel emes*), for the deceased can never return my kindness. Or in following the language of Levinas, we may call it an act of infinite kindness.

CONTINUITY AND DISCONTINUITY

If the land is to belong to Abraham, what does it mean that its first purpose is for the burial of his beloved Sarah? We may begin to understand the response to this question of what the land is for by considering the analogy of the relation of Abraham to the land. If Isaac does not *belong* to Abraham, then in a certain way neither is Abraham the proprietor of the land that forms the burial plot of Sarah. Put bluntly, this would make G-d other than a divine real estate agent. It would seem rather that Abraham and his descendants will belong to the land, or at least have a continuing relation to it. Perhaps it is important that his paying for and taking possession of a small portion of the land is recognized as a legal acquisition rather than as a gift, but it is hard to believe that the ultimate test,

---

12 I heard this from my late lamented friend and teacher R'Shmul Hecht in October of 1977.

13 I am indebted to Professor Roger Burggraeve for making this distinction between hope that originates with the self and promise with the other (conversation in Jerusalem at the Hebrew University, Institute for Advanced Studies, January 2006).

14 The *Tur* in his commentary insists, contrary to Rashi, that Sarah was as beautiful as a woman at twenty and as innocent as a girl of seven. The larger point about why her years are spoken of we take up in considering the end of the life of Abraham.

the death of Sarah, is simply the forced bargaining he engages in with Ephron, the Hittite.

The land is in the first instance for the living, not for the dead. Among other things, the binding of Isaac shows that the life of Isaac transcends the life of Abraham. Isaac will emerge as his own person. In a very different kind of way, even though he has acquired the land in Hebron to bury his wife, this is significant because it includes *her life* as well as her death. For Abraham, it is not a matter of Isaac being "mine," nor is it a matter that the land is "mine" in the common sense of proprietorship. It is commonly understood in the tradition that we are not permitted to die for even the holy land, except insofar as it is a condition for saving lives (*pikuach nefesh*). The child belongs rather to the realm of the "yours" than the "mine," and so too does the land that he will inherit. In this way, both my child and my land achieve a holiness that is the surplus of ethical life. As Levinas puts it, the achievement of the modern nation state of Israel will make it possible for the social dimension of Jewish life to be lived out in a concrete fully embodied way. How ironic then, that Hebron, the land surrounding the Cave for Burial (*machpeila*), acquired through what must have been agonizing negotiation, is in our time the source of so much contestation.

After the burial of Sarah and the mourning period for her is complete, Abraham undertakes the act of searching for a suitable wife for their son Isaac. The son, as Levinas puts it toward the end of *Totality and Infinity,* is both the continuation of the father and mother, and yet a new being who has never appeared before. In this sense, the son becomes the "yours" rather than the "mine." There is a recognizable difference between a child saying "you are *my* mother" and "I am *your* son." Logically, these statements may be equivalent, but their semantic inflections and ethical import are quite different. The "yours" expresses a certain yearning and love for the alterity of the other person.

Grammatically, we can say that the "mine" and the "yours" are on each side of the "ours." By the "ours," we are referring to the interpersonal sense of morality and responsibility that would, for Levinas, spread out to include the whole of humanity, although not in a subsuming, abstract manner. As lived out, this means that the "ours" does not in any way compromise the alterity of the other person. "The mine" includes the realm of preference or affinity but exceeds it in the sense that it is ready to be taken up in the realm of the "ours." The taste of food may remain with sensibility, but as Levinas notes, the satisfying of the hunger of the other person and his neighbor are ethical issues of the first order. Similarly, the singularity of holiness is almost always an expansion of the ethical.

However, the "yours," which for Levinas presupposes the "ours" and the "mine," is on yet a higher level. It suggests a dimension of height, or a surplus of the ethical that aspires to holiness. It is this sense of the "yours" that stirs me to a position of inescapable responsibility. There is a relation with the land of Promise before we are in it and when we have left it. What is expressed is a triangular relation between God, the land of Promise, and Abraham including his descendants. Martin Buber has already recognized this distinctive triangular bond. However, what Buber does not recognize is that the land, the people, and God all express themselves as irreducible to one another if only by virtue of the otherness that each retains in relation to the other two.

Rebecca first appears in the text in her response to Eliezer, the servant of Abraham who has been sent to find Isaac a suitable wife. She shows extraordinary hospitality and embodies kindness and compassion. She gives Eliezer water to drink, and unsolicited, water to the camels, and offers him respite and lodging from his journey. She exhibits an independence of mind and humility in agreeing to follow Eliezer back to the land of Promise, despite the protestations of her family. She has shown herself truly worthy of belonging to the family of Abraham and as a worthy successor to Sarah. This portion of the text expresses the life of Sarah in a new and dynamic way. How are we to reconcile these claims? In one sense, it is meant to be a retrospective on the life of Sarah, that she had all the days of her years to count, to show as meaningful before her Creator. Recall that the "life of Sarah was one hundred years, twenty years, and seven years." According to the Zohar, this unusual formulation is meant to call attention to the fact that Sarah had "long days" (*Arichas Yomim*) because she lived for others. About Abraham, subsequently, the text says, "He was a hundred years and 70 years and 5 years. And Abraham expired and died in good old age, mature and content, and was gathered to his people" (Gen. 25:7). He had both long days and long years. By long days, we mean fully lived: able to be brought without regret before the divine Other.

In another sense, we see in the marriage of Sarah's son Isaac to Rebecca as the continuation of the trace of the life of Sarah. It is Sarah who insists that precedence be given to Isaac over Ishmael. Isaac, unlike his father Abraham and his son Jacob, lives out his life exclusively in the land of Canaan. In this sense, continuity between Sarah and Isaac is threaded through the discontinuity of Sarah's death before the marriage of Isaac. There is a reciprocity in the fact that the outstanding features which Abraham's servant, Eliezer, finds in Rebecca are the kindness and compassion that she extends both to him and his animals, as well as the hospitality that she displays in welcoming him to the land of Charan.

GENERATIONAL RESPONSIBILITY

Toldos: Generations
(Genesis 25:19–28:9)

And these are the offspring of Isaac, son of Abraham—Abraham begot
Isaac.

—Genesis 25:19

A commonly asked question concerns the use of the plural for "offspring" or
"generations" (*toldos*) for the single offspring of Abraham and Sarah—that is,
Isaac. Rashi, following a midrash, testifies to the fact that father and son looked
virtually identical so that the issue of Abraham's paternity could not be questioned. The category of fecundity is not viewed as a philosophical one until
Levinas brings it to life in his book *Time and the Other*. As Levinas puts it, "I do
not *have* my child; I *am* in some way my child" (TO 1987, 91, author's emphasis).
This is an existential distinction that transcends the biology that it presupposes.
While this appears to be common sense, it still represents a radical departure
from the overly philosophical idealism of Greek philosophy. It is worth noting
that Plato, the most methodical of Greek thinkers, does not inform us of the
proper names of the sons of Socrates. Is this because people, whatever their
intrinsic value, are always most esteemed as vehicles that would carry us to the
higher ideas? Is Levinas really asserting then that the existent, the child, is more
"real" and, therefore, more important, than the idea of the child?[15]

---

15 In Plato's famous dialogue on the nature of love, *The Symposium*, there is an image
presented of love as a ladder with three ascending rungs. Love is described as desiring and
longing for that which it lacks. In the Greek world, this is understood primarily as mortals
longing for immortality. The first or lowest rung on the ladder corresponds to procreation.
It is characterized as the lowest rung simply because it is not understood to be uniquely

The child, for Levinas, pierces through the neutrality of Being and offers me the prospect of a future in which I have a portion as well. It is not immortality that is at stake, but rather creation and the redeeming of the imperfections in that which has been created. As Levinas points out, "[T]here is a multiplicity and transcendence in the verb 'to exist,' a transcendence that is lacking in even the boldest existentialist analyses" (TO 1987, 91). The son is not a return to the father, but a movement unto itself that brings along with it the trace of the parents. The language of generations then, involves an understanding of both the discontinuity that produces individuals and the continuity that permits the community of generations. When Scripture subsequently uses the language of "the G'd of Abraham, the G'd of Isaac, the G'd of Jacob," it is not by accident that all three are named, even in this most economical of texts. Each generation has to work out its own relation to transcendence.

Death or its advent is also a prominent phenomenon in this portion of the text. Isaac mistakenly believes that he is about to die, and yet he lives for nearly sixty more years.[16] Perhaps, more significantly, Esau sells his birthright to Jacob for a simmering stew that Jacob has prepared according to the midrash as the mourning meal for Abraham. In fact, it is likely that there is no other portion of the Torah where the oral tradition is so at variance with the written text. Most of the commentary tradition is extremely harsh on Esau, commenting

---

human. Progeny are brought about by animals as well as humans. The second rung is that of renown, fame, or recognition that comes about through great deeds and accomplishments. Aristotle describes the limitation of this effort to achieve honor as a higher form of immortality or everlasting life. Such recognition is, however, always dependent upon others, and therefore as it fades, so too does the honor that would keep "immortality" alive. This, for Aristotle, expresses the limitation of the reach of the achievement of honor. Therefore, the highest rung is left to philosophy, that in its best advertisement for itself, claims to represent the unity of the knower and the known, where the love of wisdom would be consummated (*Nicomachean Ethics,* book 1, chapter 7).

However, many advantages a theoretical child might have over an actual child, such as fewer costs pertaining to child rearing, education, tuition, and sustenance, fewer worries, and so on—all the satisfactions are imagined rather than real. A real child both is and is not the continuation of the parent and yet is expected to become ultimately someone in his or her own right. The child, in this sense, appears to be reckoned as a deficient mode of honor on Plato's ladder of love.

16 According to the commentary tradition, a person should begin to worry about his or her own longevity when he or she reaches an age of five years before till five years after the death of a parent. Isaac was clearly thinking of Sarah and did not reckon with the fact of Abraham's significantly longer life.

on the multiple transgressions he committed on this very day of the sale of the birthright. The tradition appears to go out of its way to uncover violations on the part of Esau that are by no means apparent. Still, let us keep in mind that during Rebecca's difficult pregnancy with Jacob and Esau she is prophetically informed that the elder (Esau) will serve the younger (Jacob). As we see, it is Rebecca who assumes the awesome responsibility for affecting the outcome that elevates Jacob over his brother. Rebecca has already gleaned what the commentators come to realize.

Rashi notes that the word for "swallow" is used only in regard to Esau for a human being (*hitlanei*); otherwise its use is confined to animals in the entire Torah. This is to alert us to the fact that the motive behind Esau's conduct is not always apparent. Jacob, on the other hand, appears to be acting harshly when he demands from Esau the sale of his "birthright." However, when one looks more closely, Esau, who is presumably on the verge of death, is able to both think and speak quite poignantly—"Look, I'm going to die, so what use to me is a birthright?" The Ramban notes that as a hunter, Esau was exposed to constant danger and therefore his life would surely be foreshortened. Still, if we look at what Esau says from an existential point of view, we find that it is perfectly reasonable to think that Esau understands that he, like all human beings, will die. This is made all the more emphatic by the fact that he must have already known of the death of Abraham. His reasoning would not be hard to follow. Abraham, the most perfect of human beings, has died—what am I to expect? The commentary tradition informs us that five years were taken from Abraham's life so that he did not see the misdeeds of his grandson Esau. The question is, were these misdeeds perhaps also precipitated by the death of Abraham? Esau concluded that if a perfectly righteous person like his grandfather, Abraham, could die despite all of his merits, then what could possibly become of any good deeds that might be done by him or others? It was this shock and disappointment that, according to my interpretation, brought Esau to announce that "[t]here is neither Justice nor a Judge" (BT, Baba Batra 16).

In other words, Esau, to use the language of Levinas, rejects the transcendence inscribed in the promise that one generation bequeaths to another. It is for this reason, then, that the birthright means very little in his eyes. To say that Esau rejects the notion of transcendence means, for him, that each subsequent day does not carry the promise of the meaning lived out in the previous one. Death, for Esau, is not a mystery, as Levinas would have it, but rather the annihilation of meaning that occurs with the end of my own life.

REBECCA'S FOURFOLD RESPONSIBILITY

It is Rebecca who understands that Isaac's professed wish to bestow his blessing on Esau would signify the end of the covenant made first with Abraham. This is the same Rebecca who in her youth already understood what it meant to transcend the conditions governing her home of origin. In her agreement to go out of her homeland and immediate family of origin to marry Isaac, she self-consciously goes against the wishes of the dubious morality of her father, Bethuel, and her brother, Laban. This is to emphasize that the kindness she extended to the servant of Abraham and his camels is confirmed in her willingness to accept responsibility for her past and Isaac's future.

Jacob's reluctance to dress as his brother, thus deceiving his aged, near-blind father, is calmed only when Rebecca affirms that she, not Jacob, will bear the responsibility. It says, "But his mother said to him, 'your curse be upon me, my son; only heed my voice'" (Gen. 27:13). In this respect, it is Rebecca who makes the life-transforming decision for her descendants just as Sarah, her mother-in-law, did before her, in relation to Ishmael. This is what Levinas means by the double responsibility that we bear not only to others, but for the responsibility of the second party toward the third. In other words, Rebecca is not only exercising her own responsibility, but is also taking responsibility for her son Jacob and *his* sense of responsibility. In this sense, it is Rebecca who assumes a responsibility for future generations. It may even be argued that by interfering with Isaac's professed wishes, she is taking a responsibility for Isaac as well. In the language of Levinas, this means that I am responsible for the other person's responsibility as well as my own. While this moral claim may seem extravagant, it is the way by which the interpersonal realm is elevated ethically. It is at the furthest possible remove from utilitarian thinking. By this we mean that my freedom does *not* end when it begins to interfere with the other person's freedom. For Levinas, responsibility by delimiting freedom makes the free acts of human beings already ethical and, therefore, intelligible. This is how and why I can be responsible beyond my intentions for my conduct. For freedom, as Levinas understands it, is always invested and therefore dependent upon responsibility for its very expression and enactment. This means that its investiture in responsibility makes it possible for mere spontaneity to be supplanted by a moral freedom that is durable. In fact, it is this willingness to intercede that elevates Rebecca to a superlative ethical-religious status. From this perspective, where responsibility governs freedom and alters its expression, Rebecca achieves a greater level of ethical importance than any of the other matriarchs.[17]

A problem arises where Isaac smells the fragrance of Jacob, whom Rebecca has clothed as his brother, Esau. In her article in *Levinas and Biblical Studies* (Aronowicz 2003, 37), Levinas scholar Annette Aronowicz cites the Talmudic passage interpreted by Levinas, dealing with this aspect of Jacob's deception of his father: "Rav Zera said: That is to be deduced from the following text: 'Ah, the smell of a field watered by the Lord'" (Gen. 27:27). One should not read *begadov* (his clothes) but *bogedav* (his rebels)." Building on traditional interpretations, Aronowicz notes, "The reason he smelled so sweet to Isaac is that, by putting on Esau's clothes, he was signaling his responsibility for his brother, and, through his brother, for all rebels ... to don others' clothes. In Levinas's reading, it is to put oneself in their place, to agree to take on their responsibility, and thus to become responsible for them, to do what they should have done. But to don someone's clothes is also to remain with them, to put oneself in their place, to keep them in what is human" (Aronowicz 2003, 38).

The intrigue of the blessing by Isaac of Jacob remains problematic. Isaac surely appears skeptical, if not downright suspicious. Note that when Jacob draws close to his father, Isaac feels him and says, "The voice is the voice of Jacob, but the hands are the hands of Esau" (Gen. 27:24). There are few things more personal than one's voice and one's proper name. It is the voice that carries with it the intention, or as Levinas calls it, "the saying," as opposed to the manifest content or words, or what Levinas calls "the said." To put this matter more simply, the tonality of voice gives us a clearer indication of what is meant. There is an intimacy that is revealed in this kind of saying that gives us a kind of certainty that even the feel of someone else's hand or arm does not. Furthermore, Isaac says to Jacob, almost as a last test as to who this is: "[C]ome close and kiss me, my son." This is a way of amplifying the comments made by Aronowicz. A skeptical rustic might wonder how freshly tanned goatskins might smell like the fragrance of a field. As Aviva Zornberg notes, even when Isaac is made aware of deception by Esau's outrage, he nonetheless reaffirms the blessing to Jacob. Isaac states: "Indeed, he shall remain blessed!" (Zornberg 2011, 145).

Was Isaac complicit in the deception? This is also to ask if he engaged in self-deception. If so, did he see the invisible hand of Rebecca whom he had known since her youth and whose understanding of the everyday world and

---

17 See Claire Katz, *Levinas, Judaism, and the Feminine: The Silent Footsteps of Rebecca.* In Katz's otherwise exemplary book, this elevation on the part of Rebecca, who embodies responsibility in the sense that Levinas intends it, is not yet fully explored.

its ways surpassed his own? By appearing not to take issue with either Rebecca or Jacob, does Isaac not regain a sense of his own active responsibility? At least after the fact, he appears to understand and reject the established tradition of primogeniture. This rejection yields to a higher perception of reality.

It is hard to overestimate the kinds of responsibility that Rebecca has taken upon herself. In doing so, Rebecca has quietly altered not only family dynamics, but posterity as well. She has taken responsibility not only for Jacob, but for Jacob's sense of responsibility toward others, even Isaac. In a similar way, Rebecca takes responsibility for Isaac and his responsibility toward the covenantal future, the tribes that will issue from Jacob. She has more than proven herself as a worthy successor to Sarah. She has assumed an unprecedented fourfold sense of responsibility: (1) for Jacob and his deception, (2) for Jacob's responsibility toward the third party (Isaac), (3) to Isaac, and (4) for Isaac's sense of responsibility toward the third party (Jacob, Esau). Not only has she shown herself a worthy successor to Sarah, she has perhaps exceeded her in patience and foresight, overcoming the impediments of her family of origin and self-effacement.

Nonetheless, Rebecca knows that there is a difficult road ahead for her son, Jacob. The extent, duration, and difficulty of Jacob's subsequent exile to escape Esau, his brother, yields to a path of his own, one for which he is forced to come to terms and for which he must learn to take responsibility.

LOVE AND WORK IN EXILE

Vayeitze: He Went Out
(Genesis 28:10–32:3)

According to Freud, the subjects that preoccupy a person's life are love and work (*Life and Work,* vol. 1). The biblical Jacob appears to confirm Freud's observation. Jacob leaves his father's house to escape the wrath of his brother, Esau, occasioned by the deceptions through which he took from his brother's birthright, and then his father's first blessing. According to tradition, he stops in Beersheva where he is anachronistically depicted by the midrash as learning Torah. Beersheva is associated with tranquility and serenity, not simply because of its location away from the world, but also because by self-definition, learning Torah requires calm necessary for study and contemplation hence the biblical expression of, "Dwelling in the tents of Jacob."[18] Jacob leaves Beersheva for Charan, a place referred to as the "fierce anger of exile."[19]

The notion of exile is not governed exclusively by geography. From an existential point of view, exile refers to not being at home in the world (*unheimlickheit*). Exile can also refer to the realm of speech, a kind of speaking where one does not necessarily say what one means or mean what one says. We see evidences of exilic speech in Laban's manipulative dealings with Jacob. We also find alienated labor, substituted for meaningful work. Even one's comings and goings within the family may suffer from the expectation of disharmony. The climate, on many levels, leaves something to be desired. Exile also expresses a time when sleep is short, food is scarce, and households suffer from instability. This is the new situation Jacob finds himself in upon entering Charan. This is the first of many exiles that confront the descendants of Jacob.

---

18 Rabbi Menachem M. Schneerson, *Likkutei Sichot,* vol. 1. Brooklyn: Kehot Publication Society.

19 Ibid. The fierce anger of Charan is understood by the Zohar as the fierce anger of the world. It is derived from the words *charon af.*

He also goes to Charan to fulfill the obligation of taking a wife. Near a well, he meets Rachel, the younger daughter of his mother's brother Laban, and Jacob is immediately drawn to her. He works for Laban, the master deceiver, for twenty years in all.

The interwoven themes of the life of Jacob are worthy of reflection because his life perhaps more closely resembles our own than that of his father, Isaac, or his father's father, Abraham. As we see later on, there is a reason that he says to the Pharaoh, when Joseph places him before Pharaoh in Egypt: "The days of the years of my life have been few and terrible and have not been equal to those of my fathers" (Gen. 46:9). Simply put, the life of Jacob moves through the motifs and patterns that belong to everyday experience, even if they are lived out in a sublime way. To begin with, he is exiled from his home and his family of origin. In the presence of strangers whom he encounters he must learn to hesitate before engaging in transactions of any kind.

In the language of Levinas, Jacob learns that there may be a sharp difference between the sincerity of the saying and the ambiguity of the said. In fact, he learns perhaps more than he wished about the politics of the family. The "home" or "house" (*Bayis*) that Jacob would establish is from the beginning a source of intrigue. The home, for Levinas, is not simply a place from which to leave for the marketplace of history and then to return for leisure and security. In this sense, it is not like the house of the bourgeoisie, a valuable kind of merchandise. The home is interiority par excellence. Away from the traffic of history, it makes not only the "inner life" visible but serves as the origin of intersubjective existence. It does so in this way: The home serves as the precondition for the welcome (as in "welcome home"), hospitality toward the stranger, recuperation from illness, and rest that comes before and after labor.

The home for Levinas, contra Hegel, is not sub-historical. For Hegel, the status of the home is inferior to that of the marketplace and, therefore, does not reach the level of the political. According to Levinas, the home is supra-historical. It becomes effectively my address in being. Moreover, it is the central place from which I exit from the self (*sortir du soi*) and go toward others.

Jacob's home, however, is not a place where one can simply rest, recover, and welcome others; he is victimized by his father-in-law, Laban, from the outset. He had agreed to work for seven years for Rachel, his younger daughter: "Jacob loved Rachel, so he said, 'I will work for you for seven years, for Rachel your younger daughter.' Laban said, 'It is better that I give her to you, than that I give her to another man: Remain with me.' So Jacob worked seven years for Rachel, and they seemed to him a few days because of his love for her" (Gen.

28:19). Clearly, here we see time measured by meaning and only derivatively by number. To Jacob's presumed shock and surprise, it is not Rachel that he discovers after the night following the wedding ceremony, but older sister, Leah.

Laban informs Jacob that it is not the custom to give the younger daughter in marriage before the older. So Jacob is forced to agree to serve for another seven years. Still, Rachel becomes his wife after the week of festivities with Leah. The commentary tradition holds that Rachel was complicit in this deception in order that her older sister not be brought to shame. In this way, Rachel assumes a kind of responsibility for the happiness of her sister, which should not go unnoticed. Other commentaries point out that just as Jacob deceived his father, so too is Jacob now deceived. Perhaps more importantly, however, it is with Leah that Jacob sires many children. Rachel mysteriously remains childless. What this appears to imply is a temporary disjunction between eros and fecundity. Rachel, perhaps following in the footsteps of her grandmother, Sarah, gives her servant and possibly her sister, Bilhah, to Jacob after Leah has given birth to four sons. There is agreement among the commentators that Jacob makes his home with Rachel during most of this time.

The phenomenon of love is not reducible to either voluptuosity or to fecundity. Unlike labor, the kind of love that Jacob has for Rachel and even for Leah is not faceless. There is an ambiguity in the written text that makes it possible for the commentators to claim that Leah was loved by Jacob. Only in relation to his love for Rachel could she have been considered unloved. According to Levinas, love, in aiming at the other, aims at her "frailty." He makes this more concrete when he says that "frailty does not here figure the inferior degree of any attribute, the relative deficiency of a determination common to me and the other" (TI 1969, 256). Levinas makes this more concrete when he exposes love as a "fear for another," to come to the assistance of her frailty. Love, for Levinas, is linked to tenderness and vulnerability; "[T]he epiphany of the Beloved is but one with her *regime* of tenderness. The *way* of the tender consists in an extreme fragility, a vulnerability" (Ibid.).

The Talmud observes that a man is required to acquire a home for his wife. However, even after Bilhah gives birth to Dan and Naphtali, Jacob's intentionality is toward Rachel. Leah feels abandoned and rejected, even though she has had four sons by Jacob. She asks her oldest son, Reuven, to go out to the field to secure for her some flowers (either aphrodisiacal or fertility inducing).[20] Rachel says to Leah, "Please give me some of your son's mandrakes. But she said to her,

---

20 For more information, see R. Aryeh Kaplan, *The Living Torah*, 1981 (New York: Maznaim Publishing).

"was your taking my husband insignificant?—And now to take even my son's mandrakes!" Rachel's response is taken by some commentators to be the cause of her own premature death, as she later dies while giving birth to her youngest son, Benjamin. She says, "Therefore, he shall lie with you tonight in return for your son's mandrakes." Rashi notes that because Rachel "made so light of the privilege of lying with him (for it was her night) she was not privileged to be buried with him."

It is clear that Jacob is not truly at home in Charan. He is, as he subsequently describes himself, a "sojourner (*garti*) with Laban." He lacks the stability of a home and the privacy that would permit him to return to a place without worries. In this sense, Jacob lacks a certain kind of positive solitude or interiority that is accompanied by solace. Jacob is fully aware of this, and he fights against becoming too comfortable in Charan. He is aware that he is a person who lives in exile and therefore experiences the alienation from both home and labor. His life is a struggle without respite.

Laban exploits Jacob ruthlessly for twenty years. It is during the last six years that Jacob acquires his fortune by learning the arts of animal husbandry. Based upon need, according to Levinas, labor converts the other into the same. It becomes, in effect, my possession. And yet at the same time, Jacob does not disappear into his function as a shepherd. He maintains his household. He does this by incorporating his labors into his relations with others, his wives and his children. In this sense, it is not simply a matter of need. For as Levinas notes, need is something that can be fulfilled. Desire, on the other hand, is for the infinite, and therefore, is always restless and searching.

It is desire that governs need, rather than the other way around. Levinas makes this clear when he contrasts the Greek notion of the indefinite (the *apeiron*) and the Hebraic concept of the infinite (*eyn sof*) (AT 1999, 60). The *apeiron* is connected with labor but not with the other. It is through the other that the *eyn sof* appears. To put this in classical metaphysical terms, the apeiron concerns the relation between the parts and the whole of things while the Infinite occasions the questions concerning the one and the many. Levinas poses the issue in a new and original way: "Contemplation is not the suspension of the activity of man; it comes after the suspension of the chaotic and independent being of the element, and after the encounter with the Other, who calls in question possession itself" (TI 1969, 163). The life of a shepherd, Jacob's life and that of his father, is presumably free for just such contemplation. However, as Levinas observes, contemplation is not utterly divorced from labor and acquisition: "Contemplation, in any case, presupposes the very mobilization of the thing, grasped by the hand" (TI 1969, 163). In this separated existence, having worked in the elements by laboring on materiality, the subject becomes able to give the surplus of his labor as a gift to others. This, for Levinas, is the true value and ultimate expression of meaningful work. All this is not to say that Jacob is involved in what in the post-World War II era we may call "meaningful work." He has not chosen a "career," nor has one been chosen for him. Rather, he maintains an exteriority on his labors. That exteriority originates with the love of the others.

The love that Jacob bears toward Rachel resembles but is not identical to what we would in our time call "romantic love." Scripture indicates that "Rachel was beautiful of form and beautiful of appearance." The love of Jacob for Rachel was governed by what Levinas calls "desire rather than need." Desire, unlike need, can never achieve the fulfillment of its quest. In this sense, it has a non-concupiscent dimension. Even at the corporeal level, "the caress aims at neither a person nor a thing. It loses itself in a being that dissipates as though into an impersonal dream without will and even without resistance. . . . Wholly passion, it is compassion for the passivity, the suffering, the evanescence of the tender" (Ibid., 257). On a more concrete level, this is why every caress remains incomplete, because the subject of desire exceeds my intentional grasp. As Levinas describes it, "[T]he caress consists in seizing upon nothing, in soliciting what ceaselessly escapes its form toward a future never future enough . . . in a certain sense it expresses love but suffers from an inability to tell it" (Ibid., 257–58).

"So Jacob worked seven years for Rachel and they seemed to him a few days because of his love for her" (Gen. 29:20). When the seven years are described as seeming like a few days in his eyes, there is a sense that these seven years pass quickly because the ardor of his love is expressed before its fulfillment. There is a reserve then, or as Levinas puts it, a "modesty, insurmountable in love (that) constitutes its pathos" (TI 1969, 257).

Jacob's life with Leah expresses itself, at least on the surface, in the more prosaic reflections of family life. It is Leah who bears him six sons and a daughter. The economy of marriage and family life can be seen in all of its habituated routines. It is expressed as a cycle that moves from marriage to many children with an abundance of needs, and it rests upon the stability of life at home and at work. Jacob's life with Leah is accompanied by the benevolence of their disinterested love for one another. However, there is already the problem of the third person who appears as both the complement and rival of Rachel's love for Jacob. There is both solidarity and strife within the family existing side by side. It is important to note that it is through his life with Leah that Jacob achieves a certain kind of serenity and completion, and it is with Leah, as the commentary tradition notes, that he is ultimately buried. Leah has shown the courage of restraint in her disappointment in her life with Jacob. Hers has been the achievement of constancy.

Jacob is depicted as the first biblical figure to dwell in exile in a worthy manner. However, his conditions for work leave much to be desired. Nonetheless, according to the commentary tradition, Jacob was successful in raising his eleven sons and one daughter in exile. Later on, he tells his messenger to advance the following report to his brother Esau: "I have sojourned with Laban (*Im lavan garti*)." Rashi famously comments that the letters of the word "garti" add up to the number 613. This signifies that he followed all of the *mitzvot* of the Torah even if, as it were, before the fact. Within the alienation of love and work in exile, he manages to unify his way of life by his fidelity to the path of truth, even in the midst of all of the competing claims upon him.

Surely it is not by mere chance that it is Rachel who dies along the way while giving birth to her second son, Benjamin. There is something inconsolable about the death of the beloved other. Later on, the prophet Jeremiah attributes the following words to the voice of Rachel, concerning the exile of Israel: "A voice was heard on high—wailing, bitter weeping—Rachel weeps for her children, she refuses to be consoled for her children, for they are gone" (Jer. 31:14).

It is Rachel, more of a realist than we might have imagined, who refuses to yield up all hope or meaning, even when it appears gone. Hers is the voice of consolation. The sojourn of Jacob's life recommences after he has left Charan and begins to make his way to the land of Promise. Along the way, the dramatic encounter with Esau takes place, and with it, the transformation of Jacob into "Israel."

FEAR AND ANGUISH

Vayishlach: He Sent
(Genesis 32:4–36:44)

Jacob devises a threefold strategy for his encounter with Esau, from whom he
has been estranged for many years. The strategy includes preparation for and
the implementation of diplomacy. Because diplomacy can avert war, the Talmud
informs us that the sages would study the methods used by Jacob in his meeting
with Esau before undertaking a mission to a sovereign authority, such as the
Roman emperor (BT, Sotah 41b). In Jacob's case, the diplomacy is a mixture
of fealty and words of deterrence. In addition, he prepares for battle, dividing
his camp into three parts. Lastly, but best remembered, is the solitude in which
he envelops himself for meditation and prayer. This is where he wrestles with
the angel of God.

Levinas uncharacteristically comments on this portion of the Bible directly.
He states, "In Genesis 32, Jacob is troubled at the news that his brother Esau—
enemy or friend—is marching to meet him 'at the head of four hundred men.'
The text goes on to say that 'Jacob was greatly afraid and anguished'" (AT 1999,
135). Levinas proceeds to ask—what is the difference between fear and anguish?
He cites Rashi as specifying that "he was fearful for his death but anguished
at the possibility of having to kill" (Ibid.). In fact, the anxiety or distress over
having to kill is, according to Gersonides (1288–1344), even stronger than the
fear of death (Stone, Gen. 32:8, 173n8). In the language of Levinas, the death of
the other, especially by my own hand, is more distressing than my own death.
This does not relieve Jacob of the right and responsibility to protect his family,
his children, his dependents, and even himself.

However, Levinas explicitly cites this instance of Jacob's fear and anguish
as reflecting "the ethical moment of our European crisis—reflecting on our
anguish ... the anguish of Jacob, felt at the prospect of violence to be committed
... we may wonder whether peace must not respond to a call more urgent than
that of truth and initially distinct from the call of truth" (AT 1999, 135–36).
Otherwise, we should not be able to explain the origin of speaking in a manner

that is just. The stability of a pacific relation with the other is also required to postpone the violence of war and the "truth" of domination and conquest. Levinas points out that philosophers distrust the notion of ultimate or messianic peace. He remarks, "[T]o be sure, they [the philosophers] profit to announce peace also; they deduce a final peace from the reason that plays out its stakes in ancient and present-day wars. They found morality on politics" (TI 1969, 22). For Levinas, of course, the reverse is true. Politics is founded upon morality, and peace, a stable and enduring peace, is more than the interrupted wars of history. Let us keep in mind that for him, the philosophic and existential crisis of Europe is found at the juncture of Greek philosophy and the Jewish Bible.

What concerns Levinas as a philosopher above all else is whether morality itself is still credible, or if it is rather simply a disguise for power politics that uses "moral rhetoric." The Greek philosophic tradition in all its permutations from Socrates to the present aspires to "truth." Levinas argues that peaceful relations between human beings express an inescapable condition of the search for truth. It is in this sense that he rethinks what his teacher Husserl referred to as the "Crisis of the European Sciences," but in a more urgent, ethical way. For Husserl, the search for truth was suspended so that a deeper exploration of the meanings of essences could be studied.

We might ask how truth can be suspended, even for a moment. There is both an immediate and a historical context for responding to this question. As an approach to philosophy initiated by Husserl, phenomenology insisted upon a description of "meanings" that could be agreed upon even when their ultimate truth value remained to be probed. The great advantage of this approach is that most of the philosophical problems have been argued about inconclusively for over two and a half millennia. This has created an enormous skepticism about the task of philosophy and that of the human sciences (or the humanities). This skepticism can harden into a nihilism in which all philosophic questioning is thought to be fruitless. The consequences of such a conclusion can be devastating, yielding the unacceptable notion that morality is arbitrary, that meanings have no stability, and that the world lives only from egocentric instincts and drives.[21]

---

21 And is it not this very nihilism that Esau succumbs to upon hearing the news of the death of his righteous grandfather, Abraham? According to the midrash, it is then that he thinks to himself that there is neither "justice nor a judge," and therefore begins a life unbounded by justice.

Levinas adapts Husserl's approach and aims it in the direction of rediscovering Talmudic and biblical wisdom concerning the understanding of the human. The reader need not be concerned that he or she is unconcerned with Truth. Rather, he or she believes that the Greek approach, by which "the peace of humanity, European in us, has already decided in favor of Greek wisdom which is to await human peace on the basis of Truth" (AT 1999, 131). According to Levinas, this subordinates ethics or morality to the theory of knowledge and therefore can postpone peace until absolute truth has been decided upon. During this waiting, much blood can be shed in the name of absolute truth. Levinas refers to this "conscience of Europe as a bad conscience" (Ibid., 132). He argues that we do not have time to await such peace, that we have learned this from the bloodstained horrors of the twentieth century.

It is not surprising therefore that Levinas rethinks philosophical problems based upon the originary condition of peace itself. This is at the heart of the question of the priority of peace, responding "to a call more urgent than that of truth and initially distinct from the call of truth" (Ibid., 136). Not only is peace prior to the call of truth, but also "older than that of knowledge and the politics governing history … responding to the requirement of peace" (Ibid.). Put very simply, Levinas appears to be advancing the notion that the terms that we use in the quest for knowledge and truth presuppose the terms that we are on with one another.

Levinas is by no means oblivious to the imperatives of politics. As he states in the preface to *Totality and Infinity*, "[T]he art of foreseeing war and of winning it by every means—politics—is henceforth enjoined as the very exercise of reason" (TI 1969, 21). Still, politics is subordinate to the claims of ethical life where the bases and meaning of political formulae are decided. He argues that this is not simply a *bourgeois* kind of peace. Such a peace would remain oblivious to the wars around it "at home behind closed doors, rejecting that which, being exterior, negates him" (AT 1999, 136). Levinas gives us an idea of the kind of peace that would ultimately be associated with what he calls a "Messianic Society": "[W]e must ask ourselves whether peace instead of existing on the absorption or disappearance of alterity would not on the contrary be a *fraternal* way of a proximity to the other, which would not be simply the failure of coincidence with the other, but which would signify precisely the *excess* of sociality over all solitude—excess of sociality and love" (Ibid., 137). For Levinas, there must be a third way, one that is "otherwise than suicide or murder." This represents a kind of politics based upon "an excess of sociality and love." Only a transcending humanism, an ethical pluralism that opens onto the irreducible singularity of the other person, and my responsibility for this other can affect this kind of solidarity and brotherhood.

Ethics becomes politics for Levinas as soon as it encounters the third party. By no means does this necessitate the reduction of ethics to politics. Rather, the subject, Jacob, must take account in advance of the encounter with the third party, meaning those most proximate to him—his own households. Ethics must expand into the political domain. If war can be avoided, then it must be. Hence, the protracted diplomacy that he sets in motion by meticulously sorting through the nature and order of gifts that are presented to his brother to have the most beneficial effect in avoiding war. There is also the stipulation, as was mentioned, that even in exile, Jacob had remained faithful to all the obligations imposed by the Torah. This also means that he is making room for a kind of justice for himself as well as the third party and the kind of restorative justice that he may owe to his brother. We may meaningfully call this cognizance of the third party, where I become another for others as well, "the Political." The political here does not involve distortion, but rather establishes a certain kind of synchronic time that is required for stable and just human relations. While wrestling with the angel of G-d—or alternatively a man—he is thrust back on his own sense of solitude.[22]

BEFORE DAWN: JACOB/ISRAEL

Jacob was left alone and a man wrestled with him until the break of dawn.
—Genesis 32:25

Jacob's epic struggle with the angel (or man) of G'd moves through the night until dawn. Jacob prevails and insists on a blessing before he will let go the angel or man or stranger. This results in his name, Israel, which means "he who wrestles with God and prevails." The opening of the Mishna concerns the question, up until what time can one say the creedal prayer of *Shema*: Hear O' Israel, the Lord our G'd the Lord is One. In the second chapter of the Mishna in *Berachot*, the question emerges, "When does dawn arrive?"

Here, two comments of Levinas are worth noting. He cites an opinion from the Jerusalem Talmud (Beracoth) that dawn breaks when two people can recognize each other at a distance of approximately seven feet. In other words, one is able to recognize the face of the other. For Levinas and for the Jewish Bible as well, it is the expression of the human face that serves as the origin of meaning itself. The face that alerts us to the fact that we are in the presence of another person and are more or less welcome. When I ask someone else whether he or

---

22 See Aryeh Kaplan 32:25, *The Living Torah*, 87.

she has understood what I have said, her face enables me to know my words have registered with the intention behind them. What is significant about dawn (*alos hashachar*) is that it represents the beginning of the time of the other person, and for that very reason, my own sense of time. This is what Levinas calls "diachrony"—the time of the other. The time of the other person bears a trace of my encounter with him. The night does not symbolize annihilation; rather it breaks on to a day more promising than the night left behind. For this reason, perhaps, Levinas asks why the opening prayer in the Jewish prayer book (*siddur*) expresses appreciation for the creation of the rooster who distinguishes day from night. Levinas asks an incisive question—why the rooster? Other animals distinguish between day and night. The rooster is singled out because it knows the difference just a little bit in advance. It might also be pointed out that the rooster shares his happy findings with his sleepy neighbors.

The reconciliation between Jacob and Esau is the subject of much discussion in the commentary tradition. When the heart of Esau is softened, Jacob in fact says to Esau that "your face is like the face of God." It is hard to know whether this statement is to be taken ironically or earnestly. "Esau ran toward him, fell upon his neck, and kissed him; they wept" (Gen. 33:4).

When Esau kisses Jacob, the midrash notes that there are all kinds of additional marks over the letters of the word for "and he kissed" (*vishkhoo*). Rashi cites R' Shimon bar Yochai that at this moment his compassion was aroused and that he "kissed Jacob with all his heart" (Stone, Gen. 32n4). Esau offers to escort Jacob, his wives, children, and flocks to their destination. Very diplomatically, Jacob declines. He has already been criticized by the rabbinic tradition for not avoiding Esau and for putting his family and himself in what could have been mortal danger. Jacob now realizes that the danger has not completely passed despite his temporary reconciliation with his brother, Esau. In fact, Jacob is somewhat vague about his destination and his arrival time. From this, the rabbinic tradition learns that even if there is only a hint of danger, one should not disclose one's itinerary precisely.

The uncertainty of Jacob's itinerary is perhaps expressed in the fact that he has been injured upon his thigh by the angel and from that time forward limps on his way. While the commentary tradition offers the view that he is healed shortly after this time, Sforno suggests that this signals the ups and downs that Israel and his descendants will encounter in the future. In the immediate future, the peace that Jacob desires will not easily be found within his own family or in relation to his neighbors. It makes sense, then, that Jacob desires to settle down in tranquility in the land of his forefathers.

SETTLING

Vayeshev: He Settled
(Genesis 37:1–40:23)

Jacob settled in the land of his father's sojourning, in the land of Canaan.

—Genesis 37:1

Reuven returned to the pit—and behold—Joseph was not in the pit! So, he rent his garments. Returning to his brothers, he said, "The boy is gone! And I—where can I go?"

—Genesis 37:29–31

The Torah says that after all of his years in exile with Laban, his struggle overcoming the angel, and his meeting with Esau, Jacob wished to "settle down in serenity." He appears fatigued by living as a "sojourner" in exile. Understandably, he wishes to be finally "at home" or as Levinas puts it, *chez soi*. This does not mean that he is limiting himself to a house with conveniences, a bourgeois home as it were, with window coverings and suitable furnishings. This sense of personal serenity and security is associated not so much with the retirement of old age as with enjoying the abundance of life *en famille*. Jacob simply wants a rest from his many years of turmoil. It is at this exact moment when Jacob wishes to live, as it were, in the extended present that the life of his family begins to unravel.

In other words, Jacob appears to retreat into his interiority as a subject. Rashi, however, criticizes Jacob for wanting to find tranquility in this world, something that is unbecoming of a *tzaddik* (a completely righteous person). Certainly, it would appear that Jacob is entitled to a little respite after all of these years of struggle and suffering. But, from a Levinasian point of view, perhaps Jacob is trying to draw down the time of others into a single time of his own.

When he attempts to settle in Canaan, his *needs* have been met, though need is not identical to *desire*: "Desire that comes to it from the presence of the other. This Desire is a desire in a being already happy: desire is the misfortune of the happy" (TI 1969, 62). In this sense, he appears to be withdrawing his family from the turbulence of historical time and, more importantly, from the time of others. This is why his rest and tranquility cannot endure.

What unfolds instead is the rivalry between the brothers over the special affection that Jacob shows to Joseph, preceded by the dreams of Joseph and followed by Joseph's harsh treatment at the hands of his brothers. In other words, the extraordinary sense of responsibility that has transformed Jacob into Israel is to be ongoing and relentless. Jacob, in fact, reproves his son Joseph after he reveals to his brothers and father his second dream. The symbolism of "the sun and the moon and eleven stars bowed down to me" is simply too much for Jacob to take. He sharply asks Joseph, "Shall your mother and I and your brothers bow down to you?" Scripture notes, however, that "Jacob kept the saying in mind" (Gen. 37:10–11).

Jacob's intention to rest at home turns into one of the most traumatic and haunting events in the history of the Israelites. The fratricide contemplated by the brothers and the subsequent sale of Joseph open a wound in the psyche that shadows brotherhood and shatters solidarity.

The cautionary note against parental favoritism ("and he made a tunic of fine wool") is evident from Jacob's egregious partiality. "And his brothers saw that it was he whom their father loved most of all his brothers, so they hated him, and they could not speak peaceably with him" (Gen. 37:3–4). To the credit of the brothers, Rashi remarks that they were incapable of the kind of duplicity, feeling one way with their hearts, and yet speaking another way, so as not to seem as they are. In the language of Levinas, this would mean a refusal on the part of the brothers to conceal or to disguise *the saying* in relation to *the said*. This testifies to the sincerity of the brothers. Nonetheless, the brothers abdicate a sense of brotherhood toward Joseph, and withdraw from acting toward him responsibly.

The righteous indignation of the brothers toward Joseph compromises in advance the alterity of their father, Jacob. As Joseph is arriving, presumably to monitor the conduct of the brothers on behalf of his father, the fury of the brothers is aroused. The brothers, at this moment, make the absent Jacob virtually nonexistent in their minds. This enmity toward Joseph appears to be shared, but with slightly different intentions and consequences by at least two of the brothers: the oldest, Reuven, and the brother whom they recognized as their leader, Yehuda.

"Reuven heard, and he rescued him from their hand; he said, 'we will not strike him mortally!' And Reuven said to them, 'shed no blood! Throw him into this pit in the wilderness but lay no hand on him!'—intending to rescue him from their hand, to return him to his father" (Gen. 37:21–22). In the meanwhile, Yehuda interposes the idea to sell Joseph: "[W]hat gain will there be if we kill our brother and cover up his blood?" (Gen. 37:26). The brothers assent, and Joseph is sold first to the Midianite traders, who subsequently sell Joseph to the Ishmaelites.

Let us recall that the text earlier states enigmatically: "And these are the generations of Jacob, Joseph at the age of seventeen" (Gen. 36:2). At home, Joseph was despised. He was seventeen, the perfect age for adolescent self-consciousness and narcissism. Rashi comments: "[H]e acted childishly, trimming his hair and adorning his eyes to look handsome." It is only when he comes down to Egypt that he becomes beloved. R. David Lehrfield observes that this change results from a complete egocentrism on Joseph's part.[23] Joseph's rise to political prominence is accompanied not only by suffering at the hands of his brothers and the betrayal he experiences in the house of Potiphar, but also with his growing awareness of his responsibility to and for others that limits his early egocentrism. No longer do other people, the world, and even his dreams center around himself. Later, in prison, and when brought before Pharaoh, he says that all "interpretations come from G'd, not from him, Joseph." His work for the sake of others is visible in the utterly responsible way that he deals with the Pharaoh, the inhabitants of Egypt, and subsequently his brothers. This movement out of egocentrism is found in the parallel actions of his brothers. It is the bare beginning of a kind of fraternity that founds a just society.

TESHUVA: TURNING

The two brothers who try to rescue Joseph from death and catastrophe are Reuven and Yehuda. It is Reuven whose gesture of rescue is incomplete and for which he suffers. In his suffering, however, there arises for the first time an elaborated version of the phenomenon of *teshuva*: "Reuven returned to the pit, and behold!—Joseph was not in the pit. So he rent his garments. Returning to his brothers, he said, 'the boy is gone! And I—where can I go?'" (Gen. 37:30). Reuven is referring to the shock and grief that their father experiences when confronted with the news that Joseph is gone. *Teshuva*, however, appears to be

---

23 Heard from Rabbi David Lehrfield, Rabbi of Young Israel of North Miami Beach, December 2012.

the kind of pardon that follows from the recognition of injustice. It is founded upon a paradox.

It is worth noting that the Talmudic tradition recognizes that the phenomenon of repentance or *Teshuva* (literally, "turning"), so closely associated with the phenomena of pardon and forgiveness, appears contradictory. The reason for this is that the past cannot be undone (BT, Bava Kama, 94b; Yoma, 86b). Therefore, such absolution that might come through the pardon would appear limited to transforming the significance or meaning of the event for the one who has been offended or injured. The pardon, in that respect, would remain incomplete because the event of the past cannot be changed.

Levinas states that "the paradox of pardon lies in its retroaction; from the point of view of common time it represents an inversion of the natural order of things, the reversibility of time" (TI 1969, 283). For Levinas, the paradox of pardon is at the very heart of time: "[T]he paradox of pardon, of fault, refers to pardon as constitutive of time itself" (Ibid.). For the phenomenon of pardon to be made philosophically intelligible, the very phenomenon of time must be articulated in a different manner. In fact, it must overcome the philosophic problem of the irreversibility of time.

Levinas illuminates several different aspects of the phenomenon of pardon. He begins by indicating that it is possible for the subject to reanimate the past, as if the instant elapsed can be revivified. However, such revivification must go beyond a forgetting of the past, which, as he says "does not concern the reality of the event forgotten" (TI 1969, 284). As Reuven says to his brothers when discovering that Joseph was not in the pit he had placed him: "Where shall I go?"

Levinas conversely indicates that "pardon acts upon the past, somehow repeats the event, purifying it" (Ibid., 283). Pardon does not restore innocence. Rather, it must already point beyond itself to a future that, after reconciliation, can be better than the present. Through pardon, the useless suffering of the past can be approached and mitigated. Levinas absolves pardon from its paradoxical status by liberating it from the language of totality: "Being is no longer produced with one blow, irremissibly present" (Ibid., 284).[24] Now the paradox of pardon goes into remission. "Reality is what it is, but will be once again, another time freely resumed and pardoned" (Ibid.). By overcoming the stumbling block of time past, by "opening" it, pardon allows us to move toward the future. Due to this passage, made bearable by the trace of the promise by which the past inheres in the present, and thereby engenders the future, the past itself can be both preserved and overcome. Goodness for the other can now emerge within time.

---

24 Was this not the source of Jacob's error when it says he wished to *settle* in Canaan?

Later, in *Vayigash*, Joseph reassures the brothers that "it was not you who sent me here, but G'd" (Gen. 45:8). It is only Joseph who can absolve his brothers. In this sense, both Reuven and Yehuda, through their unfolding conduct, express remorse and assume, after the fact, their responsibility for their treatment of Joseph and its consequences insofar as it bears upon their father and brothers.

YEHUDA AND TAMAR: THE FACE, RECTITUDE, AND VOLUPTUOSITY

The spiritual descent and ascent of Yehuda, subsequent to the selling of Joseph, parallels the turning of his oldest brother, Rueven. The text states that "[i]t was at that time that Yehuda 'went down' from his brothers, and turned toward an Adullamite man, whose name was Hiram" (Gen. 38:2). According to Rashi, this means Yehuda was deposed as leader over his brothers. The reason for this was the great suffering experienced by Jacob at the loss of Joseph. Subsequent to two unworthy attempts upon the part of Yehuda's sons to evade the obligations of the Leverite marriage, Tamar is told by Yehuda to wait until his third son grows up, "[l]est he die like his brothers" (Gen. 38:11). In the meanwhile, Tamar waits patiently until an encounter with her father-in-law, who is unwilling, even after the passage of time, to risk the life of his third son. To arrange such an encounter, Tamar covers her face and disguises herself so that Yehuda thinks that she is a prostitute. In order to do this, she has removed her widow's garb and covered herself with a veil.

Clearly, the veil is meant to conceal her face, and therefore her identity. What does the absence of the face connote, especially in this context? This facelessness does more than give Tamar the anonymity that she desires. It also provokes, perhaps as the commentators imply, divine intent, an attraction on the part of Yehuda. This attraction outwardly appears to be one governed by a need that is carnal in character. Levinas characterizes this as voluptuosity: an attraction that reveals only a partial nudity; the nakedness of the human body, without, as it were, a face that would give it expression and direction. Tamar requests that Yehuda give her a pledge to be redeemed when he is able to compensate her. Her request requires him to give her the intimate confirmations of his identity, "[a]nd he gave them to her, and consorted with her, and she conceived by him" (Gen. 38:18). Upon completion, the text says, "Then she arose, left, and removed her veil from upon her, and she put on the garb of her widowhood."

The most subtle and important form of nudity, according to Levinas, is that of the expression of the human face. The exposure of the face is the most vulnerable and intimate aspect of the human being. The face, as Levinas describes it, is a source of both moral rectitude and fragility. The face-to-face is characterized by Levinas as the context permitting the wisdom of love. In an event that follows we see the anonymity of voluptuousness turned retroactively into disinterested love.

Yehuda sends a surrogate out to find Tamar, and he is told that there is no prostitute there. After three months, he is informed that Tamar has conceived as a result of committing harlotry. Yehuda's response is harsh and quick, "Take her out and let her be burned" (Gen. 38:24). Tamar displays an extraordinary rectitude as she privately sends word to her father-in-law saying, "By the man to whom these belong am I with child. And she said, 'Identify if you please whose are this signet, this wrap, and this staff.'" According to Rashi, she is willing to allow herself to be unjustly put to death to save her father-in-law from public shame.

The beginning of the ascent of Yehuda arises in his response, "She is more righteous than I" (Gen. 38:26). The text goes on to tell us that he was not intimate with her again. In other words, there is a dual unveiling of the face, first on the part of Tamar followed by that of Yehuda. Discourse, righteous speech, elevates aimless passion. It is only when the face is not concealed that reason and morality, justification and knowing can be found together. Putting the matter directly, we now know what is meant behind that which is said. In this sense, Yehuda begins to atone for his original transgression against his father, Jacob, and his brother, Joseph. The Torah previously depicts Yehuda as showing to Jacob Joseph's tunic dipped in the blood of a wild goat. Jacob could draw the only conclusion—that Joseph had been torn to pieces by a wild animal. According to the tradition, this revealing of the face in the later encounter between Tamar and Yehuda is the beginning of the birth pangs of the messianic era.

It cannot be by accident that Peretz, one of the twin sons of the union between Tamar and Yehuda, is the precursor to King David. Subsequently, Yehuda is once again elevated among the brothers and plays a decisive role after his repentance in the reconciliation of the brothers with Joseph. Jacob is about to undergo a descent into Egypt for the purpose of an ascent. He experiences a richer kind of peace and tranquility during the last seventeen years of his life, because he is in the presence of Joseph as the virtual sovereign of Egypt. It is only then, in the last seventeen years of his life, that Jacob is depicted by the tradition as "settling" peaceably in the land of Goshen.

DREAMS, HERMENEUTICS, AND ACTION

Mikeitz: At the End Of
(Genesis 41:1–44:17)

Jacob learned that there were provisions in Egypt and he said to his sons,
"Why are you fantasizing?"

—Genesis 42:1

Joseph has certainly suffered at the hands of his brothers and experiences the full force of exile in Egypt before he is elevated to his position as viceroy. Recall that Joseph's descent into slavery was prefigured by his insistence on telling his brothers and his father his dreams (*cholomim*). Subsequently, through his divinely inspired, prophetic interpretation of the Pharaoh's dream, he stores bread (*lechem*) for his father, his brothers, and all of Egypt. By his work (*loichem*), he distributes bread to those who are hungry, and, thereby fulfills the prophecy of his first dreams. It is not by accident that the Hebrew words for "dream," "bread," and "work" all derive from the same source.

After he tells Pharaoh what his dreams portend, Joseph advises him to appoint someone who can alleviate the suffering that will come in the seven years of famine by preparing during the seven years of plenty. Waking life involves interpretation that is transformative. In this sense Joseph already shows the inseparable relation between text and interpretation and action, as well as between dreams, bread, and work. This is illustrative of the biblical hermeneutic according to the rabbinic tradition. The oral Torah (Interpretation) is inseparable from the written one (Phenomenon). Speaking with and acting for others is achieved in this way.

According to the commentary tradition, Joseph recognizes Pharaoh's original dream more accurately than Pharaoh himself. In fact, Joseph's ability to recall the seven years of plenty to be followed by the seven years of privation are met with receptive ears on Pharaoh's part, just because the Pharaoh himself had already intuited what the dreams portend in the first place. However, what the Pharaoh does not grasp is the importance of interpretation by the subject or dreamer, and therefore lets the interpretation escape from him. Joseph, on the other hand, immediately recalls the two dreams that he had related to his brothers and his father and now saw these dreams as clearly prophetic. One of the reasons that the oral tradition remains a living one, is that it always awaits or invites an existential interpretation on the part of the living subject or reader, who cannot help but ask him-herself, 'What does this mean for me or for others?'

This signifies that the interpretation always includes but goes beyond the verse. This, in turn, suggests that Levinas is involved in a dual method of interpretation. He accepts the rabbinic levels and rules of the hermeneutic internal to the tradition; at the same time, he remains committed to phenomenological description and philosophical explanation.

To speak of meaning, sense must be conveyed to *a someone*. This is central to Levinas's theory of explanation. The Jewish Bible, for Levinas, is irreducibly interpersonal—that is to say, human. An explanation that is always given to *a someone* must be capable of withstanding sustained interrogation and criticism by someone else. Understood in this way, explanation is not something that is given simply to 'all the world, and therefore no one' but rather whose universality is found in the transcending humanism of the Talmudic tradition that speaks to *each* one. In this way, the Jewish Bible is at once "humanized" and universalized through phenomenological Talmudic interpretation.

Explanation is dynamic rather than static. This means that it is ongoing. We are always tacitly or explicitly justifying what we are saying or doing in relation to other people. In this sense, justification is an integral part of explaining something to someone. It means giving or implying reasons. For this reason, explanation always has a moral dimension, even when it is unnoticed. What Joseph brings to the Pharaoh's dreams is a reasoned, moral account. Is this not why, perhaps, the Pharaoh is prepared to listen to Joseph, because he recognizes in him a type of wisdom?

BREAD AND WORK

The first seven years reflect the splendor of Pharaoh's dream; they are years of great material and agrarian abundance. The *Ramban* puts it this way: "Joseph gathered all food of every variety to insure there would be no waste. He apportioned rations for the people of their sustenance and stored the rest. As for the grain, he amassed it in store houses like the sand of the sea" (Stone, 230n48). What distinguished the ethical-political approach of Joseph throughout the years of plenty and poverty is his insistence on elevating and giving human beings priority over property. Even when the Egyptians later offer to sell themselves into servitude so that they will have the grain that Joseph stored during the years of plenty, he refuses. Instead, a fifth of all the profit or (the land) will revert to Pharaoh; no one is to be indentured, let alone enslaved. Rather, he does what is minimally necessary to insure compliance and abundance—that is to say, the people who grow the grain are not to be denied access to what is rightfully theirs. The elevation of Joseph to a position of such prominence reflects an ethos where the reduction of human beings to mere property is resisted.

Joseph does not separate morality from economics. All economic decisions are already moral ones. He demonstrates this by decentralizing, according to the midrash, the storehouses of grain so that they will be close to the places in which the grain has been harvested. This way, he keeps the grain fresher than if it had been held in one centralized warehouse. Furthermore, Joseph meticulously supervises the actual distributing of the grain to its producers and recipients. In this way, he takes personal responsibility, in the most direct fashion, for rescuing the people from hunger. Administration, then, is subject to moral considerations that are already personal. There is no room for faceless bureaucracy in Joseph's manner of implementing policy.

It has not been simply an act of self-interested advancement when Joseph suggests to the Pharaoh that he appoint someone wise in these matters to do something that might alter the prophetic inspiration that Joseph has gathered from the Pharaoh's dream. In other words, such a theory of interpretation has been transformative. This is to say, it has led to action. The action in this case has made it possible to secure food for Egypt and ultimately for the sons of Israel. In turn, it helps us to understand the ongoing dialogue of the commentary tradition that is distinctive to the Jewish comprehension of Scripture. All teaching implies giving someone a fact with an interpretation. Is this what Levinas means by the prophecy of everyday speech? It is what Levinas refers to when he speaks of going *Beyond the Verse*.

FRATERNITY AND RESPONSIBILITY

The work of Joseph prepares the way for reconciliation with his brothers, and the rise to preeminence of Yehuda in particular. This process gives Joseph the chance to both test *and* feed his brothers. At the same time, the brothers are given the opportunity for repentance to the extent that they expiate their transgression for having sold Joseph.

Jacob perceives that there are provisions in Egypt, and he admonishes his ten sons by saying to them, "Why do you look upon each other?" (Gen. 42:1–2). (Or in an alternative translation: "Why do you make yourselves conspicuous?") It is reasonable to infer that Jacob is disturbed by the refusal of even one of his sons to take the initiative in acquiring food in Egypt and is disappointed that they are each waiting for the other brother or brothers to do so. He wants action! Another way of interpreting this is to say that he admonishes them not to make themselves vulnerable by revealing that they still have at least some provisions to get by, at least for a very limited time.

The search for brotherhood had previously begun when Jacob sent Joseph to monitor "his brothers." Earlier, in response to the question, "Who are you looking for?" Joseph had responded, "I am looking for my brothers." It takes many tests, self-recriminations, and struggles before the brothers manage to atone, and Joseph finds "in truth" the brothers whom he earlier sought. Before the climactic reunion of Joseph and his brothers, there are important indications that the brothers, almost imperceptibly, are already on their way to recognizing the meaning of brotherhood. It is only this sensibility of responsible fraternity that makes the ethics of nearness possible.

The ten brothers have already met with Joseph in his official capacity in Egypt. While Joseph recognizes his brothers, they do not recognize him. First, the brothers must give evidence of the normative meaning of the term "brother." For Levinas, this means the gesture of what he calls "proximity." Levinas characterizes proximity in the following way: "The relationship of proximity cannot be reduced to any modality of distance or geometrical contiguity, nor to the simple 'representation' of a neighbor; it is an assignation—an extremely urgent assignation—an obligation, anachronously prior to any commitment" (OBBE 1991, 100–1).

What does it mean when Levinas says that this is prior to any representation of the neighbor? The representation of the neighbor or the third party, where there can be justice for me as I become an other for others, derives from the prior way that the other, in advance of our meeting, assigns me as a subject to a position of moral responsibility. What, then, is this proximity that is not to be confused with contiguity? Who is the other who forces upon me the assignation of responsibility? In the case of the biblical Joseph, the brothers are "as one" in recognizing the transgression of the previous degradation of Joseph. It is Joseph, then, who assigns the condition of proximity to each of them, although this assignation of responsibility is different for several of the brothers. According to the commentary tradition, Shimon has been singled out as the brother who stated "[b]ehold, the dreamer comes... let us slay him." He is therefore held as ward until the other brothers return with Benjamin, their youngest brother.

Jacob finally yields to the imprecations of Yehuda, who holds himself responsible *forever* for bringing back the youngest brother alive and safe. In the language of Levinas, Yehuda has accepted Jacob's assignation as the one uniquely responsible. This happens prior to the ultimately happy outcome. Yehuda then assumes responsibility at this moment for the safety of both Jacob and Benjamin. This sense of proximity, therefore, derives from the one outside of the subject. Yehuda surely cannot know in advance that he will be successful. It is in this way that we can say, as Levinas does, that proximity precedes commitment and even subjectivity that is itself brought about by proximity: "Subjectivity is not antecedent to proximity, in which it would later commit itself. On the contrary, it is in proximity, which is a relationship and a term, that every commitment is made. And it is probably starting with proximity that the difficult problem of incarnate subjectivity has to be broached" (OBBE 1991, 86). We can understand that this is the relationship that proximity bears to commitment. The reason for this is that the other expects me in her approach to remain committed to the obligation that she has assigned me. Furthermore, it is in this same mode that the self rises to the full level of an ethical subject, only when my promise is perpetually resumed as commitment.

SUBSTITUTION AND SOLIDARITY

Vayigash: And He Approached
(Genesis 44:18–47:27)

[A]nd Yehuda approached him.

—Genesis 44:18

Please let your servant remain instead of the youth as a servant to my lord, and let the youth go up to his brothers. For how can I go up to my father if the youth is not with me, lest I see the evil that will befall my father!

—Genesis 44:33–34

I am Joseph your brother.

—Genesis 45:5

The climactic episode between Joseph and his brothers described in the Torah portion of Vayigash epitomizes some of the most important philosophic themes of Emmanuel Levinas. These themes include, but are not limited to, the responsibility for the other person, the movement out of the self toward the other, a sense of time that originates from the other or the third party that is measured by urgency rather than number, an awareness that absence is more than a depleted or privative mode of presence, and the priority of the "saying" over the "said."

When Joseph sets up the final test for his brothers regarding their willingness to risk themselves in order to secure the release of their brother Benjamin, it is only Yehuda who steps forward: "*V'yigash alev Yehuda*" or "and Yehuda approached him." Yehuda draws near to Joseph on behalf of his brother Benjamin for the sake of his absent father, Jacob. This action of drawing near is what Levinas refers to as "proximity," where it is not merely a level of spatial nearness. Rather, it involves a movement from self to other without the assurance of reciprocity. "Proximity is quite distinct from every other relationship, and has to be conceived as a responsibility for the other; it might be called humanity, or subjectivity, or self ... nothing is more grave, more august, than responsibility for the other, and saying, in which there is no play, has a gravity more grave than its own being or not being" (OBBE 1991, 46). It is this kind of ethical nearness, proximity, that Yehuda embodies in keeping his promise to his father to safeguard Benjamin in Egypt.

In his encounter with Joseph, Yehuda shows action that involves what Levinas refers to as the ethical category of "substitution." In demarcating the irreducible importance of "substitution," Levinas contrasts this phenomenon with the philosophic tradition of the West: "For the Philosophic tradition of the West, all spirituality lies in consciousness, thematic exposition of being, knowing. In starting with sensibility interpreted not as a knowing but as a proximity ... proximity appears as the relationship with the other who cannot be resolved into "images or be exposed in a theme" (OBBE 1991, 99–100).

Yehuda recognizes the added responsibility that comes with "proximity." In substitution, I recognize that I am a hostage for a third party. This does not mean that I take his place. Still, it is a recognition that there comes a time when the responsibilities with which I am obsessed, do not, as Levinas puts it, "arise in decisions taken by a subject "contemplating freely," consequently accused in its innocence, subjectivity in itself is being thrown back on oneself. This means concretely: accused of what the others do or suffer, or responsible for what they do or suffer. The uniqueness of the self is the very fact of bearing the fault of another" (Ibid., 112). This is both the beginning and limit of self-identity. Levinas appears to make an extravagant claim regarding substitution: "This unconditionality confers meaning on being itself, and welcomes its gravity. It is as resting on a self, supposing the whole of being, that being is assembled into a unity of the universe and essence is assembled into an event" (Ibid., 116). In other words, the substitution of one for the other(s) is an action that takes time seriously, the time of the other even before my own. Yehuda is aware that not only is the fate of Benjamin and his other brothers at stake, but also that of his aged, absent father. This passage illustrates what Levinas means when he says, "The self is a sub-jectum; it is under the weight of the universe and essence is assembled into an event" (Ibid.).

While Yehuda's act of substitution is exceptional, even majestic, is this not but an exalted instance of the responsibilities that assault the human subject, thereby making him into a kind of hostage in everyday life? This involves taking cognizance of the condition and time, especially the urgency of the others, whose claims upon me are in extreme moments experienced in a kind of persecution. In this way, Levinas makes the controversial claim that I am responsible, even for the one who persecutes me. What does this mean? Clearly this is not simply a form of masochism. What it does mean is that my subjectivity remains dependent upon my own conduct toward the other person, even when the other person would cause me suffering that is not my fault. Even more so, it is not merely a matter of "attitude." It signifies the way that I must go so far out of myself that I put myself in the place of the other person, even my persecutor. This is not an interruption of moral justice. It is found both before and after just or unjust conduct. It is in this way that responsibility becomes the *surplus of justice*. However, as Levinas notes, it is not a matter of psychological poles of egoism and altruism either. My response to how the other concerns me, is for him, "the religiosity of the self" (OBBE 1991, 117). It is for him, the movement which recapitulates "the possibility of putting oneself in the place of the other, which refers to the transference 'by the other' into a 'for the other,' and in persecution from the outrage inflicted by the other to the expiation for his fault by me.... The self, a hostage, is already substituted for the others" (Ibid., 118). This is the origin of all human solidarity—the birth of generosity and, for Levinas, the bedrock of all ethical life that makes religion rational and intelligible.

Ethical life appears only with the recognition of the claims of the absent other, even all of the absent others. Let us make this more explicit:

This decisive metaphysical distinction between the phenomenon of absence and that of non-existence, so long obscured in the history of philosophy, is central to Levinas' analysis and needs to be made explicit. Absence is not that which is merely somewhere else, convertible into presence by a change of position, perspective, or interpretation. That which is absent is not necessarily an entity in another place, hidden from view, or unintelligible. Rather, the phenomenon of absence positively appears and informs our understanding of everyday events with considerable concrete significance. The disbelieving look of the innocent one in her agony horrifies us just because it expresses the absence of justice. We are able to recognize the suffering of the innocent only because the absence of justice has the power to inform us that what passes for truth, under the sway of institutional power, is not exhaustive of reality. (Sugarman 1979, 221)

To recognize the absence of justice, where justice is postponed or deformed, without succumbing to a belief in its non-existence, is a necessary pre-condition grounding the possibility of ethical existence. The demand for justice depends upon our capacity for reckoning with the claims of the absent other, whether his distance is one of spatial separation or temporal proximity. The common character of justice, in an analogous manner, then, depends upon the capacity to press the claims of all the absent others. (Sugarman 1979, 221)

To reiterate, Yehuda has promised his absent father, Jacob, that he will return his brother, Benjamin, or he will bear the blame forever. Yehuda proposes to substitute himself for Benjamin. He takes upon himself the condition of hostage, where he would become the servant of Joseph, thereby seeking to absolve and to replace Benjamin. "Substitution" is diachrony, par excellence. Diachrony is time generated by the urgency of the other, measured morally by the alacrity of my response. In "substitution," the time of the other becomes my own. Here, we see the expansion of the ethical to the neighbor of the other, for whom I may, in advance, already be obligated. In other words, in the language of the Talmud, "All Israel is responsible for one another" (BT, Shevous 39b). Levinas extends the reach of this responsibility of Israel to the nations, "Each is responsible for each, and I more so, than all the others."

According to the midrash, sovereignty and messianism play interrelated roles here. As long as Joseph is the effective ruler in Egypt, an order of justice is maintained. No one is allowed to go hungry. Joseph practices what might be called the "moral socialism" of the other person. In other words, Joseph establishes the priority of persons over property. The political implementation of an economic strategy to avoid starvation is accomplished, but not at the expense of human dignity. Joseph is effectively arguing that the inhabitants will live together in solidarity or perish. He provides for his subjects, thereby forestalling starvation. The "politics of ethical life" involves installing a just relation of the third party to the neighbor, and each to the other. Joseph introduces enactments that make property subordinate to persons and their most elemental needs. The all-for-all legislation is providently assumed in advance of disaster. The anticipation of urgent demands relies upon the prior urgency of exigent demands.

In the meanwhile of exilic history, the exteriority of just relations is played out, always imperfectly. The force of administration brings an element of injustice, through the play of forces or power. Such politics ensures self-preservation, thus securing physical safety and identity in an alien system. Joseph stores the grain in abundance from the farmers. In the years of famine, the farmers purchase the grain with money. When the money is gone they sell their property for bread for themselves and grain for their cattle. When the bread and grain are gone, they propose selling their "land and their bodies" for bread. Their horses and cattle become collateral in upholding their end of the agreement. Land of the inhabitants is acquired for the state, but the offer of servitude is rejected. Persons will retain their priority over property. As the Or HaChaim stresses, this is all the more important in a time of scarcity, especially famine, where each person is not well disposed toward his neighbor, whom he regards with suspicion: "During famine people are extremely miserly and malevolent; they are apt to commit robbery and even murder to secure a piece of bread" (*Or HaChaim* 1999, vol. 1, Genesis, 335). Joseph took great care in tracking and accounting for the grain disbursed. This, according to Or HaChaim prevented speculation in grain by reducing it to a mere commodity. In this way prices could not rise and fall artificially based upon "market value." Joseph is forced to take extreme measures with great urgency because of the political peril of the times "so that we shall live and not die" (Gen. 42:2). The silos were placed near population centers, and where necessary, people were relocated so that they would be closer to the supply of food. At the same time, according to the midrash, the grain was stored throughout the various regions of Egypt, so that it could be better watched, accounted for, and distributed, by local populations. This helps to minimize the impersonal dimension of bureaucracy and its faceless forms.

In this way, Joseph represents the domain of the political where families are kept intact, thus giving precedence to the many rather than the few. Authentic government, then, arises out of the imperatives of society, rather than imposing an artificial order upon it. In this way, he preserves the people by appealing to their common existential concern, and thus elevates fraternity over enmity. Either we will act together as brothers and live, or we shall perish separately and alone. This appears to be Joseph's overriding ethical imperative that is protracted by him into the realm of the political. Or to put it in the language of Levinas, "To think of men's hunger is the first function of politics" (BTV 2007, 18).

Levinas contrasts justice with responsibility. Justice belongs to everyone, so that there can be justice for me as well. It is through justice that just institutions are established by the stabilizing of competing demands. Still, responsibility involves the perfecting of justice, and therefore always accompanies it. In this sense, responsibility is infinite. Is this not what was meant when Yehuda promised Jacob that if he did not return Benjamin safely he would bear the blame for all time? (See Gen. 43:9.)

The solidarity within his own family requires a delicate rectification on Joseph's part. When he sees with his own eyes that Yehuda and the other brothers are willing to risk their own lives to protect Benjamin, he sees a brotherhood that surpasses all previous enmity. Joseph can no longer bear concealing himself. He has all but his brothers leave the room before breaking down

weeping and revealing himself: "I am Joseph your brother" (Ani Yosef achicha).[25]
The biblical Joseph absolves the earlier conduct of his brothers toward him by
appealing to Divine Providence. Still, it is not clear that he completely forgives
them, either. There is enough responsibility to be assigned and shared.

EGLAH ARUFAH: ASSIGNING RESPONSIBILITY

Joseph confirms the words of the brothers to Jacob by reminding Jacob of what
he and his father were learning just before his abduction and exile into Egypt.
The midrash points out that he sent "wagons" to Jacob. The Hebrew word is
close to the Hebrew *eglah* meaning "heifer." This subject, in retrospect prophetic,
discusses and rules on what is to be done when a person is found to be dead
(usually murdered) between two or more cities. Why should this arcane delib-
eration and discussion have taken place just before Joseph's disappearance? The
underlying moral question is who is responsible for the dead person? Let us
assume that the body is discovered midway between two or more cities. Are not
all the inhabitants, more or less directly or indirectly responsible? Let us keep
in mind that this phenomenon is being reawakened just after the reconciliation
between Joseph and his brothers and just prior to Jacob's descent into Egypt.

Surely this implies that the blame is to be shared without specifying how
and by whom. Otherwise, would not Jacob be likely to be consumed by his
disappointment and anger toward Joseph's brothers, who have deceived Jacob
regarding Joseph's disappearance? Does not Jacob bear some of the blame for his
conspicuous favoritism toward Joseph that arouses the ire of the other brothers?
Furthermore, why didn't Jacob, as many commentators ask, send someone to
accompany Joseph to find his brothers? Did he not know that they harbored ill
will toward him? Yet he has asked Joseph to give a report to him regarding the
conduct of the brothers.

And what about Joseph himself? The text makes clear that Joseph, at the
age of seventeen, was visibly narcissistic. He admired and groomed himself
excessively and seems to have been obsessed with his appearance. Earlier, he did
not hesitate or give thought to how his two dreams might be received centering
on his own superiority to his brothers in the presence of his father. While the

---

25 These are the first words said to have been spoken to those rabbis gathered in Rome
by Angelo Joseph Roncali to rabbis whom had invited to meet with him at the beginning of
Vatican II, as Pope John XXIII. It was at this time that the charge of deicide, which caused
so much Jewish suffering through the generations, was abolished.

dreams of Joseph prove prophetic, Jacob nonetheless rebukes him for the second dream, though the Torah says, "He kept the matter in mind." Furthermore, the oral tradition criticizes Joseph's eagerness to find fault with his brothers' conduct without properly examining the matter. From a standpoint of Jewish law, Joseph, not the brothers, had erred in his description of their conduct.

Nonetheless, the brothers themselves, with the exception of Benjamin, who was not present, appear to bear the greatest burden of guilt. Both the text and the tradition are at pains to show that there are degrees of blame and responsibility even among the brothers. The brothers said to one another: "Behold the dreamer comes; let us slay him" (Gen. 37:19). However, both the midrash and Joseph later on single out Shimon for having instigated this murderous rhetoric. It will be remembered that it is Shimon who is later made a hostage by Joseph until Benjamin is brought down into Egypt. The other brothers, aside from Reuven, appear to agree with Shimon, and perhaps Levi, as some midrashim assert.

The roles of Reuven and Yehuda are unique and different.... From the beginning, Reuven's intentions are depicted as looking for a way to save the life of Joseph without openly, and therefore unsuccessfully, opposing his other brothers. When he tries to come back to the pit, in which he had recommended Joseph be placed, Joseph is gone. Yehudah, on the other hand, makes the practical suggestion of dubious morality that Joseph be sold rather than killed "by their own hands." Whereas Reuven suffers from a deficiency in the realm of action, Yehudah still remains to be tested in relation to the purity of his intentions. The other brothers also bear enormous responsibility, even if it is only by not interfering with the plans to harm Joseph.

All this is to say that there is enough responsibility on the part of so many moral agents, that the example of social responsibility diffused through the *eglah arufah* comes to mind. Furthermore, Joseph himself does not bother to inform his father of his new exalted position in Egypt for many years, thus causing Jacob much grief and sorrow. But we do not want to diminish or conflate the responsibility of the perpetrators with that of the intended victim, Joseph. This raises a philosophically difficult, if not impossible, ethical question. Only after Reuven has done *teshuvah* and the brothers express genuine remorse; and after Shimon has been punished, however mildly; and Yehuda offers to substitute himself for Benjamin, can reconciliation within the family take place.

Levinas argues that while justice is finite, responsibility is infinite. It moves out of the self, toward the other, toward their neighbors. It is also to be grasped in the extended present which includes the trace of the past and the establishing of conditions that permit the promise of the future to proceed. For Levinas, the promise of time undergoes a kind of descent from the parent to the child.

INTIMATIONS OF A MESSIANIC TIME

Vayechi: And He Lived
(Genesis 47:28–50:26)

Then Jacob called for his sons and said, "Assemble yourselves and I will tell you what will befall you at the End of Days."

—Genesis 49:1

The last portion of the book of Genesis begins with a recounting of the days leading up to and immediately after the death of Jacob. Yet it is called in Hebrew *v'yichi*—"and he lived." The only parallel for this as we have seen is in the passages recounting the death and burial of Sarah, similarly called *chayai Sarah*—the life of Sarah. There is, however, unfinished business to be dealt with while Jacob is living. He must secure the consent of Joseph to assure that his burial takes place not in Egypt, but in the land of Canaan. In fact, Jacob forces Joseph to swear an oath that he will indeed do this. This oath, stronger than a promise, binds the life of Joseph to that of Jacob, the other sons to the father, the descent into Egypt to the ascent to the land of Promise, the anticipation of oppression to that of redemption. In fact, it is for the reason of this oath, and some say only for this reason, that Joseph was told by the Pharaoh, "Go up and bury your father as he made you swear" (Gen. 50:5). In other words, Jacob is binding the generational future to the present and, also, by insisting on burial with his fathers, creating a bond to the past. In the midst of the discontinuity that is to follow, there is a condition of hope and expectation that will appear on the horizon.

The Torah states that "Jacob lived in the land of Egypt seventeen years; in the days of Jacob the years of his life were one hundred and forty-seven years" (Gen. 47:28). There is agreement among the commentators that the emphasis is on the seventeen years that Jacob lived in Egypt. This is to say that he truly lived during this time, reuniting with Joseph and being without material worries, either for his family or for himself. However, this raises a question regarding Jacob's aging prior to his subsequent death. The reader will notice that the Pharaoh also made this distinction between days and years when he asked Jacob upon his arrival, "How many are the *days* of the *years* of your life?" (Gen. 47:8). To this, Jacob answers: "The *days* of the *years* of my sojourns, have been a hundred and thirty years. Few and bad have been the days and the years of my life, and they have not reached the lifespans of my forefathers in the days of their sojourns" (Gen. 47:9). What kind of response is this? Rashi partially answers the question by stating that he has lived most of his life as a stranger or alien (*ger*) in the lands of other people.[26] This would mean a more difficult aging than might otherwise have been expected. Perhaps Jacob has made an effort to appear as politically nonthreatening as possible to the Pharoah. Yet, the question arises as to why Joseph positions his father "before" (*lifnei*) Pharoah, or alternatively, in front of him, in the position usually reserved for Joseph.

Jacob has shown a remarkable capacity throughout his life to place himself in the position of other people. This empathy is relearned by the Israelites in the exile that begins after Joseph's death. The Torah mentions thirty-three times the care that must be shown to strangers. Levinas reflects upon the subject of aging. What does it mean to age and how is aging lived out? When we become old, we commonly say, "I can no longer." This is very similar to childhood, when, in relation to time, we say "I cannot yet." In a sense then, it is easier for us to understand the passage of time as the loss of time or what Levinas also calls "the lapse." Levinas refers to the passing of time itself as at the heart of what we usually call "self-consciousness." Self-consciousness, for him, usually involves a kind of senescence. "Aging breaks up under the weight of years, and is irreversibly removed from the present—that is with re-presentation. In self-consciousness, there is no longer a presence of self to self, but senescence. It is as senescence beyond the recuperation of memory, that time, lost time that does not return, is a diachrony, and concerns me" (OBBE 1991, 52). This is more than

---

26 I have heard an alternate interpretation from R' Shlomo Zalman Hecht, obm (1917–1979). The explanation was as follows: Joseph showed a preference for his father, even above that of Pharoah. Pharoah picked up on this immediately and said that "it must be your age."

Jacob says no, "The days of my life have been few" (compared to my father's).

"It must be your great wealth?" Pharoah asks.

Jacob responds, "No, I have lived in great poverty."

"It must be that you have had a serene and happy life."

"No."

Pharoah asks, "What then?" Jacob does not give a response. At last Pharoah is alerted to the full measure of Joseph's esteem for his father.

acknowledging that as soon as I realize what I am thinking I am imperceptibly older. It means that while my reach is diminishing the time of others bears on me increasingly. In the case of Jacob, he had acknowledged his aging before the time of his impending death. As the commentators remark, these were the seventeen good years in which it could truly be said that he "lived" together with his children and grandchildren in Goshen. This is deduced in part from the fact that the Hebrew word for "good"—*tov*—has a numerical value of seventeen.

Still, as he experiences his time coming to a close, Jacob grasps that with aging comes a surplus of responsibility. Why? Is it simply a matter of putting one's affairs in order, or giving an admonition or making arrangements for burial? While it may include all of these elements, it brings with it a sense of bodily fatigue. For Levinas, this is an expression of the duration of aging. However, it is not to be confused with the effort involved in remaining upright in the face of gravity or the binding of a person to his labor. Rather, the aging are exposed to "outrage and wounding" that derives from a kind of extreme passivity which is not negativity. Levinas says that this "Is not an act but patience" (OBBE 1991, 55). But with this passivity comes virtually at the same time an exorbitant responsibility. Everyone wants or needs a last word. Why? Because of something that goes beyond what we commonly call "closure." It is what makes it possible for us to reject the foundational claim of nihilism—that is, that the future will become present, the present will become past, and the past will vaporize into a virtual nullity.

The blessings that Jacob gives to his sons is preceded by a strange interlude where Jacob speaks privately to Joseph, both about the necessity of burying his mother, Rachel, along the way and the specific blessings that he gives to Jacob's two sons. A question arises. Why does Jacob single out the two sons of Joseph, Menasha and Ephraim, and then bless them in inverse order of age? His own sons, except for Joseph, have been raised within the more or less strict supervision of his family, and not in the cultural exile of Egypt. Nonetheless, Joseph appears mortified that his father seems intent on provoking the very charge of favoritism by blessing the younger son, Ephraim, before the older son, Menasha. To Joseph's objection, Jacob remarks, "I know my son, I know" (Gen. 48:19). This repetition of "I know" appears to indicate that Jacob knows exactly what he intends, and furthermore that he understands things that exceed the comprehension of Joseph. Joseph himself has been the source of conflict and rivalry beginning with the favoritism shown him by his own father.

"Then Jacob called for his sons and said: 'Assemble yourselves and I will tell you what will befall you in End of Days" (Gen. 49:1). There is agreement in the commentary tradition that Jacob was prevented from telling his sons about the end of days. We can wonder why this was so. Levinas links the messianic idea to ethical as well as religious life in situating the messianic ideal within the Hebraic tradition. Virtually all of his discussions on the subject derive from his reflections upon Talmudic texts. However, there is also a consistent philosophical position that he advances on messianism. Levinas seeks to move beyond the war of each against each and all against all in the direction of a time of each for each and all for all. In no way does he seek to disclose the kind of secrets that were withheld from the pronouncements of even the biblical Jacob. He still speaks in the language of philosophy while nourishing his thought from the sustenance gained from Talmudic sources.

According to Levinas, a "timeless eternity," an idea often linked to messianism, represents a philosophic distortion of time and alterity. By no means does the end of my life signal the end of my responsibility. Rather, he links messianism to an extreme responsibility for others where the "I" would bear the weight of all the world. (As he says, the self is a *sub-jectum*; it is under the weight of the universe responsible for everything.) He explores what might be called a "preconceptual messianism" that arises to awareness prior to philosophical explanation or theological conceptualization. Among the great commentators on the Talmudic text dealing with messianism there is at least one element that remains constant. As Maimonides puts it, in the time of redemption, Israel will regain its sovereignty (*Mishneh Torah*, Hilchos Melachim). However, Levinas argues that before sovereignty becomes a political phenomenon, it is already a personal, moral and social one. This involves the interior sovereignty that is already on its way to taking on a position on the ethical-messianic subject. Such a subject is the "absolute interiority of government." We find Levinas's most original reflection on the subject in his commentary called "Messianic Texts," found in *Difficult Freedom*. It centers on a statement that the Talmud attributes to R' Nachman in Sanhedrin 98b–99a: "R' Nachman said 'if he [the Messiah] is among the living, then it might be one like myself.'" The translation can also be read: "[T]hen it is me." What does this mean? Levinas appears to be saying that the 'I' must take on, according to this view, a virtual messianic responsibility for the suffering of all the others.

To speak of living in a messianic temporality is to situate oneself proximate to all the others and to take on a responsibility that cannot be given over to anyone else, even G'd Himself. Whatever else the "End of Days" might entail, it means the reversal of the order of each against each and all against all. It is far from the apocalyptic drama, which is too much with us in our own time, that links violence to eternity. Put simply, what Levinas appears to be saying, and perhaps why Jacob wishes to announce this to all his sons, is that the end of days is not found magically at the end of time. It is not simply the last act in a divine drama, but rather it is the very essence of interhuman relations that works toward a regime of peace, what might truly warrant being called "messianism."

The last portion of the Book of Genesis perhaps provides us a hint regarding the reversal of fortunes of the children of Israel. In all other cases, as found in the whole scroll of the Torah, there is at least a nine-letter space, separating one portion from the next. But, in this case, there is no space. This is why Rashi describes *Vayechi* as a closed (*sesumah)* section. What is indicated according to the *Tur* (1275–1340) is that this closure is a premonition of the enslavement that will follow the death of Jacob and all of his sons. In other words, this absence of an opening reflects the apparent closing off of a future for Israel. We immediately see that the rhetoric and tone of the Book of the Exodus is quite different from that of Genesis.

In fact, the last word of the Book of Genesis is the Hebrew word for Egypt, *Mitzrayim. Mitzrayim* contains within itself the Hebrew word for limit, *tzar.* What we lack is any kind of reason that would make the subsequent slavery in Egypt justifiable or explicable. There appears to be no single reason for these events in the Book of the Exodus, at least none that will justify or satisfy the suffering that occurs before the exodus from Egypt. While the Book of Genesis has certain political motifs, inescapable in everyday life, they largely focus on the politics of the family. As such, they are not considered by most historians, especially those influenced by Hegel, to belong to history. The politics of history in this sense, are associated with a regime of power.

Where the political does appear in the Book of Genesis, it is considered a prolongation of ethical life. That is a necessary concession to the fact that government, administration, and issues belonging to power, and therefore Totality, always, however imperceptibly, play a role. The question remains, can a sense of the future be regained in servitude? And if so, what are the dynamics of its significance?

Exodus

SHEMOS

ON EXODUS

> It is the insurmountable intimacy of the exile that still continues, and in
> which the language of accomplishment reverts to that of pure promise.
> —ITN 2007, 75

The idea of history, and an understanding that the future *can* be better than
the past, is born in the Western imagination with the opening of the Book of
the Exodus. The "event" appears as the irreducible and absolute category that
permits history as we know it to be recognized as such, to be remembered as
well as to proceed. The family of Israel now appears swept up within the cur-
rents of a political history—that is to say, a history that is measured by the force
and reach of its rulers. As the journey begun in Genesis reveals, inside of this
external history is an internal one aiming at an end that is not at all clear. This
is what Levinas refers to as *eschatology*. By eschatology, he means an eschatology that is measured not at the end of time, but at every one of its instants
(TI 1969, 23). It is ethical before it is political. More precisely, the Exodus ushers
in a revolutionary history. The rhetoric of this revolution can still be heard in
the echoes of the emancipating movements of our own historical hour, especially in the echo of the American Civil Rights Movement.

Could this oppression of the Israelites have been otherwise? This question
is not unknown to the commentary tradition, and the responses vary. We have
already been told that Abraham errs when he asks how he will *know* that the
land promised to him and his descendants will come to pass (Gen. 15:8). Could
all of this suffering of the 210 years of servitude really have been brought on by
this improper question? And if so, why is it improper? After all, isn't Abraham
simply asking for mere confirmation? Or, is it possible that he has suffered an
existential crisis of faith, however brief? This would assume that knowledge
occupies a lesser role than faith, even where faith is understood, as it is by
Levinas, as primarily and almost exclusively a kind of fidelity. Consider the
example of the closest kind of human relationship. Is there ever enough confirmation that can be given to the love of one for another? For example, when

I ask the other person, "How can I know for sure that you love me?" is this not very similar to the kind of category mistake that the commentary tradition attributes to Abraham? This is to say that such a demand, even posed in the form of a question, is an improper search for a kind of knowledge as opposed to the most intimate expression of a relationship. Otherwise, we can easily slip back into what Edmund Husserl, the founder of phenomenology, calls the "natural attitude." In the natural attitude, we are lost in the objects of our reflection and imperceptibly turn other people as well as ourselves into objects.

There is, of course, a more common explanation of the descent into slavery. It would begin with the bane of historical Jewish existence—assimilation into the dominant cultural mores of a given place and time. Here, we would lose a sense of our own identity and subordinate our time to the time of the nations.

There is yet another, more radical, way of responding to this same question. What is the quickest way of forging a collective awareness, or what we might today call "a group identity?" A shared experience of human suffering with a common adversary—is this not the quickest way of forming a people and a nation? It would make us the passive objects rather than the agents of the beginnings of our own history as a people and a nation, but such a history would begin before we were conscious of it. In this way, we would remain active agents, however unknowing, helping to shape this history.

There are multiple dimensions to the servitude of the Israelites: (1) economic, (2) physical, (3) cultural, psychological, and political, (4) religious-spiritual. The movement of the Exodus shows the embodied condition of each aspect of oppression. These modes of oppression, while discernable, are interrelated. The history of oppression gives way to the experience of freedom in each aspect where it has been suppressed. The next great movement in the Book of the Exodus is the transformation of this newly experienced freedom into justice expressed as law. The reason that the Exodus can be viewed as the paradigm of revolution is that this act of great transformation culminates neither in tyranny nor anarchy.[1]

Levinas focuses on numerous interrelated themes in the Exodus. These include a subtle reflection coming to awareness of human identity. This is a kind of remembering that, as he puts it, goes "beyond memory" (ITN 2007, 64). "The going forth from Egypt—the Exodus—and the evocation of that Exodus in which freedom was given to a people, the coming to the foot of Mt. Sinai

---

1   Michael Walzer, *Exodus and Revolution* (New York: Basic Books), 1985.
Walzer's book exposes the multiple dimensions of the movements, from oppression to freedom to justice. He applies his understanding to present-day political life.

where that freedom culminated in Law, constituted a privileged past, the very form of the past as it were" (Ibid., 65).

What does Levinas mean by the very "form of the past?" He quickly gives us an idea that this is not simply a matter of historicity—history as it was remembered to have been lived. Such lived history, which is foundational, we remember so that it can live in the present, tinging the future with hope and expectation. He acknowledges the important role of subjugation for Israel but indicates that what he is speaking of goes beyond this subjugation as such. "But by the same token, it is a thought virtually obsessed by the theme of freeing slaves—whence, perhaps (despite their particularism and tentativeness), the texts from Exodus 21, destined to their many sublimations and the rest of prophetic scripture" (ITN 2007, 66). The reference is to the beginning of the laws immediately following the ten words of the commandments. These are the laws of justice that can be understood through reason. They begin with limitations placed upon human slavery, something all too familiar to the ancient Israelites.

This is consistent with a reflection that Levinas initiates in his first book, *On Escape*. Levinas speaks about the origins and conditions of the appearance of personal identity. The human subject recognizes himself as such, only through a process of going out from what we might term "the self." The self is prepersonal—while it surely exists, it does so in the realm of the anonymous—the need to be satisfied, the elements to be absorbed in, without particular regard to other people.

He specifies: "We live from 'good soup,' air, light, spectacles, sleep.... Conversely, the independence of happiness always depends on a content: it is the joy or pain of breathing, looking, eating, working, handling the hammer and the machine.... One exists from pains and joys. Enjoyment is precisely this way the act nourishes itself with its own activity" (TI 1969, 110–11). The self that arises from enjoyment is not yet a moral subject.

The moral subject originates in the ex-odus from the self. This can happen only when the self becomes aware of the other and the claims the other person makes upon me. In the beginning of the Exodus, we see the going out from the self toward the other as a socioeconomic phenomenon that becomes aware of its condition of servitude in relation to longing for human freedom. The Exodus then generates the going out from the self with a sense of its own past, present, and future. Israel will be transformed into a nation self-conscious of itself where each self can achieve a sense of its own subjectivity. Each Israelite must be able to recognize the sufferings of others for an ethical sense of solidarity to arise. This will now take the form of the past that generates a present.

Levinas again relates the Exodus to the elevation of the moral subject from the self and the awareness of how this is continually at stake. He puts it this way: Here we have a dimension of the memorable and as it were the spirituality—or the respiration—of consciousness, which already, in its content of presence is memory of enfranchisement and lives concretely in the soul of freed men. The Jew is free *qua* affranchised: his memory is immediately compassioned for all the enslaved or all the wretched of the earth and a special flair for that wretchedness that the wretched themselves are prone to forget (ITN 2007, 66).

These themes become recurrent ones in our portion by portion reflection on the Exodus. Just prior to the outgoing from Egypt, human time is given a different inflection. The calendar is given over to human beings to establish and maintain: "This month shall be for you the beginning of months, it shall be for you the first of the months of the year" (Exod. 12:2). Prior to the outgoing from Egypt, the Israelites are told to remember, even to reenact, the events of the Exodus. In other words, a future is engendered at the same time that a past is quickened so that it will inform the meaning of the present. This is truly the beginning of existential freedom. For people free and adult, time now has three dimensions—a future and a past, as well as a present.

In a sense, we might view the historical Exodus as grounded in a moral Exodus. The first of the ten proclamations at Sinai begin with the words: "I am Hashem your G-d who has taken you out of the land of Egypt from the house of slavery" (Exod. 20:2). (Hebrew: *Anochi Hashem Elokecha asher hotzasecha maeretz mitzraim mibais avadim.*) There is a great debate among the commentators as to whether this proclamation should be regarded as a commandment, as it does not appear to command anything. The first proclamation, however, contains the manner in which G'd makes himself known to the Israelites. He does so by linking himself to this monumental event of history and therefore becomes recognized as the G'd of history. He has led the Israelites out of bondage, and therefore by implication, into *freedom*. Are the laws that follow then conditioned upon human freedom? This is to ask whether or not they must be freely assumed. The specific laws of economic and social justice, the *mishpatim*, begin with the admonition not to oppress a servant.

When Moses is summoned to return from Midian to confront the Pharaoh and to lead the Israelites out of Egypt, he is understandably reluctant. In effect, G'd makes him an offer he cannot refuse. This begins with the appearance of the bush that burns without consuming itself. Moses asks G'd, "Who shall I tell them sent me?" And He says: "I am the G'd of your father, the G'd of Abraham, the G'd of Isaac, the G'd of Jacob. Moses hid his face, for he was afraid to gaze toward G'd" (Exod. 3:6). G'd begins by binding Moses to Him and, according to the midrash, by speaking initially to him in the reassuring voice of his own father and then by linking himself to the forefathers. Despite the fact that Moses is told that G'd will rescue the people from Egypt and bring them to "a good and spacious land flowing with milk and honey," Moses appears to maintain a certain humility, reserve, and perhaps even skepticism (Exod. 3:8). First, Moses appears to sense himself as unworthy for such a task: "Who am I that I should go to Pharaoh?" (Exod. 3:11). Moses is given further reassurance when he is told, "When you take this people out of Egypt, you will serve G'd on this mountain" (Exod. 3:12). Here Moses is not asking for a sign, but G'd appears to anticipate his anxiety. Then, the conversation turns from the practical to the metaphysical. Moses anticipates that the people will ask him, regarding G'd, "What is His Name?"—"What shall I say to them?" (Exod. 3:13). G'd gives the most extraordinary answer, puzzling enough to later create a different inter-pretation between Rashi and Maimonides. He says tell them: "I *am* that I *am* has sent you." Rambam says that the words *Ehy(k)eh asher ehy(k)eh* mean "I am that I am" (GFP 1956, 93–95). The history of philosophy will understand this noncontextually as G'd's existence preceding and/or coinciding with his essence. Up until the time of the existentialists in the twentieth century, existence before essence is understood as proper only to the Divine. Very simply put, all other beings are defined by what they are—that is to say, their essence. We are what we are, whether we are defined by our function or by the nature of our soul or by what we are taken to be in an enduring way, by others. This means that what we are is a function of our *essence,* as it was for Aristotle, before it relates to our existence.[2] This is why, in the same vein, we speak with such certainty about the mystery of "human nature."

Rashi, perhaps not so metaphysical as Maimonides, insists that this is to be translated in the future tense: "I will be who I will be." Rashi is so helpful as to tell us that what this means is that G'd will be with us in future exiles as he is in this one. Very practically, Moses, anticipating whom he is to be dealing with, responds—couldn't we confine ourselves to the present exile? G'd responds, "Tell them 'I will be' has sent you" (Exod. 3:14).

The implications of Rashi's placement of this ambiguous language in the future tense is of the highest importance. We are dealing with a people who are

---

2 Aristotle, *Nichomachean Ethics,* trans. Terrance Irwin, book I, chapter 7 (Indianapolis, IN: Hackett Publishing Company, 1999).

quite literally out of breath and exhausted. The very idea of hope has vanished. In everyday discourse, when a person says, "I will meet you at such and such a place at a designated time," we regard this as a kind of promise. A promise is a unique form of speech. In a promise, we send our word, given in the present ahead of ourselves, and thereby establish a kind of future.[3]

Yet, the utterance given by G'd to Moses is doubled. Why should G'd say twice "I will be who I will be?" There is a second form of promise that is used in everyday language when we speak, for example, of the promise of springtime or a promising student or artist or child. This second form of promise binds two phases of time together. The future is now bound up with the present. That there is a future altogether is a source of expectation and hope. Such hope, if it is not to be blind hope, is dependent on the fact that something is promising.

In a more philosophical sense, it is reasonable to infer that G'd is saying "You have reason to hope, because I promise you that existence itself is promising." The future then is itself established as bound to the present, but different from and, when combined with right conduct, better than the present. The language of promising ultimately refers to the way that we are situated in relation to other people and the world that we find around us. The phenomenon of probability, on the other hand, refers more accurately to a world of objects. The moment that we can no longer identify human experience as more or less promising, the more distant we become from other people and, in a quieter way, from ourselves.

---

3   Rashi argues that the immediate reiteration of "I will be" means that G'd is saying to Moses and, by extension, the Israelites that as I will be with you in the exile from Egypt, so too will I be with you in future exiles. Moses then impresses upon G'd that one exile is enough for now, and perhaps G'd would do better to limit His self-description to this exile. Therefore, G'd responds immediately to Moses, saying, "So you shall say to the children of Israel, I shall be has sent Me to you" (Exod. 3:14). These utterances are embedded within Moses having been assured that the G'd of his father, and the G'd of Abraham, Isaac, and Jacob has already given this assurance. In other words, there is clearly a redefinition here of the covenant enacted with Abraham, with Isaac, and with Jacob. What kind of promise is then being made to the Israelites? It is a promise that affirms that the future itself is aiming at goodness. Moreover, the shape of the future in relation to the present is going somewhere that is oriented, meaningful, and purposive. This two-fold promise then binds word and deed, present and future, the theoretical and the practical. This becomes delineated in the fourfold promise given to Moses and the Israelites shortly. Nonetheless, this is an extraordinary philosophical development. Why? If there is to be any significance to the theologically laden words of "trust," "faith," and "hope," then this could only be the case if there is something before and beyond the neutrality of being or nature.

This is the absolutely minimal condition for any kind of genuine hope. For this reason, it is the condition for any kind of purposive action. This double promise cannot be made by a human being. Only the first part can be uttered from our side. The time of promise originates outside the human subject with the infinite other.

Yet still, when we ask ourselves why we embark upon any course of action, why we go this way rather than that, why we move rather than stay, why we are drawn to one way of doing things rather than another, is it not always because it appears to us as good, at least in prospect? As Levinas says, "It seems indispensible that we westerners situate ourselves in the perspective of a time bearing a promise. I do not know to what degree we can manage without this. This appears to me to be the most troubling aspect in our present situation" (IRB 2001, 185). When the people of Israel complain to Moses, after their situation worsens, that they must gather straw for their bricks as a result of Moses's mischievous interfering, the people, without perhaps realizing it, do have the stirring of a future. It is a future that first appears unpromising. However, this situation turns around before the receiving of the law. This is what the rabbinic tradition means when it says that the healing will come even before the affliction.

After the outgoing from Egypt, with the giving of the law, the Torah becomes the basis of Israel's very existence, as Saadya Gaon affirms, "The Jews are not a people except for the Torah." We examine some of the dynamics of the receiving of the law, as well as its application, in what follows.

PROPER NAMES

Shemos: Names
(Exodus 1:1–6:1)

The transition from the Book of Genesis to that of Exodus begins with a reiteration of the proper names of the sons of Jacob. With the onset of slavery, we see these proper names devolve and disappear into descriptions of economic functions. The evidence for this is that with the onset of slavery, we seldom see names given for individual Israelites. The absence of proper names of the Israelites is a function of the depersonalization that comes with the onset of oppression. Proper names are then reintroduced with the beginning of Moses's mission at the bush that burns without consuming itself. It is not by chance, then, that the Book of the Exodus in its entirety is referred to in Hebrew as *Shemos*—or, Names.

The physical slavery did not start at once. It began with a subtle kind of pseudo-patriotism. In order to prove themselves as true Egyptians, the Israelites were asked to "volunteer their labor." The midrash tells us that this volunteerism turns into obligatory work without pay. This obligatory work turns into ever more repressive kinds of servitude (MR). In other words, what begins with a loss of cultural autonomy and the increase of psychological fear devolves into economic servitude and eventually, for the last eighty-six years, into physical slavery. From what Rashi says, as noted above, there had to have been a diminishing of social solidarity for this kind of degradation to fully take place.

The text makes very clear that Moses recognizes the Hebrew slaves as his brothers for whom he has empathy and with whom he shows remarkable solidarity. "*Vayetzei el achiv*—And he went out to his brothers" (Exod. 2:11). He thereby risks his princely privilege and exposes himself to an unexpected danger in his harshest, most radical kind of response to an Egyptian man who was treating a Hebrew man abusively, "a man of his brethren" (Ibid.). The killing of the Egyptian slave master was not merely impulsive or without calculation. The text states, "He turned this way and that and saw that there was no man, so he struck down the Egyptian and hid him in the sand" (Exod. 2:12). Moses cannot abide the injustice that he has witnessed. Rashi states that Moses's prophetic sensibility was at work when he looked this way into the man's past as well as that way into his future and saw that the Israelites would be in continuing peril before striking the man (Stone, Exod. 2:12n12). Nonetheless, it is the reception that he gets the next day that shocks, saddens, and shows Moses that the Israelites have been oppressed to the point where they are not yet ready for liberation.

"And he went out on the second day and behold two men of the Hebrews were striving together" (Exod. 2:13). Moses is mortified by the reaction of the two Hebrew slaves to his bold and heroic intervention on their behalf. And is this not the way of oppressors, to have their slaves or subjects fight with each other to conceal from them the source of their oppression? According to Rashi, when Moses acknowledges that "the matter is known," he reveals his own sense of how, and perhaps why, the enslavement in Egypt could have taken place (Exod. 2:14).

Rashi states that the Israelites suffer because "they quarreled and carried tales about one another." However, this surely appears to be a consequence rather than a cause of their servitude. The commentary tradition notes that there was no permission for the harshness of their servitude. Furthermore, the midrash notes that the enslavement began by inducing them to identify with the Egyptians, and was accompanied by a "soft mouth" (*biphe rach*) or gentle rhetoric. They even receive decent pay for work until they become acclimated to it. Such rhetoric dissimulates the harsh intentions (MR). It is during this time that the Egyptians embitter their lives with crushing harshness (MR).

While the rabbinic tradition identifies the two figures, Dathan and Aviram, as the archetypal troublemakers, Rashi, following the midrash, finds their behavior as expressive of the ethos that led to slavery itself. This kind of political mystification bears the signature of all tyranny. Moses realizes that solidarity or fraternity is a precondition for the expectation of social freedom. After the daring revolutionary act in which he risks his princely privilege and puts his very life in danger, Moses is greeted with the disturbing realization that the thirst for freedom is not yet present among the Israelites. It is not solidarity that Moses encounters but rather an atomized condition—that is, the "each against each, or all against all." "And they said, 'who made thee for a ruler and judge over us? Thinkest thou to kill me as thou did kill the Egyptian'; and Moses feared" (Exod. 2:14).

According to the Rav J.B. Soloveitchik, who was eminent among contemporary twentieth-century American commentators, Moses himself becomes by turns agitated and alienated from his unreciprocated intervention and thereby seeks to flee the bonds of brotherhood by going to the distant land of Midian (DDY, 125). Soloveitchik sees this as a desire to settle permanently in Midian in tranquility, away from all the strife and contention.[4] This is something that must be rectified before Moses can serve as leader in taking the Israelites out of Egypt (DDY, 125). This is why, according to the commentary tradition, the encounter by the bush that burns without consuming itself takes seven days. First, G'd must convince Moses to reestablish his bond with his people. In the second place, Moses must be convinced that his experience of unworthiness is not a liability, but rather, a precondition for his service as leader. Only then can Moses become the stammering prophet who, together with his brother, Aaron, can act as a leader ready to assume the burden of uniting the people.

There is a point of view that holds that Moses's primary motivation involves the elevation of his brother, Aaron, whom he realizes has guided the people in their most abject condition. According to this view, this is why he repeatedly hesitates to accept his divine mission until Aaron is given a proper role. What this tells us is that Moses understands that the sense of kinship is a condition for brotherhood in the larger sense.

A slavish nation is not yet fully adult, not yet capable of taking responsibility for its own destiny. Freedom from oppression can be achieved only by a people who recognize the source of their collective suffering. For them to become a nation conscious of itself as such, a basic sense of solidarity, one-for-the-other, must also be achieved in spite of the terror inflicted upon them. This, however, takes time.

The summons to Moses by the bush that burns without consuming itself, originates with G'd using Moses's proper name emphatically. He says, "Moses, Moses" (Exod. 3:4). The midrash informs us: "The doubling of Moses' name here is an expression of love and an expression of urgency" (MR). Levinas well understands the relation of proper names to moral urgency. The people must be given back their proper names—that is to say, their personal identity, and they are to be rescued in a spirit of moral urgency. Their suffering has become unbearable.

Moses responds: "*Hineini*" (Exod. 3:4). This means "Here am I and ready" as it does in the case of the biblical Abraham or, as Levinas points out, it can be associated with a sense of prophetic urgency, where the word can signify "Send

---

4   This can be meaningfully viewed as having been prefigured by Jacob's desire to settle in Canaan.

me."[5] The exile (*galus*) in Egypt is prefigured by the redemption (*geulah*) that has already shown itself with the appearance of holiness at the bush that burns without consuming itself. This begins with the divine instruction that Moses remove his shoes (MR). In every place that a person walks barefoot, he or she can feel in a way that he or she cannot do otherwise. Is this not meant to emphasize the renewed empathy that Moses must have toward his enslaved brothers and sisters after he has lived in Midian? At the same time, we see an insistent and somewhat skeptical Moses questioning the meaning and outcome of the mission that has been proposed for him. In responding, he has been subjected to the claims of the divine other, and multiple others, and he must be prepared to answer to and for them.

In the language of Levinas, the extreme difficulty of becoming a responsible subject in relation to one's neighbor is imperiled in advance of every action. The oppression works simply by making it virtually impossible for the self to exit from its own enchainment. More than inertia, it signifies the extreme difficulty of the going out from the self where it could arise as an ethical subject. The self is overwhelmed by almost inhuman effort, fatigue, hunger, and the fear of violent retaliation for any deviation from the order of oppression already established. This is why we can say that the Israelites find themselves in a state of moral subjection. The midrash illustrates this very clearly. The taskmasters had intimidated their slaves by pointing out the futility of their even going to their homes after their labors. By the time they reach home, it would already be time for them to come back. Therefore, a new procedure is introduced whereby the Israelite slaves would sleep for a few hours near the places where they were working. The most distinctive exception to this all-against-all mentality comes from the Israelite guards or foreman (*Shitri*). According to the midrash, when the quotas established by the slave masters were not fulfilled, they would often take the blame and the punishment on themselves in an effort to protect their fellows. In recent history, during the heinous system of the Nazis in World War II, some kapos were compared unfavorably by the prisoners to the ancient Israelite foremen.

In his second great book, *Otherwise than Being: Beyond Essence,* Levinas speaks of a kind of goodness that is beyond Being (OBBE 1991, 19). Yet, the beyond of being is something to be achieved by free and right human conduct. So, from an experiential point of view, what we have before us is the

---

5   Oona Ajzenstat, *Driven Back to the Text* 2001 (Pittsburgh: Duquesne UP), 123. Oona Ajzenstat calls attention to the centrality of the word concept *hineini* in the thought of Levinas. She notes the conjuncture of prophecy to social justice, reasoning to responsibility, and the undergirding of the saying before the said: "For prophecy commands my responsibility, most of all for justice."

good-in-prospect. This is to say that the good beyond being is promise itself. While Levinas speaks of the promise of time, this cannot be separated from the time that appears more or less promising, which we may refer to as the time of promise. Otherwise, we as human subjects would be confronted with a bewildering array of possibilities, no one of which could appear better than any other. If we were to argue that value is something that is merely added to fact—external to it—we should never be able to make a claim for the seriousness of ethical life. From the standpoint of human experience, value is found together with factuality. This condition is indispensable if we are to be able to explain to ourselves why we take one course of action rather than another, why we have an affinity to some people rather than others, why we choose to live here rather than there.

In this way, several biblical categories can be given a new philosophic form. Faith, for example, is usually treated as something that I "*have*." However, there must be a more originary, preconceptual notion of fidelity or faithfulness that comes prior to every credo, or system of conceptual beliefs. The Israelites must remain faithful to one another if we are to make any sense whatsoever of creedal beliefs about faith in G'd. Fidelity, hoping for good not yet present, is bound up with the phenomenon of promise. Infidelity arises when the absent one is treated as nonexistent.

The same must be true with belief. Until the modern era, beginning with the mathematical–scientific turn leading to the Enlightenment, the existence of G'd was seldom called into question. The justice of divinity, however, had been the subject of much searching reflection long before the contemporary period. What the notion of promise permits us to do is to go below the more elevated category of "belief *in*," to the prior question of believability. The capacity of belief is itself an ambiguous term. Do I find this experience credible or believable? In giving me your word, can you be counted upon, relied upon, to keep your word? This, too, is a matter of believability. If we do not recognize this phenomenon in everyday experience, it will make little difference to us whether we say we believe in G'd or not. It is in this sense that the notion of promise precisely begins with the other rather than the self. I cannot help but recognize that I may only glimpse what I can never live out beyond my own life.

When Moses confronts the Pharaoh with the divine directives, the immediate result is one of greater misery for the Israelites. Now they have to gather straw that was previously given to them in order to make the bricks that they will build into the storehouse cities of Pithom and Ramses. Moses is at a loss when the people understandably complain to him that he has embittered their lives all the more. It is at this moment that Moses turns to G'd and asks Him urgently, why, and wherefore are we going?

THE FOURFOLD PROMISE

Va'eira: I Appeared
(Exodus 6:2–9:35)

G'd responds to Moses's complaint telling him that He will reveal Himself by his transcendent, four-letter name. The name is accompanied by a fourfold promise, setting in motion the movement from exile and oppression to freedom and redemption. According to the tradition, the four-letter name represents a new elevation in the relation between the Infinite and the human being. In the plain sense, Rashi explains that "the Name (*Hashem*) revealed to Moses represents G'd as the One Who carries out His promises, for G'd was now prepared to fulfill his pledge, to free Israel and bring them to the Land" (Interlinear Chumash, Rashi, 349). Levinas offers a reflection on "the Name and its meanings" (BTV 1994, 115–26). The name is paradoxically perhaps neither to be pronounced (under normal circumstances) nor effaced. It is associated in the rabbinic tradition with mercifulness and ultimately, as Levinas stresses, with peace. It is the consummate expression of the Infinite.

While this may appear to make it remote from the finite and, therefore, the human, there is another way of looking at this relation. The Infinite can be glimpsed, but not explained or understood. It is in this way that the Infinite appears. This is in fact what makes it Infinite. Levinas describes the name in relation to being: "[B]ut revelation by the proper Name is not solely the corollary of the unicity of a being; it leads us further. Perhaps beyond being" (BTV 1994, 120). He goes on to remark that "Scriptural tradition provides the trace of a beyond of this very tradition" (Ibid., 120). Levinas's primary concern here, as elsewhere, has to do with the relation of the Infinite to the human. As becomes more explicit, the "trace" of which Levinas speaks refers to that which 'passes by' as it happens and can only be glimpsed as opposed to registered after the event.

For Levinas, "[t]ranscendence becomes ethics" (BTV 1994, 125). To put this another way, the fourfold promise of redemption is asymmetrical in character. It depends upon the capacity for promises made to be kept. This would be the case even with those that seem to stretch the bounds of the natural.

The rabbinic tradition sees this clearly when it speaks of the primary name *Eloh(k)im*, which has the numerical value of eighty-six. The eighty-six is also a numerical value of the Hebrew word for "nature" (*tevah*). In this sense, the explicit Name *Hashem* is understood to be 'beyond nature' as well as capable of promising to bring about deliverance from the eighty-six years of slavery, which according to the rabbinic tradition was the time of the actual physical servitude.

The four expressions of redemption are specific and interrelated. As explained by Rabbeinu Bachya, they refer to the removal of the burdens of slavery: "*Hotzeisi*—I shall take you out; *Hetzalti*—I shall rescue you; *Ga'alti*—I shall redeem you; *Lakachti*—I shall take you as a People."[6] As explained by R. Bachya, the movement implied here is from physical and economic slavery to the release from political oppression and the implied restoration of sovereignty that is necessary for redemption. This is referred to as *V'Ga'alti*, meaning a release from the psychological terrors of slavery in the past.[7] The fourth promise refers to what in contemporary theology is called the "doctrine of election" or the condition of being chosen—*Lakachti*—or, "I shall take you as a People."

As we have seen, these specific promises have already been prefigured by a more existential one that pertains to the relation of the present to the future as such. Hope originates with the subject; promise with the other.[8] In *Time and the Other*, Levinas juxtaposes the very words for hope and breath (*spero—spiro*, "I hope-I breathe"). Inspiration, or prophetic understanding, as Levinas presents it, is at the heart of this matter. Still, while the specific promises announced in conjunction with the four-letter word announced to Moses are understandable in context, we need to more clearly understand how the future is affected existentially in relation to the present, and therefore, the past.

To be more precise, there is a common shared sense of what it means for someone to make and keep a promise. This means that the word spoken in the present will be tested by my completion of the action at a future time. The linking of word to deed comes before theoretical comprehension. We all know whether a promise made has been kept or not. This is one of the reasons why the Torah instructs us to make promises sparingly and to be cautious that

---

6   See Stone Exodus line 6–7, footnote.

7   This is, of course, a complex process that, as we can see from the horrors of the Holocaust, has continued to haunt the survivors.

8   I am indebted to Professor Roger Burggraeve for helping me to clarify this distinction in the thought of Levinas. Professor Burggraeve explained this to me at a conference on Levinas in Jerusalem in January of 2006, at the Institute for Advanced Study at Hebrew University.

even our implicit agreements are not to cloak solemn or emphatic promises. However, the bond between future and present enables us to gain a sense of orientation, purpose, and continuity in and through time. It is the second kind of promise that bears the signature of biblical time. It is a time when the future *can* be better than the present while redeeming the imperfections of the past. What we might say then is that what G'd is promising Israel and humanity is hope. And that hope derives from a future that is promising.

This requires elaboration. For Levinas, biblical time does not represent a fall from eternity. Rather, it is the very generating of a future that *can* be better than the past. Unlike the Enlightenment notion of "progress," the promise of time does not mean that the future will *necessarily* be better than the past. It is accomplished by the enactment of the covenant made with the divine other and expressed by the responsible conduct of free human beings toward one another. *This* is what is meant by the promise of time. It is vital to understand that the promise of time also reflects the way in which human experience is lived. We do not originally experience time in terms of neutral, mathematical possibility. Rather, possibility and the companion doctrine of probability first appear to human awareness as more or less promising. It is this phenomenon of time bearing a promise that makes it possible for us to begin to understand why we decide on one course of conduct rather than another. Or, why we are drawn to one person or one path, rather than another. Simply put, it is because it seems good. More precisely, time appears as *prospectively* good. Based upon this phenomenon, we can begin to understand the aesthetics as well as the politics of everyday life. However, this promise, as we have indicated, comes to us from without—that is to say, it originates with the other or others rather than myself.[9]

The promise of time then must exist on many levels. It includes the covenantal promise refracted in the fourfold promise given to Israel by G'd. Such promise has a historical dimension, but it is history that is open to those who live it before it is written by historians or testified to by witnesses or survivors. The language of history, in fact, only begins to make sense if it is something other

---

9   To amplify, possibility first appears to us experientially within the guise of probability. Probability originates in experience in a way that is colored by value. We must determine whether the movement from hesitation to decision to action is good for the other and/or me. Where it is both the other and me, so much the better. However, this "good" remains to be achieved. In that sense, it has a temporal dimension that is inclined toward the future. It is in this way that the promise of time appears prior to the probability and possibility that it informs. The promise of time, then, originates prior to the modern philosophical distinction of "objectivity" and "subjectivity." Nonetheless, it is closer to subjectivity, as subjectivity means the embodied life of the human subject.

than and different from the past. What G'd then is telling Moses to convey to the Israelites, is that their situation is hopeful and that they should not despair, even though things might temporarily get worse or unpromising before they get better.

In fact, the fourfold promise of redemption accomplishes the movement that transforms the physical, economic, political, and spiritual dimensions of oppression. A recurrent theme in the phenomenology of Levinas, is the alternating movement between the each-against-each and the each-for-each. Levinas emphasizes above all else that this exodus begins with a moral transposition. The condition of each-against-each and all-against-all is undergoing the transformation into each-for-each and all-for-all. While this may seem utopian, let us keep in mind that it represents the elevation of the natural order into the inter-human one. In Egypt, the force of nature ultimately symbolized by the divine power attributed to the Nile must be demystified for this transformation to take place. It is only when the subject perpetually strives to go out of himself—what we might call the exodus of the self, or what Levinas calls "ex-cedence," can human solidarity be achieved. This requires additional refinements and elevation in the Exodus that culminates with the giving of the Torah at Sinai, by which according to Saadya, "Israel becomes a nation." This means that we act as guarantors for one another. More precisely, according to the midrash it is our children who bear the promise of the covenant and therefore act as guarantors for us.

We will have come a long way from a time when Moses first experienced the desire to flee to Midian because he saw an absence of fraternity among the Israelites. Still this remains something to be accomplished then and now. The promise of time is filled with uncertainty, risk, and doubt. The world of our childlike attachments must give way so that we can reattach ourselves to others, and through them learn to go forward as one for the other. This involves achieving again a level of trust, in words and then in deeds. This trust, in turn, gives confidence in the word of others, and therefore, inspires a readiness to face a future whose outcome is not known in advance.

It is important to note that while Levinas speaks of time bearing a promise, he does not elaborate on what this might mean. For example, *cannot time appear unpromising*? Surely, this is how the Israelites reacted when they were punished further for the first intervention with the Pharaoh by Moses and Aaron. Where first they had been given straw with which to make the bricks, they now had to gather their own straw. This is an exercise of pure futility. It is at this time that the people first complain to and against Moses and Aaron. Immediately sensing that the people are about to lose hope, G'd responds with the expression of the fourfold promise and the revealing of the divine name to Moses.

Is it possible to live and act in a purposive manner without the phenomenon of time bearing a promise?[10] When things seem to be going in an unpromising direction, value is not something added to time but is instead something that is the very exteriority of time. What does this mean? It means that even living in unpromising times, we do so with the recognition, however dim, of that which is meant by something that can be better, better even than being itself. The notion of pure promise pierces through the neutrality of Being and makes it possible for one generation to form a bond with another. It also makes it possible for us to connect our own pasts to the present. The past acts like a kind of pre-mise upon which we build each day. We do not wake up to nothingness; we wake up to the traces of the previous day and the approach of a future, however ill defined. Here we can situate the beginnings and even the framework of a philosophy that is Hebraic in its roots, which is otherwise more faithful to human experience than the Greek.

To be sure, there is a realm of nature that science describes with rigor, reason, and accuracy. Attempts by various religious fundamentalisms to devalue the role of science in order to save the sacred thereby, is lamentable if not downright harmful. Nature has to be registered and understood within the realm of human meaning. This is what Edmund Husserl and Levinas after him refer to as "the life-world." It is a world in space with ups and downs, with back and forth. In other words, our world is one, to use a phrase of Levinas, in which "reality has weight" (IRB 2001, 158). However, the first task for a free people is to make time one's own. We see this even before the actual outgoing from Egypt.

---

10 If it is a case of pure futility as the Israelites experienced it, does it not seem at least for the moment like the labor of the Sisyphus of Albert Camus? Here, I am reminded of a remark attributed by Camus's one-time friend and collaborator Maurice Merleau-Ponty: Merleau-Ponty in response to Camus's insistence that "life is absurd," is reputed to have said "but Albert, don't you think that what is most absurd, is that life appears to make sense?" In other words, even when speaking of nonsense, it must be from the standpoint of an assumed sense that is absent.

MAKING TIME

Bo: Go
(Exodus 10:1–12:16)

"This month shall be the beginning of months to you" (Exod. 12:2). Rashi famously argues that the Torah should have begun here. Why? What relation does the establishment of the new month have to "Bereishis Bara" ("In the beginning of God's creating")? (Gen. 1:1). The establishing of the new month is the first law given to the whole nation. This ordering of time is given just *before* the outgoing from Egypt; a free people are able to grasp the distinction between times present, past, and future.

Time is something that is made or created, at least in the language of the Torah. We recognize this when someone asks us to "make some time" for him or her. In fact, time is something that we create. R. Samson Raphael Hirsch observes, in his monumental commentary on the Pentateuch, that the statement—"This month shall be the beginning of months to you"—means that Passover must be celebrated in the spring (*Aviv*), and the calendar of "new moons" (the beginning of each month or *Rosh Chodesh*) as well as all the holy days shall be determined by human beings. Unlike the Sabbath, divinely decreed, the holy days, and their seasons, are subject to the determination of the Rabbinical Courts of Law. This means that we must turn toward one another to establish social and communal time. "Diachronic time" becomes what Levinas calls "a time that originates perpetually with the other."

The heart of the calendar of the Israelites renders time concretely their own. Hirsch emphasizes the connection between the Hebrew word for month (*chodesh*) and the Hebrew word for new (*chadash*). For this reason, he emphasizes the dimension of *renewal* that comes with the reappearance of the moon each month. He states, "This renewal of the moon shall be the beginning of New Moons, it shall be unto you for the first of the months of the year" (Hirsch, Exod. 12:2). This is doubly significant because the emancipation from Egypt also means a transcending of the Egyptian-Greek view of nature in relation to time.[11]

Nature (*physis*) means a closed system, like a river (the Nile) that flows endlessly and in a recurring fashion without orientation or purpose. For this reason, human nature, for the Greeks and for the Egyptians before them, is something essentially unchangeable. What this implies is that for them, the future cannot be better than the present, as the present is always seen as a variation of the past. We have already intimated this point in the contrast between Abraham and Odysseus. While the journey of Odysseus permits him to deepen his character, it does not fundamentally alter his identity. For the biblical Abraham and his successors, the openness of the future, new and different from the present, makes a fundamental alteration of identity possible.

The time of human freedom is measured in more than one way. Time measured by number is modified by time measured by meaning. Time measured by meaning is, in turn, governed by a more primal sense of time measured by urgency. Time measured by number has the following characteristics: it is quantitative; it is continuous; it is homogenous; it is infinitely divisible; and it is without purpose or orientation. For example, the time measured by the clock is indifferent to human concerns, value, or urgencies. It makes no difference whether time appears to us to be going more or less quickly, whether we are enjoying what we are doing or not, or whether someone is in immediate need of our assistance.

Time measured by meaning, on the other hand, is qualitative; discontinuous; heterogeneous; bounded in the sense that it is limited by minimally perceptible happenings and therefore it is not infinitely reducible; and, lastly, oriented or purposive. For example, we speak of having had a good day or a

---

11 It must be kept in mind that the month, unlike the Sabbath, is measured in relation to a natural, astronomical correlative, the moon revolving around the sun approximately every twenty-nine and one half days. The appearance of the new moon must originally be recognized by two witnesses to the Rabbinical Court. The difference between Rosh Chodesh and the scientific term "new moon" is that while the latter is not visible, the former refer the first reappearance of the crescent of the moon. In 359 CE, Hillel II created a permanent calendar that could be used in the future for all countries in the emerging Diaspora. In this way, the calendar moved toward uniformity, based on continuous time or what Levinas calls "synchrony." Still, such calendars measure years and days as well as months, and thereby they introduce the time of diachrony, which measures the uniqueness of each passing week. In this way, the natural rhythm of the seasons is affirmed and included *within* the time of the calendar.

good week. Furthermore, when we are bored or indifferent to what is happening, time appears longer. In retrospect, however, such time appears shorter. When we are involved in something of significance, time appears to pass quite quickly, but is remembered in greater detail, and therefore appears to have been longer.

Time measured by number, then, is in the modern world referred to as "objective," while time measured by meaning is "subjective." By rendering qualitative time *merely* "subjective," we might say we devalue its philosophical significance. However, this is far from the case. If we are to account for before and after, or the phases of time—past, present, and future—we must appeal to and employ the time of human existence, lived-time. Such time is oriented, and for that very reason, can seem longer or shorter in relation to time measured by number, depending on the importance or urgency of the matter. We can account for time measured by number only if we already have recourse to time measured by meaning as criteria for measurement.

It is with the ushering in of the month in which the Passover occurs that the Israelites begin to recognize themselves as a free people. It is not, then, by accident that the Jewish calendar originates with the month of Nissan. This concept of renewal is intimately associated with the way that the Israelites understand themselves from then on. This means, as experienced, such time becomes their own. Change that yields something new is foreign to the Greek notion of nature. Nature can suffer alterations but cannot permit genuine change. This is especially recognizable in the case of the human being. It is in this way that the bewitching rhythms of nature are taken up within the narrative of human experience. As experienced, such time, then, can open onto something new. Now it begins to become more visible why the Syrian Greeks, much later, at the time of Hanukah, forbade the observance of the seemingly innocuous holy day of Rosh Chodesh.

In this sense, the Jewish clock beats according to the rhythms of the week that culminate in the Sabbath. Unlike the solar year, month, or day, that correspond to an astronomical event, the week has no natural or astronomical event with which it correlates. The days of the week are named by virtue of their proximity or distance from Sabbath to Sabbath. The first day is called "Yom HaRishon," the second "Yom HaSheini," and so on.

To ensure that Passover comes out in the spring, a time of hope, the lunar calendar must be intercalated with the solar calendar. This means that seven times in nineteen years there will be thirteen months instead of twelve. This creates a kind of synchronic time that makes it possible for the time of Israel to coincide with the time of the seasons.

Still, the ability to make and control time leads to the creation of a permanent calendar that is at the very soul of the survival of the Jews as a people. This kind of autonomy is for a free people. The time of slavery exists only in the fugitive present where the mere escape from harsh labor constitutes the length and meaning of time.

The Passover offering (the *Korban Pesach*) is prescribed in advance of its enactment (Exod. 12:3ff.). All of the practices, customs, and laws associated with Passover are announced in *advance* of the outgoing from Egypt. In the plain sense, this is a matter of simple instruction. A question can be asked—for whom are most of these educational practices given? Not to possess *chometz* or leavened bread surely did not apply for the first Passover; rather, it is for the generations to come. One reason most revolutions founder has everything to do with transmission, or the inability in fact to transmit the lessons of the founders.[12]

To specify further, the symbols, practices, and customs reenact the intent, meaning, and purposes of the outgoing from Egypt. In this way, what Levinas calls the "trace of the past," leaves an indelible mark that can be accessed, at least in part, by what we call "memory." But from phenomenology we learn that memory, like understanding, must be memory *of* something. This makes it possible for there to be a memorial as well as an immemorial past, even if the traces of the past are "beyond memory," as Levinas argues. Perhaps the reason that the detailed customs and rituals are given along with the Passover narrative (*haggadah*), ahead of its happening, is to connect interpretation to lived time and experience. It is now possible to move forward while generating a new present from out of the immemorial past.

With the Korbon Pesach and the Passover meal, the families are joined to the larger community, and the outgoing from Egypt is recalled and reenacted as a social event that includes the aggregate as well as the individual. Hirsch stresses, contra Hegel, the nation emerges from out of the family. Tensions surely arise between the individual, the family, the nation, and later, the state.[13]

---

12 The necessity of learning to transmit the outgoing from Egypt, even before it actually happened continues to inform positively all subsequent generations. Take, for example, the kibbutzim, in present-day Israel. They are quickly becoming important artifacts that belong to the past. The founding generation had great difficulty transmitting its enthusiasm for collective labor and responsibility that also meant a commitment to an austere way of living. The need to recall and commemorate the outgoing from Egypt is met before this kind of crisis can arise.

13 Surely, the eating of the Paschal lamb serves a pedagogical purpose. Sheep, like the Nile, were considered divine by the Egyptians. A dramatic illustration of weaning the people

Surely, it cannot be unrelated that at the close of this portion of the Torah the people are instructed in a new form of achieving renewal. This instruction refers to the individual, perpetually on the way to becoming an ethical subject. The ritual significance of the *tefillin*, the binding of the leather straps on the forehead and on the arm, already reflect a view of the conscious self, moving toward an ethical subject to be achieved. Each day, an awareness must dawn in the self that the diverse, and sometimes opposing forces within the person, need to be fashioned, bound together, and refashioned. The cognitive aspect of a person easily drifts off into its own dream world. The self is always to be regarded as on its way to becoming unified, or one. Is this not why sections from the creedal prayer of the *Shema* (Hear O Israel, the Lord our G'd the Lord is One) is visualized first upon the hand, which will later be designated, in the wrapping of the *tefillin* in such a way that the first two letters of one of the divine names is made to appear. The name used is *(K)el Shadi*, a name that Levinas prefers to translate as "the Most High." What happens however, when the *tefillin* are not worn all day by scholars in Talmudic times? They leave a trace as the day goes on. Perhaps, when the subject reverts back to becoming a self, adrift, the role of philosophy appears more important. As Levinas says in a late reflection, "Philosophy begins when religion is adrift" (IRB 2001, 245).

---

of Israel from the trace of idolatry is demonstrated in the "eating of their gods." What is expressed here is a recognition that some people are more proximate that others.

TASTE AND MEANING

Beshalach: Sent Out
(Exodus 13:17–17:16)

R. Mendel of Rimanov is said to have given a sermon (*drasha*) every Sabbath for over twenty years, always on the subject of the manna. Even allowing for several weeks off per year, this comes to over a thousand discourses. Why? According to Ibn Ezra, the "Miracle of the Manna" (Exod. 16:4n4, SC) was even greater than that of the crossing of the sea. Modern scholars, and Spinoza in particular, have viewed the crossing of the Reed Sea *(Yom Suf)* as the epitome of the archaic, pre-rational character of the Jewish Bible.[14] However, part of the burden of Levinas's philosophical engagement with the Hebraic tradition inherently involves a critique of the kind of rationalism that Spinoza epitomizes.

Levinas shares with Spinoza a desire to demystify the claims of religion in general when measured by the "objectivity" of the mathematical-scientific revolution. However, for Levinas, the task of philosophy also involves a calling into question of what, in fact, is meant by "objectivity." No less than Spinoza would Levinas accept the purported literalism associated with the reading of the Jewish Bible. But Levinas is more aware than Spinoza of "the tradition of the history of tradition," and therefore understands that Jewish Scripture is always accompanied by interpretation or exegesis (Ouaknin 1998, 7). In fact, the great contemporary Torah scholar Aryeh Kaplan notes in his own translation of the Pentateuch, that literalism makes no sense by itself. Kaplan uses a helpful example in his introduction to *The Living Torah*. The English-speaking reader, Kaplan notes, knows that to "have a frog in one's throat" is metaphorical language (Introduction, V). The Talmud announces eighteen times, and Maimonides repeatedly reminds us in *The Guide for the Perplexed*, that the "Torah is written in the language of human beings."

The language of human beings pays careful attention to and takes seriously the phenomenon of human experience. For Spinoza, such experience is

_____

14 B. Spinoza, *Theological and Political Treatise*, chapter 6, page 51.

111

merely "subjective," and therefore prerational. To the extent that it cannot be quantified, it is not "objective." Conversely, to the extent that a phenomenon is not measurable or calculable, it does not belong to the realm of the rational. This leads to a strange bifurcation of reality where human beings are understood exclusively as natural objects among other natural objects; their experiences cannot be regarded as rational, objective, or real.

Levinas, a most rigorous student of the phenomenological approach to philosophy, regards this kind of "naturalism" as distorting and reducing human reality to something without meaning, purpose, or importance. Emptying human reality of temporality means that "before" and "after" lose their significance. Spinoza's rationalistic naturalism does not permit us to distinguish between phases of time, of past, present, and future. This does not mean that Levinas's thinking is in any way prerational. Rather, Levinas, like Kant, takes the position that reason in the strict sense is always finite, partial, and perspectival; and it is therefore not so pure as Spinoza thought. Levinas wishes to preserve a place for transcendence within the lived meaning of everyday existence.

Surprisingly, the interpretive rabbinic commentary tradition is also acquainted with post-literal methods of interpretation. We see this in Abraham Ibn Ezra's suggestion about the preeminence of the miracle of the manna. The giving of divine sustenance was an ongoing daily event while the crossing of the *Yom Suf* occurred but once (Stone, 383).[15] Indeed, the manna is a meal fit for any hermeneute worth his salt. Beginning with classical midrashim, the manna was described as capable of taking on any taste worthy of the one to whom it has been given. It is essential to note that the Hebrew word for "taste" (ta'am) is also the word for "meaning."

According to the Torah, the "manna" fell as "dew" covering the field of early morning. We are told that it looked like crystalline or coriander seed. Most economical, this "heavenly" food was edible even without preparation, and completely digestible, thus eliminating the complexities of waste. Still, the very appearance of the manna was at first unrecognizable to the famished Israelites, who had exhausted the food that they had taken from Egypt. A moment of self-reflection follows, beginning with an explicit questioning of the manna—"What is it?" ("*Ma Hu.*") In turn, according to Ouaknin, this leads back to a questioning of the question itself. "The 'Mah' of the 'manna' is the primordial interrogative attitude that makes man a man, Adam: Mah?" Manna is therefore understood as the question questioning itself.

———————

15 In commenting on these passages, we are deeply indebted to a disciple of Levinas, R' Marc-Alain Ouaknin, author of *The Burnt Book: Reading the Talmud.*

Ouaknin links the phenomenon of manna to the Hebraic word and concept for "wisdom," *Chochmah*. Breaking the word for wisdom into its constituent parts, *koach* "power or force," and *mah* "what." This questioning-thinking refuses to allow *Chochmah* to become static. It is a wisdom, perhaps distinguishable from the Greek notion of Sophia (wisdom), that makes a space for the reader as other and as questioner. The "wise" man is at once the "student of wisdom." Ouaknin correctly observes that the *Talmud Chacham* always has something of the disciple as well as the teacher within himself.

Because Levinas understands that human questioning is desirous of answers, his responses push beyond what Ouaknin himself might have accepted. It is not enough to argue, as does Ouaknin, that "I am not, I am becoming." For Levinas, the answers one seeks must begin with looking out for and answering to other people. For this to be genuinely meaningful to others, the answers cannot evade responsibility for others "in time." The law may limit my pretension to "absolute knowledge" but cannot serve as an apology for my not knowing.

The elevation of reflection on the manna by Ouaknin opens onto an important insight into the nature of time and interpretation in the Hebraic tradition. He makes a vital distinction between *nostalgia* and *tradition* (my emphasis). Nostalgia is a returning to the past and making a eulogy of memory for the past that was always better than the present. Tradition takes the past seriously by preserving it in the present. The past and the present open onto the promise of the future. It is this that gives tradition its vitality and sense of purpose and direction. Nostalgia, on the other hand, can lead to a depressed frame of mind, where the person is always returning to the image of an earlier time that is glorified or romanticized in retrospect. We see evidence of this today, in the attachment to what are believed to be the sights and smells that lead to a "kosher style" kind of existence, emptied of its contents. As Oauknin explains, this is why, subsequently, the Israelites complain of the very manna that has sustained them: "We remember the fish that we ate in Egypt free of charge; and the cucumbers, melons, leeks, onions and garlic. But now, our life is parched. There is nothing; we have nothing to anticipate but the manna!" (Num. 11:5–6). As the commentary tradition points out, they name exactly those foods that were present in Egypt. It was "free of charge" (*chinam*) because, as Nachmanides points out, they were slaves (Stone, 789). Among some of the people there was a longing to return to Egypt with all of its servitude and primitive sense of security. This represents an absence of trust that the future can and will be better than the past by following the way of the Torah.

The rabbinic tradition views the giving of the manna day by day as raising issues of "trust" and "faith" for the Israelites. There is still a debate that has percolated into contemporary times over whether it is better for a person to work for sustenance and to devote whatever other time he or she has to the study of Talmud and Torah. The minority opinion, given by Shimon bar Yochai, argues that this is the reason that manna did not fall once a year but daily. Of practical importance is that a person should learn constantly, not worrying about sustenance, but depending upon the "Hand of Heaven." This latter position is still supported by those who believe that the best and only use of a person's time, at least that of a *talmid chacham*, is to learn constantly (BT, *Yoma 76*). In times of economic stress, both positions reassert themselves, one against the other. The ethics of the fathers holds that the normative position is to combine work with study, recognizing the excellence, but rarity, of a person of Shimon Bar Yochai's stature.

Why is the prohibition against gathering manna on the Sabbath given, instead trusting in the double portion that is to be gathered on the sixth day of the week? "It happened on the sixth day that they gathered a double portion of food … and whatever is left over put away for yourselves as a safekeeping until the morning … six days you shall gather but the seventh day there will be none" (Exod. 16:22–27). On weekdays, the food was to be prepared and eaten, with none left over; rather, it was fresh again morning by morning. The issue of trust is unstated but visible. It is not so terribly different from speaking of the unspoken trust that we have that the sun will rise each day anew. Still, it requires a degree of vigilance that is connected to one's ethical conduct. A hyperbolic but instructive midrash informs us that justice is completely transparent and connected with ethical conduct. If one acts as one should, then he merely found the manna on his/her doorstep. The farther one had to travel to gather one's single portion of manna each day indicates a transparent defect in good deeds. Such a daily reckoning makes it possible for others to see if we have been on good behavior. Ideally, this should lead to the elevating of all comportment in deed, word, and thought. This also brings with it, however, an unbearable weight of honesty and justice. Through the lens of Levinas, this is not simply adding what we might call "peer pressure" but rather a judging that goes on every instant for me that prepares rather than precludes me from a generosity toward the other. This is given as another reason why the Israelites understandably complain about the manna.

In other words, the manna is new again each weekday. In a similar way, the meaning gained through study in relation to the Torah and the Talmud is approached each day anew. This again informs us of the distinction between "tradition" and "nostalgia." It is not a matter of simply looking at pictures framing righteous great grandparents and using them as honorific emblems of pride. Rather, study of Torah is incumbent upon me and my children after me. A parent then takes on the position of a teacher with the full hope and expectation that his or her children will find their own meaning in the Torah and in life within the generation in which they find themselves.

Ouaknin rightly claims that tradition is concerned with binding the present to the past for the sake of the future. The keeping of the divine promise always extends into a time that is created in the sphere of the interpersonal. This is also what, according to Levinas, makes one generation responsible for another that has come before it and whose future is bound by those who come after. On a philosophical plane, this begins to make possible our understanding of responsibility for a world into which we did not choose to be born, and for a tomorrow or the day after tomorrow that we will only get to glimpse from a distant hill. Children enjoy the teaching that the manna could taste virtually like anything that you want, except for the foods that could be found only in Egypt. More importantly, this connection between taste and meaning is more than simply of a matter of homonyms. We can be educated in regard to our tastes, and all the more so with the infinite layers of meaning, which can be found in the teachings of the Torah. It is at least possible now to begin to understand how R. Mendel of Rimanov could have devoted a thousand discourses to the subject of "manna."

THE LANGUAGE OF REVELATION

Yisro: The Giving of the Torah
(Exodus 18:1–20:23)

The sixth day of Creation: The sixth day of the month of Sivan; the day of the giving of the Torah. The mountain turned upside down like a bucket above the Israelites thus threatened the universe. G'd therefore did not create without concerning himself with the meaning of creation.

—NTR 1990, 41

V'yedaber Hashem es kol ha'devarim lemor: Anochi Hashem, Elokecha, asher hotzaysicha m'Eretz Mitzrayim, m'bais avodim—G'd Spoke all of these words, saying: I am the Lord, your G'd, who took you from the Land of Egypt, from the House of Slavery.

—Exodus 20:2

Lo Tirtzach—You shall not kill.

—Exodus 20:13

Central to the giving of the Torah is the language of "revelation." Levinas explores this language in a radically new way, a way which involves a philosophical reflection on language itself. To understand this, a few remarks on grammar are in order. The imperative mode of discourse often strikes the educated contemporary reader as expressing, in advance of any specific prescription, a limitation on the freedom of the person to whom such speech is addressed. Levinas does not take issue with this but argues that even so there is a way in which all language begins with and returns to the imperative mode. He points out that before any conversation with the other person, the other

116

appeals to me through his face not to kill him or her. This can be extended to any kind of violence. An appeal, while it belongs overtly to the vocative mode of discourse, also carries with it an imperative that issues from the other. It is not an order, and yet it brings with it a kind of command, even if accompanied by an invocation such as "please do not." Put simply, all but the first of the Ten Divine Commandments say, "Do not do this" or "Do this." For the philosophy of Levinas, the meaning of language itself, rather than the question of historical origins, is at the heart of the phenomenon of "revelation."

The first expression of the other, according to Levinas, is not "Love me," but "Do not kill me." This may seem obvious, so obvious we never consider it, though we should. Since there are a plurality of other people, this expression interdicts murder on my part, greeting me over and over again. "To see a face is already to hear 'you shall not kill,' and to hear 'you shall not kill' is to hear 'social justice' ... 'you shall not kill' is therefore not just a simple rule of conduct. It appears as the enabling principle of discourse itself and of spiritual life ... *speech belongs to the order of morality before belonging to that of theory.* Is it not therefore the condition of conscious thought?" (DF 1990, 8–9).

Levinas suggests that the moral relation with the other person registers to human awareness at the same moment as, or even prior to, consciousness. It is therefore the moral relation that governs speech, thought, and action. This is an original position within the history of Western philosophy. At the same time, it is consonant with the teachings of the Hebraic Bible.

According to rabbinic teaching, all of the commandments, including the first ten, belong either to the category of those primarily between God and human beings (*mitzvoth bein adam shel Makom),* or between one human being and another (*mitzvoth bein adam lechavero).*[16] Furthermore, according to the oral tradition, there is a direct correspondence between the first five founding commandments and the second five. For example, the second commandment is the prohibition against idolatry—"You shall have no other gods before me"— while the seventh is the prohibition against adultery. What is the discernable logical connection? Adultery begins when the absent other is reduced to a nonexistent being. This distinction between absence and nonexistence has been, for the most part, obscured in the history of Western philosophy. This is more than

---

16 It should be noted that the rabbinic tradition seldom refers to what are colloquially called the "Ten Commandments" in a way that separates them from the commandments that follow.

a matter referred to by the common saying, "out of sight, out of mind." Rather, the capacity to understand absence as a phenomenon in its own right makes it possible for us to begin to understand the difference between a past which has never been and one that is no longer. This distinction is critical. Our relations with other people are a function of our conduct toward a third party when we are not with them as well as when we encounter them. The one to whom I am pledged recedes from the figure in the foreground and, in the case of betrayal, is out of the picture all together.

This is the beginning of all betrayal in the interhuman realm. In a parallel fashion, the worship of idols also collapses the past and the future into the present moment and therefore is the beginning of all faithlessness. The absence of God is not necessarily reducible to his nonexistence. Levinas concludes his career as professor of philosophy at the Sorbonne with a lecture titled "*Transcendent* to the Point of Absence." Absence, understood in this way as an expression of transcendence means beyond or higher than me, which virtually by definition remains invisible. He calls this phenomenon *illeity*. The demand for visibility where there can be none is the first beginning of turning toward the worship of idols.

It is the first ethical responsibility that corresponds, according to rabbinic teaching, with the first of the commandments that refers to the transcendent as having taken me out of slavery and by implication into freedom. This is why, according to many commentators, the phrase "your" God, is placed in the singular, even though this primordial statement is presumably given to all of the Israelites.[17] The reason for this is that the command is addressed to each person in his or her uniqueness. This in turn refers to the prohibition against murder, the sixth commandment—the first of those between one human being and another.

There is a commonly accepted Talmudic view in the oral tradition that only the first two commandments were heard by all of Israel (BT, Makkos, 24A). This is attributed to understandable dread on the part of the hearers. The other commandments then would be given through Moses to the people. It is not simply a modern question to ask what was heard. By no means is there universal agreement that the people heard sentences or even words. Maimonides in the *Guide for the Perplexed* (2:32) argues that they heard, rather, "the sound of a voice." In the language of Levinas, then, it is possible to affirm that what was heard was the "saying" prior to the "said"—that is to say, the intention binding

---

17 I am indebted to R' David Lehrfield for this insight.

speaker to listener is announced in this wordless utterance before the contents of its language are made explicit. This makes sense because it enables us to understand both the intimacy of the first divine command while at the same time grasping the probability that there are differing views on its status and meaning.

We already know before the other person speaks whether he or she is *"for me"* or not. How much more the case with the first divine words uttered at Sinai? One of the things that puzzles the commentary tradition is that this statement of self-identification by God relates to the going out from Egypt, rather than the creation of the world, and it does not appear to command any kind of action. However, it should be noted that it is implied that G'd is identifying Himself as a G'd of both freedom and history. It is in this sense that G'd can be understood as *for* Israel, and by extension to all human kind. If in fact He is responsible for taking them out of Egypt, by implication He has taken them from bondage into freedom. Furthermore, this means that G'd is involved with the historical reality that He transcends. This gives the commandments that follow a sense that they must be freely accepted and assumed, even while they are also understood to be obligatory upon those who received them. Perhaps this can help us understand why the first commandment is in fact written in the declarative rather than the imperative mode of discourse. We might then view this as a kind of *meta-mitzvah* that grounds the possibility for the appearance, expression, and significance of all those that are to follow. Human freedom then is immediately conjoined with responsibility, as is more visible in the commandments between one human being and another.

The prohibition against murder, the sixth commandment, is the first of those between one human being and another. The killing of another human being is the most severe of all transgressions. Maimonides argues that it is even more severe than the prohibition against idolatry, because it can never be completely atoned for. In this sense, there is a parallel between the wordless voice that is first heard and the expression on the face of another person, who stands over against me and commands me not to kill him.

This pacific relation with the other arises as the precondition for all language. As Levinas states, "[T]he relationship of language implies transcendence, radical separation, the strangeness of the interlocutors, the revelation of the other to me" (TI 1969, 73). In other words, the expression of the other is an absolutely necessary precondition for the production of meaning. If, for example, I want to know if I have been properly understood by the other person, the first thing that I do is to notice his or her expression. This is the anchor of all possible meaning, at least in the interhuman realm. This often-unnoticed fact is intimately connected to the very possibility of meaningful exchanges between people. This is why we can have what we call "wordless dialogue," tacit understanding, and itinerant speech that is halted and renewed by the glance of the other. This is also the case when we give our assent by nodding or withhold our agreement by shaking our heads. This is to say that the mystery of revelation from On High finds its trace repeated continually in the encounters of everyday life.

This relation between the other and me is, however, an asymmetrical one. This is true just because all meaning begins with expression that originates from the face of the other. "To recognize the other mandates giving to him. There is a parallel between the asymmetrical relation between the human and the Most High, and between me and the other. On the inter-personal level, it is to give to the master, to the lord, to him who one approaches as "You in a dimension of height" (TI 1969, 75). This dimension of height is also refracted in the meaning of the divine-human relation.

In a commentary dealing with subjects of revelation, freedom, responsibility, and reason,[18] Levinas offers some fresh insights that are disclosed in the Talmud (BT, Shabbos 88a, 88b). Levinas emphasizes that the written Torah is affirmed, understood, and transmitted by the oral Torah. This is what makes the Jewish understanding of the Hebrew Scripture unique. In other words, Judaism has its own theory of interpretation, or hermeneutics, built into itself. It should also be noted that according to the Talmudic apologues the assent of the people must be given to the divine edicts for them to be complete. Such agreement among the Israelites may be viewed as something unique in Judaism among the world's religions.

For the most part, Levinas does not look for the meaning of the word "G'd" outside of rabbinic or Talmudic sources. Levinas is critical of the received notion of "revelation" found in Western theology. What does it mean "to have" faith, "to have" belief, to trust something as true? The language of "having faith" assumes that the subject and his/her faith are, to begin with, two separate things. More concrete than "having faith" is the action of fidelity. The philosophic basis for making this claim is that unless we can understand what it means to be faithful at the preconceptual level, we really cannot begin to explain to ourselves what it would mean to "have faith." This does not require a higher education, nor does it depend on prefabricated credos.

---

18 NTR—"The Temptation of Temptation," 30–50.

As we have already seen, Levinas has explained the experience of "revelation" in an everyday sense. It does not project theological constructs upon the divine-human encounter but makes this originary encounter able to be expressed in language. What he is most concerned with here is the modern suspicion of the imposition of divine law upon human freedom. Is this not the question at the beginning of the critique of all of the hermeneutics of suspicion?[19]

Levinas now offers a wonderful commentary on the doctrine of "We will do and we will understand" that is actually found in the next portion of Mishpatim (24:7). The "upside down bucket" is connected with Israel being placed "below the mountain" (Exod. 19:7). "It threatens to crush the tribes of Israel if they refuse the gift of the law" (NTR 1990, 37). The Torah is given as the climax of going out from Egypt. Rather than turning into anarchy or tyranny, as often happens under revolutionary conditions, as Levinas states, "[T]he negative freedom of those set free is about to transform itself into the freedom of the law, engraved in stone, into a freedom of responsibility. *Is one already responsible when one chooses responsibility?*" (NTR 1990, 37).

TIME AND REVELATION

What does "revelation" accomplish? This is the question asked by the early medieval Jewish thinker Rav Saadya Gaon. Saadya asks, "What is the Torah for?" He gives an ingenious response to this question. He states that the giving of the Torah saves human beings time. It permits us to know, in advance, what we otherwise might only learn through trial and error. If Saadya is correct, then our lives do not need to be inscribed as inherently tragic. We can know, at least in general terms, what we need to know, ahead of time.[20] It is opposed to Greek tragedy, where the central figure discovers belatedly what he wished to have known in time. Self-knowledge comes at a crushing price—this is to say, that it comes too late and is purified only through suffering and catharsis. To paraphrase Kierkegaard in one of his journal entries, "The tragedy of human existence consists in this: that while existence moves forward, self-knowledge moves backward." Or as we commonly say, "I wish I'd known then what I know now."

---

19 Paul Ricoeur, *Freud and Philosophy. An Essay on Interpretation*, trans. Denis Savage (New Haven, CT: Yale UP), 32. Comments on what he calls the "school of suspicion," which he situates with Freud, in particular, as well as Marx and Nietzsche. The term "the hermeneutics of suspicion" is adopted from Ricoeur as well.

20 *Emumah V'deos* (Faith and Knowledge), (New Haven, CT: Yale UP), 27ff.

The most practical and yet most theoretical of dimensions of the disclosing of the Torah consists in this: "To know is to experience without experiencing, before living. We want to know before we do.... We want to live dangerously, but in security, in the world of truths" (NTR 1990, 34). Levinas refers to this as the "temptation of temptation ... philosophy itself." It elevates, according to him, "the nature of courage, courage within security, the solid basis of Old Europe" (Ibid.). The key aspiration of all philosophy has been for Levinas "the priority of knowledge." This is completely consistent with the rationalization that would accompany all actions that we come to regret: "Ah, but it was really for the best because it was 'a learning experience.'" What we cannot afford, and what we do not aspire to, is to make all of life a "learning experience."

The teaching of the Torah casts ahead of our experience and is a light that tears us out of our inertia and out of the ambiguities of life. We must penetrate the future without insisting in advance upon its experience. This does not eliminate the future but forces a rethinking of the future in relation to the present. But how can we do before we know? This is the meaning contained in the apparently paradoxical expression "Na'aseh V'nishmah." "We will do and we will hear" (Exod. 24:7). In the language of Levinas, this means that we are responsible for one another prior to our freedom, prior to our exalted privilege of personal spontaneity. According to the commentary tradition, this specifically refers to something that goes counter to what we call "human nature."

Levinas explains it this way. First, he tells us what this is not. It is not a form of theosophy where we would penetrate the "mind of G'd." This is not possible. In fact, Levinas says that "theosophy is the very negation of philosophy." He adds that "we have no right to start from a pretentious familiarity with the 'psychology' of G'd and with his 'behavior' in order to understand these texts" (NTR 1990, 32).

Levinas insists that when we subordinate primary experience to claims of certain knowledge, we are also, however unwittingly, subordinating the other to the self. What he means by this is that we would find satisfaction by incorporating the other into my ongoing autobiography that I say silently to myself. This leads to a kind of totality whereby, as we say today, we can put it "all into perspective." What in fact this means for him is that we become unable to recognize the other person as another person outside of all calculation.

THE ORDER OF MEANING VS. THE MEANING OF ORDER

The order of meaning, which seems to me to be primary is precisely what comes to us from the inter-human relation, so that the face, with all its meaningfulness ... is the beginning of intelligibility.

—IRB 2001, 165

Totality is implied by *the meaning of order*. It belongs to the realm of the political without necessary reference to the moral or the ethical. It is always amenable to rationalization, when justice comes *after* the fact. Observed in this way, the commandments of the Torah still remain to be understood. This is where the Oral Torah and the apparent force that comes with its acceptance must be made clearer.[21]

Prior to rationalization is reasoning. In the same way, justification comes *prior* to the fact. It is always a justification to a "someone." Such a discourse belongs to the *order of meaning* that arises prior to our concepts, our ideas, our beliefs, and our dogmas. It is nondogmatic in character, thereby limiting in advance all fanaticism. Why? Because it begins with the other rather than the self. The other, for whom I am infinitely responsible, pierces through my attempts to control, dominate, or tyrannize over her. By no means does this act as a formal assurance against fanaticism; however, it makes it possible to distinguish genuine devotion from the absolutism that accompanies fanaticism. Devotion is given to other people before it is given to principles or precepts, however honorable they might appear.

Devotion, unlike fanaticism, affirms an open rather than a closed system of understanding and conduct. This openness can be registered by others who do not share my views. It can also be subject to self-sabotage when my self-righteousness turns into rage against the other. Still, devotion, unlike fanaticism, assumes an asymmetry where the other comes before me. This involves an existential risk, which can make the devotee more vulnerable. Nonetheless, as we are witnessing in the disintegrating fabric of economic and social life around us, it involves a fine risk—one where we must continually be open to modifying our perspectives and placing ourselves ever again in the position of the student

---

21 Emmanuel Levinas, "Revelation and the Jewish Tradition" in *Beyond the Verse*, 146. Levinas adopts the Talmudic position that the voluntary acceptance of the oral Torah did not occur until the time of the Book of Esther. Prior to this time, the Israelites were given an invitation that they could not refuse.

rather than the master. This is why, just as a philosopher does not mean a wise man but a lover of wisdom, a Talmudic master is called a student of wisdom or a *Talmid chacham*

The *order of meaning* must return to the language of the saying before the said. This is in fact what the oral Torah reanimates perpetually. It concerns the relation between the Infinite, the others, and me, and so it must remain a constant subject of study, teaching, and transmission. This helps to explain why, according to the oral tradition, it is not simply sufficient for the Israelites to guarantee that they will keep the words spoken. Nor is it sufficient that they depend upon the merits of their ancestors, even Abraham, Isaac, and Jacob. Just because the teachings of the Torah must be transmitted, it is only the future, meaning our children, or good deeds that are permitted to act as a guarantor, as a midrash indicates.

Drawing on Levinas, we are making an epistemic distinction here. Most of Western Jewish education would consist in refinements of a kind of coercion through and by grammar or the "meaning of order." The meaning of order is always attended by a certain logic, coherence, and violence. However, when I practice self-restraint, such continence makes room for other people. Otherwise, I still simply inhabit a world of my own that never escapes the solipsism where I am not faced by anyone or anything except my own self-reflection. The Torah, while it must be internalized to be practiced, originates beyond me, outside the subject. My task is not to find my place in it. Is this not the beginning of all misguided "religious education," a kind of time-released rebellion?

Authentic pedagogy begins where teaching is no longer didactic; but rather, is expressed in the first instance as a responsibility on the part of the teacher for the expression found on the face of the student. What is he or she asking me? Perhaps beginning with the words heard at Sinai, an animated intelligence finds itself in a conversation, however asymmetrical. What this means is that the spirit of the Talmud is already there in the beginning. Why? Because, as Levinas puts it, "I have insisted, more than once, that the Talmudic spirit goes radically beyond the letter of Scriptures. Its spirit was nonetheless formed in the very letters it goes beyond, so as to reestablish, despite apparent violence, the permanent meaning within these letters" (NTR 1990, 39–40). Does not the action of doing before understanding express itself in everyday life?

Even before the steps that we take in order to go somewhere, we find ourselves already beginning to take up what we have called a "stance." This stance or series of stances orients us in advance of the steps we take. Beginning with the revelation at Sinai, there is an anticipation in each commandment, *mitzvah*, of the burdensome freedom of all the steps that we are to take, whether or not we understand their meanings in advance. As we have already indicated, we do not focus on the *halakah*. However, the *mitzvot* that guide them and the rationale behind these *mizvot* must already be something that we fasten to ourselves if we are to go in a direction that we will not regret. It is this kind of inspiration that must be continually breathed into the student. This inspiration comes even before imagination, and it brings life to the text and its multiple teachings. Levinas refers to all of this in a summary as "the pedagogy of liberation," for surely pedagogy is more than a method for children (NTR 1990, 40). He turns his attention once again to the elements of apparent coercion, risk, and outcome associated with the mountain being turned upside down, threatening the universe if the Israelites do not accept the oral or Talmudic dimension of the Torah. "G'd therefore did not create without concerning himself with the meaning of creation.... The world is here so that the ethical order has the possibility of being fulfilled. The act by which the Israelites accept the Torah is the act which gives meaning to reality. To refuse the Torah is to bring being back to nothingness" (NTR 1990, 41).

Levinas elaborates on this priority of ethics over being. Ethics indicates an exodus out of the self toward the other: "The Torah is an order to which the ego adheres, without having had to enter it. An order which decides ... this exit is not accomplished through a game without consequences.... Responsibility for the creature—a being of which the ego was not the author ... to be a self is to be responsible beyond what one has oneself done" (NTR 1990, 49). We are now at the furthest possible remove from that time in the bitterness of the exile in Egypt where oppression has achieved its goal of setting one person against the other. This is not simply a matter of reflecting on a distant past. It is a recommendation for a pedagogy of liberation in the present where the techniques of the oppressors may have advanced but not the dynamics of pedagogy. The objective of this oppression is to mystify its source and to have the oppressed believe that their identities are purchased one against the other.

What gives the Exodus its moral dynamism is the renewed capacity to be a self in relation to others. This is the beginning of a society where a dual covenant is enacted. To be sure, it is a covenant set in motion from above, but it is also the enacting of a covenant between the self and the other, involving the challenge of relating to multiple others in a just manner. Moreover, at its highest level, it is expressed in the Hebrew as *temimiut,* an inwardness or integrity that is perfected in "substituting oneself for others" (NTR 1990, 49). Levinas explains this in an utterly original and compelling manner: "All the suffering of the world weighs upon the point where a separation is occurring, a reversal of the essence of being" (Ibid., 49). Why is this the reversal of the essence of being?

Because when one goes beyond essence, in the natural order the movement is toward other rather than self, making force or power subordinate to moral or ethical life.[22]

---

22 It is important to note that a prohibition is given against making an altar of stones cut with iron tools. Rashi notes that while the altar to which the stones lead is for the purpose of "repentance and atonement, (thereby) lengthening life using iron tools to cut such stones would have iron as its 'raw material' and thereby shorten life" (Schottenstein Pentateuch, 461). Because of its capacity to make instruments of violence, iron is not compatible with establishing peaceful relations between people. Following the logic of Rashi, Nachmanides comments on the similarity between the Hebrew word for "sword," *cherev,* and the word for "destruction," *churban.* Because swords bring destruction to the world, there is no place for them in the Tabernacle. In the world of all *for* all and each *for* each, there is no place for war.

ECONOMIC AND SOCIAL JUSTICE

Mishpatim: Laws for Which Reason Is Easily Adduced
(Exodus 21:1–24:18)

You shall not taunt or oppress a stranger, for you were strangers in the land of Egypt. You shall not cause pain to any widow or orphan.

—Exodus 22:20

If men shall fight and they shall collide with a pregnant woman and she miscarries, but there will be no fatality, he shall surely be punished as the husband of the woman shall cause to be assessed against him, and he shall pay it by order of the judges. But if there shall be a fatality, then you shall award a life for a life, an eye for an eye, a tooth for a tooth, a hand for a hand, a foot for a foot; a burn for a burn, a wound for a wound, a bruise for a bruise.

—Exodus 21:22–25

Everything that Hashem has said, we will do and we will obey!

—Exodus 24:7

The attributes of God are not given in the indicative, but in the imperative. The knowledge of God comes to us like a commandment, like a mitzvah. To know God is to know what must be done.

—DF 1990, 17

According to the rabbinic tradition, the Torah portion Mishpatim directly follows the commandments first heard at Sinai. Rashi notes that the laws of social justice are visibly connected to the ten commandments. The text opens with these words: "*And* these are the ordinances you shall place before them" (Exod. 21:1). What this means for Rashi is that "just as these commandments were given at Sinai, so were these," and this is why this portion begins with the word "and" (Stone, 417). With this, we see that it deals with achieving the rudiments of a just social order.

As is widely known, the phrase "measure for measure" (Hebrew, *midah knegged midah)*, is understood as an expression of severe or retributive response to injuries incurred at the hands of others. However, Levinas explains, following the tradition, what is already well known to readers familiar with the text—the concept of "measure for measure" refers to a monetary fine exclusively. This is, after all, an expression of justice, not cruelty: "[I]t inserts itself into a social order in which no sanction, however slight, can be inflicted outside a juridical sentence. They have interpreted it in the light of the spirit that pervades the whole of the Bible. We call this method of understanding: Talmud" (DF 1990, 147).

In dealing with the implications of "an eye for an eye," the Talmud makes it abundantly clear that this was a matter that was handled through monetary compensation and restitution. We are discussing laws for which reasons are given, and the rhetoric of an eye for an eye has caused great harm when it is taken in a literal manner. It was never handled by any Jewish court as a kind of physical retribution or revenge where eyes were poked out or hands were chopped off or teeth knocked out. In fact, the Talmudic tractate *Bava Kamma* 83a–b gives us guidelines for how these situations were to be handled. The sages, drawing on this passage and another from Deuteronomy (25:11), clarify that the assailant or the perpetrator is responsible for five kinds of payment for bodily injury or harm. He is responsible for medical costs, loss of income, pain and suffering, and the diminishment that he suffers from (e.g., losing the use of an arm or foot). On top of this, he is to be compensated for the shame or humiliation that he endures.

No other section of the Torah deals more directly with laws of economic and social justice than does the portion just following the commandments on the tablets. In no case, except those that are specified, is compensation to be handled by physical retribution, especially not through capital punishment. Here biblical commandments must be understood through the prism of Talmudic understanding. These mitzvot are guideposts on the way to living a just life. This is why, according to traditional understanding, this portion of the text begins with "and these are the ordinances that you shall place before them." Levinas emphasizes repeatedly that his own Talmudic reflections deal with the *aggadah*, or non-legal portions of the Talmudic texts. At the same time, he cannot escape the burden of encountering the law as a concept and, in certain cases, its general application. This does not mean, as he repeatedly warns his reader, that on the basis of his comments one has been given anything resembling a legal or *halachic* ruling or conclusion. He contrasts *aggadah* and *halakah* in the following way: "Halakah is the way to behave; aggadah is the philosophic meaning—religious and moral—of this behavior" (NTR 1990, 194). Still, surely the very title *Difficle Liberté*, "Difficult Freedom," indicates that freedom is inscribed as responsibility and enacted through the laws of the Torah. Levinas stresses that in a capital case, a Sanhedrin that passed the death sentence for the first time in seven (some say seventy) years was called "a bloodthirsty court" (DF 1990, 144). In fact, there is a strong view expressed in the Talmud, that if a court of twenty-three judges were unanimous in finding someone guilty, the person is freed, and the court is criticized. Why? Because when no extenuating circumstance could be found by anyone, it was believed that the judges had not spent significant time deliberating.[23] The most important thing for the reader to keep in mind is that Scripture simply cannot be understood prescriptively in terms of behavior or descriptively in terms of its religious and moral philosophic meaning without the oral Torah. This is not a matter of theology but of interpretation and application. Otherwise, people in a society would simply not know how to act nor understand the meaning of their own conduct.

From a contemporary perspective, what we are dealing with in the Torah portion *Mishpatim* are those conditions that must be effected and transmitted through laws in order to engender what we might in our time call "a habitable society." By "habitable society," we are referring to a social order that must be just and reasonable. This means that it must command the kind of respect of one person for another. Just as responsibility aims at perfecting justice, so too does kindness and mercy limit the severity of justice without context.

There is not a biblical phrase that occurs more regularly in the thought of Levinas than the injunction not to harm "the widow, the orphan, the stranger, and the poor." As he states, "I can recognize the gaze of the stranger, the widow and the orphan only in giving or in refusing; I am free to give or to refuse, but my recognition passes necessarily through the interposition of things" (TI 1969, 77). Is there not implied here the possibility of reducing all human activities to giving or taking?[24] Positively, the Torah admonishes us to come to the assistance of these outsiders by extending to them material and spiritual kindness. "It is here that the Transcendent, infinitely other, solicits us

---

23 I first learned this from my mentor, R' Rafoel Zalman Levine HaCohen.

24 This might lead to a further exploration in the phenomenology of giving and taking.

and appeals to us.... His very epiphany consists in soliciting us by his destitution in the face of the stranger, the widow and the orphan" (Ibid., 78). What do these different categories of people have in common? They are all "outsiders." The outsiders are all dependent on the good will of a community to which they do not belong completely or in the same manner as others. In a more concrete way, their condition is one of economic need or even destitution. Levinas portrays every other person as a stranger for me. This is why I'm bidden to welcome him or her through the gesture of hospitality. The stranger, including the widow, orphan, and poor, do not simply belong to a sociological category. The other for Levinas is the one with whom all rationality of transcendence begins.

For Levinas, G'd takes special interest in the outsiders perhaps because G'd is, in a way, the ultimate outsider, as he says: "G'd is outside and is G'd for that very reason. What is outside save Him?.... to have an outside, to listen to what comes from outside—oh miracle of exteriority! That is what is called knowledge or Torah. The sublime forms of the human are no longer full of pathos" (DF 1990, 29). Is this perhaps the reason that R' Menachem Mendel of Kotzk answers his own question in the following way: "Where is G'd? Wherever we let Him in." Only if G'd is utterly outside or transcendent to history is it possible to appeal to an order that is not governed exclusively by the power that rules in the political regimes of the day.

The concept of the *sacred* often does seek to exclude others who do not share my religious views and practices or who are not members of my community. What is most distinctive here is that there is an opposing phenomenon, that of holiness, where inclusiveness of others, often the most vulnerable in society, is given a place of primacy.

SOCIAL JUSTICE: ITS PRESCRIPTIONS AND PROMISE

How does someone give to the poor without begrudging him or her? Midrash Tanchuma states, in regard to this mitzvah, "[W]hen according to the Mesorah, not '*if*' you lend money to one of my people" (Exod. 22:24) "do not treat him with contempt, for he is with me. *Regard yourself as if you were poor;* [this is the meaning of] 'with you'" (Shemos II, 78–79, my emphasis). The manner in which the need and urgency of dealing with a variety of impoverished people works as follows: According to Maimonides, it is in the order of proximity from the center of a circle of concern outward toward its periphery. This means you begin with your own family and the poor of your town—with the poor of your family taking precedence in your place and with the poor of your town taking precedence over the poor of another town. Still, the poor man is referred to as your "destitute brother" (Ibid., 80). Maimonides later establishes more of a formula for distribution to the poor and distinctions among them, the poor who are scholars, those who are not, the poor of Jerusalem, and so on (Maimonides, Mishneh Torah 7:7).[25]

Later, as we see, there are mitzvot that pertain to the unqualified obligations to leave a part of one's field not to be harvested. The gleanings are not to be vacuumed up after the harvest in the name of efficiency. This kind of efficiency belongs to the world of objects rather than human beings. The Torah does not deal with the so-called bottom line. If you are harsh in this matter, an objectively oriented bottom liner, then you are not following the prescription given to you. These are like the prohibition against forcing the stranger within your gates or even your ox to work on the Sabbath day. This simply is not to be done. And in the seventh year, even the ground of Israel is neither to be plowed nor harvested. In other words, society has obligations to remediate the suffering of the poor. We can surely see that the laws are meant to be experienced as moral obligations with economic and social implications.

According to one of the major compilers of Jewish law, the *Sefer HaChinuch*, there are fifty-three mitzvot (23 Performative, 30 Prohibitive) in *Parshat Mishpatim*. According to Rabbi J.B. Soloveitchik, there are two distinct promises that form the context within which the laws of economic and social justice appear. The first would be, as Samson Raphael Hirsch also argues, a universal dimension of the *mishpatim* that would be accessible to everyone. By this is meant an elevated notion of common sense. The second promise, according to the Rav, is a dimension that refers specifically to those prescriptions that are found within the covenant between the Most High, the Israelites, and their relations with one another. Here, it is meaningful to speak of holiness as the surplus of ethical life. In fact, he goes on to relate: "More than any other *parshah*, [*Parshat Mishpatim*] ... epitomizes the [Oral Torah] *Torah she'beal peh*" (DDY, 163). Why is this the case? Because so many of the Talmud's foundational texts

---

25 From my own teacher, I heard the following exchange: "How do you know if the person really is poor, or if he is a faker? He responded, 'You have to thank G'd for the faker and not look into this matter too much. Why? Because he and he alone, that is the faker, is the only one who permits you to give for the sake of heaven and not your own self-feeling. This is established because you do not know who is whom," (Conversation with Reb Rafoel Zalman Levine HaCohen [1900–1992] circa 1989.)

widely studied today express expansions of the prescriptions and prohibitions that first appear as Mitzvot announced in Mishpatim. The core of virtually all of the Talmudic tractates associated with civil damages, torts, the creation of courts, and their administration are foreshadowed here.

We proceed by recapitulating some of those prescriptions and injunctions that are most central to our understanding of human society in the movement from justice to its repeated perfecting in responsibility. Special attention is paid to Levinas's reading of the Talmudic section, "Damages Due to Fire" (Exod. 22:5). According to J.B. Soloveitchik, there is a dimension of holiness that is expressed through these laws of justice. In this sense, he links this holiness back to the specific promise of the covenant: "And now, if you listen well to Me and keep My covenant, you shall be to Me the most beloved treasure of all peoples, for the entire world is Mine. You shall be to Me a kingdom of *kohanim* [priests] and a holy nation" (Exod. 19:5–6) Here, we see that what are usually regarded as the most mundane kinds of laws are embodied in such a way as to make holiness and justice bound up with economic and social life in its most visible expressions. All of this testifies to the fact that what has been called the "chosenness" or election of the Israelites is not a matter of privilege but of tireless responsibility.

"If a man should open a pit, or if he shall dig a pit and not cover it, and an ox or donkey fall into it, the owner of the pit shall make restitution. He shall return money to its owner, and the carcass shall be his" (Exod. 21:33). How can a man be responsible to and for his neighbors' animals for an uncovered pit even if the pit had been dug on property that was ownerless? This is counterintuitive only where property is valued over the lives of human beings and animals. Even at the expense of "property rights," it does not matter if a sign is posted saying "no trespassing." The farmer who puts up such a sign must recognize in advance that he is the first trespasser even if the place is bought lock, stock, and barrel. The Torah always elevates the obligations of human beings to one another. This movement from justice to responsibility is worthy of reflection.

Let us take for example the case of the involuntary manslaughter. The person had no intention of killing his/her victim and behaved toward the victim in a sober and rational way. Nonetheless, the person is held culpable because he or she did not examine all of the instruments of potential violence in his or her possession. The classic example given is of a man who takes an ax to chop down a tree. The ax, however, is not securely fastened. It then happens that the ax flies off of its handle and strikes the man flush in his forehead. What is made clear is the difference between murder and involuntary manslaughter. This difference is visible and profound. Nevertheless, presumably through carelessness, he has contributed to the death of another person. There is a remedy for him that is discussed in detail later on.[26]

---

26 He is to go to a city of refuge presided over by the Levites. Signs must be posted clearly: "[T]his way to the city of refuge." If he is a teacher, his students must go with him; or if he is a student, the teacher must go with him. Why? Because it is assumed that the teacher was not scrupulous enough in his teaching and it assumed that the student was not careful enough in reviewing the pertinent laws.

FEEDING THE HUNGRY

Terumah: Portion
(Exodus 25:1–27:19)

On the Table you shall place show-bread before Me always.

—Exodus 25: 30

The crown of the table is the royal crown. The king is he who keeps open house; he who feeds men. The table on which the bread is exposed before the Lord symbolizes the permanent thought that political power— that is to say the King, that is, David, that is, his descendant, that is, the Messiah—is vowed to men's hunger.... Not to the end of times, to the hunger of hungry men; kingship in Israel is always Joseph feeding the people. To think of men's hunger is the first function of politics.

—BTV 1994, 18

There is an unexpected transition to the remainder of much of the Book of the Exodus. It is devoted to the making of the Sanctuary, the objects which it houses, the ways in which it is to be built, and service in relation to it. There are two questions that immediately come to mind. The first is why is such an elaborate description of these ritual practices so important. The second question asks if this part of the Torah out of chronological order.

We first comment very briefly on the second question. As noted in our introduction to this chapter of the book, most of the classical commentators appear to believe that the portions from *Terumah* onward are out of order. Rashi holds this view and the Sforno[27] more crisply.

---

27 Sforno Exodus 33, 459ff. See introduction on page 281 by Rabbi Raphael Pelkovitz to Sforno: commentary on the Torah.

The Ramban (Nachmanides) argues that the command given about the Sanctuary comes immediately after the laws in Mishpatim.[28] However, his argument is rather strange. The Ramban's view would appear to imply that there is something to be gained by the prophetic intimation of a life involved with daily human activities, which are elevated and intensified by the Mishkan. Put plainly, to survive, the first thing that people need is shelter; hence the erection of the Tabernacle symbolizing a special kind of shelter where a closer sense of the indwelling presence of Godliness can be experienced. Second, to endure, people need food. Hence as we see later, the important symbol of the show—bread, focused on here by Levinas. It is only then that the spiritual illumination symbolized by the Menorah is required. For the most part, the Tabernacle and its objects are a remedy to the unworthiness that contributed to the worshiping of the Calf of Gold immediately after the giving of the laws to Moses.

To provide a psychological as well as metaphysical remedy, there must be a diagnosis. In context, we must remember that the Israelites have only just lived through the bondage in and exodus from Egypt. This means that only very slowly do they become aware of their situation. The tangible objects of gold and silver left by the pursuing Egyptians and found after the crossing of the Reed Sea is a subject for which Moses has already chastised them. It is understandable that a people deprived of a livelihood for a century or two might find the spectacle of gold irresistible. They also might be hard-pressed to understand the radical invisibility of G'd. Therefore, there are certain kinds of service and objects that can be sublimated for a higher purpose. If this is the case, then perhaps it is not necessary to dwell overly long on the erection and service related to the Sanctuary. Now we can begin to understand why there should be a need for a Sanctuary altogether. "They shall make a Sanctuary for Me—so that I may dwell among them" (Exod. 25:8). Hirsch comments that the intention behind this divine utterance testifies to the fact that Israel has lived up to its moral obligations (See Hirsch on Exodus, 25:8). This means that they will have overcome the challenges of building and serving by uniting in such a way as to make their task a holy one.

Levinas has more to say about the *Lechem HaPanim* (literally, "bread of faces") than we might expect. Before presenting his own reflection, he draws upon the commentary tradition. Rashi, in response to his own question of why this is called the bread of faces, says that "[it is] bread which has two faces because of the shape in which it is baked. These faces being turned toward the

---

28 On Exodus, 25ff., see Stone page 444 for an overview including the Ramban's position.

two sides of the Sanctuary" (BTV 1994, 18). Let us keep in mind that Rashi deals with the plain meaning of the text. Levinas remarks, ironically, that "according to Ibn Ezra (1089–1164)—who is probably less pious than Rashi but has also said some extraordinary things—'bread of faces' is the bread which is always before the face of G'd" (Ibid., 18–19). Ibn Ezra is a philosopher, a rationalist, and grammarian of the first order.

Levinas tries to reconcile the differences between Rashi and Ibn Ezra. They represent the horizontal and vertical meaning of the religious, respectively. As Levinas says, "I think that the two interpretations (of Rashi and Ibn Ezra) are not dissimilar. What should bread before the eyes of G'd do, if not look at men?" (BTV 1994, 19). According to Levinas, the primary way that we understand the so-called vertical dimension, is by the way that other people address their gaze toward me.[29] Levinas observes that there is a preoccupation with satisfying human hunger that we cannot do without. Furthermore, he observes that in the first place, the "bread of faces" first symbolizes the "bread of the starving," and only by being such is it perhaps "holy bread" (Ibid., 19).

Much later, we have evidence of this in the Book of Samuel when David, fleeing from King Saul, beseeches the Kohanim of the city of Nov for bread for his men. When Saul discovers that the priests of Nov have aided David, he has them slain. Later still, the Gibeonites harass the Israelites and tell King David that their grievance was on account of their lost wages for serving the Kohanim of Nov.[30] All of this begins with the Rabbi's harsh assessment of Jonathan's lack of foresight in preparing food for David who is fleeing from King Saul. Levinas tells us that only when men no longer suffer the pangs of hunger are we worthy to see the holiness of the faces of others (BTV 1994, 21). "Says Rabbi Yochanan; 'Great is the act of eating for the person—one's neighbor—who is hungry,'" (BTV 1994, 24).

Levinas is suspicious of spirituality that is not accompanied by material expression. Moreover, he is not elevating spirituality and thereby devaluing all "materialism." The first obligation of the "spiritual" person is to alleviate the physical hunger of others. "The Other's hunger, be it of flesh or of bread—is sacred; only the hunger of the third party limits its rights; there is no bad materialism other than our own" (DF 1990, xiv).

---

29 By "horizontal," Levinas is referring to the relation between one person and another, and by "vertical," the relation between the human and G'd.

30 See NTR, 27–29.

Levinas surely recognizes a kind of hunger "that begets hunger." This he classifies as metaphysical *desire*, which he carefully and importantly distinguishes from *need*. According to Levinas, the distinction between need and desire has not been made sufficiently explicit in Western philosophic thought. More often than not, desire has been reduced to a system of needs. While the needs of others are finite, the faces of others bear the trace of the Infinite. Is metaphysical desire, then, to be found only in the vertical dimension of religious life of which Levinas speaks?

This depends completely on the relation between the vertical and the horizontal planes of existence. Levinas expands on what he means by metaphysical desire when he states that "desire is the misfortune of the happy" (TI 1969, 62). Another way of putting this is to indicate that not every intentional act of awareness is satisfied by or equal to its intentional object. My relation to the other person (e.g., to understand her, to comprehend him) will, by definition of the Infinite trace of the other, always fall short. This is how the vertical sphere always interpenetrates the realm of the horizontal sphere. To use the more philosophic language of Levinas, this is how Infinity pierces through the various systems of totality. In this way, human love—even eros—involves the face-to-face relation where I must turn toward the other in an act of welcome. This is perhaps best symbolized by the *cherubim*. According to the tradition, this is, as Levinas might put it, a "non-concupiscient" kind of love. It is in this way that the love of the other as the neighbor is depicted in the Sanctuary. In fact, the *cherubim* are portrayed as facing one another in times of right conduct. In order to sustain the other, it is first necessary to welcome her—to show a kind of hospitality that permits the domesticity associated with the making and consumption of bread, "the staple of life." For Levinas, such love as is symbolized by the *cherubim,* is not the mere sublimation of eros, but rather irreducible and originary. This means that such love involves concern for the other at the outset. This is why Levinas refers to it as disinterested and benevolent. In this way, by looking at the Sanctuary through the lens of Levinas, we can begin to see the ethical-metaphysical dimensions of ritual that are not so far removed in time from everyday life.

From a philosophic point of view, the overarching theme concerns the relation of the Infinite to the finite. Most of the attention is focused in the commentary tradition on the way that the Infinite "appears" in the finite space of the Sanctuary. This kind of "contraction" would extend beyond the Sanctuary to the objects within in it. Levinas appears more concerned with the temporal meaning of the word "always" (*tamid*) as we now explore.

DAILY FIDELITY

Tetzaveh: Command
(Exodus 27:20–30:10)

This is what you shall offer upon the Altar: two sheep within their first year every day, continually. You shall offer the one sheep in the morning, and the second sheep you shall offer in the afternoon.

—Exodus 29:38

Levinas notes a striking midrash where there is an attempt to determine how one might reduce the entire teaching of the Torah to a single statement. The three opinions are as follows:

> Ben Zoma said "I have found a verse that contains the whole of the Torah: Listen O Israel, the Lord our G'd, the Lord is One." Ben Nanus said, "I have found a verse that contains the whole of the Torah: You will love your neighbor as yourself." Ben Pazai said, "I found a verse that contains the whole of the Torah: You will sacrifice a lamb in the morning and another at dusk." And Rebbi, their master stood up and decided, "the law is according to Ben Pazai." (DF 1990, 19)

Prefacing his comment on this passage, Levinas states that "the second [opinion] indicates the way in which the first is true and the third indicates the practical conditions of the second" (Ibid., 18–19). He does not, however, explain why this is the case.

How, then, is this to be explained? The radical originality of the Torah consists in linking the first two affirmations together. For Levinas, the transcendent unity of the Most High can be glimpsed by its enactment through the difficult and problematic commandment to "love your neighbor as yourself" (Lev. 19:18). It is through the relation with the other that the Infinite makes its ethical appearance. This means that monotheism is not simply a numerical denotation—the one—but instead carries with it moral connotation.

What is most striking from this conclusion is the affirmation that the lamb sacrificed in the morning and at dusk (*Korban Tamid*) is superior to "loving your neighbor as yourself" and that it also affirms the unity of G'd. This is especially surprising given the fact that Rabbi Akiva is reputed to have said that "loving your neighbor … is equivalent to the whole Torah." If Levinas is correct, why does this *mitzvah* depend on the creedal prayer of Judaism, the Shema—Hear O Israel? Can it be that the fundamental law affirming a responsibility for the other, the neighbor, is itself dependent in some metaphysical sense on the ethical dimension of the transcendent unity of G'd? Why should these utterly sublime precepts yield to something so apparently plain as sacrificing a lamb in the morning and another at dusk?

About this conclusion, Levinas states that "the law is effort. The daily fidelity to the ritual gesture demands a courage that is calmer, nobler and greater than that of the warrior" (DF 1990, 19). The kind of responsibility that is announced in the statement "love your neighbor as yourself" is to be lived out continually. In the thought of Levinas, this involves the concept of *always* that is quite different from and better than the static notion of eternity. Eternity, for Levinas, is in fact "the irreversibility of time." From the standpoint of the Torah, time is *not*, as it is for Plato, "the moving image of eternity." The "always," then, can be elevated and transformed so that it becomes an ultimate sense of responsibility. Such responsibility, like our relations with others, is always being renewed. The always is an iteration that begins anew "ever again." This "ever again" brings with it a kind of novelty that is to be something that I perhaps do not need but awakens in me a desire. The expression of desire always takes time. This is why, in some mystical traditions, the practitioner is encouraged to empty himself first of all desires. In this way, he will achieve a certain kind of serenity that issues from an absence of restlessness.[31]

Levinas refers to *diachronic* time as a time that originates with the other and calls me forth to wakefulness. In this sense, diachronic time articulates temporality as the "*making of time for the other*." In dealing with the three precepts announced in the midrashic passage above, we testify to the divine unity of transcendence by taking perpetual responsibility for others on ourselves. The way that this was ritually reenacted was through the sacrifice that was

---

31 Nietzsche called this idea of emptying oneself of all desires "the last temptation," a reference to Buddhism.

offered morning and evening—that is each day—thereby giving orientation and purpose to human time.

Keep in mind the conclusion to the passage commanding the *Korbon Tamid*. The *Korbon Tamid* is described as "a continual elevation-offering for your generations, before the entrance of the tent of meeting, before Hashem, where I shall set My meeting with you to speak there" (Exod. 29:42). Is there a more fitting place for this sacrifice to take place than at the "entrance" of the meeting tent? It is here that the elevation of everyday life is consecrated and set apart as a place for acts of holiness without interruption. In this sense, it symbolizes what Levinas, when speaking of the bread of faces, called the "horizontal axis" in coming together with the vertical. In other words, everything that is ultimately holy must be taken to and from the work-a-day world.

The opening of the first volume of the Talmud in Berachot asks the question—up until when in the evening can the *Korban Tamid* be brought? Since the Korban Tamid depends upon the existence of a Sanctuary or Holy Temple, it also asks the question of up until when is the recital of the *Shema* (Hear O Israel) permitted? The second chapter of Berachot asks up until when can one bring the Korban Tamid in the morning or recite the Shema. What is being asked is no less than the question of what it means to speak of "evening" and "morning," the opening and closure of each day.[32]

IN THE ABSENCE OF MOSES

It has been duly noted by the commentary tradition that it is only in this Torah portion that we do not find the name of Moses mentioned since he first appears in Exodus. This offers additional evidence of the fact that these passages are out of order. Importantly, there is an intrinsic connection between the transgression of the Golden Calf and the absence of the name of Moses here. When Moses is

---

32 We see this in the order of creation itself. "G'd said, 'Let there be light,' and there was light. G'd saw that the light was good, and G'd separated between the light and the darkness. G'd called to the light: 'Day,' and to the darkness He called: 'Night.' And there was evening and there was morning, one day" (Gen. 1:1–5). Light and its measurement belong to the realms of optics and physics. Transforming light into "day" requires nothing less than a transcendent transformation. While Adam names the animals, only G'd can inflect the realm of physics into that of human experience. In making experience oriented and purposive, night is further contracted into evening and day further into morning. This is why only in Jewish Scripture is time, one day (yom echad), the fruit and culmination of all creation. Only in the Hebrew Scriptures does time occupy this place of preeminence in the scheme of creation.

about to descend for the first time from Sinai, the debacle of the Golden Calf is brought to his attention, and G'd threatens to wipe out the entire nation except for Moses, Moses replies: "And now, if You would but forgive their sin!—but if not, erase me now from this book that You have written" (Exod. 32:35). Since the words of any genuine biblical prophet matter (and how much more so for Moses, the prophet par *excellence*) the tradition suggests that the absence of the name of Moses is premeditated and the mildest kind of fulfillment of his conditional request. This points to the inability of the newly forming nation of Israel to tolerate the absence of Moses even for one half of one day and, more generally, with the difficulties they have in dealing with absence in general. Infidelity always begins when we treat the absent other as nonexistent. Conversely, fidelity arises in relation to the other whether absent or present. In turn, the ethical-metaphysical dimension of this absence is tested when we reduce absence to non-existence.. Is this not exactly what happens in the case of the Golden Calf?

Yet, most of the time we dwell in the absence of others, however dear they might be to me. Levinas, in his last lecture as a professor of philosophy at the Sorbonne, speaks of this kind of transcendence as "illeity"—that is, as "Transcendent to the Point of Absence."[33] Such absence is not merely a privation. It makes it possible for the third party to stand in a transcendent manner to the second and therefore to me, as well. It is worth pointing out that we can only love the neighbor when we regard his/her absence as something that can re*appear*, and therefore however distant in time or place, the person remains subject to the command to love your neighbor as yourself. The same is true when G'd's absence is noted, especially in times of distress or anguish. The traditional theological explanation of "G'd concealing his face" (*hester panim*) testifies to this sensibility.

Just as parents ask the children about their child's conduct while they are absent, G'd is understood as binding Himself to Israel through the teaching of Torah. This does not require the immediate presence or apperception of the Divine—in other words, love My teaching even more than Me. This is why Levinas can say descriptively that what matters most in our time is for morality "to know and justify itself in the fragility of the conscience, in the 'four cubits of the *Halakah*,' in that precarious, divine abode" (PN 1996, 123).

---

33 Emmanuel Levinas, "A God Transcendent to the Point of Absence," in *God, Death and Time*, 1976, 219.

THE TRACE

Ki Sisa: Take a Census
(Exodus 30:11–34:35)

Hashem would speak to Moses face to face, as a man would speak to his fellow,

—Exodus 33:11

You will not be able to see My face, for no human can see my face and live … Behold! There is a place near Me you may stand on the rock. When my glory passes by, I shall place you in the cleft of the rock; I shall shield you with My hand until I have passed. Then I shall remove My hand, and you shall see My back, but My face may not be seen.

—Exod. 33:20–33:23

The G'd who passed is not the model of which the face would be an image. To be in the image of G'd does not mean to be an icon of G'd but to find oneself in his trace. The revealed G'd of our … spirituality maintains all the infinity of his absence, which is in the personal order itself. He shows himself only by his trace, as is said in Exodus 33. To go toward Him is not to follow this trace which is not a sign, it is to go toward the others who stand in the trace of illeity.

—*The Trace of the Other*, 359

One of the most enduring images of the Bible is not an image at all. When Moses asks G'd to see His Glory, even he, who spoke to Him as a man would speak to his friend, is allowed to see His face only from its eclipsed side. Several questions immediately arise: What is it that has been glimpsed in this encounter and what is it that has "passed by?"

142

What Levinas wishes to describe is what can be seen when the goodness of G'd passes by. This is especially important given the fact that Moses cannot see the divine face; this is withheld from him as it is from every person. Maimonides concludes that the encounter results in a registering of the primary Divine Attributes, thirteen in all, beginning with mercifulness and concluding with forgiveness (GFP 1956, 75–76). Still, what is it that does appear to pass by Moses? Levinas uses this almost imperceptible time lag between appearance and disappearance of the present into the past as the very mystery of memory itself. How does the past endure? The common understanding is to say that it remains in memory. This is necessary but not yet sufficient, for a memory is memorable because it is a memory *of* something. How does that something appear and where does it go? The related question concerns what happens in the two-fold presence and absence of the original encounter.

Levinas calls that which passes by into the past "the Trace." The trace can be rediscovered simply because it leaves an indelible imprint that can no more be effaced than a thief can erase all the traces of his or her fingerprints despite attempts to erase them. In this way, it recedes into what Levinas calls "the Immemorial Past."

Levinas refers to the trace as the "insertion of space into time" (BPW 1996, 62). What does this mean and why is it important? The priority of time over space originates in the modern history of philosophy with Kant's *Critique of Pure Reason*. In its opening section, Kant argues that without a prior sense of human time, all sense of sequence, simultaneity, and cause and effect would remain utterly unintelligible. We would therefore not be able to understand either the *before* or *after* that makes it possible to speak meaningfully of time as it is lived. From this, it follows that the directionality of space as it is lived would not be intelligible either. In a similar way, without a prior understanding of space, we would be unable to signify what we mean by place, position, or direction. For example, the "near and far" and the "up and down" would not be able to be expressed in meaningful language,[34] at least in terms of its oriented human significance. Levinas's claim that the trace arises from the insertion of space into time is not immediately clear. Nor does he go to great lengths to explain it. Human space, or spatiality, however, belongs to the realm of the visible. If so, would space then belong to the realm of totality? As such, for space to become humanized, it must enter into the promise of time that binds totality to infinity.[35]

---

34 See Kant's *Critique of Pure Reason*, the section on the transcendental aesthetic.

35 To explore this problematic conjunction more fully exceeds the bounds of our inquiry.

This means that the "and," or "et" in French, between totality and infinity is an ongoing movement that binds totality to infinity and is the way whereby the promise of time is achieved.

There is an existential context for Moses's request to see G'd's glory. This comes after the first forty days in the giving of the Torah at Sinai and the divinely inscribed first set of tablets. Moses smashes the tablets just before his descent, after realizing that a portion of his people are rejoicing in the construction of the Golden Calf, which is meant to replace Moses as an absent leader. Why Moses smashes the first set of tablets is the subject of numerous commentaries. One compelling explanation consistent with Moses's role as an intercessor for Israel is that of the Maharal. He argues that Moses's act is not simply one of unpremeditated anger or even of anger itself. What the Maharal emphasizes is that if the people had already accepted a written version of the Torah, even those epitomized by the words on the tablets, this would have constituted a final breech because it would have been as though a marriage contract had been signed. On a more philosophic plane, it is a kind of righteous indignation that follows a deep disappointment with those Israelites who have apparently put out of mind the deliverance from Egypt and the receiving of the law spoken at Sinai. This opens the possibility for repentance and reconciliation, and therefore the renewal of the covenant.[36]

Whether the Golden Calf was in the strict sense an idol or not, it nonetheless shows that the people could not withstand the ordeal of the disoriented present because they could not recall the trace of the absent past from which they had emerged. In a way, they tried to put time to a stop—or, at least to put it to sleep. This also means that they could not face the contingent, absent future. This contrasts vividly with Moses, placed in the cleft of a rock, as G'd showed him His goodness and His glory while passing by. While the trace passes by, it has a permanence that can be revisited within the folds of time. In this sense, it is not limited by place, position, or direction. For time cannot be arrested, made stationary, or inhabited as even the most sacred or holy of sites can. In the case of the Golden Calf, transcendence is inserted and inverted into an immanence that would become one with the natural attitude.[37] However, there is an aspect of the other that cannot be divested of its transcendence. This means that the

---

36 I heard this from my teacher, about the Maharal's position, R' Rofoel Zalman Levine Hacohen (1900–1992); *circa* 1988, Albany, NY.

37 In the "natural attitude," everything would revert to the status of an object and is separated from any kind of transcendence in advance.

other cannot be absorbed into the same. It is the face of the other person that passes me by.

For Levinas, it is the trace of the other that is at stake in the encounter between Moses and the divine other. An aspect of this ultimately asymmetric relation is found in the interhuman sphere as well. This means that in the interpersonal sphere, the face-to-face relation can likewise be revealed one to the other. Even in the turning away of the face of the other, the face-to-face relation is presupposed.

EXPRESSION AND DISCOURSE

The *locus classicus* of divine expression can be found, for Levinas, in Exodus 33. This occurs when Moses has been summoned a second time to receive the tablets of the law. While Moses is hidden in the cleft of the mountain, the Divine Presence passes by. What Levinas asks in the first place is "What is it that Moses encounters as 'God passes by'?" He notes that "the God who passed is not the model of which the face would be an image. To be in the image of God does not mean to be an icon of God but to find oneself in his trace.........He shows himself only by his trace, as is said in Exodus 33. To go toward Him is not to follow this trace, which is not a sign; it is to go toward the Others who stand in the trace illeity" (BPW 1996, 64). What this shows is that while Levinas does not use biblical verses to make the case for a philosophic argument, he nonetheless finds in this encounter the original relation between expression, the face, and the other.

For him, the beginning of discourse is always found in the expression of the face of the other. As such, discourse can be affirmed, rejected, or ignored when the other turns his or her face away from me. Without appealing to the phenomenon of expression, we would not know if we had made ourselves understood. It could easily revert to a mere exchange of information. Expression, then, is prior to speech but necessary for its enactment. It is in this expression that the trace originates and is preserved. What appears to be paradoxical in Moses's divine encounter is that while it registers to Moses's awareness, G'd says to him: "No man can see my face and live" (Exod. 33:20). There is something about the face that breaks through all adjectives, predicates, and descriptions. This is why the divine trace cannot be a picture or an image.

This contrasts perfectly with the fabricating of the Golden Calf (*egel zahav*). The Calf of Gold remains stationary and cannot move. The "ab-solute" is apprehended only in its passing by. In fact, G'd says to Moses, "I shall make all My goodness pass before you, and I shall call out the Name Hashem before you"

(Exod. 33:19). Although he leaves the meaning of the phrase quite elusive, this appears to involve the way that the trace of the absolute makes historical events recognizable. If Levinas is correct here, he is demonstrating a way of preserving the infinite dimension of the Divine without insisting upon a static absolute that excludes other expressions of the Most High. As such, it is a fence against fanaticism based on theological absolutism.

From an existential point of view, what passes by must remain as a trace, as Levinas describes this phenomenon. It is not simply a part of what is or of what will be called "Being" by philosophers. It is rather, as Levinas describes in his second great work, something that belongs to "the otherwise than being."

It was this inability to withstand the absence of Moses that led to the transgression of the Golden Calf. Such incapacity or unwillingness is associated with a kind of angry impatience. Is this perhaps why Moses asks G'd when he intercedes on behalf of the nation Israel: "Why should Your anger burn against Your people, whom You took out of the land of Egypt with great power and a strong hand, O G'd" (Exod. 32:11). It is at this moment that G'd says to Moses, "I will pass My goodness before you" (Exod. 33:19). In so doing, according to Reb Nachman of Breslov, he states that "He is seeking to encourage Moses to arouse the good points in others" (*Rebbe Nachman's Torah*, vol. 2, 259). This, in turn, permits G'd to reveal his own attributes of goodness, mercifulness, kindness, and forbearance. Since Moses sees G'd from only His eclipsed side while protected in the crevice of a rock, let us ask again: How does this theophany show itself?

On an everyday level, the trace appears as that which unifies and preserves all phases of time. This is especially the case with respect to the past—or, as Levinas calls it, "an absolute past which unites all times" (BPW 1996, 63). While the Golden Calf would arrest time perceived to be going in an unpromising direction, it in fact represents the vaporizing of time. Levinas affirms that "the trace is the insertion of space into time; the point at which the world inclines toward a past and a time" (Ibid., 62). In this sense, what the trace responds to is the apparent impermanence of time and the way that it would bring all of our efforts and all of our striving to an incomprehensible and meaningless nothingness. But this passing itself does and must leave a trace, according to Levinas, for any kind of enduring significance. As he says, "A real trace disturbs the order of the world. It occurs by over-printing" (Ibid.).

The trace, then, is that which would remain despite my intentions and notwithstanding the lapse of time that occurs between the leaving of the trace and its discovery or rediscovery. We can understand this. However, this depends on our capacity to recognize the appearance of absence. We look at a bookshelf where a book is missing, though we do not know which one. It is premature to say that it has been misplaced or is hidden from view or submerged. It is first recognized as that which is "not there." There is a disruption that occurs. In fact, most of the rest of reality, and therefore humanity, is often not perceptually present; it is absent. Still, this would be merely a kind of "ontological absence"[38] where that which is hidden from view can be illuminated or interpreted, where that which is missing can be found, where that which is absent can be made present.

Levinas speaks of an absolute that absolves itself. What does this mean? He says, "Its wonder is due to the *elsewhere* from which it comes and into which it already withdraws. This coming from *elsewhere* is not a *symbolic reference* to that *elsewhere* as to a term" (BPW 1996, 60). In his radically original formulation, Levinas elaborates upon this in the following way: "The absolute exteriority of the exterior being is not purely and simply lost as a result of its manifestation; it absolves itself from the relation in which it presents itself." This has a concrete significance. It means that the idea of the absolute cannot be thought of as an object. Rather, instead of an object, it expresses itself as "desire, perfectly disinterested goodness. But desire and goodness concretely presuppose a relationship in which the desirable arrests the negativity of the 'I' that holds sway in the Same, putting an end to power and the endeavor of adventure" (TI 1969, 50). By absolving itself, the absolute makes a place for a multiplicity of others as individuals with an identity before one another and also for a metaphysical pluralism, which engenders a diversity of societies and perspectives. Hence we can speak of the absolutely Absent: "The other proceeds from the absolutely Absent, but his relationship with the *absolutely Absent* from which he comes *does not indicate, does not reveal* this Absent; and yet the Absent has a meaning in the face.... The relationship which goes from the face to the absent is outside every relation and dissimulation, a third way excluded by these contradictories" (BPW 1996, 60). What Levinas appears to be describing is a way that the absolute can appear to us through time and across places. This is the crowning metaphysical achievement of his transcending humanism.

Levinas points to a fidelity that obligates me even when the face of the other is absent. For him, it becomes a trace that maintains itself throughout all time and place. This is what the Israelites could not endure in the absence of Moses. When such fidelity is resumed, as it is ever and again, it makes sense to call this the *faith*fulness of fidelity. It would then become inserted into the promise of time. Now we can understand how idols, despite their physicality,

---

38 I am indebted to my colleague, Annika Jung-Baruth at the University of Vermont, for this insight.

are ephemeral in the sense that they cannot abide in this absence. What makes genuine fidelity possible is glimpsed through the trace. This is how the infinite can express itself in the finite.

This is what Levinas refers to as "illeity" (See OBBE 1991, 12–13). Illeity deals with the "third person," who is always foreshadowed by the second. Illeity is therefore a relationship, which is already personal and ethical. Otherwise, it could not command the kind of fidelity and right conduct required of a society intent on elevating itself. From the standpoint of the present historical hour, we begin to glimpse this third way where, by not treating the infinite as a natural object, we can begin to see its movement in everyday life. The moment that the Infinite is arrested by forming it into a totality, we become intent on subordinating other people in such a way as to deprive them of their own relation to the infinite.

THE INCALCULABLE: SUFFERING AND JUSTICE [39]

Levinas makes an important contribution to understanding that question that Moses, according to the sages, most wanted answered at the time of this great intimacy in the divine-human encounter (Berachos, 7). "Why are there righteous people that suffer, and wicked people who seem to be rewarded?" (Nachshoni, vol. 2, 583). Levinas astutely observes that Moses asks precisely "why are the righteous *sometimes* [my emphasis] prosperous, sometimes not, and the unrighteous sometimes prosperous and sometimes not?" (NTR 1990, 186). With this, it is noted that he did not ask the Job-like question of the present day: "Why do the righteous suffer and the wicked prosper?" Levinas gives a first response to his own question: "A rigorously upside-down order would certainly be diabolical, but it would still attest to a *governed* world. Moses is afraid only of an absolutely contingent world!" (NTR 1990, 186–87). In other words, as Levinas puts it, "There would still be a direction in Creation: an order. Order, whatever it is gives reason back its place" (Ibid., 187).

What is at stake here is nothing less than a question that appears to have no answer. At the same time, however, this question is so important that the refusal or failure to respond to it often uproots people from their sense of existential certainty. Levinas builds upon an argument of the Maharasha (1555–1632). Levinas observes that, for reasons of grammar, one term always precedes another. He asks whether or not we can infer anything from such chronological

---

39 For this section, we rely heavily on a chapter by Levinas entitled "Damages Due to Fire," which can be found in the collection *Nine Talmudic Readings*, pages 178–97.

priority. He then points out that when Abraham was interceding for Sodom that the righteous were named first. And in the case before us, Moses is also asking first after the consequences for "some" of the righteous, and only then "some of the unrighteous." This question is not allowed to expire along with Job and his troubles. Levinas links the absence of a response to this question to the "arbitrariness of extermination" (NTR 1990, 187). He asks, "Or does the madness of extermination retain a grain of reason? That is the great ambiguity of Auschwitz" (Ibid.).

Levinas does not seek to resolve the problem from a standpoint of Divinity. He refuses any kind of rationalization or attribution to the meaning of sacrifice unless it involves personal sacrifices on behalf of other people. It is as he says in his presentation "Damages due to Fire," a kind of paradoxical anthropology: "To be human is to suffer for the other, and even within one's own suffering, to suffer for the suffering my suffering imposes upon the other." He attributes his position to Chaim of Volozhin's (1749–1821) *Nefesh HaChaim* in which he says, "The *human* appears as a rupture of *being* and *perseverance in Being,* and only as a result of this rupture as a relation with G'd" (Ibid., 188).

Levinas appears to be arguing that the natural order of things appears as the each against each. It is, however, possible for human beings to surmount this condition, this so-called human nature. This reversal would consist in the each for each and all for all. Only in this way is it possible to understand the normativity of the human being.

Levinas does not, therefore, abandon the human quest for justice. Rather, he situates it in relation to absence and presence. Most of the time, we dwell neither in the presence of perfect justice nor in its complete absence. It is tempting, however, to regard the postponement of justice or its apparent inversion as equivalent to its nonexistence. This is an invitation to nihilism where a sense of aimless, even arbitrary relativity would rule in all spheres of existence.

This distinction between absence and nonexistence, so long buried in the history of philosophy, must be reanimated if we are to grasp the Torah's essential teaching on justice and to follow Levinas's own thought. For Levinas, absence is something that positively appears and informs our perception, understanding, and responses in the most concrete expressions of human life. Take, for example, the case of an innocent party who has been violated or tortured. His or her expression of suffering makes apparent the absence of justice, and by making us aware of injustice, signals a kind of urgency to be acted upon. We reduce the absence of justice to its nonexistence only at our own peril. We do not accept the notion that what passes for political justice under the sway of institutional power is exhaustive of reality. We learn to hold out in the absence of justice for a remedy that may take too much time but nonetheless testifies to a world that is contingent, yet non-arbitrary.

In context, the commentary tradition asks: What happens when the Infinite passes? Or, in other words, what happens when God passes Moses by, even from the eclipsed side? As Moses hides in the cleft of the rock, God is said to have revealed to Moses his Glory. What does this mean, this "passing by"? How does the Trace of the Infinite appear? It would manifest itself to the face of Moses, irradiating his expression. To the end, it expresses a divine glow (or Hebrew *Chein*). Is this not why Moses is forced to mask his face upon his return through the divine-human encounter? Levinas helpfully adds, "A face presents itself in its nudity; it is not a form concealing, but thereby indicating, a ground, a phenomenon that hides but thereby betrays a thing itself. Otherwise, a face would be one with a mask—but a mask presupposes a face" (*The Trace of the Other*). Again, a passing leaves a trace of what Levinas calls the "immemorial past." Only as an absolute past, uniting together all times past, does the Trace of the Infinite appear upon the face of the finite other.

The trace then, is what appears as a radical absence that can be distinguished from mere nothingness. One of the great tests that calls into question all human striving, work, and aspirations arises in the fact that what comes to be appears to pass away. Especially after having done something good but arduous without acknowledgement or thanks, we are inclined to ask ourselves—What good did it do?—seeing that eventually, it will come to nothing. This view is predicated upon a certain notion of time and being. It is this: the future becomes the present and the present becomes the past. The past, then, becomes nothing at all. And all of time threatens, therefore, to become nothing at all. This would be the case if time did not bear a promise bequeathed to us from the past. This promise is visible in the Trace that is always "passing by."

Such an affirmation of the promise of time then makes it possible for us to hold that what we do and what we say are consequential, that they make a difference to others, and thereby, to ourselves. While this does not answer Moses's question, why the righteous sometimes suffer, it begins a response to the question, how the good can meaningfully be said to endure when we are not physically present to perceive it. Also inscribed here is the notion of generational responsibility for those who come after us, whom we may not live to see, and those that have come before us, whose legacy binds the future of their past to my own present. Am I then responsible for the pasts of others? Surely I am, according to Levinas. Otherwise, the covenantal bond between one generation and another could not hold nor be explained.

Moses may not get an answer to the question of why the just sometimes suffer, but he does receive a response to this ultimate and related question—How can the meaning of my life outlast its length? Levinas puts it in the following words, indicating that the key to understanding this is not in recognizing the terror of my own death but "that patience does not consist in the agent belying his generosity by giving himself the time of a *personal immortality*. To renounce being the contemporary of the triumph of one's work is to have the triumph in a time without me, to aim at this world without me, to aim at a time beyond the horizon of my time" (*The Trace of the Other*). This is in the context of an explication by Levinas of a Talmudic passage that refers originally to one of the Mishpatim: "If someone brings on a fire which consumes wood, stones, or earth, he would be liable, as it is written, Exodus 22:5: 'If a fire breaks out and catches in thorns, so that the stack of corn, or the standing corn or the field is consumed, he who starts the fire, must make restitution," (BT, *Baba Kama*, 60a-b).

Levinas does not appear to be placated by the argument expressed in this Talmudic debate that "trials begin only with the just" (NTR 1990, 185). Levinas goes on to examine an argument from the rabbinic sages found in the prophet Ezekiel. The argument goes like this: "The righteous are responsible for evil before anyone else is. They are responsible because they have not been righteous enough to make their justice spread and abolish injustice. It is the fiasco of the best which leaves the coast clear for the worst. But, if this were so, there would still be reason in the very irrationality of war: the justice of history" (NTR 1990, 186).

Levinas does not accept this argument. He believes that it rationalizes war but is unsuccessful because it still ends in unreason. Keep in mind what Levinas has stated about his own biography: "It is dominated by the presentiment and the memory of the Nazi horror" (DF 1990, 291). For Levinas, the terrible suffering that occurred between 1933 and 1945 is "a useless suffering." The only consolation for unjust suffering, according to Levinas, appears to reside in the way that one human being "is to suffer for the other" (NTR 1990, 188). It would be consoling only because it shows that morally it is possible to hold one's ground by and through a valuation of the life of one's fellow even above one's own. The humanity of the human against even the most vile and total persecution remains an open possibility.

AFTER FIRE

Vayakhel: Assembling
(Exodus 35:1–38:20)

You shall not kindle fire in any of your dwellings on the Sabbath day.

—Exodus 35:3

For the Israelites, the text states, "Six days you may (shall) work" (Exod. 35:2). The effects of the enjoyment of light and heat, assuming that their conditions have been established beforehand are welcomed, rather than rejected on the Sabbath. It is because of the Sabbath that work and labor are for the sake of something beyond themselves. Work, for Levinas, is intimately related to the notion of the home: "The access to values, usage, manipulation and manufacture rest on possession, on the hand that takes, that brings back home" (TI 1969, 162). The Sanctuary is like the Ultimate home in that it expresses both the most inner recesses of the conscience, the solitary, and the intimate. At the same time, it is a place where everyone, at least from time to time, assembles. It is both where the holiest of possessions are kept, and at the same time where the very idea of possession is called into question. It is, after all, "the Other who calls in question possession itself" (TI 1969, 163). Is this perhaps why all of the categories of work in the strict sense (*melacha*) on the Sabbath are already connected to the building of the Mishkan? The threshold to the Sabbath represents the sum of labor, work, and creating for the sake of something higher. Still, this is the reason given why the thirty-nine kinds of work that went into the building of the Tabernacle are prohibited on the Sabbath.

It is not by accident that the Sabbath is welcomed by the lighting of candles just prior to its advent and ushered out with the candle of the *Havdalah* services that distinguishes between the holy and the not holy. This is to say that the Sabbath itself, while it operates on a level different from that of the everyday, does so in a way that elevates the notion of creation toward its consummation each week.

It is also important to point out here that fire may be understood as symbolizing destruction as well as creation. The moralists among the commentators emphasize that we should make an attempt to refrain from anger on all occasions, but especially on the Sabbath. This is because anger is associated with fire, a symbol of pride.

Consider for a moment the divinely chosen architect of the Sanctuary, Betzalel. "Moses said to the Children of Israel, 'See, Hashem has proclaimed by name Betzalel, son of Uri, son of Hur, of the tribe of Judah,'" (Exod. 35:30). The midrash adds that Betzalel was called by name, singled out, because he had earned himself "a good name." A good name is the most imperishable of all human achievements, something good in itself and something that can be bequeathed in perpetuity. Betzalel is described as a person of great wisdom and artistry. According to the Torah, Betzalel would be the grandson of Hur. According to the tradition, Hur had been slain while trying to keep the people from transgressing during the time of the rebellion over the Calf of Gold. Imagine, then, the trace of anger that had to be overcome, converted, and sublimated by his grandson Betzalel.[40] The Sanctuary was more than merely a concession to human immaturity. It was through Betzalel, whose name means "shadow of G'd," that the concession to visible, punctuated steps on the way to holiness took place.[41] The lesson that we can learn about the prohibition against fire on the Sabbath has to do with the prohibition against expressing anger, and therefore disturbing the equanimity between one person and another on the Sabbath day.

The interpretation of this prohibition regarding fire has had historical significance. The absolutely essential role of the interpretation drawn from the oral tradition is decisive. Reading the text with the naked eye, without the prism of the commentary tradition, can lead to absurd conclusions even on the part of very intelligent human beings.

Such was the case with a ninth-century sect known as the Karaites. The Karaites prohibited using preexisting fire for light or heat on the Sabbath. They

---

40 Originally heard from R. David Lehrfield.

41 This brings to mind the story of a devotee of a certain Hassidic Rebbe. The Hassid is reported to have said, when the Rebbe recommended that he do *teshuva* for the wrong that he had done, "But Rebbe, I do not know how to do *teshuvah*." The Rebbe sharply responded, "But you committed the transgression before you understood how to do it."

did so on the basis that only the words written in the Pentateuch were to be acted upon as though they understood them without interpretation. This is in opposition to rabbinic or Talmudic Judaism. The Sabbath is meant to be a "delight." Thereby, warm food and illumination are important.[42]

Levinas argues that the home is not simply a place to recuperate from the "real work" of the marketplace, of commerce, and of history, but rather is supra-historical in character, contra Hegel. The interior drama of the home can be exteriorized and enacted where I can practice hospitality and extend a welcome to others.

Levinas aims at a kind of demystification of religion in general, in Judaism in particular. He does so knowing full well the critique of religion by Spinoza and does so in opposition to Spinoza's "naturalism"—that is, his attempted destruction of transcendence.[43] For we, who come after the time of the Enlightenment, are both its heirs and critics. Judaism does not criticize the genuine discoveries of the mathematical sciences, but rather, embraces them as enhancing the promise of human dignity. Nor does Judaism seek to take its place among the world of sedentary peoples with their nostalgia for the naturalism of pagan, folk, and peasant society. This does not mean a return to irrationalism, but rather a new reflection on rationality and transcendence. Only in this way can we show how there is a resistance to treating people as only natural objects while preserving the discoveries issuing from mathematical-scientific turning since the dawn of the Enlightenment. Rather, the human journey through time and place can be depicted without false appeals to a static eternity that would devalue time and life itself.

According to the theory of time advanced by Levinas, the Sabbath is not viewed as a static eternity that would be opposed to the passage of time. Nevertheless, the toil of everyday life must reach beyond itself toward a horizon

---

42 According to legend, Saadya Gaon wanted an empirical demonstration that the Karaites were in error, hence that mysterious stew known as "cholent," was produced by Saadya's students in order to demonstrate the folly of the Karaites. Historically, cholent is the only distinctively Jewish food that is not borrowed from a host or alien culture. What is unusual about cholent is that it does not become fully edible until it simmers for a number of hours, and therefore is eaten during the daytime meal of the Sabbath. This is how thought for food becomes food for thought.

43 Spinoza's critique of religion and Levinas's response to it exceed the bounds of our study. See Richard A. Cohen, *Out of Control: Levinas and Spinoza on Ethics, Politics, Science, and Religion*, SUNY Press, 2017.

of fulfillment. Because of this, even the most seemingly innocuous acts associated with creating are proscribed.

THE PORTABILITY OF THE ARK

> Betzalel made the Ark of acacia wood.... He cast for them four rings of gold on its four corners; two rings on its one side and two rings on its second side. He made staves of acacia wood and covered them with gold. He inserted the staves in the rings on the sides of the Ark, to carry the Ark.
>
> —Exodus 37:1–5

Levinas speaks of the difference between the Ark and the mummy. He states that across the desert, a midrash tells us, the Israelites coming out of Egypt carried the ark of Joseph's remains alongside the Ark that carries the Tablets of G'd (DF 1990, 55). Levinas explains this proximity by emphasizing the fact that the righteous Joseph carried out all that was written on the tablets of the law, however anachronistically. In this way, there is a sense in which the law, unlike an Egyptian mummy, brings meaning to life. Levinas states that "the law carried by the Ark is always ready to be moved. It is not attached to a point in space and time but is continually transportable and ready to be transported" (BTV 1994, 32). This is consistent with the Ramban's position that the *Mishkan* was like a "portable Sinai." Rather, the Sanctuary perpetually had to be assembled. This is the act of holy assembling that is meant to rectify the transgression of the Golden Calf, thus demonstrating that people can be gathered for purposes that are noble or less than noble. A reminder that the justice of the law is to be administered together with divine compassion is the fact that the broken tablets are included in the Ark of the Covenant along with the second set as well. Richard A. Cohen puts it this way: "The commandments of the second tablet were the same commandments as the first, to be sure, but the stones of the second were carved and contributed by Moses not by G'd (though still according to G'd's Command)" (NwTR 1999, 9). Cohen describes the relationship between the two sets of tablets using the terms of Levinas as "expressing the time of diachrony, link and rupture at once as expressive of the divine-human encounter" (Ibid., 11). Perhaps this gives added weight to the midrash that argues that the Tabernacle was Moses's response to G'd's earlier statement threatening to annihilate the people (Exod. 32:10). According to this position, it was Moses who responded to Him: "Test them by telling them that they should make the

Tabernacle" (MR). Hence, the gold possessed by the people would now be put in the service of something holy rather than profane.

GENEROSITY

> Every man whose heart inspired him came; everyone whose spirit motivated him brought the portion of Hashem for the work of the Tent of Meeting, for all its labor and for the sacred vestments.
>
> —Exodus 35:21

Through their contributions to the Sanctuary, we see evidence of the Israelites' maturing understanding of what is expected of them. The Israelites are portrayed as giving so bountifully that Moses has to tell them to stop. This conduct may be viewed as the "surplus of justice." Generosity, unlike justice, does not stop with reason, measure or limit.

According to the midrash, "The women cherished the Tabernacle so much, that they came forth first, and brought their gifts before the men" (MeL, 214). This is consistent with the view of the tradition that the women did not transgress in contributing to the Calf of Gold. Furthermore, by way of anticipation, the women were not among those who would later complain against Moses for having sent out the explorers to spy out the land, the last and most terrible trial of the Israelites. For that reason, all of the women, but none of the men between twenty and sixty, were allowed to enter the land of promise.

According to Maimonides, this generosity, once initiated freely, had certain conditions attached to it: "One was not bound by a vow or a free-will pledge unless his mouth and his heart agreed" (*Pearls of the Rambam*, 214). Clearly such offerings had to be attended by sincerity where one says what one means and means what one says. Maimonides qualifies his statement, when he goes on to say that as soon as the matter is decided in one's heart, one becomes bound. Is this not comparable to the saying before the said?

As the surplus of justice, generosity does not only come after justice has been done. It prefigures just conduct. It does so in the following way: As John Wild, Levinas's first American expositor points out, under normal circumstances I speak to the other person of my own volition. The first question that arises for me when someone greets me: "Am I to respond or not? In one sense, this appeal is irresistible. A word must be spoken, but it may take on a definite number of variations" (POP 2006, 174). I find myself between response and nonresponse: "With words of no moment, I may pass the other by and evade his question. Or I may really speak and give an answer" (Ibid.).

We may view the greetings or summons that issue from the other as a test of the way that we take hold of our lives. Even before justifying our responses or nonresponses, we must make a fundamental decision as to whether we wish to turn in the direction of the other and meet him face-to-face. This impulse toward generosity, according to Levinas, represents an inversion of the original human desire for self-preservation and acquisition. It may be viewed as a rupture in the war of each against each. Such generosity occasions a redirection of time and place. This means that I can assign a priority to the other that forces me out of myself. This is what is meant by an open hand when I ready myself to give to the other person.

As the Zohar observes, it is perhaps worth noting that every child is born with a clenched fist, while everyone leaves this world with an open hand. The transforming of the self to the each for each signifies that there is an economic exodus with a moral signature that comes before and after the historical-political exodus from Egypt. Such generosity of spirit has to endure through the ordeals of life. It is also checked by a certain accountability that each takes upon himself for the other.

ACCOUNTABILITY

Pekudei: Reckonings of the Tabernacle
(Exodus 38:21–40:38)

These are the reckonings of the Tabernacle, the Tabernacle of Testimony,
which were reckoned at Moses' bidding.

—Exodus 38:21

Responsibility is initially a for the other. This means that I am responsible for his very responsibility.

—EI 1985, 96

Why does Moses take upon himself the auditing of all of the wealth expended
in making the Sanctuary? This is not directly requested of him by G'd or by the
people (MR, Pekudei). At the same time, Moses recognizes that he is responsible for the items donated by each person—that is, to see that they have been
properly accounted for. He takes on himself a greater degree of responsibility,
not simply by holding himself responsible in some vaguely spiritual sense, but in
relation to the everyday transactions that have been elevated to holy donations.
In a way, he is obsessed by his responsibility, not only for what he has done,
but also for accounting for the responsibility with which others have entrusted
him. This suggests an intimate connection between responsibility and value.
As Levinas puts it, "[R]esponsibility is what first enables us to catch sight and
conceive of value" (OBBE 1991, 123).

Implied is a very material expression through which economic justice is
presupposed, making the Sanctuary itself worthy of such holiness. Here we see
a common route to the quantitative and qualitative dimensions of existence
before their separation into two different spheres of measurement. In other
words, justice implies counting equitably and fairly. This justice on the part of

the sovereign subject doubles back on itself in making the auditor responsible for the justice administered. "Value," then, is not something added upon "facts." The facts themselves are already rendered valuable in the presence of others. This refusal to separate fact and value prematurely by adopting the modern philosophic prejudice of superimposing values upon facts makes accounting for human conduct both intelligible and just.

Let us recall that the Book of the Exodus that begins with the deprivation of the freedom of the Israelites, closes with the assumption of responsibility of one for the other that is possible only for people who have tasted freedom. In fact, a mature freedom is enacted only through the assumption of a vigilant responsibility for others. The transformation from servitude to freedom to responsibility is the movement demonstrated by the Book of the Exodus. The extraordinary degree of accountability demonstrated by Moses for every particular thing contributed to the Sanctuary by the Israelites is not limited in time or place to the Sanctuary, but is an enduring attribute of human excellence.

With the erection of the Tabernacle there occurs at this same juncture, the completion of the most holy place. This is a perfection of space, with its concurrent circles of holiness radiating out from the center to the periphery. When completed, the text says, "Moses blessed them" (Exod. 39:43). With what words did he bless the people? Rashi says, "Yehi Noam ... or "Let the pleasantness of G'd our Lord rest upon us. Let the work of our hands be established, establish the work of our hands" (Psalm 90:17). While this refers, in context, to the Sanctuary, it can apply to all human endeavors. In other words, let it be for good that we have labored, and let this goodness remain visible, even if as a trace. As R. Nachman of Breslov says, "Work and the building of the Tabernacle are synonymous" (*Rebbe Nachman's Torah*, II, 296). In Psalm 90, attributed to Moses, lines 12–18 are explicitly in the form of a petition, as prayer (Hebrew: *Tefillah*).

"Teach us to number our days to get us a heart of wisdom" (Psalm 90:12). The priority still belongs to time in relation to space. This is perhaps also why work associated with that of the Tabernacle is not permitted on the Sabbath. The weekdays, 'where work may be done"—the realm of the historical—are counted off in relation to the coming Sabbath, as is the case when we say, "This is the first day of the week" (Yom Ha Rishon). The Sabbath is then "the other" in relation to the days of the week, and as such, trans-historical, and therefore better than all static eternity.

The separation between the Holy Sabbath and the weekdays, concludes with the *Havdalah* or service of separation. The liturgy accompanying the *Havdalah* concludes with the words of yearning with which Moses blessed the people: "Establish Thou the work of our hands. Yea, the work of our hands establish Thou it." We may not get to see the fruits of our labors, but we can glimpse them as Moses did, from a distant hill.

The Baal Shem Tov, the founder of Hasidism, is reported to have uttered this prayer as his last words. This repetition of the refrain is also a request. The request resonates with the yearning for the infinite and aspirations of human beings who realize in advance that their years are numbered and that their days are counted. It is inscribed with an almost perfect prayer that asks that we recognize we cannot see all that we have achieved and that we understand we cannot know with certainty if what we have done has been good or enduring.[44]

---

44 See Psalm 90, especially lines 12–18. This Psalm is the only text accredited to the biblical Moses in the Hebrew Bible after Deuteronomy.

Leviticus

VAYIKRA

ON LEVITICUS

The Book of Leviticus focuses on matters of holiness. Holiness, in its narrow sense, pertains to the service to be performed within the Mishkan—the portable Sanctuary in the wilderness. It should be noted that it also applies to many ritual practices that are not so very close to us in our time. The task before us is not simply concerned with matters that are regarded as important artifacts; rather, we are concerned with what traces remain that animate and guide our present lives.

The amount of detail devoted to the Sanctuary is striking, to some readers even disconcerting. According to the Ramban (Nachmanides, 1194–1270), the material related to the creation and maintaining of the Sanctuary is chronologically out of order. The Sforno (1470–1550) is even more emphatic. He argues that the building of the Tabernacle (Hebrew *Mishkan*) was made necessary only by the near idolatry that took place with the incident of the Golden Calf (Exod. 25:1; Stone, see footnote 1). In psychology, that lapse into idol worship is often referred to as "sublimation," the replacement of one desire for another.

Much like Maimonides before him, Sforno explains that had the Israelites comported themselves properly when Moses was spending his first forty days on Sinai preparing himself to receive the tablets of the law, there would have been no need for a Sanctuary or, later, for a Temple.[1] However, the Ramban's argument runs in a different direction. Nachmanides argues that although the incident of the Golden Calf was responsible for all the myriad details associated with the Sanctuary's construction, the Sanctuary, the ark, and the Temple are continuing features of biblical Israel. The Tabernacle and its contents must therefore have a significance that is independent of the cause that brought it about.

The Sanctuary was completed and ready for service on Rosh Chodesh Nissan. Since Rosh Chodesh Nissan is the first day of the year's first months, we know that it has a distinctive relation to the marking of time. It is from this date

---

[1] This could be extended to indicate that there would have been no need for animal sacrifice, as well.

163

that all of the Jewish holy days are identified on the calendar. From its conse-cration, the Sanctuary is also understood to be the holiest place for the Israelites and their descendants. This convergence of holiness in time and place gives the completion of the Tabernacle a distinctive kind of synchrony and symmetry.

Levinas, in fact, is more sensitive to the details of the *Mishkan* than one might otherwise expect. In context, we briefly explore how these particulars relate to the responsibility of one person for another. In his third major book, *Of God Who Comes to Mind*, Levinas goes beyond the limiting legacy of what has been called "onto-theology." According to Levinas, basing the idea of God on Being—onto-theology—does not think through the problematic place of Being as the first principle of reality. It ends in explaining neither the God of philosophy nor the God of Abraham, Isaac, and Jacob. Unlike Heidegger, his former teacher (and later nemesis), Levinas does not resort to a kind of neo-paganism, as he does not invest in the elevation of the "sacred" in regard to blood, soil, temples, and places. How, then, does he proceed? What Levinas substitutes for onto-theology is the notion of transcendence. He arrives at this idea from a phenomenological point of view. Just as the other person exceeds my capacity to know him or her, so too, and even more emphatically, does the Divine Other.

The great mystery of the Sanctuary can be understood by showing how the Infinite appears in the finite gestures, actions, and rituals, not only of the Sanctuary but also of everyday life. Much depends upon the distinction that Levinas makes between the notions of the holy and that of the sacred. For Levinas, the holy refers to that which is absolutely other while the sacred is exhausted in the ontology of sameness. Holiness is based upon the human capacity to put the other before oneself. He refers to this as "the only absolute value" (EN 1998, 109).

Levinas argues that holiness is the beginning of philosophy. At first, this does not make sense. It only begins to make sense if, as he maintains, "holiness is indisputable" (EN 1998, 109). He seems to think that this is self-evident despite all of the deformations of holiness with which we are all too familiar. Levinas provides at least a prelude to his position: "This (holiness) is the beginning of philosophy, this is the rational, the intelligible" (Ibid., 109). He is aware that his view sounds all too utopian. He objects: "But we forget our relation to *books* that is, to inspired language, which speaks of nothing else. The book of all lit-erature is perhaps only a premonition or recollection of the Bible" (Ibid., 109). For Levinas, the holiness of the Bible is not to be used as a battering ram, sub-duing others into submission. Our task in opening the book of Leviticus again is to get a glimpse of how holiness works.

It is commonly known that the book of Leviticus—or, in Hebrew *Sefer Vayikra*—is not as familiar to most readers, including those who occupy themselves with Scripture, as are the preceding two books of Genesis and Exodus. The text by Talmudic times was already referred to as "Sefer HaKohanim," the book for descendants of Aaron of the tribe of Levi, who acted as priests in the Sanctuary and later in the Holy Temples. Reading the oral commentary tradition together with Emmanuel Levinas's religious philosophy offers a great advantage, as it helps us to open the Book of Leviticus that is otherwise closed or has the appearance of irrelevance to the contemporary reader.

Since the destruction of the Second Temple in Jerusalem around the year 70 CE, many practices and laws cannot be performed. This is because they are connected to the rituals of the Sanctuary described in detail in the last several portions of Exodus and later the two Holy Temples in Jerusalem. What substitutes today in the absence of these practices, observances, and laws is the study of the text and its commentaries. In addition, there are traces of the original service found in common practices today. What is necessary to recover is what these practices intend to say, before they become ornate symbols for picture books. Levinas's own reflections on speech and language are relevant to the first five portions of the text, as we try to show. These reflections are all the more important in the absence of a sanctuary or temple.

Leviticus deals primarily with questions, issues, and laws of holiness. Hirsch defines holiness as "the ultimate expression of moral perfection." This is very close to Levinas's own philosophic position on the subject. Still, there are differences. We take up this subject in the last four portions of Leviticus, beginning with "Kedoshim." In Kedoshim, we focus on what Rabbi Akiva called the "central commandment of the Torah," loving your neighbor as yourself. We do so in the context of the *sedrah* as a whole and with the benefit of Levinas's original and new thinking on the subject. The last three sections are taken up with the subject of holiness in time, the Jewish festival year.

We focus on the subject of Yom Kippur and the phenomenon of *teshuva*, with reference to the Book of Jonah as well as Leviticus. The Book of Leviticus closes with those conditions that can occur if the covenant between G'd and Israel is breeched. What can and cannot be said about human suffering based upon the philosophy of Levinas guide us in our inquiry here. In anticipating what lies ahead, Levinas helps us to penetrate some of the puzzlement of the terrible skin disease akin to leprosy that plagued the inhabitants of ancient times. Here we also briefly speak about the condition of the biblical Job.

THE SAYING AND THE SAID

Vayikra: To Call
(Leviticus 1:1–5:26)

He called to Moses, and HaShem spoke to him from the Tent of Meeting, saying: "Speak to the Children of Israel and say to them: When a man among you brings an offering to HaShem from animals—from the cattle or from the flock shall you bring your offering."

—Leviticus 1:1–2

The question arises regarding the three terms employed for speech at the very beginning of this portion: (1) "to call" (*Vayikra*), (2) "to speak" (*Dibbur*), and (3) "to say" (*Amira*). Levinas divides living discourse into what he calls "the saying" (*le dire*) and "the said" (*le dit*). It is tempting to reduce this distinction to the contents of speech—that which is said—and the manner or tone that one uses to speak to someone else—the saying. Virtually the entire history of philosophy focuses on "the said" rather than "the saying." Discoveries in the mathematical sciences in particular have very little to do with "the saying" aside from the conditions under which such discoveries were made and the implications following from them.

Levinas seeks to rediscover in everyday discourse the way "the saying" precedes and informs "the said" at virtually every level. When "G'd called to Moses," the language in Hebrew indicates that this implies a conversation preceded by a greater level of proximity than is usual in the divine-human encounter. In an everyday sense, this may be explained in the following way: we do not always wait until we have the attention of the other person before speaking to him or her. It is at the threshold of the door of speech where we often find ourselves rushing ahead to explain something to someone who we later learn was not attentive. This often leads to irritation on the part of the speaker and/or the listener, which turns into an argument and ends in the complaint, "you're not listening to me" (*Torah Temimah*, vol. 3, 1).[2] This often means that we are not facing the person to whom we are speaking.

In the case before us, G'd is depicted as calling to Moses from within the Sanctuary. This is where most subsequent directives are given to Moses from on high. This is more than a matter of protocol or etiquette that is presupposed. One does not have to say explicitly, "I want your undivided attention right now," as a classroom teacher might. Rather it is more like an announced pause whereby the listener can gather his or her attention before speech occurs.

Why then does the text use the double description of the words "speak" and "say" after the use of "And he called to Moses?" While many commentators have noted this apparent redundancy, Rabbi Samson Raphael Hirsch provides a novel explanation: "[S]peech (*daber*) denotes brief concise expression, meaning the written Torah … can only be understood with the illumination of the oral Torah … the discursive saying by means of which G'd explained the Torah to Moses" (Stone, 545). In the language of Levinas, the intention of the saying is repeatedly being recovered by the content-driven language of the said. This is the manner in which the meaning of what has been said is continually being rediscovered by us in everyday language. We see this in living conversation when we say in response to a query from the other person, "What did you mean by that?" "I mean, 'such and such.'" In other words, I do not proceed simply in a chronological fashion from having said one thing to having said a different thing with a different meaning. I mean a variation of the words I have been intending to say to you in the present tense. This could go on between speaker and listener *ad infinitum*. This is where phenomenology in fact ties into the rabbinic theory of interpretation. Meaning, for Levinas, first arises in the saying that animates the said, including, yet also surpassing motive and intention. The saying must be perpetually rediscovered if the said is to make a difference, come to life, as we say.

We immediately gain an example of what he is talking about in the opening statements of Leviticus. The word "Vayikra," in its plain sense, means "to call." To call means to gather the attention of the one to whom one is speaking. The word "Vayikra" has a second meaning that flows from the first. It means to "draw near to" or establish a certain kind of proximity to the other. Before we speak to another person or convey to him or her what we would like him or her to tell a third party, we have to gather his or her attention and respond to what

---

2   I am indebted to R. David Lehrfield for this excellent illustration.

the other person is saying to us in an attentive manner. Levinas calls this "proximity." Proximity is a drawing close on the part of the subject to the other. This
means morally, emotionally, or affectively, rather than spatially, close. In the case
before us, it is the divine other that brings Moses closer to Him by calling out
his name. Biblically, calling someone by name is usually a sign of endearment.
This is true in the case before us.

The dominant subject of Leviticus's first portion deals with various kinds
of sacrifices, a concept that appears most distant to the majority of us when we
are speaking of animals. One way of viewing this is found in the *Guide for the
Perplexed* by Maimonides. Maimonides regards animal sacrifice as a kind of
concession to human frailties and an absence of spiritual maturity (GFP 1956,
323). However, he sees this concession as one that originally the Israelites could
not have done without (Ibid.). Maimonides is not alone in this view. He has
support from Abraham Ibn Ezra, the great rationalist and grammarian, and
most emphatically Sforno. Also, it should be pointed out that the Sanctuary
itself, and the Temple later on, were viewed as a necessary way of diverting
attention of the Israelites away from idolatry. This occurred only after the
transgression of the Golden Calf, according to this point of view. However, in
his book of laws (*Mishneh Torah*), Maimonides states plainly that the Temple
will be restored and animal sacrifices will be reinstituted in the messianic era.

Dr. Georges Hansel (the son-in-law of Emmanuel Levinas) observes that
"sacrifices belong to religious traditions of all people, but always within the
framework of idolatry. In addition, they were frequently associated with super-
stitions, degrading practices, debauchery or violence" (Hansel, lecture given in
Paris). What Hansel does not focus on are possible psychotherapeutic uses to
which the sacrifices may have contributed. For example, the unintentional guilt
offering called the *asham tuluy* is an offering brought when one had a doubt
about whether or not one had transgressed. Rather than leaving such doubt as
an animating part of the human psyche, it was dealt with by bringing a sacrifice
to the Sanctuary. All sacrifices were accompanied by a verbal acknowledgement
that one had unwittingly, or may have, transgressed. This kind of practice kept
the future for an individual more open and more promising than it might have
been otherwise. It did so by dealing with the matter of guilt feelings directly and
therefore may well have kept individuals from turning their doubts into anger
against themselves or toward others. However, in no cases could the sacrifices
be brought to absolve an intentional transgression. These sacrifices, despite their
diversity of purpose, in no way could nullify the transgression of one person
against another. The reparations had to be made between people and the sacrifices were not used as a substitute for just relations with others.

This may then be viewed as a kind of vicarious way of expunging guilt feelings and other distorted human emotions. Feeling guilty may well be quite different from being guilty. The kind of guilt that exists from improper exploitation of other people can be repaired only by restitution. The clear recognition of the difference between guilt and guilt feelings recognizes that there is a moral order that one may have transgressed. Hirsch adds a more positive dimension to the understanding of some of the sacrifices. He gives the example of the offering made in the morning and toward evening, the *korban tamid*. Hirsch insists that this involves a quickening of the human spirit by renewing the sense of human creativity, morning and evening. To clarify, what Hirsch appears to be arguing for is that each morning it is as though time begins anew. What stands in the way of this creativity is a stymied and leaden past of arrested development. Or, from an ethical point of view, it deals with rectifying the conditions of somnolence, an absence of vigilance, and a refusal of responsibility. It is in this way that the individual and the community are called toward their responsibilities.

The purposes of sacrifice range from the rectification of guilt (whether intentional or not), repentance for sin, the rejoicing connected with thanksgiving, and the appreciation expressed for peace between people. In fact, most sacrifices are eaten. There is no more reason, then, for any nonvegetarian to object to the sacrifices than to the eating of a hamburger. Still, all that we know of the sacrifices, as Hansel points out, is not yet enough to reach their existential significance (Hansel, lecture). In other words, we know how the procedure was done, but there are holes in our understanding that do not permit us to grasp the larger issue of why they were done.

Keep in mind that all the sacrifices belong within the realm of those laws that are classified as *chukkim*—that is, the laws for which no reasons are specifically given or are easily adduced. Nonetheless, this does not free us from the obligation of trying to understand them. Some reasons are more visible than others. For example, a guilt offering for theft must be preceded by a rectification for that which was stolen. This means that even in the case where there is no proof, the defendant must return the money that was taken plus one-fifth, and bring a guilt offering, even if this transgression is inadvertent (Stone, 566). This also involves matters of cheating in business, especially concerning wages withheld from workers. The material reparations given to the neighbor who has been wronged are essential to the sacrifice. What this shows, more visibly in some cases than others, is that the sacrifices do have an ethical dimension.

Levinas argues, though not without critics, that I have a greater responsibility toward the other person than he or she has toward me. We see this in the very beginning of Vayikra when G'd calls to Moses in the first sentence. The aleph at the end of the word *Vayikrah* is conspicuously small. This is something that every child on the verge of school age learns to recognize. In the context of Levinas's theories, which are consistent with the tradition, this refers to the extraordinary humility that is associated with Moses. This humility is not to be confused with self-abasement. On the contrary, it is Moses who recognizes his supreme responsibility for all of Israel. A parallel to this can be found in the Book of Samuel when Saul, a visibly large man, tries out of perhaps a misguided humility to hide in the back of a baggage train: Samuel says to Saul, "Though you may be small in your own eyes, are you not king over Israel?" (Samuel I 10:22). Recall that Levinas emphasizes the asymmetrical relation between the other and the self, where the other comes first.[3]

---

3   The late American philosopher John Wild, who wrote the Introduction to the English edition of *Totality and Infinity*, first raised the question by stating that the reader "may wonder about the strange asymmetry, the complete supremacy of the other, that the author (Levinas) finds in the self-other relation" (TI 1969, 19).

SPEECH IN THE IMPERATIVE MODE

Tzav: Command
(Leviticus 6:1–8:36)

> Command Aaron and his sons, saying: this is the law of the elevation-offering.
>
> —Leviticus 6:2

> Plato says that ... no leader proposes or orders what is useful for himself, but what is useful for the one he commands.[4]
>
> —Levinas, *Collective Philosophical Papers*

The word *tzav* means "command," as in the verse "Command Aaron and his sons, saying: this is the law of the elevation-offering" (Lev. 6:2). The imperative mode of discourse, as previously discussed, is frequently associated with the sense of force or coercion. As such, it runs contrary to our sense of human freedom. Since the Commandments are by definition prescriptive and written in the imperative mode, the greatest modern critics of religion (monotheism in particular) are joined in their disparate critiques by what they together hold as the assault on human freedom. Each of these critics—Marx, Nietzsche, and Freud—are troubled by the apparent way that religions limit and delude human societies and individuals.[5]

---

4 Emmanuel Levinas, *Collective Philosophical Papers*, 15, citing *Plato Republic*, 412–21c.

5 We have neither wish nor desire to detail these critiques, as they are in general well known. However, it is important to point out some of their salient features, especially with an eye toward showing how the tradition of Scripture anticipates and responds to them. Freud affirms that religion is man's "oldest collective obsessional neurosis." At base, Freud believes that we live in an utterly insecure world and that the origins and maintenance of religion

The critique by Nietzsche is perhaps the most compelling and the most difficult to answer. Nietzsche's critique, often confused with his slogan "God is dead," is based on the ancient Greek idea that the human being is capable of being a great god. By this, Nietzsche does not mean that human beings are literally capable of immortality, omniscience, or omnipotence; rather, he believes that the "great-souled man" is the exception to all moral rules and conventions. It is in this way that he, through the self-assertion of the will, becomes a figure who frees himself from a religious morality born out of *ressentiment*. *Ressentiment* results in the devaluing of the source of all human suffering when it cannot be directly avenged. It turns inward against itself when the self remains unaware of what is happening, and therefore posits humility as a virtue. For Nietzsche as well as the Greeks, it is simply the absence of power. Religion, therefore, is the ultimate rationalization and the artificial limitation placed upon human freedom.[6]

---

derive from the self-willed delusion that we superimpose a kind of order, and therefore security, when in fact the natural universe offers us neither. Marx locates the origins of religion in a conscious attempt by the ruling class to impose its will by aggregating to itself wealth in the forms of property and power, relying on the naïve assumption that this is in fact an expression of the order of nature.

6   Just by way of a brief response, it is clear that there is a way in which the first two critics, Freud and Marx, collide with each other. Let us begin with Marx. We have already seen how the Book of the Exodus anticipates and goes beyond Marx's critique of human freedom. As Michael Walzer observes in his book *Exodus and Revolution*, the Exodus already serves as a "paradigm of revolution." All of the basic forces that govern the outgoing from Egypt begin with the recognition of the material conditions of oppression: from the economic, to the psychological, to the political. Each form of oppression, as the reader will recall, has been overcome and transformed into a kind of freedom, resulting neither in tyranny nor anarchy. Marx would have done well to pay more attention to those "miserable Sabbath observing Jews in Jerusalem," who he derides in his essay "On the Jewish Question." For those Jews, the Exodus is recalled each Sabbath and every morning and night. This is before the six-day work week was established. Long before the advent of trade unions, the Israelites already had their own "union" that placed a limit upon labor and therefore oppression.

What bothers Marx, Freud, and Nietzsche is the willingness to accept the imperative mode of discourse and what it presumably implies: forced submission to arbitrary or self-interested directives. Contrary to Freud, the biblical order of meaning is closely associated with the creative capacity of human beings. G'd is not understood as a mere projection onto a neutral nature. Rather, it is the human being who, from Genesis on, is described as a creature and, therefore, created. In fact, according to a creative midrash on the statement from Genesis: "And God said, 'Let us make man in our own image and our own likeness,'" (Gen. 1:26). Rather than *us* referring to the angels or heavenly court, this can be reasonably

So, what then can we conclude about the nature of the command? Levinas, as he does elsewhere, sees "the command" of our primary experience before it becomes expressed in the form of a commandment. He puts it this way: "We must impose command on ourselves in order to be free. But it must be an exterior command, not simply a rational law, not a categorical imperative, which is defenseless against tyranny; it must be an exterior law, a written law, armed with force against tyranny. Such are commands as the political condition for freedom" (CPP 1987, 17).

Levinas makes, as we see, a sharp distinction between the sacred and the holy that eludes Nietzsche. The sacred belongs to Same, to the ontology of power. Holiness, on the contrary, pertains to that which is other, separate, or unique. To Levinas, it is the other who is the exception, always—not the self. In this way, the self bears responsibility for the other without diminishing his or her freedom. Morality is not, as it is for Nietzsche, merely its own history expressing and asserting itself. Rather, all directives come ultimately from the

---

understood as an invocation to a co-creation by G'd and human beings together. This is to say that humans are co-responsible for their own paths. Of course, this is meant figuratively.

Freud does not explain his theory of projection. In other words, why is it that we are willing to accept that God is a projection and that Freud's theories are not governed by his own wishes and fears? Still, we are not saying that Freud is lacking in insight into certain religious phenomena. Neither would we claim that Marx does not give a powerful description to human oppression, alienation, and the conditions under which human beings labor. For example, Freud can give us a better idea of how to interpret the dreams of the biblical Jacob and Joseph than perhaps anyone else. On the other hand, Marx would have understood that people who are starving would be more likely to dream about food than about political theory. The biblical Joseph, as we have seen, anticipates a just response to ruling Egypt in such a manner as to avoid mass starvation. In this way, Joseph disputes Marx's hypothesis that religion aims at buttressing the ruling political regime.

Nietzsche has it in for the priestly class but perhaps is the first modern to begin to understand the power that they wield. He remains largely unimpressed by biblical morality. The motive-force for religion arises out of misplaced humility and guilt that culminates in terror. On the other hand, Nietzsche understands that one of the few ways in which a powerless people can become powerful is through an intricate form of rationalization that connects psychology to politics. Nietzsche does not care for the attribute of humility, comparing it to a worm that doubles up in order to avoid having to be stepped on. Only the Sacred is an ultimate expression of power. The priestly class has a virtual monopoly on sacrality, and others are therefore beholden to them and must practice a certain humility in their presence. All of this, for Nietzsche, is an excuse or rationalization on the part of the priestly class for the arbitrary expression of power, for the sacred is itself utterly arbitrary.

other, and therefore, the imperative mode of discourse becomes one not of force, but of urgency and intimacy.

What is lacking in Nietzsche's thought is the thorough investigation into the relation between the imperative and declarative modes of discourse. A thorough phenomenological investigation of this kind, not possible here, would show as Levinas does, that the imperative mode of discourse precedes the declarative, and that in this same way, the notion of command comes before the idea of freedom. This is because, for Levinas, the command always issues from the face of the other toward me. It is something that can be taken up and responded to, or it can be refused. It can be refused by simply looking away. At the very core of the Western philosophical idea of freedom is, according to Levinas, the notion of spontaneity (TI 1969, 45). While spontaneity is praised in the behavior of young children and the works of artists and poets, Levinas links it to arbitrariness and capriciousness, and he finds it to be essentially egoist. At a deeper level, spontaneity is the self-assertion of the Will. It may be creative, amusing, and reflect a sense of dynamism. At the same time, however, naïve spontaneity is at best knowingly indifferent to the claims of the other person. In this way, it reflects an existential dogmatism that is at odds with ethical life because it arrogates to the self a dominion or sovereignty that may be practiced or expressed willfully at the expense of the other. Nietzsche, we believe, understands this better than either Marx or Freud. However, unlike Levinas, he approves of this position. Levinas objects:

> A calling into question of the same—which cannot occur within the egoist spontaneity of the same—is brought about by the other. *We name this calling into question of my spontaneity by the presence of the other ethics.* The strangeness of the Other, His irreducibility to the I, to my thoughts and my possessions, is precisely accomplished as a calling into question of my spontaneity as ethics. (Ibid., 43, my emphasis)

The imperative mode of discourse may also connote a sense of urgency and importance. The Talmud informs us that "[w]herever the Torah uses the word *tsav* ... it indicates three points: a) urging on, b) that the matter must be done immediately, and c) that it also must be performed by future generations" (Talmud Kiddushin 29a). The word concept *mitzvah* is founded on the phenomenon of attachment. What must be done with alacrity are the *mitzvot*. In the case before us, these mitzvot pertain to the Sanctuary.

Corresponding to the imperative mode of discourse is the interrogative mode. It is this responsiveness to the interrogative "when?" that is lacking in most of Western ethical or moral philosophy. Levinas attempts to remedy this limitation by inserting philosophical questioning into a temporal horizon.[7]

It is this sense of urgency that is one of the defining hallmarks of the philosophy of Levinas. Urgency, in turn, reveals to us what is important at any given time and, perhaps, what is most important. One of the reasons for the continuing engagement with the thought of Levinas is, as Richard Cohen puts it, "that he raises the phenomenon of the importance of importance itself." [8]The concept of urgency is associated with the positive attribute of alacrity, in relation to another person or in relation to a task to be performed. At another philosophical level, this involves a way of measuring time as it originates from the other person. On the surface, it would not seem that keeping the fire burning on the altar and cleaning out its ashes, would fall under such a command. Yet, it is perhaps for this very reason of human inertia that the word concept *tzav* is used. Levinas remarks on the overcoming of this kind of inertia in the Torah: "and the way that leads to man draws us back to ritual discipline and self-education. Its greatness lies in its daily regularity" (DF 1990, 18).

The attachment to ritual life expresses itself most visibly in the commandments that make up the body of Jewish laws. In a more general manner, the *mitzvot* are the prescriptive modes of conduct to which we are to attach ourselves. As John Bowlby, the eminent British psychoanalyst has explained, it is illuminating to view our lives in terms of the people, places, and practices to which we become attached.[9] For example, the most intense experiences of joy, affection, and mourning are expressed in relation to those who are closest to us. It is with people who are our familiars, or people whom we care most deeply for, that we are inclined to use the imperative mode of discourse. We trust that they will understand what we mean by a single word or gesture, without elaboration. Before the attachment to specific modes of conduct, there is a prior attachment that is presupposed. As we intensify in our attachments to people, places, or things, we become more devoted to them. This devotion sometimes

---

7   In this way he differs from Immanuel Kant. Kant's moral philosophy is basically a formalism. Consider, for example, the two formulations of the categorical imperative: (1) treat others as an end in themselves, rather than a means to an end, or (2) act as though what you are doing can be done by everyone. This is exhortatory, but it lacks a sense of urgency.

8   Richard A. Cohen, "Biblical Humanism and Its Relevance to the Humanities," March 7, 2000 at University of Vermont colloquium on "Levinas and the Humanities," published in *Phenomenological Inquiry*, vol. 24, October, 2000 (Belmont, MA).

9   See John Bowlby's trilogy, *Attachment and Loss*, 1980 (London: Hogarth Press).

lacks the distance necessary for critical self-detachment. "De-tachment" is the way by which we absolve our relations to those close, if even for a moment.

The ritual conduct associated with the many kinds of sacrifices spoken about in this portion of the Torah are most often associated with psychological states, which may or may not have objective correlatives. Guilt offerings may be doubtful or certain. The doubtful offering implies that atonement will be given because the transgression was unintentional and perhaps unknown to the transgressor. In order to assuage the doubts that are at the origins of the feeling of guilt, the penitent brings what is called "a guilt offering" (*asham tuily*). This is a very clear and expedient way of unburdening himself from his guilt feelings. In this case, we are dealing with a ritual that is very much involved in the psychology of everyday life.

ON RITUAL

One of the most difficult things for us to fathom or accept is the repetition of practices that can appear empty or tiresome. Such is the case with mindless ritual. Even when we are self-critically aware of what it is that we are doing repeatedly, we must reflect upon the meaning of what we are doing in ritual and practice in both the biblical and contemporary Jewish worlds. One of the first essays that Levinas wrote on Judaism—in 1937—contains an extraordinary meditation on the nature of ritual. Levinas begins by saying, "Ritual everywhere mediates between us and reality" (Malka, 242). Levinas goes on to explain that one of the effects of ritual is to make us pause in what we are saying or doing. He puts it this way: "Everything occurs as if he had not entered the world on the same footing which has offered itself to him; as if, in a world where techniques open up pathways without resistance, ritual constantly marks a time for stopping, as if to momentarily interrupt the current that constantly binds us to things" (Malka, 242–43). This happens, as Levinas points out, when we pause before eating to make a blessing, or upon entering the home, to touch or kiss a mezuzah.

This already shows that ritual interrupts our feeling of being at home in the world. This is because, as Levinas says, "to the practicing Jew, the world never appears as a natural thing" (Malka, 243). He goes on to remark on the way that "there is something infinitely surprising for him. It strikes him as a miracle. He experiences continual wonderment at the simple yet extraordinary fact that the world is there" (Ibid., 243). This reflection is worth keeping in mind as we proceed through some of the more dense and unfamiliar practices pertaining to service related to the Tabernacle. Levinas sets himself the task of showing how the infinite breaks in upon the finite and therefore endows it with the promise of meaning.

In the spring of 2012, Dr. George Hansel presented a paper on Levinas. This essay, among other things, contests the notion that the sacrifices are meant to sublimate human violence, a notion advanced by René Girard and supported by Jonathan Sacks. Hansel correctly points out that "according to Talmudic tradition, the slaughter plays only a subordinate role in the performing of a sacrifice. Strictly speaking, the slaughter does not belong to the 'rite' or service (*avodah*) (BT, Zevachim, 14b). He goes on to remind us that

> actions involved in sacrifice have over time become strange to us. They no longer belong to our cultural environment, so that the access to their lived meaning is almost closed. The proof of it is the common mistake of placing special emphasis on the step of slaughter in the sacrifice procedure. In fact, according to the Talmudic Tradition, the slaughter plays only the role of a means, that is a subordinate role in the performing of a sacrifice. (Hansel, lecture)

As Hansel correctly points out, there are traces of the sacrifices that are still present. The table has replaced the altar. He notes, "Rabbi Yochanan and Rabbi Eleazar both explained that as long as the temple stood, the altar atoned for Israel, but now man's table atones for him" (BT, Berachot 54b).

Another trace that should not be forgotten is the phenomenon of what is called the *korban shelamim*, or the "peace offering." While there are various forms of the peace offering, one that remains of significance to this day is the thanksgiving offering, or the *korban todah*. This offering is voluntary and may be offered by men or women. Its purpose is a specific, or at times even general, reminder of personal familial gratitude on a specific occasion where one undergoes a kind of elevation that involves the giving of thanks for something. Examples include offerings after recovering from a serious illness or release from conditions of imprisonment or having been taken hostage: "Today the place of this offering has been taken by a prayer uttered in the Synagogue by someone who has survived a dangerous experience" (Stone, Lev. 7:11).

An offering that more perfectly symbolizes the trace, as Levinas describes it, is that of the Passover feast. Aspects of this are reenacted to commemorate the outgoing from Egypt (Exod. 12:8–11). "With unleavened bread and bitter herbs shall they eat it" (Ibid.). The matzah or unleavened bread is still eaten today as a reminder of the haste with which the Israelites left Egypt. The bitter herbs commemorate the lives of the Israelites as slaves in Egypt. However, the paschal lamb, *korban pesach,* can no longer be brought, sacrificed, and eaten in the absence of the Sanctuary or Temple. What is placed upon the Passover plate is a symbol that serves as a reminder, a shank bone. This, of course, is not directly illustrative of what was actually brought, but rather itself serves as a Trace of the absent past that cannot be completely filled in. In this way, the *korban pesach* more perfectly symbolizes the trace.

QUESTIONING, RESPONDING,
AND ANSWERING

Shemeni: Eighth[10]
(Leviticus 9:1–11:47)

We may ask questions about the manifestation of these things within what is said. But can we convert transcendence as such into answers without losing it in the process?

—LR 1989, 209

According to Tradition, the center of the Pentateuch, by word count of the entire Torah, is found in double expression, "Interrogate, Question" (*darosh, darash*) (Lev. 10:16),[11] or alternatively, inquire insistently. The *Chassidic* commentator Degel Machane Efraim (1748–1800) states that "this teaches us that the entire Torah revolves around constant inquiry; one must never stop studying and seeking an ever deeper and broader understanding of the Torah" (Stone, 596). To whom should we address our questions, especially if they refer to matters of Torah and Mitzvot as implied? The Torah portion, and immediate context of this statement, refers to an ambiguity about certain sacrifices that are to be brought in the Sanctuary, preceding the discussion of which animals are *kosher* to eat and which are not. However, the broader instruction clearly indicates that the kind of questioning that is associated with study is not mere preparation for study, but an integral part of an ongoing action.

---

10 It was on the eighth day that Aaron assumed responsibility for the Sanctuary from Moses.

11 "Most printed editions of the Pentateuch contain a Masoretic note that these words are exactly the halfway mark of the Torah" (Stone, 596n16).

All questioning asked with earnestness is not only in relation to the subject under investigation, but also about the one who asks—that is, self-questioning: "[T]he questioning is not to do with *one* particular question ... questioning is not interested in the object, but above all in the man who questions. I question, I mean: I question myself, I disturb myself. *Questioning is a movement where one is disturbed, but not for nothing*" (Ouaknin 1998, 179, my emphasis). In other words, the relation of the questioner to his question already anticipates the response that comes from outside—from the other person. My question assigns to me the burden of being answerable for the questions I ask, as well as the interrogation we undertake together. As Levinas puts it, "These questions concern the nature of the ultimate and put into question the rationality of reason, and the very possibility of the ultimate.... We may ask questions about the manifestation of these things within what is said (*le dit*). But can we convert transcendence as such into answers without losing it in the process?" (LR 1989, 209). Fittingly, Levinas concludes his inquiry on "Revelation in the Jewish Tradition" by asking: "And in the question, which also calls into question, do we not hear the true resonance of the voice commanding from beyond?" (Ibid., 209).

Here we open onto a multiplicity of readers, the time of whose conversation is across time. In the language of Levinas, this conversation is one of diachrony, meaning a time of discontinuity, with interruptions of give and take that begin with questions. The residue of this kind of conversation leaves questions that are expected to have been formed by the previous responses, and therefore elevated to a higher level. Elie Wiesel observes: "Questions unite people; answers divide them."[12]

When this kind of learning takes place in the House of Study, the discourse is frequently enacted in concert with a distinctive tone where one party can be heard going out from himself toward another. This is not to be confused with either chanting or ecstasy. Frequently, a wordless melody (a *niggun*) accompanies the speaking and listening and can serve to signal the welcoming of a third party.

We cannot, however, say that we are not aiming at an answer. What we have are provisional answers that punctuate the responses given to questions that invariably raise further questions. It should be stressed, however, that at no time are the laws themselves suspended before, during, or after inquiry. In this way, we may regard the laws as the steps to be taken or avoided while inquiry is underway. The applied laws (*halakah*) are in this way "answers"

---

12 Interview with Oprah Winfrey from the November 2000 issue of *O, The Oprah Magazine*.

marking the path of inquiry. There is an opening onto the future in such questioning-thinking. This would be like that opening moment Franz Rosenzweig refers to as "new thinking"—that is, "a speaking thinking."[13] After all, as Levinas says, this is "not a game." What Levinas means is that such "speaking-thinking" has a purpose even as I come upon it through overhearing my own responses to what is asked.

We learn for the sake of learning, but we also learn for the sake of doing. This is a direct continuation of the "na'ase v'nishma"—"we will do and we will understand" (Exod. 24:7). Is not doing before understanding contrary to logic? It does stand against the meaning of order announced in formal logic. There is, however, an order of meaning that arises in the traumatisms of everyday life. One of the central features that separates the biblical-prophetic tradition from that of Greek philosophy, and by this we mean philosophy from Plato to the present, is the fact that the Torah emphasizes the interrogative of "when" as opposed to "what."[14] There are certain instances where the exceptions are of such importance as to become the rule. For example, the recognition and honor of other human beings (*Kavod Habriot*) is not to be lightly regarded. We find that the law itself suspends its own rules in order not to cause the suffering of public shame or humiliation. To know when this is the case requires study. It means that we must inquire "insistently."

Why does the prescription "Inquire, Question" arise in the context that it does? This occurs just after the deaths of Nadav and Avihu. Aaron remains silent when Moses asks why Aaron and his remaining sons are refusing to eat a sacrifice brought to the sanctuary. Let us recall that whatever the cause, the text has described Nadav and Avihu, the first two sons of Aaron, as "offering a strange fire." Nadav and Avihu have experienced an unmediated contact with the Sacred. Among the various reasons given for the sudden deaths of Nadav and Avihu, the most generous appears to derive from Kabbalistic and Chassidic sources. In the language of Levinas, their transgression was one of "angelism." In "angelism," there would have been a desired 'out of body experience' in an attempt to elevate the soul. Human life is meant to be enacted with and for other people. What is commonly referred to as its "spiritual dimension," must be refracted through the lives that we live with others.

We do not wish to enter into a mystical discussion here. The commentaries on Aaron's sons who offered a strange fire and hence died, provoked much

---

13 Nahum Glatzer, *The Life and Thought of Franz Rosenzweig,* 1961 (Schocken), 190.

14 See the central question of virtually every Platonic dialogue (e.g., What is piety? What is love? What is justice?)

consternation and commentary on the part of the tradition. Were they intoxicated before offering a sacrifice, even though the punishment prohibiting the Kohanim from drinking wine was not mentioned until after this event? (MR, Shemini). Or was it for some other reason? The sacrifices, for the most part, were meant to be eaten. The priestly class (*Kohanim*), now being set aside, were to devote themselves exclusively to service in the holy sanctuary and could certainly have yielded the impression that there was a hard and fast separation of the material and spiritual realms. However, human beings, as Levinas expresses repeatedly, are not meant to be angels or even beautiful souls. They are utterly embodied beings whose very holiness is the surplus of ethical life.

Much of the Book of Genesis, as we note, deals with the stances taken towards one's destination before going or walking. This means that one must stand upright, in a moral as well as a physical stance. When Aaron learns of the death of his two sons, the commentary tradition notes, in keeping with the words of scripture, that he was silent. This silence was more than simply the absence of speech but the absence of expression. This absence of expression can be understood either as the ultimate expression of grief or its complete internalization. But he will not eat.

Moses subsequently chides Aaron, for the High Priest Kohen Gadol is distinguished by the fact that he is not allowed to engage in any act of mourning, not even for those most dear to him. Before the discussion of which animals are and are not kosher, Aaron holds his ground, and Moses learns from divine inspiration that his brother is right in not eating at this time. Is Aaron's silence, too, to be regarded as the ultimate nonresponse to a crisis that cannot be humanly reconciled? Is it not the cessation of questioning? Moses, who receives and teaches the Torah, is the one who questions incessantly. Aaron, who above all is noted for bringing peace between his fellows, assumes a kind of responsibility, or so it appears, that precedes and perhaps assumes an ultimate kind self-discipline in its apparent passivity in the face of the most terrible kind of news.

Let us keep in mind that Moses is called a "man of truth" (*Ish Emes*). *Emes*, the tradition reminds us, is consistent through and through. The letters are formed from the first, last, and middle letters of the Hebrew alphabet. Aaron, on the other hand, is called a "man of kindness"—an *Ish Chesed*. The careful reader cannot help but notice that truth and kindness, though not necessarily contradictory, are often contrary and therefore in tension with one another. Kindness involves a generosity that may not be warranted from the standpoint of a third party. Nonetheless, this expansive attribute, because it is associated with achieving peace, is found both before and after speaking of and/or enacting truth. In this sense, kindness has an ethical and metaphysical priority over truth.

Subsequently, when Aaron dies, it says that the whole of Israel, meaning the men and the women, mourned for him. For Moses, it says the men of Israel mourned for him. Why? Because Aaron sought to make peace between a man and his wife as well as between a person and his or her neighbor.

When we examine the dietary laws, Maimonides reminds us that these laws are rational: "I maintain that the food, which is forbidden by the Law is unwholesome" (GFP 1956, 370). Maimonides qualifies his position, however, by noting that there is also a component to the dietary laws grounded in the fact that they are divinely commanded. We do know that, among those birds that are forbidden, there are those that are considered particularly unkind to the point of being predators. Rashi takes up the example of the stork. There is some dispute about whether the stork (*chasidah*) is kosher—that is, permissible. Rashi asks why it is called by the Hebrew name that derives from the root word for kindness (*chesed*). If so, why then would it be classified as a non-kosher bird? One response is that this is because "it directs its kindness exclusively towards its own, but will not help other species" (*Rizhiner Rebbe*, Stone, 601). Is this understood, then, as a less than ideal example for people who would consume such a bird? In the language of Levinas, the stork is unable or unwilling to practice a kind of justice toward the third party, even if the third party is another bird.[15]

In a late book of extraordinary interviews entitled *Is It Righteous to Be,* Levinas regards Hamlet's question "to be or not to be?" as an ontological question that is morally derivative. While it may be the case that everything we do is practiced at the expense of another creature, this does not sanction our own refusal to live, and not simply that, but to live righteously. The *conatus essendi*—the effort to persevere in being—is only unworthy when it becomes a mere end in itself. When it is made righteous, it is for the sake of performing kindness to others.

---

15 One of the most puzzling aspects about kosher animals is that an animal cannot be eaten if it "dies of itself" (*nevelah*). Why should this be the case when it can be ascertained that, in fact, the animal would otherwise be permissible, and that it can be established to be healthy in all other aspect? For example, if a veterinarian sees a deer stumble and crash into a tree, thus killing itself, and can after the fact prove that the deer did not suffer from any disease, he or she may still not eat it. Why not? If our reasons for not eating meat were to be purely ethical, then this would seem to be a key exception. And yet, we are permitted to eat meat of animals that are permissible as long as we take responsibility for the violence that accompanies even the most humane kind of slaughtering. After all, we are eating the animal rather than the other way around. We are also certainly not allowed to practice cruelty toward animals—to cause them unnecessary suffering of any kind. This extends to the dubious practice of force-feeding animals for the purpose of consumption.

Even the last act of kindness, which is the burying of the dead, is referred to in Hebrew as "kindness-in-truth" (*chesed shel emes*). Why is burying the dead something that even the high priest must do when there is no one else to do it, at the risk of making himself impure and unable to preside over the holiest service of the year—the Yom Kippur atonement service? He is obligated by the mitzvah to bury the dead when no one else has happened upon a dead body. The sages say it is a kindness that truly cannot be repaid by the one for whom the kindness is practiced.

What if insistent inquiry does not yield ready responses or conclusive answers? Levinas argues in a famous essay "To Love the Torah More Than God," a searing reflection on the Holocaust, that the Torah itself provides the only framework for asking the questions that may have no ready or apparent answers. Fidelity to the teachings of the Torah does not suggest an acquiescence to the meaningless suffering of millions of others during this time of apparent abandonment. However, such "useless suffering," or the "suffering of others," as Levinas calls them, are magnified when measured against the ethical expectations of the teaching of the Torah. In this way, we are always giving responses to the questions that are asked of us by the way in which we comport ourselves. This does not mean that we have an answer for such ultimate questions. What it does mean is that we continue to dwell in the expectation of justice even when it seems too belated. This is, according to Levinas, the price for moral autonomy and, as he says, "of a Creator, against whom we can rebel and for whose namesake we can also perish." What is forbidden is not for me to try to rationalize my own sufferings, but rather to incorporate the sufferings of others into some divine plan that I presumably understand and, therefore, out of my ignorance, superimpose upon others.

For Levinas, it is not a matter of faith overcoming doubt. This dialectic dominates much of contemporary post-Holocaust theological literature, and appears to be filtered through onto-theology, often foreign to rabbinic Judaism. Levinas takes rather a more classical rabbinic approach, where learning Talmud and Torah is the very activity in which questions are asked, and in which answers and responses are given. The Torah in fact, for Levinas, "is a protection against the madness of a direct contact with the Sacred that is unmediated by reason" (DF 1990, 144).

Before questioning becomes conceptual or thematic, we are confronted with the traumatisms of everyday existence. It is out of these experiences, according to Levinas, that philosophy arises. When asked the question, "How does one begin thinking?" (EI 1985, 21), Levinas responds, "It probably begins through traumatisms or gropings to which one does not even know how to give a verbal form: a separation, a violent scene, a sudden consciousness of the monotony of time" (Ibid., 21). It is in this sense that Levinas suggests that we learn to care for others and for ourselves "without succumbing, however, to the good intentions of beautiful souls, or to the normative idealism of what 'must be.' In this sense the Bible would be for me the book par excellence" (Ibid., 22).

The "meaning of life," then, as we are inclined to call it, is not resolved for us in advance by formulae or plans, which would make G'd into a mathematician or engineer. This would reduce human beings to a set of equations or blueprints and not to a life of flesh and blood. Where then, do we go for answers? For Levinas, it depends on the kinds of questions that we are asking. Ultimately, especially when the Trace of the Divine appears absent, as it did during that terrible period between 1933 and 1945, we have as he says, "a morality which can, however, for its part only know and justify itself in the fragility of the conscience. In the 'four cubits of the *Halakah*,' in that precarious divine abode" (PN 1996, 123).

This *halakah*, while it always bears a prescription, brings with it an expectation in its fulfillment even the possibility of disappointment. Nonetheless, its logic is to be determined in the interpersonal realm, where it is spoken, questioned, and answered. It is situated within and without the questions that pertain to meaningfulness in the infinite conversation that binds listener to speaker and one generation to the next. We cannot simply devalue this as mere narrative accompanied by essential laws or suggest that the aggadic dimensions of the Talmud or the midrashic portions of the Torah, to which Levinas addresses himself, are in any way of lesser importance. For surely, human beings are responsible for the "answers they give," and this responsibility itself is reiterated as an ongoing literature of "*responsa*" to life's ordeals.

To inquire insistently does not mean that there are no resting places. When we speak of answering, we are answering for ourselves in relation to the exigent demands of life. Sometimes the answers in a specific context in relation to the law cannot be expanded to other circumstances. In this way, the halakah represents the steps taken where paths diverge on life's way. These may be considered answers, but only in a provisional sense. For after answering, there is responding to and for the other person. This kind of responding is the way that responsibility is lived out. For this reason, we are responsible both for the questions that we ask of others and for the unspoken questions that are asked of us.

THE SKIN OF OTHERS

Tazria: Skin Disease
(Leviticus 12–13)

This and the next Torah portion deal with a skin disease akin to leprosy. While it is still frequently translated as leprosy, R'Hirsch makes a compelling case that this cannot medically be leprosy as it is currently understood. According to Hirsch, not only are the symptoms significantly different from those of leprosy, but the confinement of the metzora (the diseased person) is not consistent with what is commonly thought of as quarantine. Nonetheless, the persons afflicted suffer a kind of isolation that is not so very different from those who are described in the language of our day as "suffering from leprosy." According to the commentary tradition, this disease as such no longer exists in the absence of the Sanctuary or Temple (*mishkan*). This illness is referred to by Scripture as "tazria," while the person who suffers from it is called a "metzora." These two portions are often read together, hence the name of the double portion tazria-metzora.

The difference between leprosy and tazria is not simply a matter of terminology. Similar, if not more important, is the distinction in the use of the Hebrew words for "pure" (*tahor*) and "impure" (*tamei*). For, as Hirsch also notes, the Hebrew, often translated as "clean" and "unclean," might easily be confused with the language of hygiene. This, however, is most emphatically not the case. The example that the Talmud gives to demonstrate that this is neither a matter of hygiene nor contagion is made clear from the fact that

> if the symptons of tazria appear on a newlywed or during a festival season, the Kohen does not examine the affliction or declare it to be tamei (impure) in order not to interfere with the celebration ... if the purpose of these laws is to prevent the spread of disease it would be imperative to enforce the laws at times of great overcrowding and mingling![16]

---

16 Interlinear Chumash, edited by Rabbi Menachem Davis, Mesorah Publications.

Hirsch underscores the fact that the physical ailments derive from a turning away from moral life, however temporary.

By regularly searching for the moral dimension of those commandments that appear to be suprarational, Hirsch anticipates and is perhaps closer to the thinking of Emmanuel Levinas than any other commentator within the tradition. While Hirsch first names slanderous speech, he does not see it as the only cause of the blemishes affecting the metzora. He also lists the "shedding of blood, perjury, sexual immorality, arrogance, robbery, and stinginess" (Hirsch, vol. 3, 421–22). These sources are taken directly from the Talmudic tractate *Arachin 16a*. All of these transgressions are associated with negative attributes and have a moral as well as a social dimension. The most common theme stressed in our generation is that of "bad speech" or gossip, which generally translates to language used to hurt or ostracize others: "*loshon hara.*" *Motze shem ra*, "slanderous speech," is considered an especially grievous form of loshon hara because it effaces the name of the injured party and thereby puts him or her *outside* of the social sphere.

Why the skin, and why specifically is it the face that suffers blemish? As we have stressed repeatedly, Levinas's reflections on the human face are one of the central features of his philosophy. The face is the most vulnerable aspect of the human being. It is the source of all human expression. Meaning arises and is confirmed in the facial expression of the other. In this sense, the face is the source of all signification. There is nothing more naked for Levinas than the human face. The other person's facial expression lets us know if we have made ourselves understood, and in turn gives us our first indication of how it is that we face other people in the human world.

Shame appears first as a reddening face. The rabbinic tradition states it is necessary to go to great lengths not to shame another person. This is more emphatic when it comes to shaming another person publicly. Such humiliation visited upon the other publicly diminishes the implied social covenant. The Talmud likens this to the shedding of innocent blood (BT, Bava Metzia 59a). Why is this the case? Because just as the face of another person reddens upon being shamed, so too is it likened to shedding the blood of another.[17]

Levinas accords an important place to the phenomenon of skin, particularly contact with the skin. "The skin caressed is not the protection of an organism, simply the surface of an entity; it is the divergence between the visible

---

17 According to the Talmud, the Second Temple was destroyed because of the shaming of one person by another at a public banquet. This is regarded as an act of baseless hatred (BT, Gittin 55b–56b).

and the invisible, quasi-transparent, thinner than that would still justify an expression of the invisible by the visible" (OBBE 1991, 89–90). What Levinas appears to be saying is that the skin represents the closest contact between the visible and the invisible, where the animating intentions of the psyche can virtually be shared. For Levinas, it is on the surface of the other person's face that the Infinite appears. This is what first cautions me against doing him or her harm or violence. For the person who engages in "speech that is not good" (lashon hara) or variations of this, the trace of the Infinite upon the other's face contracts to the vanishing point from my perspective. This is how I can treat the other person as a natural object rather than a human creature.

Let us keep in mind that for Levinas, face-to-face relation allows the trace of the Infinite to appear on the face of the other person. This is the metaphysical condition for the ethical enacting of genuine or ethical speech. The face of the other pierces my own skin. It turns me around to face the other rather than looking away from him or her. Hence, the biblical expression "his face was not to him as before." When I devalue the face of the other person, I separate him or her off at the level of his skin. Is this not why we have such expressions as "not being able to put yourself in another person's skin?" We also speak of a person who is ill at ease as "not being comfortable in his own skin."

According to J.B. Soloveitchik, there are three general categories and causes that the sages see regarding the afflictions of tzaraas and three stages of depravation. The three causes are derogatory speech (lashon hara), envy (eiyin hara), and bloodshed (shfichas damim).[18] The impenetrable mysteries of this condition and its progression as well as its rehabilitation are, for the most part, closed to us as contemporary readers. According to R' Nachman of Breslov, the fact that the kohen was responsible for both diagnosis and quarantine was based upon the fact that the kohen represented the trait of kindness or chesed. This is the opposite of the conduct shown by the afflicted one. As Nachman says, "Ve-hisgir" (he will quarantine) literally means "he will close up." When a person manifests kindness in the world, he "closes up"—(i.e., heals)—all illness and attains healing for all wounds" (Rebbe Nachman's Torah, Likutei Moharan, vol. 2, 339).

Closed up in himself, the transgressor may be unaware of his transgression. The severity of the blemishes and lesions of the skin progress to that of clothing and, lastly, to the house. The reverse progression occurs upon reaching the land of Canaan? Hirsch gives us a clue, suggesting that such a person "thinks that

---

18 Darosh Darash Yosef citing Babylonian Talmud, Arachin, 16a, 227.

his house is meant exclusively for himself; he does not want to lend his posses-sions and says that he does not have the article requested" (Hirsch, Leviticus 12–13). This shows that he does not regard his house to be a home where the other is welcome. In this way, he wishes to remain an isolated monadic self. He has fallen from what Levinas calls the "ethical subject." For these reasons, the transgressor must understand his or her relation to others in a new way where the other can come *before* the self. The rehabilitation, then, may begin, but does not end in his or her confinement. This, rather, is the beginning.

He or she may be viewed as though oblivious to the neighbor's economic situation or social standing, making him or her careless in his speech or conduct and leading him or her to disparage the neighbor. The second stage occurs when the identifying marks of tzaraas appear upon the garments. This can be meaningfully interpreted as a disregard for the neighbor's social situation and standing. In other words, he or she has been incapable of understanding the neighbor's economic insecurity and lack of social standing. When his or her lack of attentiveness expresses a total lack of empathy, it is the very skin that is afflicted. He or she must then go to the Kohen to receive a disinterested diag-nosis, for the Kohen embodies the holiness of purity and can therefore recognize its degradation with acute clarity. In the language of Levinas, the transgressor cannot auto-diagnose, but must instead subject him-herself to the other. After a temporary exile from the camp of the Israelites, the process is reversed. He or she cannot declare himself well or "pure" until he is scrutinized by the other— the Kohen. Still, we may ask what the skin and its vulnerability have to teach us.

The skin expresses both an exposure and protection of the body, especially the face. As Levinas puts it: "The tenderness of skin is the very gap between approach and approached; a disparity, a non-intentionality, a non-teleology" (OBBE 1991, 90). What is the connection, then, between the face and the skin? Under common conditions, when we call to mind another person, such as a friend, we see and hear three phenomena: the face, the voice, and the other person calling me by name. All of these are signs of proximity by which I am approached and through which I approach the other person. It is not merely the case that the skin frames the face. Levinas states that "proximity, immediacy, is to enjoy and to suffer by the other. But I can enjoy and suffer only because I am for-the-other, am signification, because the contact with skin is still a proximity of a face, a responsibility, an obsession with the other" (Ibid.).

It is because the afflicted one refused to accept responsibility for the other, and through arrogance allowed the one for the other to devolve into the each against each, that the very fragile form of his humanity is scarred. However, the scarring is said to be temporary and in need of rehabilitation. This means a full restoration to wholeness of body and mind on the part of the one who previously transgressed.

FROM ONE'S OWN SKIN TOWARD THE SKIN OF OTHERS (EXCURSUS ON JOB)

The biblical Job is likely the best-known case of an individual thought to be afflicted by something akin to biblical leprosy in the entire Hebrew Bible.[19] The case of Job is perplexing because G'd testifies in the prologue to his righteousness: "Hast thou considered my servant Job, that there is none like him in the earth, a perfect and upright man" (Job 1:8). Only when the matter touches him personally with the affliction of his body does he give one of the most powerful and poignant laments in literature.

Despite his loss of property, home, and finally children, the biblical Job does not distance himself from human society or cry out in complaint until he is visited with the affliction in his skin. It is not until the adversary is given permission to afflict Job that he cries out, " 'Skin for skin! Whatever a man has he would give up for his life. But send forth your hand and touch his bone and his flesh and surely he will blaspheme you to your face," (Job 2:4–5). Even at the moment of Job's bodily affliction, Job states, " 'Shall we accept the good from God and not accept the bad?' For all this Job did not sin with his lips" (Job 2:9). Apparently, this signifies that Job's complaint remained unnoticed. It is shortly after this that Job sits on his ash heap for seven days and seven nights in mourning and begins to lament his coming into the world. Does this express a subtle egoism on the part of Job, seeing that he mourns for himself not when he has lost his flocks, servants, home, and children, but the recognizable form of his appearance? Or does this tell us something about the nature of embodied subjectivity and its connection to the phenomenon of the skin?

Levinas gives us a clue in his elaboration on the phenomenon of the skin: "It is a thinness already reduced to the alternating of sense, the ambiguity of a phenomenon and its defect, poverty exposed in the formless, and withdrawn from this absolute exposure in a shame for its poverty" (OBBE 1991, 90). In the

---

19 The other most prominent case is that of Miriam, the sister of Moses and Aaron who suffers for a week for speaking against Moses. Since it is in the merit of Miriam that the well of living water is said to have accompanied the Israelites, Moses intercedes with God and the people accordingly wait a week for Miriam to be healed.

case of Job, he was aware that his friends who had come to comfort him had difficulty not only recognizing his outward figure but his human form, as well. They mourn with Job in silence for seven days and nights on an ash heap. When Levinas speaks about the exposure of the skin, is this not the first threshold through which suffering passes and pleasure can be experienced? Job's agony, which causes him to cry out, should not be devalued as "lightly physical." What he learns throughout the course of his excruciating education is to place himself in "the skin of the other." After much give and take with his friends, who do not comfort him, Job later complains on behalf of the apparent injustice visited upon other people as well. Never does he doubt G'd's existence, a more modern phenomenon. Rather, he doubts G'd's justice.

In the twenty-fourth chapter, the reader can see a marked change in Job's position. He speaks on behalf of the apparently uncompensated suffering of orphans and widows and the poor. He says, "They carry off the donkey of orphans; they exact the ox of a widow as collateral. They steer the needy off the road; together the poor of the land go into hiding ... they reap produce in the field; the wicked denude the vineyard" (Job 24:3–6). Job shows himself to have moved from self-feeling to feeling for the most vulnerable. This also appears to show that he is familiar with the ways of righteousness and that which is clearly prohibited. He goes on: "[T]hey let the naked spend the night unclothed, without a garment against the cold ... they take collateral off the backs of the poor ... they carry away a sheaf from the hungry" (Job 24:7–10). Nonetheless, Job complains that the transgressors are not singled out for guilt: "From the city the populous groans and the souls of the slain cry out but G'd does not lay guilt!" (Job 24:12). Is Job, then, to be understood as beginning to intercede on behalf of the most oppressed and vulnerable?

He goes on to question why this situation is not made right. He has not given up on the idea of justice or of a judge. In fact, he almost begins to speak as one of his friends, but in the future, rather than the present tense. Still, Job does not yet recognize his own irrecusable responsibility for the sufferings of others however inadvertently he may have contributed to them. It is not until the end of the whirlwind speech, chapter 38, that Job confesses his inadequacies. It is not simply a matter of Job having been overpowered by G'd. Job understands that divine responsibility exceeds that of a person's limited awareness of his or her own past obliviousness to the present and his or her preference for the self over others in relation to the future. It is after Job repents and sees his own fallibility that everything is restored to him. Job, who held out for justice, fares better than his three friends whom God chastises as follows: "For you did not speak properly about me as my servant Job did." Let us now return from our brief excursus on Job to a fuller understanding of how the metzora begins to put himself in the "skin of others."

The reader will note how his personal suffering matures into a sense of responsibility when he progressively asks on behalf of others who also seem to be suffering without reason. This begins in chapter 21, when Job asks his friends: "But Job answered and said, hear diligently my speech, and let this be your consolations … suffer me that I may speak." "Wherefore do the wicked live, become old, ye are mighty in power. Their seed is established in their sight with them, and their offspring before their eyes."

In this section, he is following out the logic set up for the rehabilitation of the *metzora*. He is at last able to put himself in the position of others, in the "very skin" of others. His sense of personal time began with a deep resentment for all the stages leading up to and including his birth. Job wishes that he had never been conceived or born: "Let the day perish wherein I was born, and the night in which it was said 'there is a man-child conceived.' Let that day be darkness; let not God regard it from above, neither let the light shine upon it" (Job 3:1–3). He does so in a manner that is completely transparent to him, even though he could not possibly remember a time before his having been born.

In a variation of this theme, Levinas reflects upon Macbeth's resentment of having been born: "Macbeth's final cry in confronting death, defeated because the universe is not destroyed at the same time of his life" (TI 1969, 146). More precisely, "Macbeth wishes for the destruction of the world in his defeat and his death ('and wish th'estate o'th'world were now undone')—or more profoundly still, he wishes that the nothingness of death be a void as total as that which would have reigned had the world never been created" (Ibid., 231).

This can be further contrasted to when Job is finally granted his request to personally bring his complaint and his demand for an explanation before G'd. No explanation as such is forthcoming. However, G'd does give Job a sublime response, beginning with, "Where were you, when I created the heavens and the earth?" (Job 38). His question is not simply an assertion that power governs justice. Rather, G'd would take on responsibility for everything that has happened, all of time past and all time that passes. Now Job, too, without saying a word, appears to recognize this distinction and ultimate unknowability of Divine Justice. Job appears to concede his responsibility for things that he may not have done to the upmost to relieve the suffering of the widow, the orphan, the stranger, and the poor. It is in this way that Job is restored and elevated to a society with others.

Consider the stunning reversal that forms the Book of Job's conclusion. Is this perhaps the reason that God says to Job's friends: "My servant Job has done that which is right in my eyes; perhaps he will pray for you?" Through Job's repentance, he has turned himself around and is to be readmitted to a life with others. This kind of turning on the part of Job is what is expected in the life of the one who has been afflicted and placed outside of social life.

THE SINCERITY OF THE SAYING

Metzora: The Afflicted
(Leviticus 14:1–15:33)

The term *metzora*, the one visited with *tzaraas*, is intimately connected with *motzei ra*, the term for slanderous speech. In the biblical Hebrew idiom, *motzei shem ra* refers not merely to loose speech or gossip (*Lashon ha ra*)— bad speech—but to slander. Such speech carries injustice by undermining the bond between the other and his or her neighbor. By speaking falsely "against" another person to a third party, the metzora thereby weakens the personal attachment that makes a community or congregation possible. In other words, he or she intentionally is consigning the other person to privation from human society.

Slander is an extreme and injurious form of gossip (*loshon hara*). The prohibition against *loshom hara* derives, according to the *Chofetz Chaim*, from the prohibitive commandment "You shall not go about as a tale-bearer (*rechilus*) among your people" (Lev. 19:16). *Loshom hara* can involve words that are in fact true. Nonetheless, the Chofetz Chaim states that "[e]ven if he speaks the truth, a person thus brings ruin into the world" (1990, 163). Rather than speaking directly to another person, "*loshon hara*" is always speech about a third party.

The association of gossip with "*tzaraas*" finds its first explicit biblical expression in "gossip" of Miriam and Aaron about their brother, Moses, criticizing him for distancing himself from his wife, Tzippora. According to tradition, Miriam, in the presence of Aaron, chastises her brother for withholding conjugal relations from his wife, Tzippora, during the time of his prophetic leadership in the wilderness (Num. 12:10). Although true, the reason for it is that Moses had to be ready to receive divine revelation in a direct manner at all times. Why then is Miriam punished with tzaraas, even temporarily? G'd tells Moses that Miriam and Aaron were not so very concerned about his distancing himself from his wife, Tzippora, but rather that they had not been included in the kind of direct prophesy given to Moses. The three—Aaron, Miriam, and Moses— are first told to go out of the Tent of Meeting. Aaron intercedes on behalf of

Miriam and himself, and says, "I beg you, my lord, do not cast a sin upon us for we have been foolish and we have sinned. Let her not be like a corpse, like one who leaves his mother's womb with half his flesh having been consumed" (Num. 12:11). Moses then cries out to God to "[h]eal her now" (Num. 13). Nonetheless, Miriam is quarantined for seven days outside the camp; but out of their gratitude to Miriam, the Israelites do not journey during this time. If this can happen to Miriam, one of the great heroines of the Bible, what does this mean for the rest of us?

Speaking *to* another person precedes speech *about* that person. The saying (*le dire*), for Levinas, involves what is intended or expressed prior to the contents of what is said. Three parties, then, are affected by *loshon hara*: the one spoken about, the one who speaks, and the one spoken to. In this sense, we can see the beginning of the dissolution of human relations. We can see responsible speech when one acts as a guarantor for the other. This positively affects the other, his or her neighbor, as well as the speaker. The said, or the contents of speech (*le dit*), take on ethical significance only within the context of the saying. The reason for this is that, for Levinas, there is something inescapably personal, no matter the context, about human speech that is central to the elevation of society.

"Slander" is speaking against the other and as such, is an expression of the war of each against each. Is it any wonder, then, that the *metzora* is placed outside the encampments of all Israel? He is examined and reexamined to see if he has turned himself around, achieved the full measure of repentance so that he may turn now his unblemished face toward and for his people, Israel. However, he cannot simply examine himself. He must be examined by a member of the priestly class (*Kohanim*), whose holiness acts as an assurance that the metzora is now capable of speaking and acting in a holy manner. At this juncture, holiness appears to express itself not so much as what one says, but rather how one approaches the other in speaking. In this context, holiness appears as a kind of sincerity where one addresses the other in his or her uniqueness, and perhaps with reserve, but without resentment. In this way, the holiness of speech would become manifest through its purity of intent while including an ethical relation to what is said.

It is for this reason that the *metzora* is once again able to meet with and speak to others face-to-face. His house has become a home once again. This means he can welcome the other across the threshold of his home and express to him hospitality, the very opposite of closing himself off to others. The closing of his wounds in his social convalescence must be sincere, repentant, and self-aware. The countenance, the reflection, or trace of the face itself then returns to its human mobility and defies the menace of the death mask. Through this sense of homelessness, the skin is able to repair itself just because it sets up the possibility of "an inwardness already settled on itself, already a substance. It is always to empty oneself anew of oneself, to absolve oneself.... It is to be on the hither side of one's own nuclear unity, still identifiable and protected" (OBBE 1991, 92).

THE PARADOX OF PARDON:
TESHUVAH AND TIME

Acharei Mos: After the Death
(Leviticus 16:1–17:30)

In the seventh month, on the tenth of the month, you shall afflict yourselves and you shall not do any work, neither the native nor the proselyte who dwells among you. For on this day he shall provide atonement
for you to cleanse you; from all your sins before Hashem shall you
be cleansed.

—Leviticus 16:29–16:30)

Levinas explores both the philosophical and religious significance of *teshuva*,
the central feature of Yom Kippur. He does this most openly in one of his best-
known Talmudic readings, entitled "Toward the Other" (NTR 1990, 12). While
he considers many interrelated subjects, he presses the issue raised by Rabbi
Yehuda HaNassi "who attributes to the day of Yom Kippur itself—without
teshuva—the power to purify guilty souls, so important within Jewish thought
is the communal basis of inner rebirth" (NTR 1990, 17). Levinas explores
what it means to engage in petitioning for forgiveness in relation to other
people and how this is connected to transgressions before G'd. Rabbi Yehuda's
position argues that the day itself atones. For what and to whom? How is this
possible without any kind of initiative on the part of the person? From a metaphysical point of view, Levinas asks toward the close of *Totality and Infinity* how
atonement itself is possible.

The philosophical question concerns whether and how the past can be
changed. If we refer only to the *meaning* of the past, as opposed to its fac-
ticity, then we can understand that this is not so different from the practice of

psychotherapy. In psychoanalysis, for example, the patient learns to redirect the emotions of earlier life away from the perceived sources of suffering toward a different and more realistic set of symbols and attachment. Levinas is not simply encouraging a reinterpretation of the past. He is primarily concerned with how and whether we can explain our responsibility for the pasts of other people. Furthermore, he wants to know how our understanding of time plays a role in making pardon and forgiveness possible. Is this simply done through a kind of restorative justice? Does it not seem impossible that we should be able to return to a time prior to the injustice perpetrated or suffered?

Levinas refers to this phenomenon as the "paradox of pardon." He appears to be searching for a way of showing how temporality does not consist in the annihilation of the past. He says "the paradox of pardon lies in its retroaction; from the point of view of common time, it represents an inversion of the natural order of things, the reversibility of time" (TI 1969, 283). For Levinas, the paradox of pardon is at the very heart of time: "[T]he paradox of pardon, of fault, refers to pardon as constitutive of time itself" (TI 1969, 283). For the phenomenon of pardon to be made philosophically intelligible, the very phenomenon of time must be shown to have a dimension to it that is *reversible*.

He begins his demonstration by arguing that it is possible for the subject to reanimate the past, as if the instant elapsed can be revivified. However, such an action must go beyond a forgetting of the past, which, as he says, "does not concern the reality of the event forgotten" (Ibid.). It is the reality of the past with which we must deal, and not simply its meaning or interpretation. Consider how different this is from the current idiom that speaks of simply "moving on" as though my past could be assigned to someone else and therefore become a source of indifference. Am I responsible for the past of another person, or only the other's present? The answer to this question depends on whether a trace of the past endures in the present: it would be impossible to explain why we call the past "the past" in relation to the present as opposed to something simply apart from the present. In standing before another person, I am answerable for what he or she brings to the present encounter. This is all the more the case when I have injured, insulted, or disturbed the other person in a way that might have escaped my attention.

Returning to Levinas's commentary on the Day of Atonement, Yom Kippur, he notes that the position of the *mishna*, at the core of the Talmud, states that "religious experience, at least for the Talmud, can only be primarily a moral experience" (NTR 1990, 15). "The transgressions of man toward G'd are forgiven him by the Day of Atonement; the transgressions against other people are not forgiven by Day of Atonement if he has not first appeased the other person." Levinas emphasizes the positive nature of ritual in the practices set out for Yom Kippur in awakening the moral conscience. In the Talmud's discussion of the *mishna*, Levinas notes that "the guilty party must recognize his fault. The offended party must want to receive the entreaties of the offending party. Further, no person can forgive if forgiveness has not been asked him by the offender, if the guilty party has not tried to appease the offended" (Ibid., 19). In other words, the first act on the part of the offender must be to awaken to his or her offense. the offense then draws him or her necessarily back toward *the ongoing past* of the other person. We say that the past is ongoing because the offended party can not only recall the offense, but lives it. What this requires is a case of heightened awareness regarding one's own responsibility toward others; the very kind of sensibility that usually remains enclosed within the self who easily remembers offenses committed by others.

Contrary to all formal logic, Levinas argues that the pardon, while it does not restore innocence, "acts upon the past, somehow repeats the event purifying it" (TI 1969, 283). This means that the request for pardon points beyond itself to a future that after reconciliation, can be better than the present. Through pardon, the useless suffering of the past can be approached and mitigated. Levinas absolves pardon from its paradoxical status by liberating it from the language of totality: "Being is no longer produced with one blow, irremissibly present" (Ibid., 284). By overcoming the stumbling block of time past, the reopening of the pardon allows us to move toward the future. As he says, "[R]eality is what it is, but will be once again, another time freely resumed and pardoned" (Ibid., 284). In other words, the past itself can both be preserved and overcome. The passage of time is accomplished by the promise of the other that provides me with hope. Goodness from the other can now emerge within time.

Teshuva, deriving from the Hebrew word "to turn," indicates that we are now able to turn toward or face one another directly. This is the reestablishment of a just relation. However, the condition for its possibility lies perhaps with the meaning of the idea that the day itself atones. How can this be? If the day itself atones only in relation to G'd, then does this not signify that time works in such a way as to permit me to turn myself around, at least toward G'd? This would mean that my own past can be rectified and absolved at least in such a way as to let me go forward in relation to other people.

Levinas is here speaking of the time that he calls "diachrony." Diachrony begins outside the subject, with the other person who bears the trace of the infinite Other. To put this more concretely, I must be willing to remake the time of my own past by committing myself to making time for the other. *Teshuva* begins with a recognition that I have violated the time of the Other. What is it that I grieve for myself? Does this not mean that I am aware of how I have fallen short of what I could have been in relation to others? This summons me to a higher level of responsibility with a continuing awareness that pulls me toward the future. A human being cannot, by him-herself, keep the present from receding into the past, or, on the contrary, preserve the past in the present. The condition for this must come from outside the subject. This happens when we understand that the promise of time, full and therefore more real than all possibility, is attached to the good, the good at least in prospect.

To face the future without devaluing the passage of time, we must overcome the feeling that we already have limited ourselves completely by what we have done, or that the future will be a mere continuation of the present. Only when we understand that time does not come to nothingness can we begin to take our bearings with respect to a future that may be quite different from the present, while at the same time preserving the trace of the past in the present. Nietzsche is correct when he observes that "eternity" acts like time's avenging angel, seeking to make permanent that which is provisional and impermanent. At the same time, we must understand that the urgency by which time can be measured originates with the other. The promise of time means that it can go on without me, and that this does not devalue what I have done or set out to do. The promise of time that originates with the other means that there is hope for me as well. In this sense, the past must be understood not simply as a "dead weight" limiting my possibilities to choose freely, nor is it necessary to arrive at Nietzche's conclusion *reductio ad absurdum*: "time is the eternal return of same."[20]

---

20 It is worth noting that there are obstacles to *teshuva* that must be described. In a famous Gemara, the story is told of two great sages, Rabbi Chaninah bar Chamah and his disciple, Rav (BT, Yoma, 85a–85b). Rav had offended his teacher by refusing to repeat a lesson once again in his presence that he had already repeated many times. For this apparently minor offense, Rav went to seek forgiveness for thirteen years on the eve of Yom Kippur. Rabbi Chaninah refused, however, to be appeased. Normally, this is understood as an expression of an absence of good will on the part of the offended party who needs to be asked no more than three times for forgiveness. What Rav did not realize was that he was going to be the vehicle for deposing and replacing his teacher as head of the Rabbinical Academy. How can he be responsible, though, for something that he could not have known explicitly or consciously? As Levinas puts it, "The aggressiveness of the offender is perhaps his very unconsciousness. Aggression is the lack of attention *par excellence*" (NTR 1990, 25). Levinas is making a point that one must recognize one's responsibility forcing oneself to remain awake to even unintended wishes or consequences. This discussion occurs in a context of what kind of forgiveness was possible with respect to those Germans who had directly and indirectly borne responsibility for the Nazi persecutions. Even here, Levinas sees complexity.

JONAH (EXCURSUS): TESHUVAH FURTHER EXPLORED

One of the most solemn readings of the liturgical Jewish year occurs in the afternoon on the Day of Atonement. It is the Book of Jonah. Jonah is often referred to as the "reluctant prophet." He is told by G'd to return to the city of Nineveh, and to proclaim that "in forty days, Nineveh will be overthrown" (Jon. 2:4). According to the commentator Kimchi (1160–1235), regarding the wickedness of the Ninevites, violence is specified. These are moral and social sins that include brutality toward the people whom they conquered. What Jonah realized was that the Ninevites were being invited to do *teshuvah*. This thought was unbearable to Jonah, who prophetically saw that the inhabitants of Ninevah would be instrumental in wiping away the Northern Kingdom of Israel.[21] This highlights the tension between justice, or more precisely, injustice and repentance. Therefore, Jonah flees from the presence of G'd, as it were. He then heads out to sea with a group of non-Israelite sailors (Jon. 1:3). This is to say he leaves, or metaphorically wishes to depart from his embodied earth-bound life. The estrangement from both G'd and earth is complemented by his alienation from the sailors on the ship. He is now estranged from G'd, other people, and the human world. When a terrible storm breaks out, Jonah is found asleep in the depths of the ship (Jon. 1:6). Finally, Jonah has had recourse to a deadening of his consciousness and conscience. All the obstacles to *teshuva* are virtually complete: G'd, other people, the natural world, and lastly, the vigilance that attends consciousness. Then we see the beginnings of a kind of *teshuvah* that requires human choice and action, as well as the underlying conditions that make purposive conduct possible.

The sailors refuse to throw Jonah overboard as he wishes, to stem the tide of the great storm against them. Finally, the sailors accede to Jonah's imprecations. Jonah, in a great reversal, takes full responsibility for the misfortune of the sailors (Jon. 1:12). He has turned himself around and refuses to be the agent responsible for the sufferings of the sailors near him. As the story goes, Jonah is swallowed up by a great fish, and after prayer and repentance, is vomited back out onto the land.

This time he heeds the words of G'd and goes to proclaim his prophecy in Nineveh, thus risking his life again. Not only do the Ninevites respond by repenting, but so too do their animals, and the king of Nineveh himself (Jon.

He remarks: "One can forgive many Germans, but there are some Germans it is difficult to forgive. It is difficult to forgive Heidegger" (Ibid.).

21 Kimchi and Abarbanel, "Book of Jonah," *The Twelve Prophets* (Soncino Books), 138.

3:7). All of this makes Jonah very resentful. This is expressed by his sitting in the shade of a gourd that has grown up overnight as a shadow to protect him. Suddenly the gourd withers and dies. Jonah is depicted as finding his new exposure to the elements as unbearable. He mourns over the loss of the gourd. G'd says to him, "For the gourd which grew up in a day and perished in a day, you mourned, but not for the Ninevites, who do not know their right hand from their left. You have no compassion" (Jon. 4:10). This not knowing their "right hand from their left," according to most commentators, refers to their perpetual lapse into a pre-moral condition.

Jonah's mourning is comprehensible. There is an inherent conflict between justice and the manner of kindness that we might call "mercifulness." In this way, mercifulness toward the Ninevites would temper treating them strictly from the standpoint of justice. The second philosophic obstacle to accomplishing *teshuva* is intimately involved not simply with regretting the past and promising to do differently in the future, as Maimonides holds, but rather, absolving and taking responsibility for the past of the other. In this way, I open up a radically contingent future that comes from the other as well. Otherwise, the kind of turning around toward the other makes little or no difference, as I would become chained to a perpetually vanishing past of my own.

The openness of time is engendered in such a way that *teshuva* has been made possible for many people on many levels. All the contradictions are not resolved or synthesized, but lived through as evasion, estrangement, resentment, and even mourning. Jonah had to come to grips with an explicit awareness that *teshuva* is enacted by and for human beings and, therefore, must be accompanied by direct expressions of responsibility that go beyond our intuitions, feelings, and intentions. It is, therefore, fitting that this humble book, the book of Jonah, is read at the most exalted time of the Jewish year, for it demonstrates that the day can atone for transgressions between humans and G'd (*adam l'makom*) and must be lived out between human beings (*adam l'chaveiro*). Still, it is not prayer but pardon and forgiveness that must be practiced between human beings for *teshuva* to be lived out (*adam l'chaveiro*).

Returning briefly to the Book of Jonah may help us to better understand Levinas on the "paradox of pardon." In chronological order, the sailors are first presented as repenting, and the sea is restored to its former calm. Then, Jonah does *teshuva* in the belly of the fish, and his life is restored. Even G'd can be depicted as relenting on his previous decision to destroy the inhabitants of Nineveh. Jonah's prophesy, "Forty days and Nineveh will be overturned" (Jon.

3:4)[22] appears to have been contravened. Another plausible way of reading this same statement is that the Ninevites are no longer who they were. In this sense, we may say that the words commanded to Jonah have been verified, not contradicted.

What Levinas frequently refers to as the "miracle of temporality" must make it possible for the openness and promise of time to inhabit the past, as well as the future. As he puts it, "We must make a distinction between forgetting, which does not alter the reality of the event, and pardon, which acts upon the past. This is not a return to a kind of naïve innocence that would place innocence above pardon" (TI 1969, 283). Levinas argues that "the paradox of the pardon of fault refers to pardon as constitutive of time itself" (Ibid., 283). In this way, we can explain what sense it makes to speak of the "day atoning." How so? It must be something akin to a divine gift. That is to say, temporality itself: "The instants do not link up with one another indifferently but extend from the other unto me" (Ibid., 283). Diachronic time originates with the absolutely Other. If it did not, we surely could not speak of the day atoning or offering the prospect of resolving the paradox of pardon.

---

22 Rashi notes the ambiguity of the term "overturned." He indicates that if they repented and their hearts changed from evil to good, they would not be destroyed. Otherwise, they would have been destroyed. They did repent and were, therefore, no longer who they had been ("Jonah," in *The Twelve Prophets*, ed. A Cohen, 146).

HOLINESS

Kedoshim: The Laws of Holiness
(Leviticus 19:1–20:27)

You shall not be a gossipmonger among your people, you shall not stand
aside while your fellow's blood is shed—I am Hashem. You shall not hate
your brother in your heart; you shall reprove your fellow and do not bear
a sin because of him. You shall not take revenge and you shall not bear
a grudge against the members of your people; you shall love your fellow
as yourself—I am Hashem.

—Leviticus 19:16–19:19

"Love your neighbor, he is like you." But if one first agrees to separate
the last word of the Hebrew verse, kamokhah, from the beginning of the
verse, one can read the whole thing still otherwise. "Love your neighbor;
this work is like yourself"; "love your neighbor; he is yourself"; "it is this
love of the neighbor which is yourself. Would you say this is an extremely
audacious reading?"

—GWCM, 90

Levinas takes pains to distinguish holiness from sacrality. The sacred, the subject
of so much reflection by modern scholars of comparative religion, belongs to the
realm of power and totality and is, therefore, quite far from what Levinas understands by the biblical notion and philosophical meaning of holiness. Holiness
suggests an otherness that cannot be represented as an expression of ontological power. *Kedoshim* refers to the laws of holiness, while the Hebrew word
kadosh means "other" or "separate from." It is very far from the notion of divine
possession that is commonly found together with the sacred. Levinas maintains that holiness can begin to be understood only in a world that is rendered

free of possession, mania, and above all, enchantment (NTR 1990, 141). This comes after, rather than before, the Enlightenment, with its triple superlatives of progress, objectivity, and efficiency. Here we are speaking thematically rather than historically. Unlike the sacred, the holy is always associated with goodness.

William Paden, teacher and scholar of comparative religion, places emphasis on the notion that sacred order deals primarily with "the constraint of *upholding* the integrity of one's world against violation."[23] Importantly, Paden demonstrates that the concept of the other in the sense of sacred order has the function of excluding all persons, places, objects, and actions that do not belong within the order of sacrality. In this sense, the sacred order is arrived at by subtraction and *exclusion* (my emphasis).

What Levinas argues has a different purpose. What he shows is how otherness is essential to holiness and is inseparable from benevolence and right conduct. He thereby indicates an order of *inclusion* that is arrived at by addition and multiplication. Levinas understands, for example, that "the widow, the stranger, the orphan, and the poor" are already outside the established social order, and therefore special attention and care must be paid to them. This involves material support, as we shall see, and makes the relation to the vulnerability of the other a notion of founding importance. Is this not why G'd is presented as judging the oppression of the widow, the orphan, the stranger, and the poor so forcefully? We might ask what these different groupings have in common. They are not only outsiders to me but also outsiders to others, and perhaps, even to one another. In this sense, they help define the parameters of what is outside the subject. Perhaps this is why Reb Menachem Mendel of Kotsk' answer to the question, "Where is G'd?" is so often repeated, "Wherever you let Him in."

The biblical portion that specifically deals with holiness (Lev. 19) appears at first glance to simply reiterate a number of the commandments given at Sinai (Exod. 19–23), however, so important is this section that it says it was spoken to all of Israel, reversing, according to the Talmud (BT, Eruvin 54b), the normal order of transmission. The usual procedure of transmitting the *mitzvot* to Israel

---

23 In his article, "Sacred Order," William E. Paden argues that there are two models of sacrality. As he says, "For its members, a religious world is simultaneously 1) a set of objects imbued with trans-human power or significance *and* 2) a matrix of obligations which upholds the world of those objects. And only focusing on the first aspect, the revelatory nature of objects, phenomenologists of religion have typically ignored the second aspect, namely the sacrality of the system itself." New Patterns of Comparative Religion (Bloomsbury, 2016), 59.

would be that Moses would first teach Aaron and the sons of Aaron, and Moses would repeat the teaching; the elders would then enter, and Moses would repeat it again. The Alshich (1508–1593) explains that the reason that Moses called everyone together in this case was to make them aware that holiness involves a heightened responsibility to others and to see to it that such responsibility was binding on each one, so that everyone, even in their ordinary actions, had the capacity for holiness (cf. Stone, 656).

Holiness does not supersede morality. Rather, holiness is the surplus of morality, involving not only what we do and what we refrain from doing, but *the manner* in which we act as well. Perhaps this is why, after virtually every utterance, we have the refrain "You shall be holy, for Holy am I, HaShem, your G'd"—or in shortened form, "I am HaShem your G'd." The prohibition against idolatry could not be more clearly spelled out. Why then does the prohibition against idolatry follow inevitably upon the imperative of human holiness? According to Rashi, it involves a *turning* toward idols before one begins to regard them as if they were truly *gods* (my emphasis) (cf. Stone, 657).

Prior to the epochal statement "you shall love your fellow as yourself," we find what this means, in part, expressed through the laws of holiness. The groups of people who are the recipients of such conduct are perhaps just as important as the actions themselves. Rather than neglect the widow, orphan, stranger, and poor, we are told to be mindful of them while harvesting a vineyard: "When you reap the harvest of your land, you shall not complete your reaping until the corner (*peah*) of your field, and the gleanings (*lekhet*) of your harvest you shall not take. You shall not pick the under-developed twigs (*ollol*) of your vineyard, and the fallen fruit (*peret*) of your vineyard you shall not gather; for the poor and the stranger you shall leave them—I am HaShem, your G'd" (Lev. 19:9–10). This transcendent decree is bound up with the most vulnerable among Israel and humanity.

This is far from the model of corporate productivity in late capitalism, in which a supreme value is placed upon efficiency. Would it not be more efficient to let everyone proceed as he or she wishes and then to recommend a system of voluntary allotments to different groups or individuals, based upon what is presumed to be merit? Such corporate efficiency makes every other person utterly *replacable* and therefore disposable. There is an instructive story attributed to Reb Mendel of Kossov. Early one morning, he was found weeping profusely. His attendant (Gabbai) asked him what the problem was. He is reported to have said to the attendant, "You must not have heard, Moshele, the water carrier, who lives at the edge of town, died last night." The attendant interrupted, "Is that all? We can get a new Moshele, a new water carrier." The Kossover shot him a sharp look and responded, "That's funny, I was thinking the same thing about you, just now."[24]

For Levinas, every person is irreplaceable and therefore singular and unique. This uniqueness stems from the fact that people must regard themselves as responsible for all Israel, a burdensome freedom that Levinas would extend to all of humanity.

This is all the more important in a time when we tend to devalue the wisdom of age and to discriminate against those who are old, presumably because they are no longer as productive. Contrary to the contemporary tendency of warehousing the elderly under profit-making institutions with sunny names and often abysmal conditions, the Torah insists that "[i]n the presence of an old person, you shall rise, and you shall honor the presence of a sage, and you shall revere your G'd—I am HaShem" (Lev. 19:32). The Talmud explains this means a person of seventy years or more (BT, Kiddushim, 32b). In other words, one does not even have to be a sage in order for the other person to rise up in his or her presence.

Levinas cautions the reader that to interpret any verse of the text meaningfully, one must have the entirety of the book in view as the context of the verse: "It is not at all the two or three verses that proceed or follow the verse upon which one comments! For the absolute hermeneutic of a verse, the entirety of the book is necessary!" (GWCM 1998, 91). In this context, Levinas is referring to the oral tradition, the Talmud, the midrash, and the commentary tradition. He then gives a rare glimpse of the way that he proceeds. He does so by keeping in mind some of the central themes that guide his ethical-religious reading of Scripture: "Now in the entirety of the book, there is always a priority of the other in relation to me. This is the Biblical contribution in its entirety and that is how I would respond to your question; Love your neighbor all that is yourself; this work is yourself; this love is yourself." What does this mean?

"*Kamokhah* does not refer to your neighbor, but to all the words that proceed it. The Bible is the priority of the other (*l'autre*) in relation to me," Levinas explains (GWCM 1998, 91). Before I can recognize this specific widow or orphan or stranger, I am aware of and always see in another the widow, the orphan, and the stranger. The reason for this is that "the other always comes first and this is what I have called in Greek language the dissymmetry of the interpersonal relationship" (Ibid., 91). It is this predisposition that Levinas brings to the text when he interprets. In fact, he states that "[i]f there is not this

---

24 Story from *Hasidic Anthology* by Louis I. Newman, New York: Schocken Books, 1972.

dissymmetry, then no line of what I have written can hold. And this is vulnerability. Only a vulnerable 'I' can love his neighbor" (Ibid.).

Still, if we keep in mind that we are always looking at the figure of explicit language against the ground of its before and after, then it makes sense to look at the passages leading up to the statement "to love your neighbor as yourself." We do so fully aware that there are multiple interpretations that can be given to this entire portion of the Torah. We will follow the general line of Levinas's thought and interpretation and note when indicated views of other commentators within the tradition. It is perhaps worth noting that the Kotzker Rebbe expressed his astonishment to his followers when he came to the statement "love your neighbor" and remarked in horror "as yourself?"[25] In other words, what Menachem Mendel of Kotzk was asking was, is there really a mitzvah to love yourself.

Notice, in particular, the careful laying out of a logic of the heart leading up to loving your fellow as yourself. To begin with, we are told not to engage in gossip (loshon hora) among our people. The Torah continues, "You shall not stand idly by while your fellow's blood is shed—I am HaShem." Gossip (see Tazria/Metzora) has a way of setting up other people as objects rather than subjects, undesirable outsiders, far from the perfect stranger. This kind of speech leads to discord and, in the commentary tradition, is likened to the shedding of innocent blood. Maimonides, in fact, directly links this statement to the one following about not standing idly by while someone's blood is shed (Mishneh Torah: Hilchos Deòs, 7:1). These words of not standing idly by were repeated to exhaustion to encourage, even demand, efforts at rescue during the time of the Holocaust of European Jewry. Such indifference does not reduce bystanders to perpetrators but rather serves as a test of one's worthiness in relation to others.

For Levinas, this opens up an entire philosophic problematic dealing with the relation of the third person and his or her neighbor to the other and me. Levinas finds it understandable that justice as defined in the Torah cannot sanction pacifism, at least in most instances. It cannot because I am not permitted to stand idly by the "blood of my brother." For Levinas this means your neighbor. In a world of two, it may be possible for me to argue that I am morally entitled to surrender my life rather than take the life of another. However, the Torah allows, even commands me, to preserve my own life first. The appearance of the third party already involves me in justifying an order of precedence. To clarify, the third party, the neighbor, is always adumbrated in my regard for the second party. Thus, I cannot permit a fourth party to want to take the life

---

25 Chaim Feinberg, Leaping Souls (Hoboken, NJ: Ktav, 1993), xvi.

of my neighbor without protest, without taking even the extreme measures of defending him and thus endangering the life of the perpetrator.[26] Nonetheless, for Levinas, I must take responsibility for the one who persecutes me as well as my dealings with my intervention on behalf of my neighbor. For Levinas, the political is almost always a prolongation of ethical life.

Immediately after telling us not to stand idly by, the Torah admonishes us: "You shall not hate your brother in your heart." R. Samson Raphael Hirsch interprets this statement to mean that you shall treat even your antagonist as your brother. However, in a simpler sense, it is likely that such inward hatred, unreflected upon and not guarded against, will result in unintended violence toward the other. Is this why the Torah then states that "you shall reprove your fellow and do not bear sin because of him?" There is an entire school emphasizing such moral thinking and conduct referred to as "The Mussar Movement," which came of age in the nineteenth century to refine what were considered higher levels of ethical sensitivity in relation to other people. Levinas himself takes this very much to heart. In fact, he helps to philosophically ground one of

---

26 This complex issue has been the subject of considerable inquiry, criticism, and some confusion in the political philosophy of Levinas. For example, Howard Caygill, in *Levinas and the Political (Thinking the Political)* (Routledge, 2002), takes the false and extreme position that Levinas condoned the infamous massacre at the Sabra and Shatila refugee camp on September 28, 1982. He cites, out of context, a statement made by Levinas in response to a question: "Is not the other, above all, the Palestinian?" Levinas responds, "The other is the neighbor, who is not necessarily kin, but who can be. And in that sense, if you are for the other, you are for the neighbor. But if your neighbor attacks another neighbor, or treats him unjustly, what can you do? Then alterity takes on another character, in alterity we can find an enemy, or at least then we are faced with the problem of who is right and who is wrong, who is just and who is unjust?" What Caygill refuses to acknowledge is that Levinas unequivocally praises the people and state of Israel for demonstrating against the massacres immediately and bringing the negligent parties to account before tribunals and courts. He argues that the soldiers of Israel who were in the area were surely "responsible" but he withholds judgment as to their guilt. This can hardly be compared, as Caygill does, to Heidegger's "silence" on the Holocaust. This is a grotesque misrepresentation. In fact, as we have learned in recent years, Heidegger was not at all silent on the Holocaust. Regarding the Holocaust, Heidegger wrote: "This is why man can die if and only if being itself appropriates the essence of man into the essence of being on the basis of the truth of its essence" (The Bremen Lectures of 1949). This is why Emmanuel Faye correctly concludes that "after having denied, in a revolting way, the extent of the Shoah, by speaking of 'hundreds of thousands' whereas several millions of human beings were exterminated by the Nazis, Heidegger gives us to understand that no one died in the death camps because none that were liquidated were 'able' to die there" (Emmanuel Faye, *Heidegger and the Introduction of Nazism into Philosophy* [New Haven, CT: Yale UP], 305).

the essential theses of the Mussar movement: where possible and appropriate, one should tread lightly in correcting others and deal more harshly with oneself. Love of the other, for Levinas, begins in an extreme vigilance for the other in all of his or her uniqueness.[27]

The penultimate statement in the logic leading up to love of one's fellow, we find inscribed in the Torah: "You shall not take revenge, you shall not bear a grudge against the members of your people." Is this perhaps the hardest of all of the *mitzvots*? Why? Is it because it involves a turning toward rather than a turning away, a transformation in one's feelings as well as one's intellect? Such a grudge can lead to a subtle devaluing of my relation to the other person, after all there are a lot of people. How can I be meaningfully expected to love every one of them with equal intensity and concern?

Franz Rosenzweig criticizes the tradition of philosophy for elevating an idea of a person above the person him- or herself. In the opening of Rosenzweig's work *The Star of Redemption*, he argues against those philosophers who commend death as a special protégé of philosophy. The ill or dying person, as he says, cries with his every breath not for a "there" that he does not desire, but for a "here" to which he is utterly attached.[28] In Nietzsche's view, this is the origin of the false idea of eternity that goes back to Plato. Eternity would be expressed as an unchanging now that would remain both time's limit and its avenging angel.

Levinas criticizes this view when he more soberly argues that "eternity is but the irreversibility of time." But for Levinas, it is the suffering of the other, even more than his death as in Rosenzweig, that is utterly unintelligible, in the sense that it is forbidden for me to rationalize it. It is now possible to begin to approach with seriousness the statement of "loving one's fellow as himself—I am Ha Shem." The secret consists, for Levinas, not in the other's eternity, but in making time for him or her in an immediate way.

How does holiness enter in here? Immediately after the opening words, "You shall be holy for holy am I, HaShem, your G'd," Rashi connects this statement to the love of the stranger, in this case meaning the proselyte (Lev. 19:2). The Torah reads as follows: "When a proselyte dwells among you in your

---

27 This further means that difference would then arise from uniqueness rather than the other way around. What Levinas opens by predicating difference on uniqueness is what we might characterize as

"an *infinite-egress*," where holiness would appear as the source as well as the surplus of morality.

28 Franz Rosenzweig, *Star of Redemption*, translated by William W. Hallo (Boston: Beacon Press).

land, do not harass him. The proselyte who dwells with you shall be like a native among you, and you shall love him like yourself, for you have been aliens in the land of Egypt—I am HaShem your G'd" (Lev. 19:33–34). A meaningful question arises: why should the stranger be singled out in relation to the statement "you shall love him like yourself?" Rashi comments, "I am your G'd and his G'd." Is this simply a matter of emphasis? The stranger has an experience similar to the Israelites who were strangers in the land of Egypt. Nevertheless, the stranger may be thought of in a more general sense than simply as a proselyte. For Levinas, every other person approaches me in the manner of "*a stranger.*" However near to or far from me that he or she may be, there is a way that, in advance of encounter, he or she transcends my understanding of who this other person is. This thesis is at the very heart of his philosophy; all begins with the other rather than the self. It is in this way that my own journey out of myself begins—that is, with the questioning glance of the other.

For Levinas, this is the origin of all ethics:

> We name this calling into question of my spontaneity by the presence of the Other, ethics. The strangeness of the Other, his irreducibility to the I, to my thoughts and possessions, is precisely accomplished as a calling into question of my spontaneity, as ethics. Metaphysics, transcendence, the welcoming of the other by the same, of the Other by me, is con-cretely produced as the calling into question of the same by the other, that is, as the ethics that accomplishes the critical essence of knowledge. (TI 1969, 43)

While Levinas links the phenomenon of love to that of justice and holiness, he remarks that the word concept "love" has become "a worn-out and ambiguous word" (EN 1998, 108). Still, he affirms that "love is originary" (Ibid.). What, then, is the relation of love to holiness? Using the language *via ementiae,* Levinas states, "*the only absolute value is the human possibility of giving the other priority over oneself*" (Ibid., 109, my emphasis). Much is at stake for the philosophy of Levinas in this claim. He appears to invite the reader to compare this with one's own intuition on the subject. He states, "I am not saying that the human being is a saint, I'm saying that he or she is one who understood that holiness is indisputable" (Ibid.). Why? Rather than simply affirming the position that holiness is a surplus of morality, he appears to be asserting that holiness itself is the source of all morality. In regard to holiness, he states, "This is the beginning of philosophy, this is the rational, the intelligible" (Ibid.). Here he appeals to philosophical sensibility and rigor, indicating that we are not "getting away from reality" (Ibid.).

212 Levinas and the Torah

Love of the other, for Levinas, expresses an extreme vigilance for the other in all his/her uniqueness. When we come upon the statement commanding us to love the other as ourselves, we are already conditioned by Western philosophic thought, which holds that we must first learn to love ourselves properly in order to love others. Hence the proliferation of so many books and articles on the importance of self-esteem.[29] It is clear Levinas does not agree, either practically or theoretically with this kind of emphasis. Rather, he is arguing that my ability to go out of myself, to go out of my way, to go out of my own egoism, is the "moral exodus" that precedes the historical Exodus from Egypt. My self-esteem, then, becomes a reflection of the way that I exercise my own sense of "election" or being chosen by taking responsibility for the other person. This other person, like me, is not reducible either to a species of humanity where I would love all the world with the same urgency and importance. My humanity is something that I achieve. It is not the human species that I love, nor is it a set of sociological constructs. When in *Kedoshim* we hear the words, "[Y]our mother and father you shall revere," father and mother are not reducible to the scientific language of proximate protoplasmic progenitors. In other words, a mother or a father precedes the biology that each presupposes and thereby surpasses. It is, as Levinas says, "Love without concupiscence, in which man's right assumes meaning; the right of the beloved, that is the dignity of the unique" (EN 1998, 194).

It cannot be by accident that the admonition to be holy is followed directly by the apparently redundant iteration, "and you shall observe My Sabbaths" (Lev. 19:3). From the words inscribed on the tablets at Sinai, the word *kadosh*, or "holy," is used only regarding the Sabbath day. In yet another transposition, more visible, perhaps, than any of the others that Levinas reconfigures, the Sabbath is itself holy because it represents the ultimate achievement of divinely conditioned, but humanly enacted time. It is a time freed from the yoke of labor where the transcending diachrony of time becomes palpable.

Love of others obviously also involves justice. This means not only "social justice," as we like to call it, but a more tangible economic justice that is the subject announced in the Torah and amplified in the Talmud. "An Israelite cannot regard his land as his own, that is, he cannot take crops for himself and his family, according to R' Hirsch, until he has left the mandated portions of gleanings, underdeveloped twigs, and fallen fruit for the poor" (Hirsch, Leviticus, vol. 3, 505ff). Why else should it say, "[Y]ou shall do no wrong in justice, in measurement, in weight ... you shall have correct scales, correct

---

29 See books by Abraham Twerski and Zelig Pliskin on this subject.

stones … I am HaShem, your G'd who brought you forth from the land of Egypt" (Lev. 19:35–36). There is a well-known maxim found in the Talmud that the first subject that a soul is asked about on High is "Did you have just weights and measures?" In other words, were you righteous in your material interactions with other people? Levinas puts it this way: "The love of one's fellow man, and his original right, as unique and incomparable, for which I am answerable, tend of their own accord to make appeal to a Reason capable of comparing incomparables, a wisdom of love. A measure superimposes itself on the 'extravagant' generosity of 'for the other' on its infinity" (EN 1998, 195). Justice implies that there is a continuity of expectations, obligations, and manner of dealing with others in all exchanges. It is not simply a matter of marketplace economics governed by the invisible hand of the laws of nature. This is an economics of transcendence that includes me as the other for others as well. Notice how often the prophets who come to admonish Israel draw on examples from everyday economic life. By this, we are not suggesting a divinely planned corporate economy. Rather, human beings are themselves transcendent to the merchandise in which they traffic, especially in the sphere of commodities.

Recall that it is a central dictum of rabbinic tradition that there are only three kinds of actions that one cannot transgress, even for the sake of "saving a life" (*pikuach nefesh*). These include idolatry (*avoda zora*), the shedding of innocent blood (*shfichas damim*), and gross acts of sexual immorality (*arayis*). Regarding idolatry, Levinas is at special pains to make sure that we do not confuse holiness with aesthetics. In the case of aesthetics, Levinas finds himself in a minority position in the history of Western philosophic thought, aligned with Plato, Marx, and Tolstoy, but above all with the Hebraic tradition. For something to be beautiful, it must already be good. For it to be good, it must already be holy. For it to be holy it must be other and not reducible to the sublimity of self-feeling. The prohibition against the representation of the Divine forbids us to elevate anything else above the transcendence of the divine other. The prohibition against shedding innocent blood means that the other person arises, for Levinas, in his or her face, even before I am commanded that murder is revealed as divinely forbidden.

Levinas clearly regards the phenomenon of eros as a central philosophical concern. He links the phenomenon of eros to that of the face, and therefore, the transcendent. It is for this reason he states that the face precedes eros, and that these forbidden relations are meant, in part, to preserve the otherness of order. Forbidden sexual relations are not always those that are con-sanguinary. For example, one is not permitted to marry his stepmother, the wife of his father, even after the father's death. When it is holy, such love of the other must always be capable of detachment from eros. This is why Levinas uses the unusual phrase, "disinterested, non-concupiscent eros." For to love the other means in the first place to preserve the otherness of the other and not to amalgamate her to my interests or desires. To be for the other is the way that our love can show itself prior to its specific expression. If for the other is the central direction of the interhuman sphere, then it prevails *ad interim* over the mere striving to persevere in being.

TIME, HOLINESS, AND ALTERITY

Emor: Say
(Leviticus 21:1–24:33)

Holiness is expressed in and through time. The divinely appointed festivals punctuate and orient the time of the Jewish year. These include the three festival holy days commemorating the exodus from Eygpt (*Pesach*), the giving of the Torah at Sinai (*Shavuous*), and the time of rejoicing and redemption (*Sukkos*). These appointed festivals each involve a time of sociality.

R' Samson Raphael Hirsch notes that there are three different accounts given of the festivals. What is distinct about the recounting of the festivals in Leviticus is the manner in which each set of holy days can be viewed as "Festivals in Time." Hirsch puts it this way: "And just as Time is the conception of the changing succession of things one after the other, so do G'd's Sanctuaries in Time—the Festivals—deal with the manifestations of the G'dly in the course of time, i.e. the revelation of G'd in nature and history and the human element in time" (Hirsch, Leviticus, 644).

In his masterful reflection on the Star of Redemption, Levinas continues to develop his ideas concerning time and the breakup of totality.[30] Such time is reflected for Rosenzweig, and similarly for Levinas, in the irreducible moments of creation, revelation, and redemption. Together these comprise what could be called an "existential eschatology."

These three moments appear both in the Sabbath day and in the festivals. Friday evening reanimates the notion of creation on its way to completion. The blessing over wine that initiates the Sabbath meal begins with the words, "And it was evening and morning, one day." The central moment of the Sabbath morning is the reading from the Torah scroll of the weekly portion of the Torah. Revelation is a transitive action, spoken and studied. The afternoon is associated with a longing for redemption, expressed by a third festive meal in the

---

30 *Franz Rosenzweig: His Life and Thought*, edited by Nahaum N. Glatzer (Hackett Publishing), 307ff.

215

awareness that the work week with all its trials awaits. The festival holy days bear this same kind of movement, both in themselves and in relation to one another. Passover perpetually is recalled as the beginning of liberation and the formation of the Jews as a nation no longer subjugated to a harsh servitude. In this sense, Passover is linked to the past, not simply as a historical event, but as the founding possibility of all social consciousness. The outgoing from Egypt is also an exodus of the people, Israel. To use the language of Sartre, it represents at the first, a group "*en fusion.*" Such solidarity is the precondition for self-consciousness of a people conscious of itself as such.

In a Talmudic reflection called "Beyond Memory," Levinas examines the relation between this past and the transformative condition that it establishes for Israel. He states: "A consciousness that is immediately narration, an interiority in which some story stirs, giving the present its meaning. Consciousness is not, in this case, just the actualizing of the new, but also the narration of the past by which consciousness is sustained and ordered" (ITN 2007, 66). In other words, the Exodus refers to a past that is still present as a new beginning and, therefore, a future as well.

For this reason, the recounting of the outgoing from Egypt and its ritualized retelling, must be reexperienced at the yearly Passover Seder. Seder, meaning "order," is a meal that retraces the Exodus. The narrative from the Haggada spells out the four questions to which the unfolding of the Haggada responds. The meal "within a meal" begins to reenact the movement from the harshness of slavery to the fourfold expressions of freedom and redemption accompanied by the drinking of four glasses of wine. Matzah, the unleavened bread, replaces leavened bread, symbolizing the bread of affliction and haste in departure. All traces of the leavened bread have been removed prior to the onset of Passover.

The Exodus calls us to wakefulness, the very precondition of prayer: "This past of the Exodus and the Law forms the heart of the Jewish weekday morning prayer. Or, more precisely perhaps, this memory is already prayer, morning prayer, prayer of awakening, awakening as prayer" (ITN 2007, 66). This wakening is, for Levinas, a vigilance to go out (sortir) of ourselves toward the other. In this sense, it is "Beyond Memory." It goes beyond the finite duration of human beings, and thereby "punctuates the time of the total history of humanity" (ITN 2007, 69).

At the same time, the outgoing from Egypt is intrinsically related to the giving of the Law at Sinai. This is the holy day of Shavuos, meaning "weeks" yet derived from the word "oath." It is, therefore, an inscribed responsibility enacted as law, a freedom engraved with the responsibility lived within the anticipation and aftermath of the giving of the Torah. The festivals delineate the movements toward exteriority. Passover expresses freedom. Levinas argues that freedom is always already an "investiture" on its way to justice. The law of the Torah expresses this justice. Because such freedom is "inscribed" on the tablets of the Law, we are free from the anarchy of arbitrariness or the tyranny of totalitarianism.

If the Exodus may be viewed as a foundational past of which we are reminded daily, weekly, and yearly, the giving of the Torah at Sinai may be viewed as a kind of pure present. It is through the perpetual prism of the Torah that we interpret the context out of which all the laws and imperatives arise. Levinas's diachronic conception of time helps to elucidate this phenomenon. Between Passover and Shavuos, we are commanded to count seven weeks, forty-nine complete days (from the second night of the Passover), until the receiving of the Torah: "You shall count for yourselves—from the morrow of the rest day, from the day when you bring the Omer of the waving—seven weeks, they shall be complete. Until the morrow of the seventh week you shall count, fifty days" (Lev. 23:15–16).

Why is this counting so significant, especially given the fact that the sacrifice associated with it does not begin until the entrance into the Promised Land? The seven weeks are counted in expectation, where each day and each week means an ascent in moral maturity and the willingness to take on the responsibility of freedom, meaning of one for the other. This is no small task for a people just experiencing the disburdening of slavery. Is there, then, also a counting, not just for myself, but for all the others for whom I will bear responsibility? This counting is a serious business that also marks the distance that I have come from my own sense of shame and limitation experienced in the social, as well as geographical Egypt. It is a mathematics of expectation where a kind of maturity is born and progresses. Such time originates in its imperative form from the other, and it positions me as subject to the elevating claims and obligations directed toward me.

The revealing of the other is already experienced by me as an imperative that comes from outside the subject. Such responsibility of one for the other goes beyond the people, Israel, with whom it begins. This kind of conduct takes time to learn and to practice: "You shall count for yourselves—from the morrow of the rest day" (Lev. 23:15). This means that the observance of seven Sabbaths will take place from the beginning of the counting until the receiving of the Torah. At the same time, there is a connection reestablished between the Sabbath, the sabbatical year, and the Yovel (Jubilee). In other words, the celebration of the outgoing from Egypt leads to freedom invested as justice in the giving of the law of the Torah. This is to say, that *Pesach*, or Passover, finds its expression in the just relations and institutions delineated through the laws of the Torah given at Sinai.

There is an implied oath that Israel will take upon itself the covenant at Sinai that, above all, guarantees the keeping of the Torah, its laws and practices. As such, spirituality will, from this time on, be enacted as conduct practiced in the concrete material world. This is a responsibility that continues through time and history, still waiting upon its perfection. Levinas, in his commentary "Beyond Memory," asks whether the observing of the original exodus from Egypt will be remembered when the sovereignty of Israel is reestablished. He situates this question within the context of a Talmudic argument over whether the memory of the original exodus will remain in messianic times. Why is this important? It is philosophically significant because he understands holy history as building upon the past that it does not annul. One illustration he gives is from our own time. He specifically references the catastrophes of the twentieth century, above all the Holocaust of European Jewry: "Savagery and wasteland, the memory of which may yet fade but the death of the starving children thrusts us into the snake pit, into places that are no longer places, into places that one cannot forget, but that do not succeed in placing themselves in memory, in organizing themselves in the form of memories" (ITN 2007, 73). The trace of the past as it passes by will continue to make it possible to initiate memory, even where the recollection of the past has dimmed. Nonetheless, the past, as such, will be exceeded. The exodus from Egypt will still be remembered as a formative event in relation to the time and times preceding the messianic era, but it will recede into the background.

As a midrash has it, just before the Torah was to be given, the Israelites were asked: "Who will guarantee that you will keep this Torah?" The people volunteered themselves. This was not considered adequate. Abraham, Isaac, and Jacob, then, would vouch for their reliability in keeping the Torah. This too was rejected. Only when the children promised to receive the Torah from their parents was Israel elected. Does this mean that only the perpetual receiving and transmitting of the Torah from generation to generation invests the Torah with generativity?

There is an ancient custom to remain awake learning Torah the night of Shavuous. One reason given for this custom is that the Israelites were overcome with such excitement just as they were about to receive the Torah, that they fell into a deep stupor likened to sleep. Were they thinking in the same way as Nadav and Avihu, that they would become angels, rather than human beings? According to the Kabbalistic understanding, our staying awake and learning the Torah until dawn serves as a rectification (*tikkun*) for the sleep suffered just before the giving of the Torah. We can also understand this through Levinas's insistence that the ethical life begins with a wakening and vigilance, to the point where it can be counted as a kind of moral perfection or holiness. Now we can better understand what is meant by the affirmation that the children will act as the guarantors for Israel.

This study, practice, and teaching of the Torah remain the primary prism through which the promise of Israel is realized. The hope for the end of human alienation and oppression resides in what Levinas refers to as the "pure promise to which the language of accomplishment reverts" (ITN 2007, 75). Levinas observes that "it is memory surviving forgetfulness. It is a tired man opposing the violence and lies of the earth, having had many misfortunes, who continues the struggle. The greatness of Israel is still in Jacob" (Ibid.). Even after he is named Israel, the trace of Jacob's embodied sojourn through life's most formidable obstacles remains visible.[31]

The festival harvest of *Sukkos*, then, would celebrate the anticipation of a justice based upon the interior sovereignty of responsibility toward others, where the world of each-for-each and all-for-all would extend to the whole of humanity. The surplus of justice is expressed at the time of *Sukkos* holiday harvest as generosity and mercifulness. The sages refer to *Sukkos* as "the season

---

31 According to the tradition, the counting begins on the second evening of the Passover holiday. The counting involves a measure of a combination of days and weeks culminating after forty-nine full days with the giving of the Torah (*shavuos*). The Talmud takes special note (BT, Yevamos 62b) of the fact that the students of Rabbi Akiva, some twelve hundred pairs of students, stopped dying on the thirty-third day of the counting (*Lag B'omer*). This became a time of semimourning. The question is asked, why did the students of Rabbi Akiva die before this time? As the matter is commonly explained, because they did not have proper regard and respect for one another. But this does not make evident sense since, as the most recent Lubavitcher Rebbe (M.M. Scheneerson) argues, they would not have been true students of Rabbi Akiva, who emphasized the love of one's neighbor above all of the other mitzvot. The Rebbe suggests rather that this a more complex moral matter. It could not be said that the students did not honor one another properly, nor could it be said that they did not value the opinions that were different from their own. What then? Perhaps it could be argued that while they entertained one another's opinions with sincerity, they did not truly express the wisdom of love for one another required. As the Rebbe explains it, they could not inhabit fully the positions held by their fellow students and therefore were lacking, at a very high level, the deepest kind of love that one person can have for another. In the language of Levinas, this begins with recognizing the inviolable alterity of the other person. This means that, for Levinas, the uniqueness of each person must be the source of both love and justice. In this way we learn, as Einstein observed, "Not everything that counts can be counted, and not everything that can be counted counts."

of our rejoicing" (*zman simchaseinu*). This seems paradoxical, given the fact that such rejoicing is done primarily in impermanent homes or huts away from the comforts of our houses. Every activity usually associated with the home—eating, learning, and for some, even sleeping—occurs in the *Sukkah*. Biblically, the Sukkah represents the clouds of glory that are said to have accompanied the Israelites during their sojourn in the wilderness, protecting them from the heat of day and the fear of night. It is in the merit of Aaron, whose primary attribute is kindness, that the clouds of glory are said to have endured through the stay in the wilderness. *Sukkos* has elements that serve as a premonition of redemption.

The organic, vegetative, animal, and human realms are all included in the mitzvah of *Sukkos*. This can be achieved, however provisionally, through the work of the human agent. The *sukkah* must be built with an impermanent roof. Four species of vegetation are to be acquired, to be employed in the liturgy of the seven holy days. Feasting is prescribed, strong drink is permitted. The whole of these holy days is inscribed with a certain transience, but how and why should we associate the fragility of the Sukkah and the awareness of life's ephemeral character with rejoicing and even redemption? It is not by chance that the Book of Ecclesiastes is read during this period. If everything is fleeting, Koheles (Solomon), the author of Ecclesiastes, says, despite the fact that there is "a time to be born, as well as a time to die, a time to laugh, as well as a time to cry," then why should we care about anything at all?

Do we rejoice despite the fleeting character of earthly life? Recall that it is a time of harvest where one remembers others through acts of kindness and generosity that surpass the demands of justice. According to the *Torah Temimah* (1860–1941), on Sukkos there is an extra measure to rejoice. He goes on to say that such rejoicing was connected with the peace offerings (*Torah Temimah*, vol. 3, 432). This conclusion is compatible with a description of the sukkah of peace (*sukkah shalom*), where, according to a prophetic portion, all of the nations will gather together with Israel in Jerusalem at the fallen sukkah of David in the messianic time. In other words, this will be a time when Israel will have regained its sovereignty and lives in peace with all the other nations, to whom it will extend hospitality. Sovereignty, for Levinas, involves a moral self-rule and the companion doctrine of responsibility for others before it takes on a political shape and authority.

Rav Hirsch notes that the sukkah introduces an added dimension of equality between peoples. He says that the *skach,* the temporary and fragile roof, is "the same for all. The beggar and the millionaire, both alike, are to reject the combination of human and natural powers as protective of their lives" (Lev.

7:11). This is why, according to one opinion, the sukkah may not be above a certain height, again emphasizing the egalitarian nature of the holy day.

During the days of sukkos, the Israelites brought sacrifice, seventy in all, or the symbolic equivalent of all of the nations of the world. Only on the eighth day—technically its own holy day, *shimini atzeres*—did the Israelites bring but one offering for themselves. This is indicative of an extra measure of intimacy between them and their Creator. In the terms of Levinas, this means that they were to understand that they were singled out for one degree of responsibility more than the other nations. This responsibility was both for one another as well as for the other nations.

This entire holiday culminates with a rejoicing in the Torah (*Simchas Torah*). We conclude the reading of the Torah and immediately commence its beginning again. Joy would appear to be capable of undergoing an education. Our greatest joy is something that resists impermanence. This is the glory that appears not with a blinding light, but with the capacity to renew, ever again, the love and appreciation that is associated with the Torah. For most of this holy day, the mantle of the Torah is covered, and the custom is to dance with it before uncovering the scroll and reading it. This gives a perpetual continuity to the study of the Torah. The end of Deuteronomy is read and immediately the beginning of Genesis is opened and read aloud. The last letter of the Torah is a *lamed*, or "L," and the first letter of Genesis is a *beis,* or "B." Together they spell out the word for heart, *lev.* The trace of the beginning is found in the end and does not disappear. In a similar way, we are reminded that it is through our attachment to the teachings of the Torah, leading to deeds of goodness, that the impermanence of time is imprinted in the traces of a future.

ON BIBLICAL SOCIAL ECOLOGY

Behar: At the Mountain
(Leviticus 25:1–26:2)

Justice, society, the State and its institutions, exchanges and work, are comprehensible out of proximity. This means that nothing is outside of the control of the responsibility of the one for the other.

—OBBE 1991, 159

What is likely the first record of any body of laws governing what we today refer to as "the environment" is found in Leviticus 25. Here we are informed that "[w]hen you come into the land that I will give you, the land shall observe a rest for Hashem. For six years you may sow your field and for six years you may prune your vineyard and you may gather its crop. But the seventh year shall be a complete rest for the land. A Sabbath for Hashem; your field you shall not sow, and your vineyard you shall not prune" (Lev. 25:2–5). Like the Sabbath Day, the observance of the sabbatical year is social, economic, as well as ecological. The triangular relation between the transcendent, the people, and the land suggests a dimension of the Jewish Bible that has until recently been overlooked, when it has not been misunderstood. The tendency to emphasize noncontextually the statement from Genesis: "And man shall have dominion over every living thing that creeps upon the earth," (1:28), often creates this misunderstanding. Viewed in isolation, this statement is often used to justify anthropocentrism. A kind of biblical ecology emerges more clearly when we understand the other-self relation through the lens of Levinas.

The commentary tradition notes that the beginning of this portion specifically mentions the intimate connection of the laws concerning the sabbatical year with the giving of the Torah at Sinai. This is why the portion is called *bahar,* meaning "at or by the mountain." The common understanding is that of Rashi, who states that "this is to teach that, as this law was ordained there, with its general rules and its minute details, so too is it with all the commandments of the Torah" (Soncino, 764). Still, Rashi's instructive comment is not specifically responsive to why this sabbatical year should be the paradigm of the law expressed both in its generality and in its details.

Long before his contemporaries, S.R. Hirsch recognized the centrality of what we today tend to call "the environment." Hirsch prefigures Levinas, arguing that there is a general significance to the responsibility that human beings have for one another in relation to the natural "world around them," which is most clearly seen in the laws pertaining to the land of Israel. In fact, Hirsch reclassifies the laws of righteousness toward those beings that are subordinate to the human in such a way as to make them belong to the realm of the "suprarational" or *Chukim.* He begins by specifying the kind of righteousness that pertains "towards earth, plant (and animal)" and makes this parallel to "one's own body, mind, spirit, and word" (*Horeb,* 277). Notice that long before recycling became a popular environmental and social concern, Hirsch writes against the destruction and wastefulness of the animate and even inanimate worlds: "The first prohibition of creation is thus not to destroy anything, large or small, if it may still be of use, from the fruit-tree, which may still refresh the latest grandchild with its fruits, down to the smallest piece of thread—in short, anything which can still serve some purpose or other" (*Horeb,* 280). This is not to be confused with mere fiscal frugality. Hirsch is in fact rediscovering a new dimension of meaning to the biblical law of destruction and waste (*bal tashkis*). This is to say that Hirsch discovers a logic that comes before the specific prohibitions and enactments pertaining to the sabbatical year.

The seriousness of the sabbatical year begins with the recognition that, to cite the Psalmist, "the earth is the Lord's and the fullness thereof" (Ps. 24). The earth belongs to us only conditionally and contingently. Hirsch puts it this way:

> God's call proclaims to you "do not destroy anything! Be a man! Only if you use the things around you for wise human purposes, sanctified by the word of My teaching. Only then are you a man and have you the right over them which I have given you as a man. However, if you destroy, if you ruin—at that moment you are not a man, you are an animal, and have no right to the things around you. I lent them to you for wise use only; never forget that I lent them to you." (*Horeb,* 277ff.)

Hence, it becomes much easier to understand why, in the seventh year, our awareness of our contingent relation to all property becomes more visible. This position tears at the anthropocentrism of European Enlightenment humanism.

There is an intimate connection between the laws pertaining to the sabbatical year and the prohibition of idolatry found at the conclusion of the Torah portion *Behar*. Levinas recognizes that the prohibition against idolatry has meaning for the contemporary human situation that permits us to take a position toward one another that we are characterizing as "a transcending humanism." For the ancient Greeks, the human body was itself the highest expression of a work of art, and therefore subject to being viewed with adoration. For the Torah, human beings are not the measure of all things. He or she may remain the one who measures, but what is measured is Infinite. For Hirsch and for Levinas, the biblical formulation does not permit us to worship inanimate objects, including those in the Holy Land or the land itself that is holy. Notice the language at the end of this portion: "You shall make no idols, neither shall you rear up a graven image, or a pillar. Neither shall you place any figured stone in your land, to bow down to it; for I am Hashem your God. You shall keep my Sabbaths and reverence your sanctuary, for I am Hashem" (Lev. 26:1–2). All the prohibitions against oppressing one another, especially those who are most vulnerable—the widow, the orphan, the stranger, the poor—are found expressed once again but in a new, more positive way in the portion dealing with the sabbatical year.

It is not charity but righteousness that demands that there should be no harvesting or planting during the seventh year. The fruits of this land that remain over in the seventh year are considered ownerless (*hefker*) and therefore, according to Rashi, everyone must be allowed equal access to them, including ownerless beasts or animals of the wild. How much more so shall this food that is left over in the fields be available to landless laborers, the poor, the stranger, the widow, the orphan? In this sense, the land has a claim of its own, not to be harvested for the sake of people, specifically people and creatures other than those who claim it as their property.

There is a kind of radical alterity that engenders both a sensibility of dependence upon that which is given by the divine other and an extreme vigilance for other people. The limits of egocentrism are thereby announced long in advance of those critics who seem to know only the statement from the earliest part of Genesis that states that "man shall take dominion over the earth." Even the trees of the field have "rights" of their own. This is not to dispute that the human being has a place of primacy in the philosophical anthropology of the Jewish Bible. But, just as domestic animals are not allowed to work on the Sabbath Day, so too do trees have a certain purpose that must be respected: "When you come in to the land, and you shall plant any fruit tree, you shall treat its fruit as forbidden. For three years they shall be forbidden to you, they shall not be eaten" (Lev. 19:23). According to the commentary tradition, this is an exceptional law because it not only relates emphatically to the land of Israel, but also generally to all places where fruit-bearing trees are planted. This may have a practical ecological purpose of its own. However, in the context of the laws of holiness, including those that pertain to the sabbatical year, there appears to be a degree of respect and dignity that is recognized in the restraint and regard that must be shown with respect to the order of creation.

If we look at this from an Aristotelian perspective, the trees, like other "natural" beings, have a promise to be achieved. In a sense, the fruit-bearing trees are taken up within the covenant between God and every living being (Gen. 9). However, this covenant positions human beings at the center. While man is compared to a tree of the field (Deut. 20), the human being, unlike trees and animals, has a twofold promise.

What we might call "generational responsibility" binds the future of others to that of our own present. The "land" becomes the third term in this self-other relation. To live well, human beings need a habitable environment. In turn, this requires that we leave a sustainable environment to others. On either side of our own generation, we have a communal as well as a personal responsibility. How is this to be enacted in the present? Vigilance is required that we not use up in a wasteful manner what is not ultimately ours. Vigilance also requires that we face the demands of our children and their children in advance. The claims of my neighbor and their neighbors are no less important from a moral point of view.

Just as the unharvested land of the sabbatical year is for the sake of other people, so, too, does the sabbatical year appear as time that is other, that is set aside by the Other. Just as the days of the week are a time of creativity, so too are we enjoined to endow our labor with meaning and purpose for others. This is not simply work that is devoid of content. To leave a habitable, sustainable environment is a precondition for a purposive existence. It is in this way that I, too, have a future that arises from a responsibility that originates with others. Water, food, and in our time, even the very air we breathe, cannot be taken for granted. The appearance of the Sabbatical Year, when there is neither to be planting or harvesting, sowing or reaping, is an expression of diachronic time. The natural world becomes more philosophically comprehensible and existentially meaningful when it is taken up within the horizon of interpersonal time and place.

This is the conjuncture between the imperative "not to oppress one another" and to provide for one another. This makes the idea of a covenantal relation between the other and the self, concrete and embodied. It cannot exclude what must include the common places that we inhabit together. This does not mean that the future will necessarily be better than the present or the past. As Richard Cohen points out, the future at this radical level is unforeseeable: "The future is always the prospect of the new, the different, the otherwise—the unforeseen" (UH, xiv). The biblical notion of "time bearing a promise" cannot be reduced to the Enlightenment concept of inevitable progress based upon scientific discovery. The future may be either promising or unpromising. However, it cannot revert to the realm of pure neutrality, that which Levinas calls the "il y a," without divesting the human of its humanity, or the person of the personal. The reason for this is that the il y a collapses all time into a formalist present in which neither the past nor the future can be experienced or understood.

In the same discussion of the sabbatical year, Scripture states, "Each of you shall not aggrieve his fellow. And you shall fear your God, for I am Hashem your God" (Lev. 25:17). This reiterates the responsibility that each has for the others, so central to the Torah and the philosophy of Levinas. My hope for the future is dependent upon and originates with the promise of the other, most emphatically the other person. We see this movement out of egocentricity cataloged in its logical sequence by Rashi. The movement that begins with loving your fellow as yourself is expanded in detail in the laws of the sabbatical year. After seven cycles of the sabbatical year, comes the remarkable announcement of a second sabbatical to follow in the fiftieth year. A special place is set aside for the fiftieth year called in Hebrew the *yovel* (the Jubilee Year): "You shall sanctify the fiftieth year and proclaim freedom throughout the land for all of its inhabitants: it shall be the Jubilee Year for you, you shall return each man to his ancestral heritage and you shall return each man to his family." Once again, we are cautioned. The text indicates that the *yovel* involves the restoration of all injuries and insults to people and land.

In this context, the prohibition against idolatry represents a warning against the suffering caused by egocentricity, the ultimate source of idolatry. The movement toward the other from the self is the very itinerary of ethical life in the philosophy of Levinas. The philosophical anthropology that accompanies this movement is found in its embodied expression in the portion of Scripture dealing with the sabbatical year. It is perhaps not by accident that in the absence of a Court or Sanhedrin that the time of the *yovel* is not able to be enacted. Is this because the *yovel* requires the capacity for perfect justice that is presently unable to be legislated?

AN ETHICAL ESCHATOLOGY

Bechukosai: Laws for Which Reasons Are Not Given
(Leviticus 26:3–27:34)

One of the most difficult philosophical problems in the Hebrew Bible is that of the relationship of history to divine justice. Since the early part of the eighteenth century, we are accustomed to refer to this problem as that of "theodicy." Theodicy means justifying the ways of G'd to human beings. Yet this would mean penetrating "the mind of G'd," as it were. We call this would-be discipline "theosophy." This is paradoxical because in order to "know G'd" directly from his own side, as it were, we should have to be G'd.[32] Levinas rejects theosophy as the very negation of philosophy. According to Levinas, theodicy received its name from Leibniz in 1710. Levinas goes on to remark that theodicy is

> as old as a certain reading of the Bible. It dominated the consciousness of believers who explained their misfortunes by reference to Sin.... This theodicy is in a certain sense implicit in the Old Testament, in which the drama of the Diaspora reflects the sins of Israel. The misconduct of the ancestors, still unexpiated by the sufferings of the exile, explain to the exiles themselves the length and harshness of that exile. (EN 1998, 96–97)

Levinas situates his reflections on theodicy within the context of European humanity in general and the Holocaust of European Jewry in particular. The power of the idea of theodicy is one that Levinas clearly recognizes, yet it is one that he believes has exhausted its meaning. Until this moment in our reading of the Jewish Bible, Levinas appears as a thoroughly orthodox Jewish thinker whose reading of Scripture, while original and vibrant, is nonetheless consistent with other received commentaries.

However, Levinas cautions against what he calls "explaining" the suffering of others to them. He regards this as an act of ethical imperialism. The logical

---

32 I first learned this from my late-lamented friend, Rabbi Shmuel Hecht (1948–1978).

consequence of his position is founded on the moral impossibility of justifying the suffering of innocents. If there is consolation for the survivors of the
Holocaust, it is for them to determine, not me. These are the words of a man
whose entire family of origin—his father, his mother, his brothers, his mother's
father and mother—were all murdered during the Holocaust. These are the
words of a man who himself spent five years as a Jewish prisoner of war in a slave
labor camp near Hanover, Germany. It is not, however, for autobiographical
reasons that Levinas presents his views or that we should accept them.

If we look at Levinas's reflections on theodicy more carefully, we find a very
subtle and complex philosophy that perhaps leaves open a role for divine providence in relation to human affairs. What this position raises for Levinas is
perhaps the least defined aspect of his philosophy—that is, the notion of divine
providence, or its absence, and its intelligibility. His view of human suffering is
subtle and involves what we might call a "bimodal logic." Keep in mind that he
sees himself first and foremost as a phenomenologist who describes and explains
to others only that which appears within the context of possible experience. This
is why he calls the last of his three great books, *Of God Who Comes to Mind*,
his major work on "religion." This means that the trace of divine understanding
remains for us in the realm of Torah study, *mitzvos,* and everyday experience.
He is not interested in penetrating the mind of G'd, something that he believes
is philosophically impossible.

Before examining his philosophy on this important subject more carefully, let us look at the text of Scripture itself and some alternative explanations.
According to tradition, the order of the Torah, as well as its contents, have an
inherent meaning and logic. Peace and prosperity are promised in relation to
the observance of mitzvot. The security of dwelling peacefully in the land of
Israel is closely linked to the observance of the laws of the sabbatical year. As
we have seen in the previous portion, this kind of wellbeing or blessing is associated with a transcending of egocentrism. This kind of egocentrism applies not
only on a personal level but also on a social and national one. It is important to
remember that it is Israel as a people who are addressed in the keeping of the
sabbatical years and the *Yovel*. The oral tradition holds that the inability to keep
theses observances is associated with exile and all the insecurities and tribu-
lations that follow from the loss of sovereignty. The laws of the sabbatical year
pertain to the kind of self-mastery that permits an economic and social justice
to be expressed with an unreserved generosity towards the "widow, the stranger,
the orphan, and the poor." This generosity, which is most severely tested with the
absence of planting, plowing, and harvesting, reveals an attitude toward other

creatures as well as the earth. In the language of philosophy, it is a refusal to permit the earth to be viewed from the perspective of "naturalism alone." The human subject is to treat others with the kind of respect owed to created beings (*kavod habrios*). When this does not happen, then the laws of nature, most especially, the law of preserving and extending the self or the *conatus essendi* takes over and rules. Hence, the curses that follow the blessings represent a return to the state of nature.

We should not overlook the important commentary of Rashi on the beginning of the Torah portion before us. Rashi comments on the opening statement: "[I]f you will go in My decrees and observe My commandments and perform them; then I will provide you rains in their time, and the land will give its produce and the tree of the field will give its fruit" (Lev. 26:3–4). Rashi states that you should be "laboring" in Torah and you shall study them (mitzvoth) and you shall observe them to perform them (Rashi, vol. 3, Saperstein edition, 348). Keep in mind that the kinds of laws alluded to in the name for this Torah portion are *chukkim*, those laws that transcend reason. In this respect, such laws may well be rational but are not necessarily transparently so. This is how they differ from the laws for which reasons are given or for which they can be easily adduced. These latter laws are referred to as to the *Mishpatim*. About the Mishpatim, Saadya Gaon is reported to have said that "in an infinite amount of time, all rational beings can concur with their rationality." However, as Saadya points out, we are finite beings, and therefore the Torah makes it possible for us to have knowledge prior to our experience and avoid the tragic sense of life (Saadya, 27). Is it any wonder, then, that Rashi says our "laboring" in Torah is necessary for purposes of observance and the application that comes with performance. *Mizrachi*, in the standard supercommentary on Rashi, notes that observance is a higher level than study but not yet actual fulfillment[33] (Rashi, Sapirstein, 348n3).

Levinas appreciates the central and even normative role that Rashi occupies in approaching and interpreting the Jewish Bible.[34] Commenting on a vital aspect of this Torah portion, Rashi notes that this blessing or that curse is the kind of divine attention or direction in relation to Israel that is at stake. More precisely, Scripture states "and I will direct my face against you … you will fall

---

33 This refers to the classic super-commentary on Rashi's Pentateuch. It was authored by R'Eliyahu Mizrachi (1450–1525 of Constantinople.)

34 As noted before, for thirty years Levinas taught an ongoing course on Rashi, which was open to the public and took place each Sabbath afternoon in connection to the Torah portion of the week. We do not as of yet have access to Levinas's reflections on Rashi's commentary.

but there will be no one pursuing you" (Lev. 26:17). Rashi indicates that the words "I will direct my face" means "I will direct my attention." Maimonides, in *Guide for the Perplexed*, notes that the Hebrew word for face, *panim*, is derived from the verb *panah*, "he turned," and signifies also "aim," because people generally turn their faces toward the thing they desire (GFP 1956, 16). The revealing or turning away of the divine "face" is associated with the revealing and concealing of providence. In the language of the medievals, this is referred to as *Deus Revelatus* or *Deus Absconditus*. To return briefly to Rashi's commentary, Rashi calls attention to the fact that "if you will not engage in Torah study ... it is inevitable that you will not perform ... these commandments" (Stone, 711). The admonition (*tochacha*) that begins with the refusal to labor in Torah study ends with the denial of the existence of God Who made the covenant (Ibid.).

Prior to Levinas, most philosophic discussions of God belong to the realm of what Levinas calls "onto-theology." Onto-theology involves an approach to God through a prior understanding of Being. Such a notion, according to Levinas, is unfaithful to the absolute transcendence of God. This is the case because by opposing the God of philosophy to the God of Abraham, Isaac, and Jacob, one winds up reducing the latter to the former and therefore presumably penetrating the impossible—that is, the mind of God. As theosophy is at the furthest possible remove from philosophy for Levinas, theosophy would arrogate to itself the capacity to understand the mind of God. This means nothing less than to be God. In other words, it would involve comprehending the infinity of that which is absolutely other. This is not for him a task proper to human understanding or philosophy, for philosophy always begins in the recognition that the other transcends me. How much more so in the case of the absolutely Other. Let us keep in mind that Levinas is not interested in the human contact with the sacred; rather he is concerned with the relation of human beings to the holy and holiness.[35] As previously stated, Levinas understands the role of the Torah as a "protection against the madness of a direct contact with the Sacred that is unmediated by reason" (DF 1990, 144).

Let us begin by again reflecting on what Levinas insists is the "end of theodicy" (EN 1998, 97). The Holocaust of European Jewry, for Levinas, is a suffering that cannot be rationalized. As he says, "It renders impossible and odious every proposal and every thought that would explain it by the sins of those who have suffered or are dead. But does not this end of theodicy, which imposes itself in the face of this century's inordinate trial, at the same time and in a more

---

35 The sacred, such as it is understood by Eliade and others, belongs in the realm of ontology and therefore of power.

general way, reveal the unjustifiable suffering in the other; *the outrage it would be for me to justify my neighbor's suffering*" (Ibid., 98).

Does this not put him at odds with the normative tradition? Yes and no. Levinas does not say anywhere that I cannot attribute reward and punishment, happiness and suffering to and for myself. However, to place the other person, whose face reflects the trace of the Infinite, under such systematic constraints is ethically impermissible. Just as I cannot forgive on behalf of another who has been aggrieved without his or her assent, I cannot absolve the other person of his or her suffering by explaining it away. One can do this only for oneself. That is, if he or she is the one who has suffered offense, a third party cannot pardon the perpetrator without the consent of the offended other.

Regarding forgiveness, Levinas's position is grounded in Talmudic reflection. As Levinas explains, in his Talmudic reading "Toward the Other," "the offended party can grant forgiveness when the offender becomes conscious of the wrong he has done." He goes on to ask: "[I]s the offender capable of measuring the effect of his wrongdoing? Do we know the limits of our ill will?" In his reflection, Levinas states, "There are two conditions for forgiveness. The good will of the offended party and the full awareness of the offender. But the offender is in essence unaware. Aggression ... is the lack of attention par excellence" (NTR 1990, 25). In the context of the Torah portion before us, this becomes important in connecting both the origin of the Exile (in the time of the First Temple) as a result of the awareness that must accompany the refusal to honor the sabbatical years: "The Land will be bereft of them; and it will be appeased for its sabbatical (*shemittah*) years having become desolate of them; and they must gain appeasement for their iniquity" (Lev. 26:33). It is important to emphasize here that it is the Torah itself that explicitly makes the connection between the nonobservance of the sabbatical years and exile. This would suggest, in the language of Levinas, that the national calamity of exile follows upon an absence of generosity toward the other that is associated with the depth dimension of the observance of the sabbatical years. This is known in and through "laboring" in the study of Torah and not from the superimposition of the rationalizing of suffering associated with theodicy.

That Levinas accepts the holiness of transcendent justice is beyond dispute. However, what remains unclear is his position on the relation of such justice to a judge who is transcendent to history. Here there appears to be a tension in his thinking. In the opening pages of *Totality and Infinity*, we find Levinas's reflections on eschatology. There he states, "We are judged not only at the end of time, but at each of its instants" (TI 1969, 22). He opposes theological and political positions where the last act alone would change beings into their essential selves.

In order to comprehend Levinas's reworking of the notion of eschatology, it is necessary to understand that, for him, politics originates with ethics. This is not merely a utopian politics, nor is it at ease with the idea of eschatology commonly understood in theology. The more common position would depend upon additional information about the future by presumptuously knowing in advance "by revealing the finality of being." Eschatology, for Levinas, institutes a relation with being "*beyond* the totality or beyond history, not with being beyond the past and the present" (Ibid., Levinas's emphasis). The ethical eschatology that frames the thinking of Levinas relies on "a surplus *always exterior to the totality* ... as though another concept, the concept of infinity, were needed to express his transcendence with regard to totality, a non-encompassable within a totality" (Ibid., 23). From the standpoint of eschatology, such time is always beyond itself. By remaining on this side of the "accomplishment of history, while there is still time ... where existents can speak rather than lending their lips to an anonymous utterance of history" (Ibid., 23).

Inscribed here is a philosophy of history waiting to be written. Such a position would situate justice proximate to the events undergone and not leave judgment simply to the historiography of the survivors. In this way, there is a refusal to reduce the transcendent to the immanence of the economy of historical events written as though one knew in advance what Levinas calls "the finality of being." Such an account, however, must sharply distinguish between the Enlightenment notion of progress and the biblical idea of time bearing a promise. Time bearing a promise originates with the other and therefore with his or her urgent demands that transform me from a self to an ethically elected subject, thus making me infinitely responsible for all others far or near, absent or present. This excessive responsibility is modulated by a justice that makes room for my claims, as well. It is a justice that is always wanting to be perfected and therefore can be found wanting, as well. Still, the covenantal notion of justice is visible from the human side as subject to the responsible actions of free human beings. In this way, it differs from the impersonal and ineluctable progress that issues from the discovery of the laws of nature and the advances made by technological innovation that would assume a neutrality toward conduct.

Levinas's critique of theodicy rejects the reduction of the biblical notion of promise, with its infinite dimension, to the totalizing concept of progress that can remain indifferent to the extreme inversion of justice. In relation to the Holocaust, Levinas asks, "Who will say the loneliness of those who thought themselves dying at the same time as Justice, at a time when judgments between good and evil found no criterion but in the hidden recesses of subjective conscience, no sign from without?" (PN 1996, 119). Using the language of the

Talmud, Levinas remarks about morality that it can only "know and justify itself in the fragility of the conscience, in the 'four cubits of the *Halakah*,' in that precarious, divine abode" (PN 1996, 123). In other words, from our side, from the human side, what is left and what gives us our moral compass is to labor in the study of the Torah.

Before the Talmudic phrase that Levinas refers to, the four cubits of *halakah* refer to the study, observance, and practice of Jewish law. This is what remains after the time of the Roman exile, beginning with the destruction of the Second Temple around year seventy of the Common Era. Even in the apparent absence of the *shekinah*, the in-dwelling presence of God, this does not alter the way we are asked to study, act, or live. In fact, the study of the law is done both for its own sake and for the sake of practice. It is this space of *halakah*, beginning with the common shared study of the Talmud, that makes it possible for us to act ethically and therefore rationally toward one another. Levinas is fond of citing the discussion between two scholars of the Talmud: R' Eliezer and R' Joshua. In a Talmudic dispute, the latter invokes miracles to prove that he is right in his proof. However, the miracles are dismissed as irrelevant by his interlocutor, and all those present, as not having bearing on the subject at hand (BT, 59b). This means that our concerns may be directed toward on high, but what remains of surpassing importance is the resolution of problems in the interhuman sphere, with or without blessings or miracles.

Numbers

BAMIDBAR

ON THE BOOK OF NUMBERS

The Book of Numbers traces the movement of the Israelites from the teachings given at Sinai through the journeys that precede the going into the land of Israel. As such, there are important historical developments that become progressively more concrete regarding human aspirations, their disappointments, and achievements. The first three portions deal with a great variety of social relations and how they are to be conducted, managed, and adjudicated. Above all peace is the desired end.

The next five portions, beginning with *Shelach*, discuss the reasons given for not being able to enter the land until a new generation has arisen. Each of these provides a different Levinasian lens on the challenges to true peace. In *Korach*, we see the beginnings of a mutiny against Moses and Aaron. This section focuses on the conjuncture of ethics, politics, and holiness. The portion called *Chukas* deals with those laws that are, unlike the *mishpatim*, suprarational in character. *Balak* deals with the relation of morality to prophecy, personified in the relation between Israel and the nations. *Pinchas* deals with zealotry and its limits. It is particularly timely in our age, when fanaticism threatens to overtake devotion. The last two portions, *Mattos* and *Masei*, deal with the relations between words and deeds, promises and their fulfillment, and the normative relations that value persons over property. According to the rabbinic tradition, the Book of Numbers concludes the original events that took place from the outgoing of Egypt to just before the entrance to the land of Promise.

ON THE IRREPLACEABILITY OF THE HUMAN

Bamidbar: In the Wilderness
(Numbers 1:1–4:20)

Perhaps the names of persons whose saying signifying a face—proper names, in the middle of all those common names and common places—can resist the dissolution of meaning and help us to speak.

—PN 1996, 4

The opening of the Book of Numbers records a census of the Israelites. In the commentary tradition, there is a continuing question as to what this adds to what we already know. The discrepancies between this census and the two previous countings, when the Israelites left Egypt (Exod. 12:37) and after the sin of the Golden Calf (Exod. 28:36), is a subject for reflection on the part of the commentators. Rashi comments that this census of all males between the ages of twenty and sixty, by their tribes, is a reflection of God's love for the Israelites. However, the *Ramban* adds additional reasons for the census. Like Rashi, he notes the fact that this time, each individual tribe, family, and their leaders are specifically named. This is seen by the *Ramban* as an indication of their "individual, personal, worth" (Stone, Num. 1:1n1, 726). The philosophical commentary of R' Yitzchak Arama, *Akedas Yitzchak,* notes the conjuncture of numbering and naming. It suggests that while generations can succeed one another, at another level every person is irreplaceable (Akedas Yitzchak, vol. 2, 682–84).

This relates to Levinas's reflections upon the dissolution of language and the possible loss of its claiming power: "Time no longer conveys its meaning in the simultaneity. Statements no longer succeed in putting things together. 'Signifiers' without signifieds play a 'sign game' with neither sense nor stakes" (PN 1996, 4). He goes on to suggest the importance of proper names in forestalling the dissolution of language and perhaps restoring its signifying power: "*Perhaps the names of persons whose saying signifying a face—proper names, in the middle of all those common names and common places—can resist the dissolution of meaning and help us to speak.* Perhaps they will enable us to divine, behind the downfall of discourse, the end of a certain *intelligibility*, but the dawning of a new one" (PN 1996, 4).

One of the increasing worries of our generation concerns the relation of quantity to quality. Is it possible to count that which is irreducibly unique or qualitative? The homogenization of society, propelled by the mathematical-scientific turn and the Industrial Revolution, has been succeeded by the economic reduction of virtually everyone, as well as everything, to a commodity. As compensation for this, there is a strong pedagogical emphasis upon "cultural diversity." In the understandable quest for uniqueness, we seek out differences—between people, between cultures, between versions of reality or the world. These differences, however, are more often apparent than real. Virtually all of the great universities of the West emphasize the importance of understanding cultures and traditions different from one's own. But language betrays this pedagogical inspiration.[1]

We are different *because* we are unique, we are not unique because we are different. What, then, do we mean by "uniqueness"? An expression of uniqueness is found when we associate people with proper names, rather than reduce them to a series of economic, social, or grammatical functions. Uniqueness, for Levinas, is associated with irreplaceability. Irreplaceability refers to moral responsibility. It signifies the manner in which I become responsible for others. No one can take my place, not even G'd himself, for making me answerable to and for the claims of other people. How does this work?

The arrangement of the Israelites into four distinct groups positioned in relation to the Sanctuary and the Ark of the Covenant involves these different groups facing one another. Thereby, each group recognizes its responsibility for itself but also maintains a concern for others that radiates out from a center of responsibility toward the periphery. This represents the way in which the Divine

---

1   We speak, for example, of "non-Western" traditions. This of course hides, for Levinas, a cultural and even an ethical imperialism, however unintended. Rather than defining another culture in its own terms first, its identity is one of being "non-Western," hence giving the first and last word to whatever might be intelligible in terms of the West. Instead of this endless series of self-assertions and negations with some syntheses, Levinas proposes that we start with the other (culture) rather than our own.

Other turns me around. By turning me around, the other makes it possible for me to be an ethically elected subject. Here we find that the gatherings of three tribes together on each side indicate a fraternal solidarity that is not in opposition to the other groupings but complimentary to them. Taken together, the four groupings do not, however, form a static totality. Rather, there is a recognition that there is something unique and irreplaceable in a way that the subject assumes responsibility for each other person.

The reader will note that on each of the four sides, three tribes are grouped together with the Sanctuary guarded by the Levites in the center. Originally, the first and second tablets given at Sinai were placed within the ark (*aron*) in the very center of the Sanctuary. Subsequently, the entire scroll of the Torah is placed there as well. Each of the groups, then, is facing the other three, mediated only by the Torah itself. It is the Torah that indicates how one comports oneself in the face-to-face relation, with all of its ethical prescriptions and implications. This pertains immediately to the leaders of each of the tribes and to the members of each tribe individually.

Does this, then, form a way of uniting that does not end in a totality? Recall that this is not a rigid, fixed system. The ark is transported only by the Levites (or, more precisely, a subgroup of the Levites) without actually touching it. Rather, they use the staves designated for upholding the ark to bear its weight. There is an adage that it is the Torah that bears the weight of the people and not the other way around. We are told by the tradition that the entire encampment, including the Sanctuary and the *aron*, were moved forty-two times on the journey through the wilderness or desert (*midbar*) (cf. Num. 33:1). In other words, the original event of the Torah given at Sinai travels through time and place while its principles remain constant. The teachings of the Torah become actual only when attended to and safeguarded, as at the coming together, face-to-face, of the tribes through the prism of the Torah. To put this simply, the uniqueness of each person is preserved even though that person is succeeded by others, beginning with one's own children, who also have proper names.

INTIMATIONS OF PEACE

Nasso: Count
(Numbers 4:21–7:89)

Peace is produced as this aptitude for speech.

—TI 1969, 23

Emmanuel Levinas observes that philosophers distrust the notion of peace, especially "messianic peace." He comments: "To be sure, they profit from it to announce peace also; they deduce a final peace from the reason that plays out its stakes in ancient and present-day wars. They found morality on politics" (TI 1969, 22). Levinas contests this idea. He argues, rather, that politics is founded on morality and that truth itself cannot exist or endure without peace. He states: "To tell the truth, ever since eschatology has opposed peace to war, the evidence of war has been maintained in an essentially hypocritical civilization that is attached to both the True and the Good, henceforth antagonistic" (Ibid., 24). The human activity of philosophy rests upon a non-violent, nonallergic, and ultimately peaceful relation with the other person. Otherwise, we should not be able to speak philosophy together.

In the realm of ontology, or the meaning of Being, modern philosophic thought beginning with Hobbes and Spinoza is governed in the first place by the effort to preserve oneself in being, and therefore, if necessary, at the expense of anyone else with whom one might have to struggle in order to secure one's place under the sun. This kind of peace is the mere interruption of war that is incessant. Levinas provides an alternative view of peace and war, where peace would achieve the normative condition of being human, and where it would, in fact, be a precondition for a philosophy based in ethical life. The biblical version of being human begins not with the self but with the other. Here, we can begin to understand how a peaceful relation with others makes the search for truth possible. It is disinterested benevolence that allows us to gain a kind of critical distance on our own self-interest that precedes all mathematical objectivity. It is only in the face of a plurality of interlocutors that speech takes on a living meaning so that the interplay between questioning, answering, and responding can be enacted.

One of the names for G'd in Hebrew is Shalom, or "peace" (BT, Shabbos, 110b). It is also a word used commonly in everyday discourse, associated with comings and goings, greetings and farewells. In other words, it is a transitive rather than a static term when used between people. The priestly blessing or the *Birchas Kohanim*, uttered every day in the morning service in the land of Israel, but only on holy days outside of the land, reads as follows: "The Lord bless thee and keep thee, the Lord make his face to shine upon thee and be gracious unto thee. The Lord lift up his face, lift up his countenance upon thee and give thee peace" (Num. 7:24–7:26, Soncino). The prescribed priestly blessing is placed immediately after the laws of abstinence associated with the Nazirite and just before the offerings of the tribal leaders. There is an assymetrical dimension to its performance, though both elements reference the face or countenance. The people avert their gaze from the *Kohanim* only when peace moves from the vertical to the horizontal plane, where there is peace between one person and the next. For peace to be truly divine it must be played out in the face-to-face relations of the interhuman sphere.

So important is the peace between husband and wife, idiomatically referred to as peace in the home (*Shalom Bayis*) that under certain conditions, G'd demands that His name be effaced in order to restore this kind of peace to the home. "Ordinarily it is forbidden to erase the sacred Name, and one who does so is liable to lashes, but G'd demanded that His Name be erased in order to bring peace between man and wife" (Stone, Num. 5:28n28). The case concerns the *sotah*, a woman suspected of adultery by her husband but for which there is no proof because there are no witnesses. The husband has specifically prohibited his wife from secluding herself with a specific man, a named individual. This is a very rare event, to which all kinds of conditions are attached, including the requirement that her husband cannot be guilty of the same conduct of which he accuses his wife. In addition, the wife always has the alternative of refusing this rite of sotah renouncing her wedding contract (*ketubah*). Moreover, if she is found innocent, then he is never allowed to divorce her. Furthermore, G'd will give her "a child to compensate for her ordeal" (Ibn Ezra, cited in Stone, 757n23). Divorce is then allowed in favor of peace. The effacing on the scroll that included G'd's name further signifies that peace takes precedence over virtually everything else (TB, Shabbat, 116a.)

Close to the portion of the *Sotah* is that of the Nazir, a person who takes a vow of abstinence, usually associated with a limited period of asceticism. The rabbinic tradition sees the description of the Nazir as following, logically, as well as sequentially, from that of the *Sotah*. Just as the *Sotah* is charged because of excessive seclusion from the larger community, the Nazir's asceticism is viewed with a certain degree of suspicion and discouraged. After all, engagement with the world, not withdrawal, is the normal state of affairs.

Under most conditions the Nazir's remove is understood to be a temporary state of affairs, usually for a period of thirty days. The vow of the Nazir emphasizes abstinence from wine, cutting of the hair, and keeping away from anything that would render him impure—especially that of a dead body awaiting burial. When a person transgresses, the reason given by the tradition is that "the spirit of folly" has entered into the person. This is more likely to happen when there is an excess of wine. Hence, an attentiveness to sobriety is recognized as a measure of caution. Not only will specific actions that are prohibited be more likely to be avoided, but placing oneself in such problematic positions is also less likely. In other words, not only is a person responsible for his or her specific actions, but for the conditions in which one places oneself.

Such unusual restraint is associated with a holiness devoted to the purpose of promoting peace between human beings. Why is this the case? Most transgressions are spurred by egocentrism, or in psychological language, narcissism. It is for this reason that the Nazir can be elevated only by separating himself from the community. He lets his hair grow to render himself unattractive. With his isolation, he achieves a new sense of elevation, although provisional, in which he can respond to others in a non-self-involved way. Levinas, in a brilliant reading of the Talmud on this subject, calls this non-self-involvement, "disinterestedness" (NTR 1990, 127).

In this reading, Levinas opens up the ethical-metaphysical dimension of the Nazir. He makes several distinct yet interrelated observations. He notes that "most Nazirites make vows, either when they are in trouble, or to atone for a sin" (NTR 1990, 127). He also cites at length the reaction of Shimon Hatzadik, who was also the *kohen gadol.* Shimon Hatzadik recounts (BT, 4b) the case of a young shepherd whose motivation for becoming a Nazirite was considered proper, a vow for the sake of heaven. The story is quite simple at one level. It resembles the Greek myth of Narcissus, but with a vital variation. Like Narcissus, the young shepherd became enamored of his own beautiful hair and fine form when he looked into the water. Unlike Narcissus, this realization concerned him, and so he became a Nazir.

Levinas asks why an act normally viewed as self-interested is, in this case, considered exceptional and something to be emulated. What insight did the young shepherd have into his own conduct? "It is that self-contemplation he shunned: What he objected to was not being beautiful but looking at oneself being beautiful" (NTR 1990, 127). Levinas goes on to say: "He rejected the narcissism which is self-consciousness, upon which our Western philosophy and morality are built" (Ibid.). For Levinas, the young shepherd represents what he calls "disinterestedness"—another more radical way of doing philosophy, by beginning with right conduct. To put it succinctly, as Levinas does elsewhere, "[T]o know God is to know what must be done" (DF 1990, 17). Disinterestedness is one of the most basic categories of the thinking of Emmanuel Levinas. It is not to be confused with an absence of interest, but rather is associated with a kind of benevolence that goes beyond the exclusively moral and creates in a soul a generosity of spirit.

What the young shepherd resisted was to see his image eternally frozen in a timeless youth. It is this that made him ready to reenter the world of aging and even dying of those around him. In this sense, he finds not the infinite regress of self-consciousness, but the *infinite egress of self-transcendence.*

Implicit in Levinas's discussion of the young shepherd, or noble Nazir, is a radical critique of philosophical idealism. But like much of Levinas's thought, these lines revealing the narcissism of idealism are encrypted. Frequently, he will use a single word or two to refer to a philosophic train of thought. Here, he uses the uncommon word "maieutics" which brings to mind the pedagogy of the Platonic Socrates. He is pointing out that since the time of Plato and Aristotle, *the idea* of the self, and even more so, *the idea* of the other person, represents a higher kind of reality than the actual phenomenon of the other person. This is at the core of Levinas's objections to philosophical idealism. To be more precise, Levinas does not object to self-consciousness, but rather to the idea that such awareness remains an end in itself. Self-consciousness, as it arises in the accusative mode of discourse and grammar, is always already aware that it finds itself "outside the subject" on its way to responding to and for the other in a responsible manner. At rock bottom, the same would be true of morality, which philosophy would include. That is to say, *the idea* of morality has been viewed as greater than its practice. So, too, the idea of the self, the other, the world, is greater than each of these subjects. The other, the world, and the self, become part of an *idea* where external reality is diminished and devalued. As he puts it, "But the young shepherd of Shimon HaTzaddik rejected thinking itself, by which Aristotle's G'd is defined, and with which Hegel's *encyclopedia,* and perhaps Western philosophy, end" (NTR 1990, 127).

Self-consciousness can become a kind of end in itself, where nothing falls short of the importance of *contemplating* the self. In this way, disinterestedness is experienced as a claim made upon the self by the other. The other exceeds my idea of him or her, always. The infinity of the other is met at the very outset of any relation, not simply when all the facts are not enough to presume an understanding that would be complete. The latter is closer to the Greek concept of the indefinite, also referred to as the *apeiron*, which lacks the dimensions of height, depth, and accountability. In the case of the Infinite, it becomes more difficult to make the other into a caricature. This is what the narcissist can never understand nor accept. The other's relation to his or her neighbors then, is also reckoned in terms of my responsibility for him or her. The diminishing of self-gratification on the part of the young shepherd is meant not to evade, but to take on an added degree of responsibility. We must point out here that this responsibility goes deeper than the division between "objectivity and subjectivity" engendered by Descartes and, thereby, set in motion for modern Western philosophic thought. Responsibility refers us back to a kind of reality that precedes both positions within consciousness. Or, as Levinas puts it, "At issue here, is a disinterestedness opposed to the *essence* of a being, which essence is precisely always persistence in essence, the return of essence upon itself, self-consciousness to complacency in self" (NTR 1990, 127).

In isolating oneself from others, one has also chosen to cut oneself off for a time from responsibility for others. It is for this reason that one's self-isolation is completed by bringing an extra offering, a "peace offering" (Num. 6:14). This peace offering symbolizes that he or she is now elevated to a place of membership within the community. The community, in turn, is thereby elevated by his higher level of sanctity, and greater sense of responsibility for others.

One of the longest and apparently most repetitious series of passages in the entire Torah concerns the offerings brought by each of the twelve tribes to the Sanctuary. A commonly asked question is why this could not have been said more simply. In other words, why is it necessary to report all of the items of each of the tribes if they are identical? Furthermore, why did the leaders of the tribes have to bring the offerings themselves, since it included labor that is often thought to be menial in character? As tradition explains, it is to prohibit strife in the interhuman sphere that might develop through jealousy, should one tribe bring something more valuable than another. The offerings, however, do not form a homogenized totality, even though the tally of all the items offered is identical. Each group is represented in its uniqueness by having established a relation with the guardians of the holy Sanctuary that is their own. In other words, even though they have brought the same items, it would appear to be sufficient to amalgamate them so that they still form the kind of social unity that derives from totality. In Levinas's view, they must derive from the irreplaceable uniqueness of responsibility.

We have seen a kind of image of a peaceful society refracted through the prism of justice. Such justice must be achieved at every level of the interhuman order. It applies to those who are close and those who are far, to the neighbor and to the stranger, to husband and wife, and to the diverse dimensions of society. The peace between human beings recognizes the transcendence of every person for every other person. While the administration of the Sanctuary, and then the Temple belongs to the tribe of Levi, it is the Kohanim, the priestly class, who supervise, if we may put it this way, the ordering of holiness. There are divisions even within the Levites, dealing with the outer and inner dimensions of the Sanctuary. And yet, despite this seeming elevation, the priestly classes, including the Kohanim, are not permitted to own any land. Not only are the Levites deprived of owning land, but they are dependent upon the good will of the people and their sacrifices for their very wellbeing. What then, are we to make of the priestly blessing? The *Birchas Kohanim* (the priestly blessing) is not a substitute for justice, but the surplus of a just and ethical society through which peaceful, and therefore loving relationships, can be established.

The priestly blessing speaks of the Divine Countenance that would turn one person toward, rather than against, the other. There is an asymmetry here, between the divine and the human, and within the interhuman sphere, which Levinas describes in an original and penetrating way. The asymmetry of the interpersonal order begins with the recognition that the other person transcends my comprehension. This necessitates rather than precludes the responsibility that comes with proximity. As he says, "The proximity of my fellow man is the responsibility of the *I* for another" (EN 1998, 186). He continues, "Responsibility here is not a cold juridical requirement. It has all the gravity of the love of one's fellow man—of love without concupiscence—on which the congenital meaning of that worn-out word (love) is based, and which is presupposed by all literary culture, all libraries, and the entire Bible, in which its sublimation and profanation is told" (Ibid.). Is it surprising, then, that Moses hears the transcending voice issuing between Cherubim—the symbol of non-concupiscent love—only after peaceful sociality of the offerings brought by the twelve tribes?

Peace, then, is not to be regarded as merely an alternative to war. Rather, it is the very foundation of the social order. Therefore, it becomes a condition for a just society to fully realize its promise. Levinas is aiming at the transposition of the dream of philosophy—namely, the love of wisdom into the wisdom of love. In a very active and transitive sense, it turns each person toward rather than against the other, and, therefore, opens the possibility of what Levinas has called "the wisdom of love." This is why, in everyday usage, when we bid someone "Shalom," either by way of farewell or by way of a word of welcome, the first approach to the other is a peaceful one. This is how proximity becomes a moral as well as an experiential category. This is the way in which peace conditions the search for truth in the world of everyday life.

THE ITINERARY: REDIRECTION

Beha' Aloscha: To Raise Up
(Numbers 8:1–12:16)

He fed us manna. Miraculous food: The real miracle is not that the manna falls from heaven, but it corresponds exactly to our needs. To be nourished on manna: not to need to stock up; messianic times.

—NTR 1990, 65

The journey from Sinai to the land of Promise proves to be longer and more arduous than originally expected. We get a clear, even graphic, idea of the halting interruptions posed by the itinerary of the Israelites. Two statements are set off from the rest of the entire text of Scripture in such a way as to make the commentary tradition ask if this involves a short but separate book of the Hebraic Bible. Before and after the two statements, there is an inverse Hebrew letter, a "nun," the fourteenth letter of the Hebrew alphabet. The text states, "When the Ark would journey, Moses said, 'Arise, Hashem, and let Your foes be scattered, let those who hate You flee from before you,'" (Num. 10:35–36). The inversion of the two Nunnim has been the subject of considerable discussion and debate.

The more important controversy concerns *the reasons* for this apparent break in the narrative, rather than whether or not this constitutes a separate, sixth or even, perhaps, a seventh, book of the Torah. Very simply, in order to speak of seven books, one would speak of the portion before the set off statement and that which comes after it. But clearly these are not considered separate books in practice. Most commentators, classic and modern, believe that the bracketing of this passage is a kindness to the Israelites to interrupt three successive transgressions.

The first transgression, according to the midrash occurs after receiving the laws at Sinai; the Israelites took off as fast as they could like schoolchildren wanting to avoid more homework or, in this case, more laws and, therefore, more restrictions. The second concerns the reiteration of the objection to the manna as tiresome and the developing of a craving for meat. After the insertion of the interruption, there is the complaint made by Miriam and Aaron against their brother, Moses, concerning his separation from Tzipporah, his wife. As we have noted, this separation was understood by Moses to have been commanded so that his readiness to receive divine prophecy and instruction would not be compromised or postponed in any way.

There is a legal tradition that holds that three consecutive repetitions of the same kind of conduct constitute a permanent practice. In Hebrew this is called a *chazakah*. What these three incidents appear to have in common is a kind of ingratitude that would call into question the worthiness of the generation to move so quickly from a slavish to a free and responsible people. Whether or not this portion is chronological is beyond our concerns.

In fact, commenting on the structure of Talmud rather than that of Scripture, Levinas observes about his own work,

> My effort to comment starts from the hypothesis that the Talmud is not simply a compilation. Of that I am persuaded in spite of the appearances to the contrary. And I always ascribe my difficulties in discovering this coherence and this profound originality of the Talmudic statements to the paucity of my means. Perhaps nothing should be published under the title of "Jewish thought" for as long as this logic has not been found. (Ouaknin, 149)

Of course, this does not keep Levinas from commenting on the Talmud any more than it does the Scriptural commentaries. Rather, he appears to be suggesting is that even now, after these thousands of years have passed, we must still regard our own findings as inadequate and, therefore provisional, as long as we have not elicited the logic for reading the texts with greater certitude.

We have already touched upon the complaints concerning the manna (see *Beshallach*). However, the longing for those foods that could be found "free" only in Egypt under the conditions of harsh servitude are exactly those tastes that the manna does not contain—"[l]eeks, fish, garlic" (Num. 11:5). This appears to be a harbinger of the fact that a number of the people are not yet ready to embrace the responsibility attendant to their new freedom. Rather, the nostalgia for a slavish and childlike security forces itself upon their consciousness and creates an oscillation, or at least a hesitation, in the decision to go forward; above all, it would appear to represent a forgetting and, perhaps, a moral insensitivity to the surpassing of slavery and the outgoing from Egypt.

It is in this portion of the Torah that the unique phenomenon of a second Passover offering, one month from the first, is presented. It is for those who were unable, for various reasons, to make the appointed time. Is this a second chance at another level to embrace the significance of the exodus from Egypt? The most recent Lubavitcher Rebbe says that the more general message of the second Passover (*pesach sheni*) is that it is never too late as long as one is still able.

It should be kept in mind, however, that while the order of the passages considered here are subject to some dispute regarding their placement by the commentators, there are some instructive positive developments as well. After the complaints directed toward Moses because of the manna, and perhaps because the path of freedom inscribed for the Israelites is an arduous one, Moses turns to G'd and pleads with Him for assistance. G'd responds to Moses with the instructions for the formation of the first Sanhedrin. The Sanhedrin is composed of seventy men according to the Mishnah (BT, *Sanhedrin* 2a). It emerges as a judicial body in response to Moses's plea for assistance in providing the people with guidance (Stone, Num. 11:16n16). To ensure fairness among the different tribes, a lottery of sorts was held so that two members at large would be selected. The two new prophets, named Eldad and Medad, were selected. They were infused at once with the spirit of prophecy, as were the other elders upon whom the spirit rested. The text says about the others that "when the spirit rested upon them, they prophesied, but did not do so again" (Ibid., 11:25). However, the other two kept on prophesying in the camp. Joshua, the attendant and subsequent successor to Moses, is described as agitated and concerned, especially after he hears their words. According to Rashi, what they said was, "Moses will die. And Joshua will bring Israel into the land" (Ibid., 11:26n26). Moses responds to Joshua, chastising him for being zealous for his sake. He goes on to state, "Would that the entire people of Hashem could be prophets, if Hashem would but place His spirit upon them!" (Ibid., 11:29).

Levinas takes these words of Moses most seriously. He states, "It is true that all men are prophets," enlarging upon the statement that Moses makes to Joshua. He goes on to comment in relation to the prophet Amos, "The eternal G'd has spoken. Who shall not prophesy?" (IRB 2001, 226). Levinas characterizes prophecy as a basic dimension of human discourse: "We call prophecy this reverting in which the perception of an order coincides with the signification of this order given to him that obeys it. Prophecy will thus be the very psyche of the soul: the other in the same, and all of man's spirituality would be prophetic. Infinity is not announced in the witness given as a theme" (OBBE

1991, 149). In other words, before specific prophecies, there is a prophetic intentionality connected to the animation of the soul itself.

Let us keep in mind that the prophet, unlike the oracle, is responsible to others for the inspiration of his own words. The praise that Moses appears to be bestowing upon the prophetic spirit of Eldad and Medad does not appear specifically with reference to the contents of what they have said regarding the death of Moses and the ascendance of Joshua. The inspiration of the prophetic breath, however, bears the trace of the present along into the future. In other words, the actions of the present can be criticized for the sake of a hope for transformation. This would imply that the prophetic element of speech makes itself answerable to and for others in the moment that it is inspired, as well as the moment that it is spoken. Implied here is an elevation of speech itself, not to some rarified realm but rather in daily discourse and exchange, where human beings bear the burden through speech tied to conduct, of looking out for one another.

All speech has a prophetic moment to it for Levinas. Yet not all prophetic speech is on the same level; it has moments of descent and ascent. After Miriam and Aaron speak against Moses, Miriam and Aaron say, "Was it only to Moses that Hashem spoke? Did He not speak to us, as well?" The text interposes the statement, "Now the man Moses was exceedingly humble, more than any person on the face of the Earth!" Is this the very precondition of the asymmetry between G'd and the human that makes it possible for Moses to be the bearer of divine revelation? Regarding Moses, G'd says: "With him I spoke face to face in a vision not containing allegory" (Stone, Num. 11:12).

G'd renders Miriam leprous (k al na refah Nalah, please, HaShem, her now). Moses's intercession is until this day the basis for all liturgical prayers asking for the healing of those who are ill. The willingness of Moses to put himself in the position of his sister, even after she has spoken ill of him, is a sublime example of what Levinas calls "substitution." Substitution begins with placing myself in the position of the other person even to the point of taking responsibility for the one who is against me. It begins with a self-effacing that makes it possible for me to take the place of the other without divesting her of her alterity or me of my subjectivity. It continues to the point where I assist the other in her expiation. The Israelites, upon hearing the news that Miriam will be stricken for seven days, wait for her out of a disposition of gratitude for her benevolence toward them, especially the well of water that has accompanied them because of her merit.

We now have a better understanding of the "additional book" sequestered within Numbers. The breakup of continuous time, of "diachrony" as

Levinas calls it, arises from the need of the Israelites to regain their composure and direction. This, in turn, arouses them out of their temporary stupor and occasions in them a gratitude that had receded too far. It also calls to mind elements of the beginning of the Torah portion before us, including the two silver trumpets that call for the order of the breaking of the camp and the direction of motion oriented forward, toward the land of promise. The trumpets, according to Maimonides (*Pearls of the Rambam*, Num. 10:9, 635–36), represent a summons to wake up from the dilation of the momentary, as though it were authentically tied to the future. It is the occasion for a "re-iteration" of the prophetic conscience. Through this punctuation of time, a sublime moment of *teshuvah,* it becomes possible to reorient oneself toward the original, promised itinerary.

PERMISSION FOR THE PROMISED LAND: GRANTED, DENIED, POSTPONED

Shelach: Send
(Numbers 13:1–15:41)

The explorers undermined the legend of sacred history; they said that
G'd would not be able to fulfill his promises; but now, in addition, they
are contesting that He has ever promised anything at all.

—NTR 1990, 57

Moses sends out twelve explorers to spy out the land of Canaan, one from
each of the tribes. This incident, according to the oral tradition, occurred in
the second year following the outgoing from Egypt. Another thirty-eight years
would await the entrance to the land. The entire generation of men between
the ages of twenty and sixty would perish in the wilderness. Only Joshua and
Caleb would be spared. Our primary question is, why? Can it really be concluded that ten of the twelve spies made a grievous error of judgment through
interpreting what they had experienced rather than merely reporting the facts?

Levinas gives his own commentary on this episode: "[O]n the two pages
of commentary that the Babylonian Talmud (Sotah, 34b–35a) devotes to this
narrative" (NTR 1990, 54). Levinas makes clear that he is interested both in
explicating some problematic issues in the Talmud and pointing out their continuing, contemporary relevance. The most common question asked both by
a careful reader of the text and by the commentary tradition concerns the dis-
proportionate punishment meted out to the entire generation of the wilderness
and the seemingly minor nature of the transgression. In its plainest philosophical sense, the issue appears to be one of dealing with perception and interpretation. Ten spies see a land flowing with "milk and honey," bearing gigantic
fruits, but a land that is also inhabited by giants in relation to whom the spies

are like grasshoppers. According to most commentators, the ten explorers go beyond merely reporting what they have seen, "We were like grasshoppers in their eyes as well" (Num. 13:33). According to the midrash Rabbah, this is the crux of their transgression—that is, claiming to grasp how they were seen and experienced by others. The explorers permitted themselves to be defined not within the context of their own unfolding history, but through the eyes of others.

They give the report after returning from their mission of forty days. Then they announce to Moses and the people of Israel after they "showed them the fruit of the land" that they had encountered the offspring of giants and therefore concluded, "We cannot ascend to that people for it is too strong for us" (Num. 13:31). The ten explorers, each princes of their own tribes, go on to add that, "The land which we have passed, to spy it out, is a land that devours its inhabitants! All the people that we saw in it were huge!" (Ibid., 13:32).

Levinas cites a Talmudic commentary: "It is a land which uses up its inhabitants" Raba taught: "The Holy One, Blessed be He, said: I had a good intention but they interpreted it for the worst. My intention was good: wherever they went the leading citizens died so that, in the confusion, they could not be noticed. Some say: It was Job who died, and all the inhabitants were in mourning. But they interpreted it in a bad sense: it is a land which uses up its inhabitants" (NTR 1990, 67). Levinas immediately uses contemporary language to show the direction of his thought. He is, after all, ultimately dealing with lived experience: "It is a land where one gets used up easily. Heart attacks are frequent there. People work too hard and die early. The proof! There were only funerals around us during the exploration! The explorers want to frighten. In the desert, obviously, one lives much better!" (NTR 1990, 67).

Caleb and Joshua give a dissenting report just before the ten spies draw their conclusions. The text states that "Caleb silenced the people towards Moses and said, 'We shall surely ascend and conquer them, for we can surely do it!'" (Num. 13:30). According to Rashi, Caleb was posing as an ally of the ten spies a moment before in order to get the people to listen to him (Stone, Num. 13:30). This was to no avail, however. The reaction of the Israelites seals the fate of most of that generation: "The entire assembly rose up and issued its voice; the people wept that night. All the children of Israel murmured against Moses and Aaron, and the entire assembly said to them, 'If only we had died in the land of Egypt, or if only we had died in this wilderness! Why is G'd bringing us to this land to die by the sword? Our wives and young children will be taken captive! Is it not better for us to return to Egypt?'" (Stone, Num. 14:1–3).

Joshua then tries to placate the people who had torn their garments as an act of mourning for themselves. He tells the Israelites again how good the land is and then adds, "If G'd desires us, he will bring us to this land and give it to us." He urgently tries to refocus the fear of the Israelites: "But do not rebel against G'd! You should not fear the people of the Land, for they are our bread. Their protection has departed from them; G'd is with us, do not fear them!" (Stone, Num. 14:6–9). The reaction to Joshua's exhortation is catastrophic: "But the entire assembly said to pelt them with stones" (Ibid.). The result is that none of the men from the age of twenty to sixty, except for Caleb and Joshua, go into the land of Promise but perish in the desert. The wives and young children over whom they worried are, however, spared from this edict.

It is important to note that not all the commentators see this event in the same light. And here it is more than simply a matter of emphasis. The *Akeidas Yitzchak* suggests that the spies did not wish to achieve "the perfection of the world" (Nachshoni, vol. 4, 1007). The Lubavitcher Rebbe, Menachem Mendel Schneerson (1902–1994), expands on this theme and argues that "the spies did not wish to descend from their heavenly spiritual level to build society" (Ibid., 1009). He goes on to argue that, in fact, all physical needs and material life were provided for at a minimum. The commentary tradition indicates that the spies were the elect of each tribe. They were attached, then, to a purely spiritual life. More precisely, they were sustained by the manna, which, as Emmanuel Levinas points out, is miraculous in that it "conformed perfectly to their real needs" (NTR 1990, 65). They did not have to worry about their clothing or any sort of diversions or adversity that would keep them from a life of pure Torah study. Above all, they did not have to worry about the future. Levinas compares the spies, in his Talmudic reading on the subject, to the "beautiful souls" of Paris, who do not wish to be bothered with everyday matters, let alone the founding of a just society. The midrash points to Miriam's strategy for rescuing the baby Moses from the Nile and her leading the women and rejoicing after the crossing of the sea. The clouds that encompass them make life between the Israelites and the outside world quite frictionless and peaceful, in the spirit of Aaron, who loves peace and pursues peace. Such peace, however, cannot be at the expense of devaluing the material world. Human beings are not meant to live as angels; "The deed is the essential thing." Actions that make it possible for holiness to permeate this world through divine instruction cannot escape the diachronic time of mitzvoth in a life lived with others.

Yet another phenomenological perspective for viewing these events might be employed. In order to do so, we must ask how their perceptions were skewed or distorted. Their fear turns into panic, strong enough that they perceive the appointed time of entering the land with fear and contrast it unfavorably with the comparative "security" of slavery in Egypt. The people fall victim to nostalgia for the past of oppression that they selectively remember, and only in its narrowest terms. The ten spies clearly wish to dwell in the fullness or presence of the present, where anxieties about the future are controlled or bracketed. G'd, on the other hand, is directing the people of Israel toward their future and, in that sense, endowing their present and their past with direction and meaning. This glorification of the present is the beginning of a kind of letting go of the attachment to the divine promise and the attempt by Israel to escape from its own covenant, a kind of recoiling from its own future. It is in this way parallel to the transgression of substituting the calf of gold for Moses in his absence in a less evident way.

According to Levinas's commentary dealing with this Torah portion, "Promised Land or Permitted Land" (NTR 1990, 51 ff.), the philosophical issues here are ultimately ethical in character. Levinas begins his Talmudic reading with the lengthy analysis of the meanings of the names of each of the spies sent out. He moves from there to a discussion of the sacred history of Israel. He opens up this history with a questioning of the universal conditions of ethical and religious life, at the juncture of society, morality, and holiness. Levinas sees the names of the spies as giving us a clue to the tension of the exposition in the Talmud. He cites Rav Isaac, who says, "We have a tradition according to which the explorers are named after their actions, but we only know how to interpret one name, that of Sethur, son of Michael." Levinas points out, drawing on the Talmud, that the name Michael may be interpreted from the Hebrew *mak*, "he has weakened him" (NTR 1990, 57). However, this could be extended to suggest that Michael means "weak G'd" (Ibid.). Levinas stresses that Michael can also mean "who is like G'd." He appears to be alluding to a kind of ambiguity or enigma within the phenomenon of the name itself. It is instructive to see how Levinas develops this reflection.

Levinas asks: Are the explorers actually arguing that God cannot fulfill his promise, or are they contesting at the same time "that He has never promised anything at all?" (NTR 1990, 57). He augments the first proposition by arguing that G'd promises nothing. In other words, He promises nothing because "He is weak." This, of course, makes no rational sense because either God is God or there is no God, as Plato has Socrates argue in the first systematic philosophic reflection on religion, the *Euthyphro*. However, Levinas advances the view that the rationalization of the spies harbors a subtle kind of psychological atheism. If G'd can do nothing, He "has never done anything, He has promised nothing and does not care at all if virtue is rewarded and vice punished" (Ibid.). The explorers dwell only in the present—that is to say, a present that would be detached from future and past. This means that it is easier for them to forget the significance of the founding commandment: "I am G'd your Lord, who took you out of the house of Egypt, out of the land of bondage." It is not by accident that this command is reiterated at the very end of the entire Torah portion before us (Num. 15:41).

The explorers then, are obsessed with what is immediately around them. They neither wish to think about the conditions out of which they came, nor of their promised destination. This frame of mind is captured by what phenomenology calls "the natural attitude." Everything is the way it is simply because that is the way it is given—by nature. In other words, the spies see only measurable objects in the world around them. Everyone is susceptible to transformation into a thing or an object. The natural attitude takes its orientation from a purely mathematical-scientific description of perception. This is true of trees, fruits, people, friends and foes alike. Hence, the atonement demanded for public, unintentional idol worship is announced just after the episode of the spies (Num. 15:24–26). As such, G'd is mistakenly represented as the most powerful visible thing or object. Such a God simply becomes one large piece in the puzzle of totality.

This kind of idolatry may be subtle in its expression and represents a refusal of transcendence. Hence, the fear of the giants who then, from the standpoint of the natural attitude, would be pitted against G'd, who would Himself be reduced to a competing natural object. This leads to confusion that, in turn, is capable of transforming unintentional idolatry to a more premeditated kind. According to Rashi, this is why, in the giving of the Ten Commandments, the prohibition of idolatry follows directly after the declaration where G'd identifies Himself with the founding event of the liberation from slavery in Egypt. That, in turn, signifies both His involvement with and transcendence to history. And is this not why, after the episode of the explorers, a specific prescription is given for the atonement of public, unintentional idolatry (Num. 15:24–26)?

Levinas attempts to understand the transgression of the spies in a very concrete way: "Fear seized them; they said to themselves, 'this is what awaits us there. These are the future children of Israel, those people who make holes wherever they set foot, who dig furrows, build cities, and wear the sun around their necks. But that is the end of the Jewish people!" (NTR 1990, 61). Is Levinas making the point that the spies are advocating a philosophic position that is understandable but dubious? The anticipation of settling the land, reverting to agriculture (furrows, cultivation, and holes) and exalting vital values will deprive them of their essential identity as spiritual beings. This would be the end of Israel's unique moral responsibility.

By no means is Levinas critical of the meaningful and self-sacrificing work involved in the forming of modern-day Israel. In a vital passage from his Talmudic reading, he raises the question of founding a just society without encouraging conquerors and colonialists. He adds decisively,

> [B]ut here one must answer: to accept the Torah is to accept the norms of a universal justice. *The first teaching of Judaism is the following: a moral teaching exists, and certain things are more just than others* [my emphasis]. A society in which man is not exploited, a society in which men are equal, a society such as the first founders of the kibbutzim wanted it—because they too built ladders to ascend to heaven, despite the repugnance most of them felt for heaven—is the very contestation of moral relativism. What we call the Torah provides norms for human justice. And it is in the name of this universal justice, not in the terms of some national justice or other that the Israelites lay claim to the land of Israel. (NTR 1990, 66)

Simply then, how are these principles to be applied to the founding of a just society, especially when the elements of displacing others are always in the political foreground or background? Even more so, where is the evidence or internal justification for having established a society based on justice? Here Levinas gives an original response. This is not a matter for "beautiful souls," content with their own lot but not with those of others. In advance, the builders must be committed to justice. And, as Levinas says, "also apply it rigorously to themselves" (Ibid., 68). The governing premise of this moral and existential logic lies in the fact that exile is always already an alternative. Redemption, on the other hand, derives from recognition that responsibility without indulgence must be continually established and meticulously maintained. This is why the language of "going up" before going into the land is used. It must come as a time that achieves justice for others as well as for one's self. But since the neighbor is also owed a certain measure of responsibility, only the laws of moral justice can make a place for him and her and give me guidance in resisting those who would violate my neighbor. In this way, there can also be a place for me in the order of justice.

In 1951, Levinas published an essay entitled "The State of Israel and the Religion of Israel," (DF 1990, 216–21) affirming the reason for the modern nation-state of Israel while offering a cautionary note on its *raison d'être*: "The Jewish people craved their own land and their own state, not because of the abstract independence which they desired, but because they could finally begin the work of their lives.... All the same, it was horrible to be both the only people to define itself with a doctrine of justice, and to be incapable of applying it. The heartbreak and the meaning of the Diaspora" (Ibid., 218). The creation and maintenance of justice is, for Levinas, the link between the state and the religion of Israel.

He insists that this goes beyond the political event of the founding of the state and the distinction between those Jews who are religious and those who are not. He advances a concise distinction to drive the point home: "The subordination of the State to its social promises, articulates the significance of the resurrection of Israel, as, in ancient times, the execution of justice justified one's presence on the land" (Ibid.). The precise formulations of how this kind of justice is to be achieved is not specified. But Levinas gives an important clue. He states, "This means that between the Jewish State and the doctrine which should inspire it, we must establish a science, a formidable one. The relationship between the Jewish State and the Jewish Religion … is that of study" (Ibid., 219). Levinas continues, "The State of Israel will be religious because of the intelligence of its great books which it is not free to forget. It will be religious through the very action that establishes it as a State. It will be religious, or it will not be at all" (Ibid.). Levinas speaks here about a work that has been contested both from within and from without, but whose necessity in incontestable. Levinas is not advocating a dogmatic approach to what is already understood as something quite breathtakingly new, the establishing and maintaining of the modern nation-state of Israel. On the other hand, he is not merely seeking out new variations on the Enlightenment understanding of Judaism. Rather, he sees much study, thoughtfulness, and ethical discourse leading to what we have referred to as his "transcending humanism."

Toward the end of the Torah portion before us, there is a mitzvah announced: "You shall not explore after your heart and after your eyes" (Num. 15:39). In other words, in the context of going toward and retreating from the promised destination, one can easily be misled by the senses and lose sight of the figure-ground relation. On the fringes of my awareness, there are always horizons pointing me beyond myself and my present situation where I am mindful of the past and vigilant for the future of others. It is not at all difficult for the future and the past to become occluded by the overwhelming nature of what is immediately in front of our eyes. This is, in fact, the beginning of all infidelity. When the absence of the other is devalued to the point of being nonexistent, I momentarily slacken my responsibility toward him or her. In order to remedy this, the Torah commands us to "make fringes (*tzitzis*) on all four cornered garments." The numerical value in Hebrew for tzitzis is 613, the number of mitzvahs that are in the Torah (Rashi on Num. 15:39). But how can one be aware of all the 613 mitzvot at the same time? It is not clear that this is what is asked for.

A more practical question concerns the remedy that only fringes would supply. What are fringes? Fringes on most garments are functionally unnecessary. They express something that is otherwise merely decorative. However, according to the American philosopher William James, fringes are what keep the stream of consciousness moving along.[2] The way this happens is that every present moment has a fringe beyond itself, toward a future, sometimes easily perceptible, sometimes less so. This is true for the whole temporal, spatial field. Thereby, we are constantly reminded by the tzitzis when we would tarry overlong, lost in our own thoughts or pleasures, to uproot ourselves. The fringes then, point beyond the figure to a ground of which we may become forgetful. In this sense, the fringes help us to keep refocusing on the context that defines the limits of my situation and the horizon beyond it. This present context leads on to a future one and is at the same time mindful of the contexts from which we come.

It is not at all clear that the facts, as we say, "speak for themselves." Of course, there are facts that are not reducible to interpretation and appropriation. At the same time, as William James and Emmanuel Levinas would tell you, facts are always perceived in relation to value—that is, they are understood as more or less significant or meaningful. The episode of the spies, then, has a contemporary significance. It is this very dimension of depth that belongs to perception to which Levinas refers when he says that "reality has weight" (IRB 2001, 160). While our emerging systems of analytics and metrics are very good at counting things, they do not necessarily measure things that count.

There is, then, a self-distancing dimension signified by the fringes that appear to have been a practical, if partial, remedy to the dilemma of the explorers. The fringes remind us of the importance of context at all times. It means that we are called upon to see the present not in isolation nor the past as something that recedes to nothingness. Rather the future opens onto and informs the present, just as the present carries with it the trace of the past.

Just before this mitzvah that ties together the flawed exploration of the promised land, there is another, related, mitzvah that orders that a separate portion of dough be separated from the making of *challah*. There is a minimal, but not a fixed maximum amount of the *challah*, which is to be set aside and

2   William James, *The Principles of Psychology*, vol. 1.

given to the kohen. Keep in mind that when entering the land of Promise, the Kohanim are ordered to look after the Sanctuary and have no land of their own. They are dependent on the people for their very bread. In other words, the actions arising from the growing of the wheat, the making of the wheat into bread, and the awareness of its purpose all involve activities that render the work, the land, and the bread, as holy. This means that the working of the land can serve a higher purpose.

When Levinas speaks of "time bearing a promise," he refers to the echo of biblical times in our own generation. The reader will remember that the Israelites who perished in the wilderness because of the transgressions of the explorers earlier expressed deep concerns about how their children could possibly bear up under such difficult and unyielding conditions. In this way we see that time bearing a promise extends beyond the present generation to the one that comes after it and the one that we cannot yet envision. This is how the covenant would endure from generation to generation.

BEYOND POWER POLITICS: MUTUALITY AND THE ASYMMETRY OF ETHICAL LIFE

Korach
(Numbers 16:1–18:32)

Morality will oppose politics in history and will have gone beyond the
functions of prudence or the canons of the beautiful to proclaim itself
unconditional and universal when the eschatology of messianic peace
will have come to superimpose itself upon the ontology of war.

—TI 1969, 22

The rebellion by Korach against Moses and Aaron is placed immediately after
the episode of the explorers. This portion begins with the words, "And Korach
took" (Num. 16:1). Ramban interprets this as follows: "His interpretation is
'Korach took thought," (Rashi in *The Metsudah Chumash*, vol. 4, 212). The
question of what Korach was thinking is not revealed until later in the text.
On the surface, he seems to have a reasonable and reasoned argument against
Moses. He asks if the entire assembly is holy, why then do Moses and Aaron
have a place of preeminence? Virtually all of the commentary tradition is in
agreement that Korach is driven by a desire for power. In this sense, we might
note that "Korach *took, but did not give*." He wishes to assume a place of prominence that he would deny to Moses. However, at a deeper level, he appears to be
challenging the asymmetrical ethical relation between one person and another,
in the name of a purported egalitarianism.

There is an understandable skepticism that philosophy brings to religious
life, especially when carried out in a national context. This "hermeneutics of suspicion," as Paul Ricouer calls it, derives in good part from explaining morality
as a rationalization for political power. We are today witnessing an almost
undreamed-of revival of religious imperialism, or "triumphalism," as it was

commonly called by historians of religion. Awareness of this situation often leads to the precipitous conclusion that religion is a subterfuge for political rule. In the contemporary world when the claims are advanced in situations of conflict, there is an appeal to a lofty version of what is referred to and understood as "international law." Such laws are presumed to be predicated on moral considerations or upon ethics itself. Such is the case with the Nuremberg trials, consequent to the destruction of European Jewry.

The very creation of the modern nation-state of Israel was authorized by the General Assembly of the United Nations. The ratification and recognition of Israel by the United Nations in 1948 was widely understood to be an expression of international law. For the countries voting, the ancient tie between Judaism and Israel was an afterthought, at best. Surely it was a political decision. Does this not mean that by being a political decision with international legal ramifications it was presumed to be based on moral reasoning? The revolution affected in Turkey after World War I by Kemal Ataturk advanced the secular ideal over that of religious Islam. However, since 1979, a resurgent and often absolutist form of Islam has sought to repudiate secularism. The key question for Levinas that we can only ask here, is this: Are political as well as religious claims based upon a foundation of justice, a justice that is itself understood in terms of a kind of irreducible expression and application of ethical life? If Levinas is correct, then international law can be understood only as a commonly shared, public morality, therefore secular.

There are over fifty nations in the world presently ruled by Islamic law. What kind of fact is this? Is it a political fact, a religious fact, or a moral fact? *Realpolitik* dictates that Jewish religious claims to the land of Israel are largely believed to be irrelevant to international political bodies. If this position is true, then the position of Israel among the nations is even more tenuous and fragile than it appears. If, however, politics is based upon morality and religious claims can compete with one another in moral rather than theological language, then there must be a dimension of political life that is founded upon morality. This would be the case in one of the few direct political forays of Levinas when he speaks about the relation of Israel to its neighbors in the title in one of his essays, "Politics After!"

Since the appearance of *Totality and Infinity*, Levinas has also had to defend his ethical position against charges that it is anti-egalitarian. John Wild, who authored the Introduction to the English edition of *Totality and Infinity*, an acknowledged master of the Western philosophical tradition and pioneer of existential phenomenology in America, lavishly praises the originality and rigor of Levinas's thinking. He believes that it opens up a new vein of philosophical inquiry. Nonetheless, he is fully aware that by elevating the other over the self, Levinas's commitment to egalitarianism would be called into question. He says, speaking of the reader, "He may wonder about the strange asymmetry, the complete supremacy of the other, that the author finds in the self-other relation" (TI 1969, 19). Wild's difficulty with this position is qualified by his excitement over the idea of starting with the other rather than the self, and thereby opening contemporary philosophic thought to a path beyond egocentrism. Beginning with the other rather than the self makes it possible to understand how just conduct can be explained rather than rationalized. In this way, justice is enacted as a concrete expression of human relations and not simply a theory where it is assumed that equality is self-understood. It would involve justifying one's conduct to and for the other. It also suggests a way to understand that while fairness is a part of justice, it cannot be the whole of it.

Korach's question is a thoroughly modern one. Either everyone is equal to everyone else, even in the realm of holiness, or we are left to draw a conclusion that both Moses and his Torah are antidemocratic. It is not by accident that Korach, seeking to replace Aaron as the *kohen gadol* (high priest), should turn his attention first to the tribe of Reuven to enlist them in his rebellion. Let us keep in mind that Korach wants to gain favor with the leaders of the tribe of Jacob's oldest son, who have seen the custom of primogenitor overturned. Nonetheless, what Korach is advocating in the name of "fairness," is what is called a "formalism" in the language of phenomenology. Briefly, while fairness is an indispensable part of justice, it surely is not the whole of it. Misery, for example, can be equally distributed to everyone. Yet no one asks for or desires unnecessary suffering. Korach's philosophical misunderstanding is a very deep one.

By starting with the self—himself—he is interpreting the importance and place of everyone else as a function of his desire to rule. In a language of psychology, we might say that he is seeking a pretext to overthrow Moses and Aaron—that is, to displace them from their positions and put himself, presumably in the place of Aaron, thereby calling into question both the legitimacy of Moses, and his teachings.

What Korach does not appear to understand at all, and chooses not to recall, is Moses's own reluctance to assume the burden of responsibility that has been assigned to him. Such responsibility, Korach confuses with privilege. In this way, he is already involved in the modern game of power politics. He wishes to turn his personal grievance into a national complaint. He needs the backing of other powerful people to succeed and is not interested in taking a democratic vote that would be based on numerical supremacy. Korach would undertake something much closer to a coup.

Nonetheless, Moses can be understood as proceeding in a way that is consistent with the ethics of otherness that Levinas describes. He offers reproof to Korach and seeks out ways of saving the leaders of the tribe of Reuven from themselves. He appears to be doing this with an awareness that each must understand that holiness begins with a sense of responsibility that each has for the other. In this scheme, Moses has one degree of responsibility more. He finds it deeply troubling that Korach has made it impossible for him to succeed in suppressing this rebellion in a completely peaceful manner.

More simply put, Korach is a man who values practicality above study or, as the Lubavitcher Rebbi, R'Menachem M. Schneerson, puts it more sympathetically; Korach's transgression is the inversion of that of the explorers. While the explorers wished to remain apart from a life of action and its consequences, Korach and his followers are interested exclusively in a world of mitzvot. Nachshoni notes this: "Now, states the Lubavitcher Rebbe, the assembly of Korach made an opposite claim." The Rebbe is referring to the spies' refusal to give up the manna and involve themselves in a spiritual descent. In the case of Korach, the argument is reversed: "If this is the case, that we must descend from the ethereal to the concrete, how do you remain superior to us? The path that you propose is easy, it is open to all. Why should you be exalted over this nation?" (Nachshoni, vol. 4, 1036). The Chassidic approach taken by the Lubavitcher Rebbe is earlier articulated by the *Kedushas Levi*: "Korach and his assembly ... did not believe that the Torah can assume the trappings of the world of action, (*olam ha'asiyah*). They thought that it is mainly a code of speech, not of action in everyday life." He goes on to explain Korach's punishment: "Therefore, in just retribution, the earth opened its mouth and swallowed them up" (Ibid.).

Moses realizes that Korach's stubbornness is accompanied by an unwillingness to seek out a peaceful argument or path. Moses has in fact been deprived by Korach of his ability to make peace. From this, the *Mishna* states: "Any controversy which is for the sake of Heaven will have an abiding result; and that which is not for the sake of Heaven will not have an abiding result. Which is a controversy for the sake of Heaven? The controversy of Hillel and Shammai. And which is not for the sake of Heaven? The controversy of Korach and all his faction" (*Ethics of the Fathers/Pirke Avos,* 5.)[20] Korach's argument is in the last analysis for the sake of achieving power and status. For this reason, he appears to be allergic to a peaceful solution. Such controversy is not merely abstract but ends in premature and unnatural death.

From a Levinasian perspective, Korach is trapped within an ontology of power. Korach views the domain of the ethical simply as a rationalization of the political, or what in contemporary language we might call "power politics." His rhetorical egalitarianism on this view would mask a desire for Korach himself to take the position occupied by Moses, as well as Aaron. The ascendancy of Moses and his brother Aaron would, then, be arbitrary and a mask for their own positions of preeminence. As we shall see, there is a reason Moses does not answer him in a political manner, but rather in an ethical one. The reduction of ethics to politics swallows up the asymmetry of the ethical order and ultimately marks a refusal of transcendence. What Korach fails to realize is that the positions of Moses and Aaron require a higher degree of responsibility and a heightened degree of patience, and that holiness itself is exactly that which is characterized by being nonarbitrary. He does not understand why, for example, the order of genealogy does not establish the order of holiness. It is for this reason that he appeals to the descendants of Jacob's firstborn son, Reuven.

At the simplest level, we see the attachment of Korach to power in the opening statement: "And Korach took." He took but did not give. He wished to seize and appropriate for himself holiness, the value of which he could not explain nor even see as worthy of desire. The midrash tells us that Korach was the wealthiest man among all of the Israelites and that, furthermore, he was a person of high intelligence. According to this view, what Korach really aspired to was oligarchical rule arrived at by the rhetoric of democracy.

Korach appears to have believed that the order of society was completely intelligible. This begins with his claim that not only is everyone equal, but the concealed presupposition that everyone is the same. R' Hirsch makes the argument that since Korach denied the divine mission of Moses, he is in fact denying the source or origin of that mission. It is in this sense that we may speak of his having denied the divine origin of the Torah and therefore as a refusal of transcendence. Another proof of this is Moses's refusal to insist that his own sons take over for him in his absence or the eventuality of his death. Rashi and the Ramban offer another argument: "If Moses could be suspected of appointing his brother *kohen gadol* (high priest) in an act of gross nepotism, why could he not be accused of fabricating commandments that had no basis in logic or God's will?" (Stone, Num. 16:28–30).

The language of the opponents of Moses linked to Korach shows that they regard all relations as functions of power. Moses summons Dasan and Aviram, longtime rebels and archetypal troublemakers. Baiting Moses, they accuse him: "Is it not enough that you have brought us from a land flowing with milk and honey to cause us to die in the Wilderness? Yet you seek to dominate us, even to dominate further." Speaking toward and beyond the Israelites, Moses gives an ethical response that is indicative of his selfless service: "*I have not taken even a single donkey of yours, nor have I wronged even one of them*" (Stone, Num. 16:15, my emphasis).

This portion of the Torah ends appropriately with the emphasis on giving rather than taking. Even the Levites are required to give a portion of the tithe that has been given to them to the Kohanim. It is in this willingness to place the other before oneself that Levinas situates the gesture of holiness. In fact, Moses is aghast at the fact that Korach does not recognize that he has already condemned himself in a way Moses cannot reverse. According to the *Midrash Tanchuma*, Korach has condemned himself by his own words: " 'If you alone heard, and they did not hear, you could say, but now all of them are (equally) holy, etc., (so) why do you raise yourselves?' Immediately Moses trembled on account of the dispute." The reason for this is that Moses can no longer argue on behalf of Korach and his group because they claimed to have heard equally with Moses and still disobeyed. Moses's first thought was to abase himself in front of the Divine on behalf of the others, but he is now unable to do so because his prerogative was annulled by his responsibility, a responsibility Korach did not acknowledge Moses carried with him (*Midrash Tanchuma*, Bamidbar). Korach and his assembly are, therefore, involved in an existential contradiction in attempting to elevate themselves to a level of holiness that they could neither explain nor accept. To accentuate this contradiction, Korach, who embodies conflict, wishes to supplant Aaron, who represents the perfection of peace.

Levinas shows the intimate link between ethics and holiness. He states, "*The only absolute value is the human possibility of giving the other priority over oneself.* I do not think that there is a human group that can take exception to that ideal, even if it is declared an ideal of holiness" (EN 1998, 109, my emphasis,). What Levinas has established is the irreducibility of holiness. If we begin with the political, as Korach does, we shall never be able to establish the category of the religious except as a function of the political or the economic. "A transcending humanism" does not lose sight of economic justice or social responsibility that is expressed in the one-for-the-other. Philosophically, this position can be sustained only if the other already transcends me in terms of my grasp and intelligibility. By establishing this position, the ethical and its prolongation in the political can begin to make sense. As Levinas puts it, "This [ie., holiness] is the beginning of philosophy. This is the rational, the intelligible. In saying that, it sounds as if we are getting away from reality. But we forget our relation to *books*—that is, to inspired language—which speaks of nothing else. The book of books, and all literature, which is perhaps only a premonition or recollection of the Bible" (EN 1998, 109, authors emphasis).

THE MYSTERY OF DEATH: TRANSCENDENCE
AND THE LIMITS OF INTELLIGIBILITY

Chukkas: Laws That Are Supra-rational
(Numbers 19:1–21:1)

Impurity is the name of an always already sordid egoism, which death—
my death—awakens like an ultimate wisdom.

—NwTR, 116

The great detail involving the procedure of the *parah aduma*, the law pertaining to the red heifer, is found in Numbers 19:1–22. This Torah portion is
both important and extremely difficult to approach contextually. To do so, it is
important to note that the deaths of Miriam and Aaron are also described in
this Torah portion, and the impending death of Moses is announced. All of the
events that occur after the discussion of the *parah aduma* arise in the last year
of the Israelites' journey in the wilderness. But the decree of the *parah aduma*
itself was given, according to tradition, on the second day of Nissan, the day
after the inauguration of the Sanctuary (Stone, Num. 19n1). What then, is the
connection, if any, between this virtually impenetrable commandment dealing
with the red heifer to purification of those who care for the dead and to the
deaths of Miriam and Aaron?

According to tradition, the ultimate example of a decree of the Torah, chok,
a law for which no reason is given, is that of the red heifer or parah aduma.
Simply put, "it is a mitzvah to burn a red heifer and to use its ashes as part of the
process of purifying those people who become ritually impure through contact
with the dead."[3] The Shlah[4] states that despite the fact that the parah aduma is a

---

3 Rabbi Aharon Yisrael Kahan, *Taryag Mitzvos* (CIS Publishers, 1988), 239.

4 See The Shlah, vol. 3, num. 19, on the parah aduma.

chok (decree) par excellence, a subject "sealed with many seals," he nonetheless sees it as his obligation to explain what he can. What remains for Levinas to explicate is the moral dimension of performing this ritual.

The parah aduma was used in the purification process of people who had become ritually contaminated through contact with the dead. The paradoxical aspect involves the fact that the ashes of the parah aduma purify the person involved in caring for the dead while at the same time defiling those involved in the preparation of the ashes. In a very plain sense, this law appears to testify to what Levinas calls the "preeminent importance given to the death of the other," even over my own death. Richard A. Cohen states that "Levinas nevertheless thinks most about the death of the other person. Indeed, it is precisely when and only when thinking least about one's own death and most about the others death … that the human subject achieves its true humanity, and hence the proper height of a morally and socially responsible selfhood" (Cohen 2010, 60–61). Those members of the priestly class, who prepare the ashes of the red heifer, in turn, have to immerse themselves and have their garments washed in order to become ritually pure again. So resistant to understanding is this practice that King Solomon was reputed to have said that he understood all the mitzvahs of the Torah except this one. "I said I would be wise, but it is far from me" (Prov. 7:23).

The paradox of the parah aduma testifies to a rupture in human existence. The sprinkling of the spring waters mixed with the ashes of the parah aduma does not assume that death is contagious. Still, to affirm the fact that having lived is different from the mere idea of life, that what we have done by having lived continues to make a difference, exceeds the capacity for adequate explanation. Yet, all explanation presupposes this paradox—(i.e., that the meaning of life outlasts the length of life itself). This is affirmed as part of "time bearing a promise," that at least for me, the meaning of the lives of others outlasts the meaning of my life itself. In his last Talmudic reading (NwTR 1999, 109–26), Levinas comments on the ashes of the red heifer. In a reflection entitled "Who Is the One-Self?" Levinas asks the fundamental question: "In human existence, is a person's 'as-for-oneself' preserved? … does not the very sense of self, which drives the problem of the 'as-for-oneself,' require prior clarification?" (Ibid., 112–13).

Levinas refers to the discussion in the Talmudic tractate Chullin (88b–89a). He notes from this Talmudic passage a statement linking the ashes of the red heifer to a reward, according to Rabbah, for Abraham having said "I am but dust and ashes." Levinas notes here that these words spoken by Abraham occur in the midst of his pleading for the inhabitants of Sodom. He refers to Abraham's description of himself as but dust and ashes, as a "complaint in which the destitution of the human creature is admitted in the midst of a dialogue conducted nonetheless at the highest level" (NwTR 1999, 114). For this self-description, in the midst of his intercession for-the-other, Abraham would win the reward of the red heifer as well as that of the sotah, where G'd allows His very name to be effaced in order to make peace between husband and wife.

Try to follow out the logic of Levinas insofar as it bears on the parah aduma: "Contact with a dead body is always a shock quite sufficient to recall death itself in its negativity without discrimination or exception: the death always already my death" (NwTR 1999, 116). Reflecting on the finality of death, he says, "Already to think about death overturns the natural and habitual equilibrium of our values; it troubles the moral order that this equilibrium supports or expresses" (Ibid.). For Levinas, the death of the other represents one of the ultimate ways in which my own sense of responsibility is called forth. Cohen puts it this way: "It is also the most 'individuated,' in the sense that moral agency, moral responsibility is irrecusable and non-exchangable: it is incumbent upon me—in the first person, me, myself—to respond responsibly to the suffering of the other, independent and regardless of whether others are or are not responding responsibly" (Cohen 2010, 63). Perhaps this is also why Levinas does not regard death, especially that of the other, as something "natural." It always approaches from without—that is, outside the subject. There is a violence connected to it. In a sense then, death approaches the other and me as the ultimate kind of violence, as though it were murder. The "Angel of Death" (BT, Sotah 46) plays a prominent role in rabbinic literature and it is always this angel who comes to claim me. Therefore, we need not be surprised by what might otherwise appear to be an extravagant claim by Levinas.

Speaking of the pure and the impure, Levinas links these categories to the moral order: "The notions of the pure and impure thrust themselves upon reflection, independent of any superstitious or mystical recollection. Impurity is the name of an always already sordid egoism, which death—my death—awakens like an ultimate wisdom" (NwTR 1999, 117). And here is the original turn in Levinas's thinking, that despite my consciousness of my mortality, I am not free from my responsibility toward the other: "That the consciousness of being 'dust and ashes' does not estrange Abraham from his disinterestedness, from his care for the other—near or far—that all the true values remain true for him, despite the death for which everything is the same. This is the purity of the truly human humans, of which Abraham is the father" (Ibid.).

Levinas is asking whether and how it is possible to escape this "sordid egoism." How can the life of the other person become as important, if not more important to me than my own? Here, it would be necessary to seek out all the dark corners within which such a "sordid egoism" can hide. If the life of the other is important to me because it represents my own continuity, then is this not readily unmasked as my concern for myself? This would assume that the other, like my child, would outlive me and therefore carry me with him to a future that I will not see. For Levinas, the phenomenon of filiality does, in fact, serve this very function, among others. Yet, according to Levinas, the child is also different from me, a rupture with my ego and, therefore, an intimation of a genuine kind of transcendence: "As rupture, repudiation of the father, commencement, filiality at each moment accomplishes and repeats the paradox of a created freedom" (TI 1969, 278).

The parah aduma, on the other hand, belongs to the realm of the neighbor rather than that of the child. It is my responsibility, in the midst of shared communal responsibility, to see to it, upon death, that the decedent has a proper burial. In fact, in the order of urgency, no commandment takes precedence over that of properly burying the dead. Even the kohen gadol, the high priest, on his way to perform the Yom Kippur service in the Holy of Holies on behalf of the entire people, one time a year, must risk defilement rather than forego what is called the "mais mitzvah," burying a dead body found unburied. A discussion in the Talmud informs us that this eventuality never occurred, but highlights the importance of the obligation, nonetheless (BT, Yoma 18a–19b). The Shlah notes that we cannot infer from this even the obvious—that it is the dead body that confers the impurity. Rather, we must assume that the language that introduces this commandment pertains only to the suprarationality of the decree itself. "This is the decree of the Torah" (Num. 19:2).

Commenting on the meaning of dust and ashes, cited in relation to the ashes of the red heifer, Levinas states: "The red heifer remains the symbol of this purification in its rustic traits, perhaps in this way capable of bringing purity or altruism closer to the material duties of the neighbor, which are essential to spirit" (NwTR 1999, 117). Levinas goes on to remark that this is vitally connected to what we have called his "transcending humanism." He makes a remarkable claim for which he does not offer immediate support: "Without suppressing death, victory won over death! It is Abraham, dust and ashes, who has won the victory for his children, for Israel, for the numerous nations, and for all the humanity of humankind" (Ibid.). What does this mean?

Levinas has already offered the beginning of a philosophical explanation in *Totality and Infinity*. He affirms: "Paternity is produced as an innumerable future; the I engendered exists at the same time, as unique in the world, and as brother among brothers" (TI 1969, 279). The very notion of choseness presumes a society of equals among whom the "I" has been burdened with excessive responsibility. For Levinas, it is freedom invested as responsibility that makes the I elect or chosen. As noted earlier, "choseness," for Levinas points toward responsibility rather than privilege. This is his response to the question, "Chosen for what?" It is a doctrine that goes beyond numerical equality, or fairness, to justice. Justice means that it is linked to the good. He explains as follows: "The I as I, hence remains turned ethically to the face of the other: fraternity is the very relation with the face and which at the same time my election and inequality, that is the mastery exercised over me by the other, are accomplished" (Ibid.). Is this not the extravagant, indeed, infinite responsibility that the I has for all of the others, one by one? And, therefore, the elevation to a holiness that belongs to the unique, a transcendence that forms both the limit and the promise of intelligibility. In his own words, "The election of the I in its very ipseity, is revealed to be a privilege and a subordination. Because it does not place it among the other chosen ones, but rather in face of them, to serve them and because no one can be substituted for the I to measure the extent of its responsibilities" (Ibid.).

In his Talmudic reflection, "Who Is One-Self?" Levinas is at pains to distinguish the formula "ashes and dust" from the language of Moses and Aaron, "What are we?" This should not be seen as an exercise in comparative humility. He notes that the latter formula, in Hebrew "Venachnu ma," translated idiomatically, means "And us, what are we?" He goes on to note the graduating humility as noted in the Talmudic passage marking the moral asymmetry required for holiness. Levinas assures us that "Abraham's existence, such as Rabbah [the Talmudic commentator] understands it, is not pure perseverance in being" (NwTR 1999, 122).

Commenting on the humility of Abraham, Levinas sees it as the first emphatic step in the discovery of an excellence greater than oneself. However, one must be careful that this humility does not result in an attachment to what he calls "pure complacency in being" (Ibid., 123). This needs to be explained. It is not simply a matter of experiencing a sense of one's own limitations in relation to other beings, in their being, that is at stake here. Levinas is commenting on a notion of humility that is but the beginning of an aperture to holiness, in the context of a Talmudic passage that compares Abraham to Moses and Aaron and the latter to King David, with respect to certain utterances of each.

Yet another version of the same Talmudic passage regards the "what are we?" of Moses and Aaron as "a new modulation of the 'as-for-oneself': retaining its fire but quitting a quarrel—this is the primordially human!" (Ibid.,

124). It would make the universe possible, because it would pertain to one who "restrains himself in a quarrel." This version, according to Levinas, of the "what are we," interprets "Peace as the foundation of being" (Ibid.). This peace, however, is not the peace of the dead. This is the peace of the living, who face death themselves, but who in doing so, recognize that the lives of others can take precedence over their own. And is this not the humility and holiness of Aaron the high priest and his descendants? For the text says, upon the death of Aaron, that he was mourned by all of Israel, implying, according to the commentators, the women as well as the men. Why? Aaron exemplified the pursuit of peace and the love of peace, beginning with husband and wife, and extending to the friend and to the neighbor.

It is the fraternal peace that would restore time bearing a promise. Not by accident do we see the ultimate example of the decree that is beyond understanding thematically linked to the deaths of Miriam and then to Aaron, and finally to the belated recognition that because the Israelites did not shed tears at the time of Miriam's death the well dried up (Num. 20:22). It is at this time that Moses is first told that he will not live to enter the land of Promise. The death of Miriam prefigures the deaths of Aaron and Moses. "As soon as that righteous woman died, the water stopped" (Rashi, Stone, 843).

Thus, commences a quarrel. The people demand water and Moses and Aaron are described as responding imperfectly. G'd commands Moses and Aaron to bring forth water and "speak to the rock before their eyes that it shall give its waters. You shall bring forth for them water from the rock and give to them water for the assembly and for their animals" (Num. 20:8). As understood by the commentary tradition this is not an unreasonable demand upon the part of the people.

There is a great dispute as to what constitutes the transgression of Moses. The text itself states, "Moses took the staff from before G'd as He had commanded him. Moses and Aaron gathered the congregation before the rock and he said to them, 'Listen now, O rebels, shall we bring forth water for you from this rock?' Then Moses raised his arm and struck the rock with his staff twice; abundant water came forth and the assembly and their animals drank" (Num. 20:9). Earlier, in Exodus, Moses had success in striking the rock. At this time, however, he had been precisely informed that speech, not force, was to be used. Rashi concludes that Moses's transgression was precisely this—he struck rather than spoke to the rock. Maimonides offers an alternative explanation that he refers to the people as rebels. Maimonides goes on to note that "[w]e do not find anywhere in the chapter that God was angered by the people's complaint" (Num. 20:9). After a lifetime of patient service and intercession on behalf of

Israel, Moses appears propelled by an angry impatience and quarrels with the people. This quarrel further disturbs, rather than promotes, the peace between the Israelites. Why, though, is Aaron punished as well? Is it perhaps because he refused to admonish his brother or criticize his conduct? Aaron, as we have noted, embodies the love of peace at every level of the interpersonal sphere. But peace is not always achieved through silence or compromise or delaying tactics. Previously, all of these strategies have been praised when practiced by Aaron. Is it for these reasons, then, that Moses and Aaron are punished, or is it because the rock was struck twice, or because Moses had said, with an uncharacteristic absence of humility, "Shall we bring forth water?" This explanation appears to establish a link between humility and the kind of patience associated with fidelity. More precisely, this is a fidelity to others, ultimately the transcendent other.

God speaks to both Moses and Aaron in forbidding terms: "Because you did not believe in Me, to sanctify Me in the eyes of the Children of Israel, therefore you will not bring this congregation to the land that I have given them" (Num. 20:12). The waters are referred to as the waters of strife, merivah, as they were on the earlier occasion of Moses bringing water from the rock in Exodus. Such strife cannot endure because it is not stable. Peace, rather than strife, between people, is the precondition for the promise of time. It is only later, after pleading with G'd, that Moses, the man of G'd (Ish Elokhim), will see the land of Promise from a distant hill. And is this not, in a way, the condition of every person? In advance, he is aware that the meaning of his life will not coincide precisely with its length. In the Hebraic tradition, unlike Greek tragedy, this is not a source of ultimate lamentation. Despite the fact that his body returns to dust, and that there are limits imposed upon life's intelligibility, the sanctification of life is mandated. There is a difference between the absence of someone who is no longer here and his never having been at all. Were it not for this distinction between absence and nonexistence, we should not even begin to understand that there are limits placed upon our capacity to make life intelligible and bearable.

PROPHETISM: INSPIRATION
AND PROPHECY

Balak
(Numbers 22:2–25:9)

According to the tradition, the Hebrew Prophets begin with the Book of Joshua and conclude with the Book of Malachi. The prophets do not come, as is often thought, to challenge biblical law. Rather, they focus on the underlying moral dimension of the law. They are concerned with such phenomena as justice, righteousness, sincerity, peace, the plight of the poor, the widow, the orphan, and the stranger. Moses is understood by Maimonides and the entire tradition to be the prophet par excellence. Unlike the biblical scholar and expositor on the prophets A.J. Heschel, Levinas explores the phenomenon of prophecy neither from a historical or a scholarly point of view. Rather, he is concerned with the prophetic moment in everyday discourse. This means that prophetic understanding is not understood as a thing apart, but rather incessantly intertwined with daily life and speech, especially its moral dimension. It is by his vigilant attentiveness to the moral dimension of daily life that the prophet carries with him a responsibility that distinguishes him from the Greek oracle. The Torah portion before us deals most explicitly with this subject. As such, it also focuses on prophecy in its universal dimension as well as its singular expression in the context of the Bible.

The prophetic moment of everyday life derives from primary experience, and Levinas understands it as a basic, irreducible moment of human discourse. For Levinas, the prophetic mode originates in a preparedness that signals the readiness of the subject to act as witness to what is heard, "Here I am in the name of God" without referring directly to His presence. Levinas affirms that this originates not as a theological expression. The "here am I" (in Hebrew, *heneini*) is a fact from which, as he puts it, "The word God is still absent from the phrase in which God is, for the first time, involved in words" (OBBE 1991, 149). Levinas emphatically affirms that this is a form of bearing witness and not a matter of theological belief. In fact, he goes on to say, "It does not at all state

'I believe in God," (Ibid., 149). This latter point has been the subject of much misunderstanding on the part of critics and defenders of the religious philosophical thought of Levinas.

The moment of prophetism originates outside the subject with "the sound of my voice or the figure of my gesture—the saying itself. This recurrence is quite the opposite of return upon oneself, self-consciousness. It is sincerity, effusion of oneself, 'extraditing' of the self to the neighbor. Witness is humility and admission; it is made before all theology" (OBBE 1991, 149). Prophetism arises then from this act of bearing witness, by which I am commanded by the other to speak to him or her and to his or her neighbor, even in the absence of complete understanding on my part. This is why, perhaps, the biblical prophets were not allowed to withhold what it is that they heard or saw. Does not all speech have a moment where it is halting, like that of Moses, the stammering prophet, who recollects what he has heard, as he sets it out in words? We might refer to this as a moment of proffering, or 'pre-offering,' to the other for the sake of the neighbor and myself as well. It is here that the authentic prophets of ancient Israel are found always in the accusative mode, as if given an assignment for which they did not ask. Is this perhaps the origin, also, of the not uncommon persecution that they face for speaking words that are just but not always welcomed?

Perhaps the prophetic moment of discourse is more clearly grasped when speaking is directly understood as a reaction of thinking aloud in relation to the neighbor. In simpler language, expressed by Franz Rosenzweig in the "New Thinking," all thinking is already "a speaking thinking." This means that "speech is bound to time and nourished by time, and neither can nor wants to abandon this element. It does not know in advance just where it will end. It takes its cues from others." [5] In fact, it is often after one speaks that he or she discovers the source of the intention that is bound to speech in the presence of another person, far or near, real or imagined. Is not all that passes for psychotherapy modeled on this kind of speaking thinking?

Oona Ajzenstat presents a penetrating analysis of Levinas's understanding of the Bible and prophecy. In *Driven Back to the Text*, she states "that the word of God appears only in the mouth of the human subject ... these phenomena, which in its basic or paradigmatic form Levinas calls witnessing, is manifest, he argues in varying degrees in the entire range of human expression, from the

---

5 Nahum Glatzer, *The Life and Thought of Franz Rosenzweig*, (Shocken: New York, NY, 1998), 199.

saying that underlies all speech through to specific forms of speech" (Ajzenstat 2001, 85–86). In other words, this is the source of prophetic understanding that is both open to all and exemplified in the biblical prophets. It is prophecy before it rises to the level of conceptualization. This helps to explain rather than to compromise the singularity of the prophets of the biblical-prophetic tradition.

Ajzenstat states that the work of a prophet for Levinas "entails that the commanded subject commands" (Ibid., 122). The primary textual source of Levinas' original contributions on prophetism are found in a section entitled "The Glory of the Infinite" from *Otherwise than Being: or Beyond Essence.* He devotes a separate subsection to what he calls "Witness and Prophecy." He begins by affirming that "[i]nfinity is not announced in the witness as a given theme" (OBBE 1991, 149). The authentic prophet, as Levinas identifies him, is first present in the accusative mode, whereas he says, "I bear witness to the Infinite." What follows is a trenchant but most important phenomenology of what we might call the "prophetic moment."

The logic of the prophetic moment can be described in the following way: It is when the "I" finds itself called upon or summoned to "bear witness" prior to all specific contents of a command. It begins, as Levinas indicates, with a kind of assignation that presupposes a readiness on the part of the subject, already without ambition and purely passive in this sense. Levinas associates the prophetic modality with the sincerity of the saying and the response to "here-I-am" (*heneini*). The biblical word *hineini* has the sense not of simple spatial location, but of readiness—that is, "here am I, ready to serve." This readiness is tested when the prophet as respondent says, "[S]end me." Hence, the astonishing conduct of the prophet Jonah, when he attempts to evade his call to prophesy to the inhabitants of Nineveh. Notice the vivid contrast to Balaam, who is cannily all too ready to comply with the request of Balak to initiate prophetic condemnations of Israel. Despite or because of Balaam's disclaimers, he is quite receptive to receiving remuneration for his prophetic vocation. Still, he is calculating enough to know that he cannot proceed without divine permission.

In no way is Levinas contesting the traditional understanding of the conditions required for attaining divine inspiration (*Ruach HaKodesh*). Maimonides has already distinguished between the "degrees of prophecy" and the specifications which "qualify a person for the office of prophet" (GFP 1956, 241). The prophet anticipates his dual responsibility for others as well as his superlative responsibility in making his listeners responsible for the neighbor and the neighbor's neighbor *ad infinitum*. In this sense, he is a friend to no one, but a neighbor who would speak to galvanize justice for all. Still, he is not a populist, for he "speaks truth not only to the powerful" but "the people" and the powerless as well. The people are also held responsible for their own ignorance as well as their misconduct, such as the oppression of the neighbor.

Hence, the vocation of the authentic prophet is a precarious one. How does the prophetic moment arise prior to conceptualization? Levinas explains this as follows: "I find the order in my response itself, which, as a sign given to the neighbor as a 'here I am,' brings me out of invisibility, out of the shadow in which my responsibility could have been evaded" (OBBE 1991, 150). The genuine moment of prophecy is also attended by an extreme sincerity. This sincerity is guided by the phenomena of the one-for-the-other. In other words, there is an existential risk undertaken on the part of the subject. Most prophecy is accompanied by an element of reserve or reluctance for this very reason. The prophet, however, is not free to disregard his own prophecy. "When a prophet is sent with a message for others he is compelled to reveal it, even against his will" (Kaplan 1979, vol. 1, 109). Perhaps this is why even Balaam could not escape disclosing the good words that he spoke about Israel when his intention was to do otherwise.

As Levinas says, "To bear witness, G'd is precisely, not to state this extraordinary word, as though glory would be lodged in a theme, and be posited as a thesis, or become being's essence" (OBBE 1991, 149). This does not preclude witnessing to a theme or a message that is commanded for commanding others and calling them to their responsibility. However, "The trace of the witness given, the sincerity or glory, is not effaced even in its said" (Ibid., 151).

Levinas explicitly affirms the positive relation between language and the role of the witness elevated to that of prophetic speech. "I can indeed state the meaning borne witness to as a said. It is an extraordinary word, the only one that does not extinguish or absorb its saying, but it cannot remain a simple word. *The word God is an overwhelming semantic event that subdues the subversion worked by illeity*" (OBBE 1991, 151, my emphasis).

How is this to be explained? "Illeity" is a coinage by Levinas that refers to the transcendence not only of the second person, the one with whom I am speaking, but to the third as well, extending outside the subject to the transcendence that belongs to the Infinite. It is the third party, and his neighbor with whom language in fact originates and who establishes the order of justice. For this reason, the second party has ethical obligations to the third, and to me as well. This is how, as Levinas puts it, "I can become an other to others." It is with the third party that justice begins, because "it is the third party that interrupts the face to face of the welcome of the other man, interrupts the proximity or approach of the neighbor" (Ibid., 150). The claims of the third party delimits the infinite responsibility that I have for the other person. If it were only a matter of the relation between the other and the self, then according to Levinas, "I owe everything to the other," at least in terms of my responsibility for him or her. Justice, unlike responsibility, originates with the appearance of the third party.

In the case of authentic prophetism, I address myself beyond those present to all of the absent others. This responsibility reasserts itself in the imperative to perfect justice *ad infinitum*. Synchrony gives way to diachrony, and the political to the ethical. The one who comes from afar means that, while I may owe everything to the one who is near, I cannot give him or her everything that he or she would deserve in a world of the couple alone. The absent third both threatens to disrupt the love of the I-You relation and conditions the possibility of the I-You entering into the world of justice: "The presence of the face, the infinity of the other, its destituteness, a presence of the third 'that is,' the whole of humanity, that looks at us" (TI 1969, 213).

In his last parable, Balaam intimates the ultimate messianic redemption of Israel. He says, "I shall see him, but not now" (Num. 24:17). Even though his curses have been transformed into blessings, Balaam gives some parting advice to Balak on how to sabotage Israel. He recommends an elaborate scheme that will lead some of the Israelites to sexual immorality and from there to idolatry. Balaam's prophetic understanding is linked to a deformed version of justice. What separates Balaam from Moses and the authentic prophets of Israel is the exclusion of ethical life from the prophetic gift. While Balaam's mission as a prophet falls short, his advice on how to undermine Israel yields some bitter fruit for the Israelites. For Balaam, the spiritual dimension of prophecy and ethical conduct are totally separate. The division between the material and spiritual spheres could not be more complete.

Why is Balaam given a talking donkey, which can see what Balaam cannot? The Hebrew word for "donkey" is also the source of the word for materiality (*Chamor*). In his everyday conduct, in its material expression Balaam is utterly corrupt. His spiritual radar makes it possible for him to discern that daily, fleeting moment in which divine ire is expressed. This capacity is not used to arouse righteous indignation against injustice, but for purposes that are self-aggrandizing or harmful to others. The interhuman world, and the animal realm as well, has been turned into a series of events that are strictly for self-gratification. He still understands the difference between morality and its absence but decides for the latter. His prophetic gift, in potentiality, is equal or superior to that of Moses, and therefore, works against his intentions. His curses are transformed into blessings. He reverts to a cunning remedy to thwart and undermine the Israelites. He partially succeeds by debasing the Moabite woman, with whom Israelites in turn, debase themselves. From such carnal immorality (*Giluy arayos*), Israel weakens the bond between the material and spiritual. As Levinas observes: "There is no bad materialism, except my own" (DF 1990, xiv).

In this way, Balaam represents the inversion of the Hebrew prophets. For example, the prophet Amos testifies, in a very sharp manner, against the economic injustice practiced in Israel: "Thus saith the LORD; For three transgressions of Israel, and for four, I will not turn away the punishment thereof; because they sold the righteous for silver, and the poor for a pair of shoes; That pant after the dust of the earth on the head of the poor, and turn aside the way of the meek" (Amos 2:6–7). Rather than coming to testify against unjust conduct and practices as well as social transgressions leading to repentance and return, Balaam stirs others in the opposite direction. Rashi points out Balaam's avarice in the moment when he cannily tells Balak that he would not curse the Israelites "for all the money in the city."

His words could not be more different from those of the prophet Isaiah, referring to the absolutely other, who says, "Before you ask, I will answer," or more precisely, "It will be that before they call I will answer; while they yet speak I will hear" (Isa. 65:24). This for Levinas is a verse that epitomizes his own view on prophetism at the juncture of ethical life. This means that I find myself ready to answer, even before the other asks something specific of me.

Levinas specifies that in responsibility for the other, I become responsible for the death of the other: "Is not the rectitude of the other's look an exposure par-excellence, and exposure unto death. The face in its uprightness is what is aimed at … the order is not to let the Other alone, be it in the face of the inexorable. This is probably the foundation of sociality and of love without eros. *The fear for the death of the other is certainly at the basis of the responsibility for him*" (EI 1985, 119, my emphasis). The authentic prophet, then, can be concerned with the well-being of other people because he fears for the other and thereby is commanded to support and redirect him on the way to righteousness. For Levinas, the inspiration of the biblical prophets is situated at the juncture of morality and materiality in primary experience. It would link speech to right conduct as it is occurring or in the moments before.

URGENCY: DEVOTION VS. FANATICISM

Pinchas
(Numbers 25:16–30:1)

Before they call, I will answer.

—Isaiah 65:24

There is an ongoing connection of the Torah portions Balak and Pinchas, not just in the fact that Balak introduces the Midian threat into the Israelites' camp; each offers a different perspective on the same question of devotion. The commentary tradition refers to Pinchas, the central figure of this portion, as a "zealot" (*kinoy*). This is not necessarily a term of approval. In our contemporary world as in biblical times, zealotry is usually linked to fanaticism. Religious fanaticism, remarkably and unexpectedly re-ascendant in our times among the world's global religions, has helped to put the world in danger.

The rabbinic tradition, and even the supreme Jewish religious court, the Sanhedrin, followed the most stringent criteria, announced in advance by the Torah, for anyone who "took the law into his own hands." However, it is necessary to make an important distinction between "devotion" and "fanaticism." Devotion opens onto the realm of what Levinas calls "the Infinite." More often than not, fanaticism belongs to the ontology of power—that is, the realm of totality. Devotion from a biblical and Talmudic point of view means that one is devoted above all else to a rigorous adherence to the teachings of the Torah. In one of his late interviews, in 1983, Levinas, when asked about his personal conception of and relation to G'd, responds: "Listen, G'd is not in heaven, he is in men's sacrifice, in the mercy men show for one another. Heaven is empty, but men's mercy is filled with G'd."[6] There are, however, special cases that demand

---

6 Emmanuel Levinas, *Conversations with Emmanuel Levinas, 1983–1994*, trans. Gary D. Mole, ed. Michael de Saint Cheron. (Pittsburgh: Duquesne University Press), 2016.

immediate action. Such cases are regarded as exceptions to the law, such that they cannot necessarily be used as precedent for other cases.

This is so in the urgency expressed by Pinchas, who ultimately assuages the plague that befalls the Israelites, a result of the seduction recommended by the prophet Bilaam to Balaak, the king who has employed him to curse the Israelites. The great gift that Pinchas brings to the Israelites is the attainment of peace, the ultimate achievement. This is what is meant by the statement that God makes to Moses, in reference to Pinchas: "[H]ere I grant him My covenant, peace" (*Akeydas Yitzchak*, vol. 2, 778). Despite the fact that his action was sanctioned and praised in this case, Pinchas does not succeed Moses for the very same reason—his zealotry. Moderation is preferable to zealotry in a leader. Moderation brings with it stability, a sense of balance, and a kind of vigilance for others that is often absent in the case of excessive zeal. What we learn from this is that the tradition places all kinds of limitations upon such actions that, with the slightest variation, would not have been allowed. Therefore, the action of Pinchas in slaying Zimri, is the radical exception to the safeguards against taking the law into one's own hands. It is not simply the purity of motive that distinguishes devotion from fanaticism. An apocalyptic spirit, so ascendant in our own time, is anticipated and subordinated to forbearance. A nonresistance to evil, however, is not an acceptable position, not for my own sake, perhaps, but on behalf of my neighbor, whose life is menaced.

The timing of the conduct of Pinchas opens onto the question of time measured by urgency. Time measured by urgency, diachrony, arises from the other and for his or her sake. While Levinas does not call the time of multiple others "polychrony," such a term makes it clear that he is talking not only about the other but the third person and his or her neighbor. Sometimes the neighbor and the other make divergent claims upon me as an ethical subject. Reason measured by justification, and therefore justice, deals with a multiplicity of others. It must recuperate and stabilize the phenomenon of responsibility so that justice can be done for the third party and the neighbor as well. It is, then, in polychrony that justice not only arises, but is maintained. This kind of time is required for the stability and maintenance of society. Polychrony, then, must accommodate time measured and maintained by number and meaning, even if it arises with urgency. This helps us to understand not only the exception to the rule, but when, under the most exacting of conditions, the exception becomes the rule.

While the prophecy of Balaam is transformed from a curse into a blessing, he succeeds in giving advice to his employer Balak. He advises him to have the Midianites deploy some of their daughters for the purpose of seducing the

Israelites into acts of sexual immorality, something that in turn leads to the equivalent of idolatry. These are two of the three cardinal prohibitions that, according to the Torah, one must give up one's life rather than transgress. In the midst of this moral chaos, Pinchas, the son of Elazar, the son of Aaron the Kohen, urgently intervenes. We can now look at the conduct of Pinchas and the reaction of the Israelites with greater care. The text states,

> [B]ehold! A man of the children of Israel came and brought a Midianite woman near to his brothers in the sight of Moses and in the sight of the assembly and the entire Children of Israel. And they were weeping at the entrance of the Tent of Meeting ... and he (Pinchas) stood up from amid the assembly and took a spear in his hand. He followed the Israelite man into the tent and pierced them both, the Israelite man and the woman into her stomach—and the plague was halted upon the Children of Israel. (Num. 25:8)

This plague had resulted in the deaths of twenty-four thousand Israelites. The consensus among the commentators is that these were members of the tribe of Simeon, who, because of their consanguinity felt an undeserved sympathy toward their prince, the offending Zimri. The reader is informed that the slain Israelite man was Zimri, a leader of the house of Simeon, and that the slain Midianite woman was Cosbi, daughter of Zur, whom the commentators identify with Balak.

Under normal conditions, Pinchas would not have been allowed to take the law into his own hands. All capital cases presuppose that the potential perpetrator(s) be informed ahead of time that he or she is not to violate a specific law of the Torah; at least two witnesses must be present, and no circumstantial evidence is allowed. Such cases are to be brought to a court of scholars and be solemnly deliberated upon. For the accused to be convicted, the Sanhedrin cannot be unanimous in its decision of guilt. To our modern ears, this sounds counterintuitive. However, Talmudic tradition reasons that under normal circumstances, if not a single judge can find exculpatory evidence, then the accused is let go on the grounds that the court could not possibly have examined all of the evidence. Such is the presumption of innocence! Levinas notes that "when the Sanhedrin, the Supreme Court of our people, passed the death sentence for the first time in seventy years, the judges were looked upon as murderers" (DF 1990, 174). Therefore, there was consternation at the action of Pinchas ranging beyond that of the tribe of Simeon. "When I speak of justice, I introduce the idea of the struggle with evil. I separate myself from the idea of nonresistance to evil.... There is a certain measure of violence necessary in terms of Justice;

but if one speaks of justice, it is necessary to allow judges, it is necessary to allow institutions and the state; to live in a world of citizens and not only in the order of the Face-to-Face" (EN 1998, 105).

This action by Pinchas was at the risk of his own life. The Talmud informs us (BT, Sanhedrin 82b) that multiple conditions had to come together at a single instant for the action of Pinchas to be regarded as acceptable, even righteous. Rashi tells us that Moses and the elders had providentially forgotten the laws that pertain to such a circumstance. This, in turn, made it possible for Pinchas to be elevated to a position of prominence, if not ultimate leadership. While the action of Pinchas was judged to be righteous and within the law, the law itself falls under those conditions regarded for an emergency.

It is worth contrasting the behavior of Pinchas with that of Balaam. According to the sages, Balaam could recognize the instant that occurred each day when the attribute of divine severity prevailed completely over the attribute of mercifulness (BT, Berachot 7a). His reluctance to undertake the offer of his employer Balak did not stem from conscience. Rather, we are told by the sages that on that single day, this moment of divine severity did not appear. For this reason, Balaam's own sense of urgency was replaced by delay. As we have noted, it appears that the donkey of Balaam understood, in a visceral way, what his master did not.

Pinchas, on the other hand, risked his life in order to spare the Israelites from further suffering. *This moment of his intervention disrupts the continuity of time and action.* As an extreme expression of diachrony the intercession of Pinchas can most plainly be called an "emergency." The most acute sense of responsibility arises with time measured by urgency. The model most familiar to us is found in the medical phenomenon of triage. In triage, the living are separated from the dead, those who are able to be treated differentiated from those who are not, and the ability to give assistance in the most timely way is measured out. Such time is governed by urgency deriving from the gravity of the time of the other. The medical model of triage is found in the primary human experience. It is derived from the elements of everyday life rather than the reverse. Otherwise, we should have no idea of how to make the kinds of medical distinctions that have become established protocols. Is there, then, an order of urgency as well as an urgency of order? Such urgency is the basis of meaningful action, action that makes a difference. It was Pinchas who, through his radical and decisive act, ultimately stopped the catastrophic plague that had already taken the lives of twenty-four thousand Israelites.

Triage in medicine deals with the urgency of order. This makes reference, tacit and explicit, to who can be rescued and treated, according to established or predetermined criteria. The death and suffering of others are always in the background of such extreme ethical considerations. This means, however, that it is only by appealing to the order of urgency that we can even begin to think about the medical model of triage. For example, it is not uncommon for multiple claims to be placed upon me by others. We commonly resort in everyday discourse to the only mildly helpful suggestion that I "prioritize" what comes first, who comes second, who comes third. In the urgency of order, we make appointments. For such an occasion, Levinas often suggests for the subject to follow the maxim *après vous*. Let us say, however, that this is not merely a conflict between the subject and the other, but between the urgency with which to address multiple others. While Levinas does not offer a formula or even a schematic way of applying the order of urgency, he does maintain a governing principle that can serve as a meaningful beginning: "*The only absolute value is the human possibility of giving the other priority over oneself*" (EN 1998, 109).

In *Otherwise than Being*, Levinas bundles various categories that surround the phenomena of substitution. These include, but are not limited to, proximity, obsession, and recognizing myself as the other's hostage. By this is meant that I take responsibility for the other person's own responsibility in relation to me and to the others. Levinas says, in "Proximity and Obsession" (OBBE 1991, 87–88): "The extreme urgency of the assignation precisely breaks up the equality or serenity of consciousness which espouses its visible or conceivable object … extreme urgency is the modality of obsession—which is known but is not unknowing. I do not have time to face it." Obsession, rather than being understood by him as a neurosis, is an ethical expression of hyper-focusing on the urgent claims of others. Levinas observes that "[t]he subjective does not only undergo, it suffers" (Ibid., 88). By itself, obsession involves the most careful and focused kind of attention that comes prior to the active agency on the part of the subject. This is not to be confused with neurotic obsession, where openness to the other is closed.

Obsession belongs, then, always in advance, to a time prior to making appointments. It is here that I get an intimation of something being asked of me, something of importance. This importance is related to a time that is not reversible. Already it opens onto a past that "takes apart the recoupable time of history and memory in which representation continues" (Ibid.). Before it is an experience, "the making of a fact precedes the present of experience, [its] memory [and] history" (Ibid.). In other words, there is a singular approach by the other that announces itself to me before any kind of comparative analysis or grids. The nearness of the other has already claimed me prior to all rehearsing of a response on my part. This singularity calls for a response that is the exception to the rule of "waiting in line." It does make a difference who is approaching me. The voice of my child, my brother, my sister, who is also my neighbor, but from out of a shared past, makes an extravagant claim upon me and the present. This is what Levinas means when he says that "this difference is my non-indifference to the other. Proximity is a disturbance of the memorable time" (Ibid., 89).

The order of urgency is based upon a time that is radically contingent, found at junctures that do not necessarily synchronize for my convenience. This is why in obsession and proximity, my responsibility can be pulled in different directions. And yet for all that, I cannot simply ask myself what my mentor or teacher would have done. The burden on me to respond is an expression of my irreplaceability, my singularity.

Who comes second? Here it is necessary to ask, for whom do these questions arise? Such questions arise for the ethically elected subject who before, during, and after, becomes an agent of action. This means that he or she cannot possibly enact his or her responsibilities fully with each and every other. All the good that can be done may not be done by him or her alone. This is why we are aware of the need in primary experience for surrogates, assistants, and aids. The most important thing is not that the good be done by me, but that it be done for the sake of the other who precedes me in the order of importance. That responsibility, which is assigned by the other, means that he or she is not free from engaging in the effort to remediate suffering, oppression, conflict, and strife. Levinas emphatically states that only the hypocrite says, "I have done all my duty" (EI 1985, 105–6). Why is this the case? Because in this very utterance, he or she exposes the fact that he or she has acquitted him-herself by saying "Enough is enough. Surely, there must be a place under the sun for me as well." For Levinas this place under the sun always belongs to the realm of the not yet.

The combination of considerations includes, but is not limited to the following: Can the affected person's life be saved? Is the matter one of overriding importance to other people as well as to myself? How, and in what way, can the hemorrhaging be stopped? What is the most immediate way to intercede? Is the situation irreversible? Is there anyone who can act as a surrogate on my behalf so that more suffering can be alleviated and more lives saved? It is unclear whether Levinas gives us the preliminary indication of who comes second and third.

In the intervention by Pinchas, there is agreement that he acts with a sense of urgency, purpose, and disinterested sobriety—all of the criteria for time measured by urgency are in play.

Still, his actions do not endear him to everyone, especially those who tried to shield Zimri, the leader of the tribe of Simeon. Most commentators conclude that the reason Pinchas is rewarded with the covenant of peace is to shield him from retaliation and to indicate that his action, in stopping the deaths of others, was justified. Is it not sometimes necessary, in order to protect the neighbor, to respond to the attacker with force, even great force?

S.R. Hirsch reads this much more broadly and is very close to Levinas on this point concerning the covenant of peace. Hirsch even provides an alternative translation of the Scriptural passage. According to Hirsch, the statement should read, "Therefore proclaim it: see I have given him My covenant: peace." As Hirsch puts it, "the Pinchas-covenant is just the 'rejoined' peace. Where Pinchas's zeal is required is just where the real peace is broken" (Hirsch, on Num. 12:1).

In a more philosophic vein, Levinas argues that an eschatology of peace belongs to the realm of infinity that the historical totality of war presupposes. In other words, the war of all against all is derivative. What comes first in the order of importance, in the order of ethics, and in the realm of the religious, is the each-for-each and the all-for-all (TI 1969, 20–24). The midrash emphasizes that the ways of peace always remain to be achieved. It states: "If a man comes in from the way he is greeted with peace (*shalom*) also in the morning he is greeted with peace, and in the evening, he is greeted with peace" (*Midrash Tanchuma*, vol. 4, 246). Peace is the expression through which the other is welcomed at the beginning and the manner in which one escorts and leaves him. It should be emphasized that the covenant of peace for the Torah, and for Levinas, involves a vigilance that Pinchas has already achieved in regard to preserving the lives of Israel from death.

Moses is told to take Joshua, rather than Pinchus, who is said to have been desired as his successor. The purpose of all struggle must be for the sake of peace. In that sense, devotion, which opens onto the other, rather than fanaticism, is what is praised and called for. Such a view opens onto a metaphysical pluralism for which ethical life must begin and end for the sake of the other. This is the way of peace.

Toward the close of this portion of the Torah, Moses receives the divine instruction that he will see the land of Promise but not enter it. Levinas asks what life after me might mean to me, as well as to the others who come after me: "The significance of the authority signifying *after and despite my death*, signifying to the finite *I*, to the *I* doomed to death, a meaningful order signifying beyond this death" (EN 1998, 172–73). After this sobering announcement, Moses immediately asks for a successor. He asks G'd to "Appoint a man over the assembly, who shall go out before them and come in before them" (Num. 27:16).

G'd responds to Moses accordingly: "[T]ake to yourself Joshua, son of Nun, a man in whom there is spirit, and lean your hand upon him. You shall stand him before Eleazar the Kohen and before the entire assembly, and command him before their eyes. You shall place some of your majesty upon him, so that the entire assembly of the Children of Israel shall pay heed" (Num. 27:18–20). As Moses first thought, it is to be Joshua, not Pinchas, because of Joshua's steadiness and even predictability throughout his long apprenticeship.

As he has throughout his life, Moses places the wellbeing of others before his own. It is not the personal quest for immortality that preoccupies Moses. Rather, he pleads for the continuing well-being of those whom he has shepherded. From an ethical point of view, Moses shows an acute sense of generational responsibility. "Time bearing a promise," the notion that the future can be better than the past, is the governing assumption of my relations with others—this is, as Levinas describes it, the enactment of the time of infinity. By no means does this indicate that we are indifferent to our own mortality. Rather, we proceed despite this knowledge. This is the first affirmation that carries us beyond the sheer neutrality of Being.

The radical discontinuity of human time that separates one generation from another presupposes a continuity of expectations, hopes, and dreams. This continuity in turn is interrupted, but not ended, by my death. In this sense, the life of Moses and Israel continues through that of Joshua and the generation poised to enter the permitted land of promise.

WORD AND DEED

Mattos: Tribes
(Numbers 30:2–32:2)

He shall not desecrate his word; according to whatever comes from his mouth he shall do.

—Numbers 30:3

To create a being that has the right to make promises—is not this the paradoxical task that nature has set itself in the case of man?

—Nietzsche, *Genealogy of Morals*

Our relation to time finds itself in crisis. It seems indispensable that we Westerners situate ourselves in this perspective of time bearing promise. I do not know to what degree we can manage without this. This appears to me to be the most troubling aspect of our present situation.

—IRB 2001, 185

The covenant with Abraham and his descendants gives further specificity to what is promised and what is expected in return (Gen. 17). In the Book of the Exodus, G'd makes both a specific and a universal covenant with Israel and to the nations when He assures Moses and the Israelites of deliverance. G'd's self-identification to Moses, "I will be that I will be," according to Rashi as we have noted earlier, should be understood in the futural sense, even though Maimonides translates it in the present tense "I am that I am" (*Ey[k]eh asher Ey[k]eh*) (GFP 1956). In other words, it can be read from the human side as G'd saying, "I promise you that existence is promising." This notion that existence is ultimately promising, is the basis for genuine rather than blind hope. It is also the affirmation in this promise where we find faith situated.

Such fidelity testifies to the first premise of all existence. The first premise is that to be is to be in a state of promise. This is both beyond, and to use the language of Levinas, otherwise than being. Being, by itself, expresses sheer neutrality. As such, Being, by itself, does not permit us to glimpse the transcendence that makes the asymmetrical promise. There is a distinction that needs to be made more explicit here. It is between what Levinas calls "the promise of time," and what we might call "the time of promise." The latter, for Levinas, is much more problematic than the former. The latter assumes that there is, in fact, a purpose to the unfolding of time. He seems uncertain about this, and this is understandable as he was a witness to the unfolding catastrophes and calamities of the twentieth century. Yet, if we are to live oriented, purposeful, just, and reasonable lives, how can we manage without this idea?

As is intimated in the last portion of *Mattos*, dealing with the impending death of Moses, we may glimpse this kind of promise as the first pre-mise of all hopefulness. There is a prior bond between the future and the present that includes the past and exceeds my own temporal life and that of my generation. This is what we mean when we speak of the "promise" of a new generation, moving beyond the imperfections or limitations of the present one. To reiterate, a human being embodies a twofold sense of promise. The first, the concrete sense, is the bond between word and deed, which does much to inform the shape of everyday life. The second, which comes from outside the subject, signifies that there is something worthwhile about life even though it is limited— that is to say, that it involves "Time Bearing a Promise" (IRB 2001, 185).

Moses is quite aware that once he initiates the battle against Midian, the corruptors of so many of the sons of Israel, his own death is imminent. We might wish to ask why the language of vengeance is used in connection with the war against Midian. Revenge is not a substitute for justice, but rather an attempt, most often violent, to rectify a past injustice with some kind rationalization.

According to a midrash, Moses implored G'd to go into the land of Promise, whereupon he was told that his desire could be granted, but only if the Israelites were not allowed to go with him. By allowing Moses to peer into the land from a distant hill, Mount Nebo, we have an image of the life of Moses as one that exemplifies time bearing a promise. It is not a promise that he will get to see completed. At the same time, it is perhaps for this very reason that the humanity of Moses appears with such clarity and definition. A sense of hope, our sense of hope, depends upon the promissory nature of time. What appears to be affirmed by the image of Moses looking over into the Promised Land is that the meaning of life outlasts our conscious awareness of it. It is this promise to which we can maintain fidelity.

Levinas speaks very clearly of the resistance necessary to protect my neighbor from gratuitous violence that would be visited upon him or her. I am not, however, permitted to practice a nonresistance to evil. If the spirit of revenge shadows the desire for justice, as Nietzsche acutely observes, then we cannot speak of a future that is something different from the injury suffered by past sufferings (Sugarman 1980, 94). More precisely, if justice can be reduced to the spirit of revenge, then all ethical life is compromised in advance. Levinas refuses to conflate justice with revenge. For the future to be genuinely open to us, the past must be taken up within the present in such a way as to make the future different from the present and past. According to Rashi, it is particularly noteworthy that "Moses did not delay; he proceeded with alacrity to carry out the Mitzvah" (Stone, Num. 31:3, 905). The proximity of vengeance to justice in the case of the war against the Midianites derives from the way the Midianites had attempted to eradicate morality itself. It was for this reason, then, that the war against Midian proceeded as a way of restoring the moral dimension central to the identity of the way of life of the Israelites.

INFINITE TIME

Toward the end of *Totality and Infinity*, Levinas takes up the phenomenon of infinite time in relation to time that is finite. He states: "But infinite time is also the putting back into question of the truth it promises.... Truth requires both an infinite time and a time it will be able to seal, a completed time" (TI 1969, 284). Levinas's metaphysical affirmation that time is indeed infinite is most striking. We might wish to ask, "Why is this still called time, if it is no longer understood as finite?" That time is no longer understood as merely finite does not conflate time with eternity. To paraphrase Levinas, "[E]ternity is but the irreversibility of time." To speak of the future of the other is already to speak of the infinity of time.

The confluence between the legislation pertaining to vows, the war of vengeance against Midian, and the impending death of Moses is troublesome and needs to be thought through. At first glance, it appears to have traces of the Homeric myth of Achilles and the war against Troy. Still, there is no sense at all that Moses is either brooding over his own mortality or relishing the war that is undertaken. How then are we to interpret this? Is it perhaps the case that for the future to become something other than an eternally recurring image of the past, that the "evil of the past" must be exposed and confronted? For only in this way is it possible for the promised future to be something other than a readiness to make war in the spirit of revenge. Here, the metaphorical dimension of the text is more open to understanding than a presumably actual historical narrative.

It is not simply a matter of fighting the "last war," as we say. It is a matter of not letting the sufferings and imperfections of the past dominate our decisions, our commitments, and our promises. Otherwise, what we take to be new, is in fact governed by an obsession and compulsion with settling scores by displacing our anger and rage onto other people. What concerns Moses much more than his own mortality is the new generation of Israelites, who are now preparing to go into the Promised Land. There is no attempt here to rationalize or to cover up the kind of bloodshed that, as Plato says, accompanies the "founding myth" of every new state. Surely here there is a tension between the ethical and the political in which the ethical is not carried over in a direct or visible way into the domain of political life. Was the decision then really to kill or be killed? Was there no third term (or tertium quid) that would show a way between war and suicide?

It is Joshua, the successor to Moses, and not Pinchas, the zealot, who carries out this war. In the conquest of Canaan, as we shall see, the inhabitants are always offered a choice of settling the matter peaceably, though, understandably on the terms of the victor. In other words, while there is no enthusiasm whatsoever for the war against Midian, it appears as though the waging of war is regarded as preemptive in relation to the harm that will otherwise befall the Israelites. Could this be read as an anticipation of modern warfare: "The art of foreseeing war and of winning it by every means—politics—is henceforth enjoined as the very exercise of reason" (TI 1969, 21)? This does not make it good. As Levinas puts it, "[P]olitics is opposed to morality, as philosophy to naïveté" (Ibid.).

Here we are reminded of Nietzsche's formulation of ressentiment, whereby a necessity is transformed into a virtue. The second part of the *Genealogy of Morals* opens with this problematic formulation: "To create a being that can promise; is this not the paradoxical problem that nature has set itself with regard to man, and is this not man's true problem?" For Nietzsche, the future becomes the present, the present the past, and the past vaporizes into nothingness. This would mean that only in the fleeting present do human beings have access to life and to joy. For this joy to be perpetuated, all of the future and all of the past would have to be drawn down to a single eternally recurring "now." All time that passes on this model would become time past. In this way, it inhibits and limits the will to be-come. When it can be demonstrated that there is a difference between non-being and absence, the absent past is something that, as Levinas indicates, secretes a trace into the present. When my future becomes the future of others, it is not simply relegated to becoming nonexistent and therefore inconsequential.

Only when the neutrality of Being or nature is pierced, when it becomes something otherwise or better than Being, does it make sense to situate everyday life within a series of promises, commitments, and compromises. For this reason, we affirm that life is consequential, even though my life is limited. We make a fundamental decision to remake reality in a way that is perpetually attaching itself in our relation to others, through the promise of time. While affirming the promise of time, Levinas does not necessarily see "an ultimate stage of history, where humanity would no longer be violent, where humanity would have broken through the crust of being and where everything would be clear" (EI 1985, 114). In this way, he leaves the possibility of the time of promise open, but undetermined "to be worthy of the messianic era, one must admit that ethics has a meaning, even without the promises of the messiah" (Ibid.).

A DIFFICULT PIETY: KEEPING A PROMISE

The Torah portion Mattos begins by establishing the importance of words leading to deeds and will subsequently be completed by the carrying out of actions promised. Toward its close, the children of Reuven and Gad appeal to Moses to dwell on the eastern side of the river Jordan. Their appeal is based upon the fact that they have much livestock, and that this will be better for their own children. Moses objects on two grounds. Moses reproaches the leaders of the two tribes for apparently seeking to free themselves from the wars that will involve the other tribes in the taking possession of Canaan. Moreover, he chides them for mentioning their livestock before their children. In response, the children of Reuven and Gad promise to go out in front of the other tribes to battle, which in fact they later proceed to do under the order of Joshua for a period of fourteen years. They stand corrected by Moses and speak of their children before their cattle, thus affirming the biblical axiom that persons take precedence over possessions.

Just as the making of a promise can, under certain conditions, be annulled, the divine promise itself, for Levinas, is subject to critique and question. He argues that our obligations to one another are in no way open to evasion simply because we do not see either the beginning or end of the time of promise. For him this phenomenon becomes radicalized with the Holocaust of European Jewry. He states explicitly: "Contrary to a religion that feeds on representations, it (Judaism) does not begin in promise. Should we recognize in it the difficult piety—all the certainties and personal risks—of the twentieth century, after the horrors of its genocides and Holocausts?" It is not clear that a phenomenon of promise necessarily belongs to the language of representation, at least in its originary form. Is there not a kind of promise expressed by the countenance of the other person, even before language? My own hope seems to be predicated upon a promise that may be altogether held in abeyance for the other. As such, I can neither justify his or her sufferings nor preach to him or her about the time of promise. This would constitute, for Levinas, an illicit theodicy. The superimposition of meaning cannot take the place, even after the fact, of what Levinas calls "the useless suffering of others." He goes on to say "to be sure, one may wonder whether the time of promises ever stands at the beginning elsewhere than in pedagogy, and whether service without promises is not the only one to merit—and even to accomplish—promises" (EN 1998, 177). With the sharpest kind of self-critique, he concludes that these two questions "seem already suspect of preaching" (Ibid.).

This, too, expresses another moment in the Exodus from the self to the other. Such explanation, always in advance, directed toward another, is a way of enacting an aspect of the covenant within the promise of time.

JOURNEYS AND REFUGE
BEYOND OUR INTENTIONS

Massei: Journeys
(Numbers 33:1–36:13)

This portion of the Torah reiterates the journey beginning with the outgoing from Egypt to the preparation for entering the land of Promise. In this way, it retraces the forty-two encampments of the Israelites, and it names each one. Further, the text delineates the boundaries of the land of Israel, and the character of the cities, fields, and vineyards given to the Levites, who as guardians of the Sanctuary and future Temple, have no specific inheritance of their own. In this way, the Levites and the *Kohanim* who emerge from them can better serve the spiritual needs and ritual practices of all Israel. Because they have no land of their own, they are not subject to the same kinds of competitive rivalries and tensions as the rest of Israel. Their work is to be solely in the service of maintaining, guarding and carrying out the actions that are connected first to the Sanctuary (*Mishkan*) and later to the Temple.

The text then describes the unique institution of the cities of refuge (*Ari Miklot*) that are set aside for those who have taken the lives of others unintentionally and without premeditation. Under normal circumstances, the determination of guilt or innocence would be handled by a court, in accordance with the stringent criteria mentioned previously in Pinchas. In emergency cases involving involuntary manslaughter, the perpetrator can flee to one of the cities of refuge that serve to mitigate against an act of revenge upon the part of a family member, or "avenger of blood" (*goel ha'adam*). We might ask, once again, why the Torah would permit any kind of vengeance. Because of the stringencies involved in convicting someone in a capital case, it is a virtual certainty that the one who commits manslaughter will be found innocent by the courts, almost by definition. In cases of manslaughter, there is no intention and no possibility of proper warning, making witnesses to such an event irrelevant. It is not even clear that the unintentional agent of homicide would be turned over to the courts.

Yet for all that, the Torah does not affirm his complete innocence. All actions, intentional or unintentional are ones for which I am always responsible. If, for example, the handle of an axe flew off, struck, and killed someone, I may not have examined well the integrity of the axe beforehand, or I might have remained oblivious to the people in whose midst I found myself. The close family member who experiences such a death is not asked to look on this with equanimity. Otherwise, it could be argued that every person desires to do only what is good and is, therefore, not responsible for what he or she does. In a sense, this represents a breech in the order of justice. It is, therefore, not simply a matter of giving in to the desire for revenge as part of what is vaguely called "human nature." A remarkable strategy and institution are set aside for the accidental perpetrator. Nonetheless, this does not alleviate the sorrow and anger of those who still seek an understandable, if rough, justice.

Signs must be clearly posted to make it easier for the negligent one who has shed innocent blood to arrive at the city of refuge safely. The situation is deemed an emergency because the impulse of the avenger of blood is understandable and cannot be held accountable if he slays the perpetrator before he reaches the city of refuge. And yet, this is not some elaborate or potentially lethal game of tag. It is important to keep in mind that prisons were unknown in the biblical world and jails were used only as holding places for the person to be brought to trial.

According to Levinas, the order of justice established by the cities of refuge puts an end to the ability to take revenge. The claims of the avenger of blood cease when the accidental murderer enters the protection of the city of refuge. A life of holiness is then possible, even for the negligent perpetrator of homicide, Drawing on Tractate Makkos 10a. Levinas remarks that

> there are cities of refuge because we have enough conscience to have good intentions, but not enough not to betray them by our acts. Hence the manslaughters. Reality is not transparent to us; we take confusion of feelings for a conscience, and hatreds for fraternity. . . . We are no longer submerged by events, we no longer fear the avenger of blood, there is no longer an avenger of blood. We no longer risk committing the murders which give rise to the blood avengers. We escape the disorders where every person existing is concerned with his existence to enter into an order where the other man is finally visible. (BTV 1994, 50)

Levinas expands his meditation on the cities of refuge to a reflection on what the city means as a phenomenon in contemporary life. He appears to be asking whether the city is itself—that is, all cities—are in a certain way, habitations of refuge. He asks, "Does not the avenger or redeemer of blood 'with heated heart' lurk around us, in the form of people's anger, of the spirit of revolt, or even of delinquency in our suburbs, as a result of the social imbalance in which we are placed?" He responds to his own question as follows: "The cities in which we live and the protection that, legitimately, we find in our liberal society (even if we find it a little less than before) against so many threats of vengeance, fearing neither God nor man against so many heated forces; is not such protection, in fact, the protection of half-innocence or a half-guilt?—does not all this make all our cities cities of refuge or cities of exile?" (BTV 1994, 40). Within his broader philosophy, the commentary on the cities of refuge makes what he is saying here more visible.

Cities then, become a refuge from the primal natural law that sets people off, one against the other. The first intervention comes from authorities who recognize that the outer limitations of my person are formed by my own skin. This is exactly why the political thinker Thomas Hobbes argues that the first form of equality is found in the fact that all people equally fear a violent death. The corollary to this thesis is that each person, therefore, has the inherent right to flee from such an impending violent death. This would be a purely negative freedom, although it could account for the flight of the one who commits manslaughter. At a deeper level, are the ideas of moral rejuvenation and cultural rehabilitation. This requires a serious recognition of replacing the blind eye of natural law with the look of disinterested benevolence found in the city of refuge. In order to sustain themselves, all cities, beginning with the cities of refuge, must create, within their established limits, what Levinas calls "the responsibility of each for each."

Levinas refers, therefore, to the "humanitarian urbanism" of the cities of refuge. Above all, life in the full sense of the term must have the conditions that make life worth living and prohibit those that do not: "Exile, of course. But no prison, no hard labor, and no concentration camp … as life to the full needs clarification, clarity of the sun, but also Torah" (BTV 1994, 43). The refugee is not allowed to leave the city of refuge under any conditions, as this would reawaken the impulse for injustice and invite disorder. The refugee is to be treated humanely, however, and his or her material and spiritual needs are to be met by the Levites who dwell in and administer the cities of refuge.

The Talmud points out and Levinas emphasizes the fact that when the student is sent to a city of refuge, the master is also exiled. After all, "[T]he disciple needs Torah" (BTV 1994, 43). Levinas asks, what happens if a master is exiled? R. Yochanan says that "a master who goes into banishment is joined in exile by his colleagues (his *yeshiva*)" (Ibid., 43). Levinas is emphasizing the "strict social structure between teacher and student." How strong is this relationship? If "the disciple has the right to demand that the master join him in the city of refuge," and the master follows him, then the master may ask "[t]hat the (other) disciples follow him." All this is predicated on the assumption that a person cannot live without culture, or truly live without Torah. It is for this reason, as Levinas notes, the dictum from the Mishnah, "Let no one teach the Torah to a disciple that is unworthy." This is a call to extreme vigilance. It is also a recognition of the asymmetrical responsibility that the teacher has for the student and in turn, for the colleagues who comprise the other students. It is at the same time a call to conscience. Levinas states, "Our conscience is not yet holy conscience. It is a twilight, the transition from the non-intentional to the intentional is noticeable. We are not awake enough" (BTV 1994, 43).

Levinas observes that a teacher is also responsible for an unworthy disciple. The risk is great. Nonetheless, both the unworthy disciple and the teacher must be supplied with their material and cultural needs. Levinas asks, "Can one truly live without Torah?" (BTV 1994, 43). He responds by saying, "And so the Torah makes its appearance in the city of refuge." Levinas goes on to observe that while the unworthy disciple is not counted as a criminal, "he is nevertheless not (yet) a worthy man" (Ibid., 43). Levinas emphasizes that the person guilty of manslaughter must come to be aware and fully alert to the position of the other person. This is the continuing responsibility of the teacher. Levinas concludes his reflection on the teacher-student relation by stating that "the spiritual relation between master and pupil is as strong as the conjugal one" (Ibid.). To do this in full measure, his or her maturity is to be gained through an adherence to the law of the Torah borne out within the context of his or her life with other people. The Torah itself then becomes a kind of ultimate refuge. This is not to be confused with bibliotry, however. For the study of the Torah must lead to practice: "This study is the highest level of life, where knowledge is no longer distinguished from imperatives and practical impulses, where science and conscience meet, where reality and justice no longer belong to two distinct orders. It is as if the human were to rise to it by attaining a new condition, a new mode of the spirituality of the spirit" (Ibid., 47).

What is created in the city of refuge is a new kind of community where the fullness of human fraternity can be learned and enacted. Thus, Levinas sees what is promised in Jerusalem as the fullest expression of the humanity of the Torah. In concluding his meditation, he cites *Pirkei Avos* (*The Ethics of the Fathers*): "Without government men are ready to swallow each other alive." By this he means, a living, embodied city where the humanity of the human can manifest itself, a place "not outside all places in pious thoughts" (BTV 1994, 52). This appears to signify that spirituality can be found embodied only in relations with others and surpassing even my deepest and most pious thoughts.

Deuteronomy

DEVARIM

ON DEUTERONOMY

The word *Devar* means both "word" and "thing" in biblical Hebrew. The sages refer to Deuteronomy as *Mishneh Torah*, most commonly translated and understood as a repetition or, more precisely, a reiteration, of the Torah. However, the Torah is never understood as "mere" words without referring to "things." We mean "things" here in the broadest sense as people, events, and mitzvot. There are two hundred commandments which are contained in this book; more than seventy are completely new. To whom, then, is the Book of Deuteronomy addressed? There is a consensus among the commentators that the new commandments of Devarim are directed to life in the land of Promise. This also implies that Moses is addressing a new generation that is poised to go into the land and, therefore, must be both reeducated and given specific direction about how life is to be lived there.

According to Onkleos, whose Aramaic translation appears on every page of a traditional *Chumash*, "Deuteronomy began as the Oral Law conveyed by Moses, and then when G'd commanded him to inscribe his words in the Torah, it became part of the written Torah" (Stone, 939). This is a novel and ingenious way of explaining the first writing down of the oral Torah that was given in its entirety at Sinai.

Both Rashi and Onkleos before him point out that in retracing the steps of the past forty years, that Moses indirectly reminds the Israelites of their transgressions along the way. He does this, however, to prepare them *not* to repeat these same offenses upon entering the land. Rather, Moses mentions the places that they have stopped without directly calling attention to their transgressions. In this way he speaks to rather than about them, and without causing them public shame or humiliation.

S.R. Hirsch observes that the distinctiveness of Deuteronomy, from an ethical point of view, can be put as follows: "Not as a powerful nation, master of the art of war, but as the People of God's laws of morality. Is Israel to enter its path in the history of nations?" (Hirsch on Deut. 1:5). In a more general way, Hirsch asks why and how this fifth book of the Jewish Bible both stands on its own and is related to the four books that precede it. He begins by recalling that the last chapter of the fourth book reports the commands and regulations which God had given through Moses regarding taking possession of the land, which was now imminent (Hirsch on Deut. 1:1). Hirsch remarks that the people are about to live on their own without the guidance of their teacher, Moses.

The mode of transmission is understood by the tradition as changing in the Book of Deuteronomy. According to most commentators, Moses is here speaking in a manner that is divinely inspired but the transmission is not directly from God to Moses to the people. Therefore, what Moses now has to say has a special poignancy and urgency. Hirsch indicates that Moses is now talking to the people as individuals, though assembled together at "the imminent transition from the Wilderness into the Land, there being committed to writing (the laws) having been reserved for this compendium, or from the written repetition appearing necessary for this purpose" (Hirsch, Deut. I, 4). This is why, according to the rabbinic tradition, Moses will be referred to from this time on as "Moses, our teacher" (*Moshe Rabbeinu).*

FIRST REITERATION

Devarim: Words
(Deuteronomy 1:1–3:21)

Levinas's distinction between the saying and the said helps to clarify the matter of reiteration. Reiteration, for Levinas, involves not merely repeating what was previously said, but reinstalling the saying or the intention of what is meant along with what is spoken. Mitzvot are introduced here that deal with the inner life, the life of prayer, as well as laws pertaining to individual and communal conduct.

In a sense, the Book of Deuteronomy (*Sefer Devarim*) serves as a model of the relation between the oral and the written Torah. We are witness to a kind of speech in which the saying (the oral Torah) is visibly taking on written expression (the written Torah). Once again, what is decisive about the traditional Jewish reading of the Bible, and what separates it from other readings, is the way in which the oral Torah provides an explanation of the written one within its own framework of hermeneutics. It might appear that Deuteronomy is sealed because it is the last of what are also called the "Five Books of Moses." But, rather than canonically sealing the Torah, the task here is an ongoing one that is taken up and communicated orally before being written down in the Mishnah, Talmud, and Midrashim.

The Book of Deuteronomy is also referred to by the tradition as *Sefer HaYashar*, meaning the book of or for righteousness (literally straight or upright). All of the words contained in this book would have been spoken to all of Israel during the last thirty-seven days of the life of Moses. Therefore, they are spoken with an additional urgency, as a lasting exhortation to the Israelites for their moral responsibility to conduct themselves in the manner that is expected of them by the Torah. Necessarily, then, the traces of their previous errancy must instruct them in what had led them astray. In this way, the various places to which Moses refers, beginning with their exodus from Egypt, is itself a signpost of what is still to be achieved. Keep in mind that the entire journey in the wilderness is now into its fortieth year, rather than the simple, original geographic destination that was to have taken eleven days.

A novel explanation for Moses's present manner of discourse is given by the *Sefas Emes*. The Sefas Emes indicates that it was necessary for Moses to retrace the people's journeys in order to erase the burdens and limitations that some of these misguided adventures took. In a sense, then, the new generation is more easily able to begin their undertaking afresh in the land of Israel. Levinas confirms what the Sefas Emes intuits: "To be *leaving a trace*, is to pass, to depart, to absolve oneself" (BPW 1996, 62). In this way, the actuality of the past is affirmed, but the capacity to be open to a future new and different from the past is made possible. For those commentators who maintain that Moses is speaking not just to the generation about to enter the land, but to all future generations, Levinas offers philosophic support in his tying together time and the trace: "The trace-qua-trace does not simply lead to the past, but it is the very passing towards a past more remote than any past and any future which still are set in my time—the past of the Other, in which eternity takes form, an absolute past which unites all times" (BPW 1996, 63).

The relation of time to the trace does not deal simply with memory as a cognitive function. When we remember, we are remembering *something*. The key question concerns the relation of that which is remembered to our memory of it. *Every historical account* presupposes this distinction. What interests Levinas is not history as it unfolds, or "historicity," but rather the conditions that make times past memorable and meaningful. Time past registers to us as an absence rather than a presence. Still, it is an absence *of* something. When we speak, for example, of "remembering" the exodus from Egypt, we are of course relying on a memory that has been transmitted to us by those who have come before. Still, there are different perspectives, versions, levels of meaning, and recollecting what happened. This absence is very real, and not to be confused with nonexistence. The nonexistent never was; the absent past bears with it the promise of time that helps to orient time passing into the present toward the future. This is what Levinas means by the "trace." It leaves an imprint that cannot be effaced utterly even with attempts to conceal it.

It will be remembered that the great error of the explorers was that the significance of the absent past, beginning with the exodus from Egypt, had for them receded from absence into the realm of nonexistence. As we have already indicated, the explorers could not accept or deal with facing a future that would be different in kind from a mere prolongation of their present. The time of futurity is not wholly discontinuous from the past and present, but nonetheless remains radically contingent. There is something new about it. Here we are speaking not only of the near future, but the distant future which eclipses the limits of our vision.

There are only two mitzvot introduced in the first portion of Devarim. On the surface, both pertain to justice administered by courts and the judges who preside over them: "You shall not recognize a face in judgment" (Deut. 1:17). The companion mitzvah states: "You shall not be afraid of the face of any man." What is established here are the necessary conditions for the administering of any kind of justice. The former refers to those qualifications required pertaining to the integrity and wisdom of a judge. Aaron Yisroel Kahn states, drawing on Talmudic sources, that a judge is required to have the following character traits: "Wisdom and Torah knowledge; modesty; G'd fearing; respected by his fellows; a seeker of truth and justice and one who does not attach any importance to money (bribes)" (*Taryag Mitzvos*, 251). The reason given for knowledge in Torah is that otherwise the guilt and innocence cannot truly be ascertained.

Maimonides elaborates on this. He states that "he who appoints a judge who is unfit for his vocation, is as though he has set up an idol" (*Pearls of the Rambam*, 759). Here we are given a clear indication, from a phenomenological point of view, that the face and expression of a litigant conveys his disposition in such a way as to make us follow our natural inclinations and affections. This is, however, far from what Levinas calls "disinterested goodness." Maimonides adds that where there are two litigants and the expression of one alters the disposition of one of the judges in a court of three, that judge need not recuse himself. He must work instead to overcome his inclination or bias and judge the case regardless (Ibid., 760).

Regarding the second mitzvah, not to be afraid of the face of any man, he cannot say to himself or to others: "So-and-so is wicked, and he may slay my son, set fire to my stock of grain, or cut down my plants" (*Pearls of the Rambam*, 760). While Levinas does not offer any commentary on such a decision where the mitzvah becomes applied law, nonetheless, it is through his description of the face that we learn that the saying is expressed before and after the said. The judge, like any person, must be aware of this and take responsibility for the way in which the face may dissuade him, even to the point where he averts his gaze. This would, in turn, lead to an undermining of a just system. More precisely, justice, which operates in the realm of synchronic time, makes possible the establishment of stable institutions, reliable judgments, and justice for the self as well as the other. Still, as we have seen, this justice is not wholly impersonal; rather, it is disinterested. This does not absolve the judge from acting in a self-critical manner. This helps to explain why a judge has to make discrete judgments along with his two peers. The decision deals with finite matters but the petitioners, as well as the judges, draw their wisdom from the infinite dimension of the teachings of the Torah.

The importance of this issue reflects the central position taken by Levinas; the humanity of the human is expressed in the face of the other and that of his or her neighbor. Ultimately Moses is called upon by G'd, to subordinate his fear of the other to his fear of heaven. This happens every day in contemporary life, where we are constantly pushed and pulled in a direction that might lead to the subordination of justice to power. In effect, it doesn't matter that someone else may intimidate you, you must reckon with the neighbor and the other in accordance with a just measure.

PRAYER AND PEDAGOGY

Va'Eschanan: Pleaded
(Deuteronomy 3:23–7:11)

Without the theoretical activity of study, without the exacting regime of
listening and reading, without the limod, we can absorb nothing. But it
is also necessary to teach what one has learned in order to hand it down.
This transmission, the lelammed, an obligation distinct from the simple
receptivity of study.

—LR 1989, 221

Inspired by the *Nefesh ha'Hayim* (*The Soul of Life*), by Chaim Volozhin, Levinas
reinterprets the main purpose of prayer as involving "a reversal of subjectivity."
For Levinas, prayer is not for myself in the first place, or my own salvation, but
rather it is a way that the inner life exteriorizes itself in relation to others. This
means that the institution of prayer that guides Israel, particularly after the
return from the Babylonian exile, fashioned by the "men of the Great Assembly,"
transforms the inner life into the ultimate form of the word spoken (LR 1989,
77). He then notes that the Talmud, of course, is not dominated by individual
petitions. Such prayer, however, even when on behalf of the people of Israel, "is
not in the name of any nationalist egoism" (Ibid., 233). Prayer must be a kind
of speaking of the just person on behalf of others. Levinas asks, "Is prayer, then,
the soul itself?" (Ibid., 232). In responding to this question, Levinas reminds us
that there remains what he calls a "pre-oratorial prayer"—that is, a prayer that
arises prior to liturgical formulation. It is the kind of speaking that proceeds in
an atmosphere of not knowing and is at the same time, an acceptance of responsibility prior to the very understanding that is sought for. Even this kind of
prayer is not completely private. It relates to "the traumatism of my enslavement

in Egypt, (which) constitutes my humanity, that which draws me closer to the problems of the wretched of the earth, to all persecuted people" (Ibid., 202).

This, in turn, leads the individual to the love of the Most High. Prayer is intimately related to the phenomenon of uniqueness: "My very uniqueness lies in my responsibility to the other; nobody can relieve me of this, just as nobody can replace me at the moment of my death. Obedience to the Most High is defined for me by precisely this impossibility of running away. Through this, myself is unique. To be free is simply to do what nobody else can do in my place" (LR 1989, 202). By linking prayer to the remembrance of the condition of Israel in Egypt, does one not elicit the kind of compassion for others, strangers, that binds me to my past and reorient my responsibilities for the future of others?

Citing Chaim Volozhiner, Levinas singles out the first verse that follows the creedal prayer of Judaism, the *Shema*. "And thou shalt love the Lord thy God with all thy heart, and with all thy soul, and with all thy might" (Soncino, Deut. 6:5, 1022). This expresses the asymmetrical relation between the human being and G'd. At the same time, it binds us to the human community. This reminds the individual that such love is not without need of the guidance and wisdom of the Torah. It is what Levinas calls, in a transposition of the formula for philosophy, "a wisdom of love."

Addressed to each of us personally, the details of the Shema recognize that the self needs to be put together each day, anew. In other words, the subjectivity of the subject is open to elevation and is not static or imaged as the "little person inside of me." In the second passage of the Shema, the commandment pertaining to the tefillin is also given. The tefillin are the leather straps placed upon the head, the hand, and the part of the arm opposite of the heart, "and these words, which I command thee this day, shall be upon thy heart; and thou shalt teach them diligently unto thy children . . . and thou shalt bind them for a sign upon thy hand, and they shall be for frontlets between thine eyes" (Soncino, Deut. 6:6–8, 1022). The word "tefillin" comes from the same root word as the word for prayer, *tefillah*. Putting on the tefillin exteriorizes the binding together of the intellect, the emotions, and the strength of one's character.

From a phenomenological perspective, the tefillin appear as an active reminder that the moral and metaphysical unity of the person is something to be achieved each day. The cognitive, emotional, and volitional aspects of the human personality are always in need of a kind of vigilance that calls for integrating, corresponding to the head, the heart, and the hand. This is far removed from the spirituality of what Levinas calls "angelism." The leather boxes containing the portions of the Shema are made from the hide of a kosher animal. To be capable of responding for my neighbor, before the Most High, I do so as an embodied, oriented, alert human subject. The animal in the human is not left behind but sublimated.

"And thou shalt write them upon the door-posts of thy house, and upon thy gates" (Soncino, Deut. 6:9, 1023). Why are the inscriptions from Deuteronomy placed upon the doorposts of the house, called the *mezuzah* in Hebrew? Like that of the subject of tefillin, this deserves more phenomenological exploration. The phenomenological approach, which Levinas takes to his philosophical and Jewish writings, refers to that juncture between experience and meaning as it arises to human awareness. The doorpost leading from the inside of the home to the outside is more than simply a wooden framework, as it would be regarded in the "natural attitude." The threshold of the door out of my home expresses the fact that I am moving from one kind of space to another.

Under usual conditions, the home represents the sphere of the interior, the private, the personal. The "outside," as we call it, is less certain. When I am leaving home, I am aware that I am entering into a sphere that is less secure, if more adventuresome. Yet, in a sense, it is during transition, exemplified by leaving or returning home, that I pause to collect myself. Such transitions occur more than once or twice a day when I leave home, go to work, and return. They may happen within the interior of a home that has more than one room. Hence the word "doorposts" is put in the plural, to remind me, perhaps, that there is a difference between the kitchen and the bedroom. At the same time, despite the alterations that I undergo in my itinerary, even when repeated many times, I am awakened to the fact that the responsibilities of the "I" for others remains at the heart of my uniqueness. The common greeting "Shalom," upon welcoming someone into the home, signifies peace. The word *Shalom* signifies peace and is also one of the divine names. It is the common greeting upon welcoming someone into the home, and also when saying farewell, whether the other person is leaving my physical home or, as Levinas puts it, my "being at home with myself" (*chez soi*). Therefore, it would seem, peace is the precondition for the welcoming of the other and bidding him or her "A-Dieu"!

Pedagogy originates with prayer: "And these words, which I command thee this day, shall be upon thy heart; and thou shalt teach them diligently unto thy children, and shalt talk of them when thou sittest in thy house, and when thou walkest by the way, and when thou liest down, and when thou risest up" (Soncino, Deut. 6:6). This commandment refers in the first instance to the study of the Torah: "This mitzvah applies to every man, old and young, rich and poor alike. Every man must set aside a specific time to study Torah each day" (*Taryag Mitzvos*, 254). It is said of King David, sweet singer of Israel, that he kept a lyre suspended above his bed, so that he could arise with ease to pleasantly study.

Those who learn the Torah also are responsible for teaching it to children, whether their own or others'. Such learning and teaching is understood to be a lifelong responsibility. The more people learn, the more responsible they are for transmitting their understanding to others. Levinas puts it this way: "Without the theoretical activity of study, without the exacting regime of listening and reading, without the *limod*, we can absorb nothing. But it is also necessary to teach what one has learned in order to hand it down. This transmission, the *lelammed*, an obligation distinct from the simple receptivity of study" (LR 1989, 221). Levinas emphasizes the dynamic dimension of the learning-teaching-transmitting activity as one that involves constant interrogation between colleagues, as well as student and teacher. He goes on to argue that this cannot be confused with fossilized, accumulated knowledge of humankind. As he says,

> [I]n the tradition, the lesson (is) taught by the other and taken up by him. Without these qualities no revelation—no truly authentic thought—is possible. The activity of transmission therefore involves a teaching which begins to take shape, even in the receptive attitude of study, and adds something to that attitude: true learning now consists in receiving a lesson so profoundly that the student is compelled to pass it on to another. The lesson of truth cannot be contained within the consciousness of a single man, it bursts out of those bounds, towards the Other. (Ibid., 221)

While addressed to Israel, the lessons of the Torah, different from their obligations, extend to all. Levinas puts it this way: "There is a further reason why the particular should be seen within the Law as a principle which is independent of the universality that every particular law reflects" (LR 1989, 220). The Torah portion before us gives an illustration of the point that Levinas is making when it reminds us not to forget G'd, "G'd Who Brought You Forth out of the House of Egypt, Out of the House of Bondage" (Soncino, Deut. 6:12, 1023). The conditions of oppression must be transformed into just actions and institutions for everyone. This is a step on the way to achieving "a transcending humanism."

SANCTIFYING EVERYDAY LIFE

Ekev: Hear
(Deuteronomy 7:12–11:25)

This Torah portion involves a mixture of reiterating the journey that has led up to entering the land of Promise while anticipating the transformation that comes to a new generation, no longer in the wilderness. Here, Moses instructs the nation about the seven species of the land of Israel that are to be planted, grown, harvested, eaten, and blessed. The seven species include "wheat, barley (including oats, rye, and spelt), grape (or grape wine), figs, pomegranates, olives and dates" (*Taryag Mitzvos*, Mitzvah 430). Entering the land means helping to codetermine the order of creation. This surpasses the natural attitude that it presupposes. Of course, the plants referred to are organic in nature, but it is their meaning or significance in relation to the inhabitants that is at stake here. There is a gratitude that is expressed as one of the irreducible categories of a life that is purposeful and sanctified. It involves an appreciation, recognition, and expression of thanks to the Most High for our sustenance. The miracle of the manna that sustained the people for close to forty years is coming to an end. Giving thanks is not an empty piety, but a reminder of the asymmetry between creature and Creator. This appreciation, in its sublime form, that we call "gratitude," is in Hebrew called *ha koras ha tov,* a simultaneous recognizing, appreciating, and thanking for that which is good. The good is not something that has to be. Rather, the good is something to be achieved. For Levinas, the ultimate question is not the one asked by Hamlet, "To be, or not to be?" Rather, he insists that both in a personal and eminently philosophical way, the preeminent question appears as, "Is it righteous to be?"

What does the language that would subordinate being to righteousness imply? To begin with, it implies, for Levinas, that my place in the sun may be at the expense of another's, that it may even involve violence and usurpation. This appears to recognize a material scarcity that belongs inherently to the order of things. However, the material scarcity, at least according to the *Or HaChaim*, does not apply to the land of Israel. By this, he means that such material scarcity can be surmounted through the establishing of just human relations. He translates the text as "a land in which you will not eat bread out of scarceness." The *Or HaChaim* continues "that at least upon first entering the land, there will be no distinctions between the 'haves' and 'have-nots'" (1999, vol. 5, 1827). He connects this with the following verse: "You will eat and you will be satisfied" (Deut. 8:10). His logic is as follows: "The reason Moses had to mention this cardinal fact, was that the perfection of the land does not merely consist of its fruit, its harvest, but the land must be able to provide basic materials to enable its people to build shelters in order to enable the possibility of life in the city" (Ibid., 1827). He continues: "Many successful farmers in various countries who employ outside labor are nonetheless forced to sell all their produce in order to acquire building materials, clothing, and tools . . . nothing essential would be scarce *after* he had described the seven most valuable foods and fruit the land would produce" (Ibid., 1827–1828). Is this, perhaps, an intimation of the Kibbutzim, present at the founding of contemporary Israel? Levinas anticipates an objection: "You will say that everyone can imagine that he is founding a just society and that he is sacralizing the earth, and will that encourage the conquerors and colonialists?" (NTR 1990, 66).

Levinas answers his own question in the following way:

> But here one must answer: to accept the Torah is to accept the norms of universal justice. The first teaching of Judaism is the following: A moral teaching exists, and certain things are more just than others. A society in which man is not exploited, a society in which men are equal, a society such as what the first founders of the Kibbutzim wanted—because they, too, built ladders to ascend to heaven, despite the repugnance most of them felt for Heaven—is the very contestation of moral relativism. (NTR 1990, 66)

In this way, Levinas attempts to generate the universality of a just teaching addressed to the people, Israel: "What we call the Torah provides norms for human justice. And it is in the name of this universal justice and not in the name of some national justice or other, that the Israelites lay claim to the land of Israel" (Ibid., 66).

It is the conjuncture of humanism and transcendence that is of the utmost importance here. It begins with the recognition of the source and abundance of goodness. The other person's deprivation would then suggest the manner in which the "I" is obligated to provide for the other because she already transcends me. As such, we are free from the kind of self-adoration that can end in an anthropocentric idolatry. At the same time, we are thinking, in the first instance, of that which is the source of all goods beyond the creation of my own hand. We work and proceed together not simply side by side but temper our justice with a certain mercifulness that comes from the originary face-to-face relation. This sense of deep fraternity does not preclude, but rather enables the appearance of uniqueness. It moves beyond a numeric equality by becoming an embodied justice that permits the generating of abundance not by the exploitation of other people, but rather through nonalienated labor that makes prosperity and generosity possible in the former and obligatory in the latter.

Once again, we are reminded in this context, "And you shall love the stranger" (Deut. 10:19). Thematically, we were strangers, outsiders, in the land of Egypt. Phenomenologically, every person remains, at some level, an "outsider" to every other person. For Levinas, from an ethical point of view, there are no insiders, despite what they may think of themselves or what others may think of them. The ethical zone of human reality is, in the words of the title of one of Levinas's books, "Outside the Subject." The love of the neighbor is possible only when we emphasize the love of the stranger, the other, in the deepest and broadest sense.

In this way, even Divinity itself remains an outsider to the creation of history. Otherwise, we should not be able to account for even the possibility of transcendence. "The God of history must remain transcendent to the world which he has created in order to provide for the promise of its redemption. Otherwise, the regime ruled by power would always administer ultimate truth and be the standard of the justice that it dispenses" (Sugarman 1979, 222). This does not preclude, but enables the subject to assume an additional degree of responsibility for other people. Such responsibility aims at the perfecting of justice. For Levinas, this implies an inescapable responsibility on the part of the elected human subject for all of the others: "Responsibility for the other, this way of answering without a prior commitment, is human fraternity itself, and it is prior to freedom . . . the non-interchangeable par excellence, the I, the unique one, substitutes itself for others. Nothing is a game: *Thus being is transcendent*" (OBBE 1991, 116–17, my emphasis).

ECONOMIC JUSTICE

Re'eh: See
(Deuteronomy 11:26–16:17)

And there will not be any more poor among you.

—Deuteronomy 15:4

And the poor shall not cease in the land.

—Deuteronomy 15:11

In the next three portions of the Torah, there are inscribed, according to the *Sefer Hachinuch*, one hundred and seventy mitzvahs. These three sections deal with a variety of subjects, while tending to focus on the overarching theme of justice. Justice is not discussed as a separate, philosophical problem but is embedded in human relations and expressed through a body of applied laws. One of the most distinctive features of these teachings, their commandments and laws, focuses on the interrelatedness of economic justice, morality, reason, and transcendence. There is no hard and fast separation between morality and economic life. And under no conditions can one be regarded as holy; when one turns ones face away from one's neighbor and acts as though one were self-made. The self-made person is thought to practice a subtle form of idolatry. Social justice is understood, to a large extent, to be a function of just economic relations. In advance, as Levinas points out in the introduction to *Difficult Freedom*, the hunger of the third party limits my philosophical aspirations. Feeding the hungry is not simply a matter of personal goodwill or discretion; rather, there is an explicit body of laws that bears upon my obligations for the physical, social, and economic well-being of other people. Very different from the political autodidacts of today, we encounter limits on the use of private

314

property, protections for animals and trees, and above all, for the other person for whom I am thought to be utterly responsible.

In all juridical matters, each person is to be treated as having an irreducible standing regardless of wealth or reputation. Still more, there is a kind of curvature to the ethical space of biblical Israel. There are limits imposed upon agricultural efficiencies, ownership of land, and commercial relations. Keep in mind that the Infinite is never reducible to a Totality, and therefore, God Himself remains as the ultimate outsider.

The social regime of the Torah depends upon the enactment of economic justice. Repeatedly, Levinas deplores the spiritualism of "beautiful souls." One of the defining aspects of human beings is that we are not angels. Levinas remarks that one of the distinguishing features of the Hebraic tradition is that it represents a "type of rationality, a reason far less turned in on itself than the reason of the philosophical tradition" (LR 1989, 206). For Levinas, this is "a rationality of transcendence." The transcendence of the other person has an economic dimension. I do not greet him "with empty hands."

Levinas finds secure support for his position in the approach of the *Or HaChaim*. What is vaguely called "social justice" in our time is not sufficient for someone to be considered an upright person, let alone a holy one. The *Or HaChaim* explains the statement "there shall be no poor among you . . . that if there are poor people among you, it is because of you in that the other man's portion is in your hands. Whatever he is lacking, you have in excess" (Nachshoni, vol. 5, 1277). How then do we explain the apparent contradiction between the two biblical statements, "there shall be no poor among you" (Deut. 15:4) and the much more widely heard statement seven lines later that asserts, "The poor shall not cease in the land" (Deut. 15:11)? Very simply, the *Or HaChaim* resists the spiritualist temptation to rationalize the inevitability of human poverty. If the others are impoverished, it is because of my actions. Although it must be acknowledged that the Torah is precapitalist, nonetheless, it anticipates a fundamental critique of bourgeois society as well as a critique of the 'latest progressive thinking from the Left Bank of Paris.' Both views share a political formalism that does not do justice to the socioeconomic dimensions of a fully human society.

The Torah provides a more radical position, one grounded in a more empirical reality where there is "a divine dictate regarding the individual's money and property" (Nachshoni, vol. 5). It can be plausibly suggested that the specific proscriptions provided in this portion of the Torah are anachronistic and therefore of no contemporary relevance. The very specific dictates expressed as laws binding upon the Israelites are not, however, limited in principle or in application to a given historical hour. The economic exploitation of one person by another is proscribed. Keep in mind "that the Torah does not oppose private property, but it places limitations on the use of that property so as to prevent a person from exploiting his property for evil purposes" (Nachshoni, vol. 5, 1277).

There is the appearance of a concession to economic inequality in the fact that despite the original equal distribution of the land according to the population grouped for the most part into twelve portions, there will arise again some disparity between rich and poor. There are, however, continuing correctives placed upon this kind of economic inequality. The traditional sabbatical year (*shemittah*), still in effect, provides for the cancellation of debts. At the end of fifty years, all land is to be returned to its original inhabitants. This is not simply a yearning for nostalgia, where the past would appear to memory as "golden time" subject to reimagined reflection. What this means ethically is that there is a time limit on the appropriation of land in excess of that which is needed. This phenomenon, called *yovel*, or the "jubilee year," awaits the time of complete redemption before it can be reinstituted. It is, for this reason, that the time of the fiftieth year remains what Kant called a "regulative idea," a hope, and an aspiration—that is to say, an idea that we cannot do without, even as it perpetually remains to be implemented.

Other conditions that pertain to use of private property are reiterated here. Most of these laws and practices pertain to an agricultural society. While there are prohibitions against waste, there are also limits placed upon consumption practiced in the name of efficiency. For example, during the time of harvesting, one is not permitted to reharvest single or double stalks of wheat that may have been dropped during the harvesting. Rather, these gleanings (*leket*) must be left for the poor. This also applies to bales of wheat left forgotten. These remnants (*shichecha*) must also be left for the poor. Perhaps the best example of this occurs in the Book of Ruth when Ruth is told by Boaz that she may take as she wishes: "Let her glean even among the sheaves; do not embarrass her. And even deliberately pull out some for her from the heaps and leave them for her to glean; do not rebuke her" (Ruth 2:15–16). For Levinas, this kind of generosity is both a condition for and effect of economic and, therefore, social justice. A more commonly known practice is that of leaving a corner of one's field for the poor to harvest for themselves. This, too, is a fence against regarding one's own field as completely belonging to oneself or thinking that one is self-made.

JUSTICE AND CHARITY

It is important to distinguish between justice and charity. Charity is not a substitute for economic justice but rather is understood as its surplus. This distinction implies that justice (*tzedekah*) is incumbent upon everyone. Charity (*chesed*) refers to the kindness that is expressed through generosity. In a logical sense, generosity presupposes the expression and achievement of justice. The kindnesses and generosity of everyday life can be practiced meaningfully even when such justice is absent, compromised, or postponed. Levinas speaks of "the exigency of holiness" He goes on, "At no time can one say: 'I've done all that I can.' (EI 1985, 105). This is the case because my sense of responsibility exceeds my abilities. He speaks of "the little acts of goodness' of everyday life" (IRB 2001, 217). He remains tentative, even skeptical, about organizing goodness as a regime or a social system.

Totalizing these acts of goodness and regimenting them through bureaucracy can lead to a form of totalitarianism. Commenting on Vassily Grossman's book *Life and Fate*, he observes "that every attempt to organize humanity fails" (IRB 2001, 217). Presumably by this he means that every totalizing system is inadequate, even if some are better than others. This does not preclude the constant responsibility to renew and work to perfect society.

The sabbatical year itself expresses the complementary relationship of justice to acts of benevolence that might rightly be called "generosity" or "charity." Since there is neither plowing nor harvesting in this year, and the fields are declared "ownerless" (*hefker*), we understandably worry more about our own sustenance than in other times. In fact, according to one commentator, the Kli Yakar, "The major purpose of the *mitzvah* of *shemittah* is to undermine a person's confidence in his own possessions" (Nachshoni, vol. 5, 1282). Since the land is rendered ownerless, we might begin to think that we are free from the obligation to pursue justice and to practice only *chesed* (or charity) in its place. This is not the case, however. In the language of Levinas, this is the constant movement out of egocentrism toward alterity.

The Torah warns us against withholding "tzedakah" (justice, righteousness) from your destitute brother as the seventh year approaches. It states specifically, "[R]ather you shall open your hand to him, you shall surely hand him his requirement, whatever is lacking to him" (Deut. 15:8). There is a poignant moral lesson drawn by the Kabbalistic commentator Alshich on what this signifies. "Whatever you do now, when you die, you will have to open your hands. At that time, none of your gold and silver will go with you. All that will accompany you will be your good deeds" (Nachshoni, vol. 5, 1279). To this we might note that when we come into the world, we do so with clenched hands, though we leave it with our hands open. What we must learn is to open our hand toward others in a timely way.

Again, the question is raised. How are we to reconcile the two statements that appear to promise there will be no poor among us, and yet the poor will not cease from out of the land? When we transpose this apparent contradiction from formal logic into the realm of time measured by urgency, then we can begin to resolve the matter more clearly. Justice is something to be achieved. We are commanded to act justly. If we do so, the lost portion of the other will reappear through my taking responsibility for him. Assuming that the institutions of economic justice are practiced and there remains an imperfection, then I have the responsibility of generosity, of kindness.

The first step must be to heed the warning of the Torah, "Beware lest a wicked thought appear in your heart" (Deut. 15:9). This is put proximate to the laws concerning the sabbatical year. According to the great moralist, the Dubno Maggid, this means that we cannot allow ourselves to believe or accede to the "fraudulent belief that it is only natural there are different classes in society. That is simply wrong. It is not naturally so. We must rectify this position and give back to the poor his portion which we have in our hands" (Nachshoni, vol. 5, 1278–79). This measurement is not accomplished simply on the basis of econometrics; rather, it is found in the recognition that morality is inseparable from socioeconomic life.

ON RIGHTEOUSNESS AND RESPONSIBILITY

Shoftim: Judges
(Deuteronomy 16:18–21:9)

Justice, justice you shall pursue.

—Deuteronomy 16:20

A central theme of contemporary life, and a recurring question within the Torah, concerns the relation of knowledge to morality. For Levinas, both knowledge and justice, the central pillar of morality, arise at the juncture between one person and another. In the interpersonal sphere, there is always a third party, seen or unseen, with whom I must reckon in my relation to the other. The third party also stands in relation to the neighbor and adumbrates a relation with the neighbor's neighbor ad infinitum. Hence it is impossible for a society to endure without laws and legal institutions.

The statement *tzedek tzedek tirdof*, "justice, justice you shall pursue" (Deut. 16:20), has been subjected to many commentaries. Most of these commentaries are exhortatory or pedagogical in character. For example, R. Simcha Bunam of Pshischa observes that "just ends must be achieved through just means" (Stone, n20, 1025). Rashi argues that cases must always be taken before a reliable or just court. Ramban indicates "the repeated word *justice* is an exhortation both to the judge and the litigant." Ibn Ezra says that "the repetition of justice denotes whether the judgment would be to their (i.e., the litigants') advantage or disadvantage" (Soncino, Deut. 16:20).

Levinas stakes out a much more radical and original claim with regard to justice. There are philosophical questions that remain to be asked: given the fact that legal justice is continuous with social and economic justice, how do we know, generally and precisely, what is just and what is not? Furthermore, *what is the relation of knowledge to justice?*

Levinas stresses that ethics, rather than ontology or epistemology (theory of knowledge) is first philosophy. This means that true philosophy cannot be put in the service of political injustice, as has often been the case. Levinas says that "we name this calling into question of my spontaneity by the presence of the Other, ethics" (TI 1969, 43). Against the majority position in Western philosophy, Levinas asserts that "[f]reedom does not resemble the capricious spontaneity of free will; its ultimate meaning lies in this permanence in the same, which is reason. Cognition is the deployment of this identity. It is freedom. That reason, in the last analysis would be the manifestation of a freedom, neutralizing the other and encompassing him, can come as no surprise once it was laid down that sovereign reason knows only itself, that nothing other limits it" (TI 1969, 43). In modernity, reason and morality represent cognition and conduct respectively. Reason is related to freedom, while justice belongs to the realm of ethics.

Levinas argues that unless ethics and knowledge have a common root, then we shall not be able to explain the philosophic basis of either knowledge or ethical life. One would belong to theory (knowledge) and the other (ethics) to action. To reason, however, in the interhuman sphere, is to give justification. To justify oneself and one's speech in the presence of the other is to begin to give reasons. In this sense, justice is not simply an inanimate substance but the basic theme of everyday speech, at least insofar as it belongs to the realm of questioning and responding.

One of the distinctive features of the rabbinic court, at least in the case of the Sanhedrin, is that its members formed a semicircle, "so that its members could see each other." As Levinas notes, "The special feature about it was that no one ever saw anyone else's back, only full faces or profiles. Never was the interpersonal relationship suspended in this assembly. People saw each other face-to-face. The 'dialogue,' as they say today, was thus never interrupted, nor did it get lost in an impersonal dialectic. It was an assembly of faces and not a joint-stock company" (NTR 1990, 72). As we have stressed, the human face plays a central role in Levinas's depiction of ethics. It is impossible for anyone to understand anyone else, or for the speaker to know if the meaning of what he or she has said was understood, without turning toward the face of the other. Anonymous reason, unattended by the human face, is incapable of rendering itself into the personal, the singular, and the temporal dimensions of human existence. Prior to speech with the other is the face-to-face encounter, and it is here that original expression arises prior to any language. It is from the face of the other that an appeal prior to thematization appears. The appeal arises "in the uprightness of the face, its extreme exposure without defense" (TI 1969, 86). The face is the source of original expression, mandating a relation that opens the realm of the ethical. "The face is as necessary for meaning as the category of quantity is for counting" (Sugarman 2002, 415).

Levinas asks, "[I]s not the model of revelation an ethical one?" (BTV 1994, 146). In other words, justice is not something merely added on to reason. Nor is revelation itself free of an ethical dimension. The great medieval conflict between reason and revelation depends upon a separation between the G'd of Abraham, Isaac, and Jacob, and the God of philosophy. It ends in explaining neither. Revelation originates, as does all meaning, in expression. The transcendent nature of expression is the locus of all meaning-giving. Its transmission is always for someone else, without whom it makes no sense to speak of the language of revelation. Rationality and transcendence are not opposed to one another. On the contrary, it is transcendence that makes it possible for the trace of a teaching to be maintained, preserved, and disseminated.

THE LIMITS OF WAR

War, as Levinas notes in the preface to *Totality and Infinity*, threatens to make morality, and all of its aspirations to justice, laughable. He does not advocate a nonresistance to evil. Rather, he argues that if I am responsible for the other person, and for the other person's neighbor, then I am not free to refrain from going to his or her assistance. The Torah seeks to promote peace, not pacifism: "When you draw near to a city to wage war against it, you shall call out to it for peace" (Deut. 20:10). Moreover, there is no argument over conscription for battle. The exceptions come first:

> Who is the man who has built a new house and not dedicated it? Let him go and return to his house, lest he die in the war and another man will dedicate it. And who is the man who has planted a vineyard and not redeemed it ... and who is the man who has betrothed a woman and not married her ... the officers shall continue speaking to the people and say, "who is the man who is fearful and faint-hearted? Let him return to his house and let him not melt the heart of his fellows." (Deut. 25:8)

The man who is fearful is not to be regarded as a coward, surely not in the Greek sense. Rather he is understood to be someone who senses himself unworthy and therefore unable to present himself without risk to the well-being of his fellow soldiers.

The Torah asks: "Is the tree of the field a man, that it should enter the siege before you?" (Deut. 20:19). Even when human passions are at their most destructive, caution, which checks one's spontaneous self-assertion, is in place.

The law requires that before attacking the other side must be offered the chance to surrender, thereby demonstrating the limits to war. Does this not suggest that it is war, not peace, which must remain the exception? As Levinas states, "[W]e oppose to the objectivism of war, a subjectivity born of the eschatological vision" (TI 1969, 25). In other words, war makes people into objects against their will, turns them into bearers of historical forces, thereby divesting each one of his or her uniqueness and alterity. It precludes the aptitude for speech and justice. It is something to be overcome.

INFINITE RESPONSIBILITY

At the close of the portion of Shoftim, we learn about the responsibility and atonement for someone who has been murdered in the area between cities, and whose perpetrator is unknown. According to the tradition, it is customary for a stranger or guest in a town to be escorted to the edge of the town fortified with food and directions. As Levinas argues, responsibility for the other has no limits. The city closest to the corpse has an additional responsibility and must perform, in addition to a proper burial, an expiation known as the *eglah arufah* (Deut. 21:1–9). The murder of a single person is unacceptable, morally and religiously. Even if there is no known perpetrator for the murder, the death must not go unnoticed, unmourned, or unrepented. Although there may be no mitzvah to accompany a wayfarer all the way to the next city, implied is an insufficiency of communal concern that would in turn have led to an extra measure of divine protection. In this case, the *eglah arufah*, or the "heifer that is axed," is a recognition of communal dereliction.

Let us briefly revisit, in light of Levinas's teachings, the imperative "justice, justice shall you pursue" (*tzedek tzedek tirdof*). The achievement of justice must be sought over and over again. For Levinas, this means that justice must follow injustice if we are ever to escape the unending cycle of conflict or revenge. In this way, even if we can speak of justice as finite, the perfection of justice is not, for responsibility is ongoing. This is the only way that justice can be perfected. An inexhaustible responsibility announces itself before and comes after justice. In this way, we can understand how what may have passed for justice at one time needs rectification at another. This is to say that even the just city is not just enough. It needs to be tempered by benevolence and the small kindnesses of everyday life.

SOCIAL JUSTICE

Ki Seitzei: Go Out
(Deuteronomy 21:10–25:19)

We are all responsible . . . for all men before all, and I more so than
the others.

—Levinas citing Dostoyevsky, EI 1985, 98

If you see your brother's ox or sheep going astray, you must not ignore
them. You must return them to your brother.

—Deuteronomy 22:1

After concluding with the infinite responsibility of communities, the Torah
resumes a very elaborate teaching primarily detailing the order of justice to be
established. This section contains more mitzvot than any other portion of the
Torah, seventy-three in all. Here we comment on only a few.

The basis of economic justice is emphasized and elaborated upon in the
Talmud. For example, it is an obligation to return lost property to its owner. The
finder is obligated to make a public announcement that the owner of the object
can reclaim with certain specifications, assuring that he is indeed the owner of
the object. It does not matter whether the object is small or large, or whether
it belongs to one's friend or one's foe. What is prohibited is glacial indifference.
"You may not withdraw yourself" (Deut. 22:3).

This kind of justice must be practiced in a disinterested manner. Human
beings must practice right conduct to animals as well. If one person is unloading
an animal and the other is loading it, the person must first assist the one who is
unloading the animal. Why? Because in unloading, you are relieving the animal
of its burden and suffering. In this case, if you are faced with a choice of helping
to unload the animal of a friend or an enemy, you must assist the enemy first.

The tradition is not indifferent to economic practicalities. If you are assisting an Israelite to load a burden on an animal, you may ask for pay, but not when helping unload another's animal. Why? Because the action of loading the animal is presumably not as time-sensitive in terms of the animal. This means that you want to diminish the pain of the animal in a timely way.

The detailing of the laws of justice is here expressed in a comprehensive and foundational manner. Justice is itself mitigated, however, by a deep sense of mercifulness. We see this in what is referred to in Hebrew as the *Shiluach HaKen*. This particular mitzvah forbids one from taking an ownerless mother bird when it is sitting on its eggs or its young. It is consonant with the prohibition against the killing of an animal with its young on the same day (Lev. 22:28). Maimonides states, "If the law provides that such grief should not be caused to cattle or birds, how much more careful must we be that we should not cause grief to our fellow men?" (GFP 1956, 372). In fact, the sending away of the mother bird is singled out, along with the obligation to honor your father and mother, as one of the two mitzvot for which long life is promised. This kind of compassion does not substitute for justice. Rather, according to Levinas, such compassion, or *rachamim*, is both the surplus and precondition of justice itself.

This law is immediately followed by one that calls for anticipatory responsibility. "You shall make a railing for your roof" (Deut. 24:8). The railing on the roof is called a *geder*, or "fence." Many of the other mizvot will have ancillary imperatives aimed at distancing the person or preventing the person from a transgression. Presumably this is the roof that people would have access to and use, at least from time to time. Moreover, you are responsible for not leaving dangerous objects casually lying around your property, so that injury does not befall others.

WORKERS' RIGHTS

The Torah advances a position on the rights of workers. Levinas places great emphasis on this issue in a Talmudic discourse that he gives on "Judaism and Revolution" (NTR 1990, 94–119). It should be noted that this discourse occurrs just after the 1968 uprising by students in Paris. Levinas takes his position on the rights of workers from biblical and Talmudic sources. In fact, one of the foremost leaders of the student uprising in Paris, Benny Levi, an Egyptian Jew, later Sartre's assistant, became a most serious student of the Talmud spurred by his admiration for the thought of Levinas. Levinas felt that the rhetoric and symbolism of the protesters separated, in a facile manner, economic obligations from social trends and political fashion. There was a parallel movement in the

United States at this same time. Aimed initially at the war in Vietnam, the desire for cultural libertinism continued long after and the struggle for workers' rights became something of an afterthought.

Keep in mind that the Torah has already installed a union of sorts that accords all workers and all of those bound by the law approximately seventy days a year free of toilsome labor. This involves counting the Sabbath and Jewish holy days, on which it is stipulated you shall do no work. Such conditions are established long before the reforms instituted in modern industrial society.

The issues before Levinas here are quite circumscribed. One particular issue involves what we would today call "overtime." The Talmud forbids forced overtime as a condition for compensation: if an employer were to pay a higher wage, it would be possible to think that he is saying to the workers, "I agreed to pay you a higher salary, assuming that you would begin earlier and finish later." Levinas observes that the Talmud already places constraints upon such conditions. It does not matter if the person is willing to pay a higher price than the normal wage, if in so doing he or she compromises the humanity of the workers. Levinas asks: "Isn't it possible to buy the leisure time of workers on the black market?" (NTR 1990, 101). He tells us what the heart of the Talmud, the Gemara, recommends as the workers' response. "The Gemara would like the worker to answer the boss who becomes generous so as to obtain extra working hours thus: Sure, you have paid me more but that is so I should work better. The quality of my labor I am willing to discuss, but I will not bargain about my human condition, which, in this particular case, expresses itself as my right to get up and go to sleep at the regular hours" (Ibid., 101).

It is, in the view of Levinas, a grave error to think in a disembodied way of the "spirit of sacrifice" demanded by all movements in the name of some higher historical end that treats the worker strictly as a theme or object of history. Levinas goes on to remark that "revolution must be defined by its content, by values: revolution takes place when one frees man; that is, revolution takes places when one tears man away from economic determinism. To affirm that the dignity of the working man is not negotiable, that he cannot be bargained about, is to affirm that which begins a revolution" (NTR 1990, 102).

THE "PACT"

Ki Savo: Enter
(Deuteronomy 26:9–29:8)

"Moses and the elders of Israel commanded the people, saying, 'Observe the entire commandment that I command you this day.'" Perhaps no other reflection of Emmanuel Levinas more succinctly describes both the content and method of his approach to the Jewish Bible than his discourse on the Pact. The passages on which Levinas comments deal with chapter 27 of the Book of Deuteronomy, which include the staging of the blessings and curses on Mount Gerizim and Mount Ebal, respectively, when the people will have crossed the Jordan. The Talmudic commentary is an amplification of the discussion found in the Mishnah regarding the scope, meaning, and purpose of these curses and blessings. The discussion in the Talmud, Tractate *Sota* 37a–b, involves a staggering, if somewhat playful, mathematical complexity. What is at stake here for Levinas is primarily the meaning and reach of responsibility as it affects the law in its interpersonal dimensions. Twelve large stones were to be established after full entry into the land was made under Joshua. There is a dispute as to whether the stones conveyed simply the biblical mitzvot, all six hundred thirteen according to the Talmud, or whether the entire text of the first five books was written on them (Nachshoni, vol. 5, 1354–55). There is even a third opinion that holds that the inscription on the stones, in all seventy languages of the nations of the world, referred only to the prohibition against idolatry (Ibid., 1358). Furthermore, the biblical text indicates that "you shall not raise iron upon them" for, as has been explained before, it is from iron that the instruments of war are fashioned, as well as the first condition for all industrial activity. The text says, you shall inscribe on the stone all the words of the Torah, "well clarified" (Deut. 27: 8). In Hebrew, the words "well clarified," *Be'er haTiev*, could mean "plainly written," or clearly expressed. There is agreement, however, that this should be readable in the seventy languages representing all of the other nations of the world in addition to Israel.

During the annual conference of Jewish intellectuals that was dedicated to the theme of community, Levinas remarks upon "the unease felt by man today within a society whose boundaries have become, in a sense, planetary" (LR 1989, 212). He adds that "certainly, the conduct of State and nation is less abstract than that of the planet, and the universal ties of the law guarantee a condition in which men find themselves side-by-side rather than face-to-face" (Ibid.). The choice of the words "side-by-side" are an implied critique of Levinas's former teacher Heidegger, whose idea of community appears to be modeled after that of a triumphant military parade. Levinas believes that a genuine community, one that endures through time and is linked to the idea of the good must be fashioned on the notion of face-to-face encounter and the attendant responsibility that follows, and most certainly not on the triumph of the will, founded on an ontology of power. In order to establish community, it is necessary to demonstrate "interpersonal relations whose members turn their gaze towards humanity as a whole" (Ibid., 218). In fact, according to Levinas, "[T]he distinction between community and society belongs to an immature stage of social thought. The adoption of the Law which is the foundation of this society, brings with it for those men who adopt it in the proper manner, the possibility of remaining intact face-to-face with each other" (Ibid.).

Clearly this Talmudic text is about covenant and community. The decisive issue involves the tension between personal and communal responsibility. In the language of Levinas, found already announced in a slightly different manner by the Talmud, it deals with the issue of "personal responsibility and responsibility for others" (LR 1989, 225). This is not simply an assertion but the result of a rigorous argument. The conclusion again is that "one is not only responsible for everyone else, but responsible for the responsibility of everyone else" (Ibid.). The genealogy of the argument begins with the delineation of the four dimensions of every law: "to learn (*lilmod*), to teach it (*lelammed*), to observe it (*lishmor*), to perform it (*la'asot*)" (Ibid., 218). Simply put, there are four obligations associated with each commandment.

The law here is understood as the manner in which the covenant is expressed. Therefore, there are four specific covenants within each mitzvah. According to the view that the covenant is in fact enacted three times—once at Sinai, once at Mount Gerizim, and once in the plains of Moab, or alternatively in the Tent of Meeting—then there are forty-eight covenants within the Pact. The mathematics of justice, if we may call it this, which is set out here, are arrived at in the following way: the four levels of each mitzvah are squared, one binding upon me and one binding upon my acting as a guarantor for the other person. Since there are three enactments of the covenant and given the agreement that the Torah was taught three times, we multiply three by sixteen and arrive at forty-eight. Given that the number of Israelites at Sinai is 603,550 multiplied by the 613 mitzvot, we arrive at a very large number. The matter does not end here, however, as the total must be multiplied once again by 603,550. This is the case because each person acts as the guarantor of every other individual person.

While this number is not infinite, it is staggering yet conceptually accessible. The four levels of a mitzvah explain how this mathematical progression takes place. Theoretical activity or study of the law implies its transmission. The transmission of the Torah implies that the student will in turn be able to speak. This speaking involves observance and the keeping of the law as studied, understood, transmitted, and clarified. Each person then is in the position of teacher and student ad infinitum. What is achieved then is a society based on and absorbed in study, able to act in a just way through the transmission of speaking and listening. Each person becomes the guarantor of every other person, both personally, and as a full member of society.

Levinas is not advocating any kind of political or religious imperialism. He is very much aware not only of the philosophical but of the specifically ethical problems of trying to bring a Jewish teaching to bear upon our commonly held human condition. Regarding the obligations from a religious point of view, he understands very clearly the Talmudic position that charges the people of Israel with 613 commandments, even if according to the Chofetz Chaim (Rabbi Yisrael Meir haKohen), only about three hundred are presently able to be observed (*The Concise Book of Mitzvot*, Feldheim Publishers).

Levinas clarifies the rabbinic teaching that only seven commandments suffice for the children of Noah. Let us keep in mind that these seven commandments are binding upon Israel as well. They include the prohibition of idolatry, interpreted less stringently upon the nations than upon Israel, murder, or the shedding of innocent blood, and gross acts of sexual immorality. Emphatically, the establishing of courts of justice are obligatory upon every nation and society.

Regarding this distinction between the minimalist foundation for ethical life and the burdensome freedom demanded of the children of Israel, Levinas argues, "I owe the Other more than is asked! A cursory glance blinded by the too-bright sun of the West sees in this only separation and pride. This is fatal. For it would be our right to ask if this apparent limiting of universalism is not what preserves it from totalitarianism, if it does not awaken our attention to the murmur of inner voices, if it does not turn eyes towards those faces that illuminate and allow the control of social anonymity, towards the defeated and the reasonable history of humanity" (LR 1989, 287). It is in this way that the mathematics of justice is to be affirmed, taught, studied, and applied. Or as Levinas puts it, "[T]he arithmetic is undeniable!" (Ibid., 218).

TIME AND COVENANT

Nitzavim: Standing
(Deuteronomy 29:18–30:20)

You are standing today, all of you, before HASHEM, your God; the heads
of your tribes, your elders, and your officers—all the men of Israel; your
small children, your women, and your proselyte who is in the midst of
your camp, from the hewer of your wood to the drawer of your water.

—Deuteronomy 29:9–10

The commentary tradition understands the renewal of the covenant in the
Torah portion Nitzavim as focusing on the responsibility of one for another.
This theme, already very familiar to us, is here expanded and elevated. It is made
clear that this responsibility is binding on each person of whatever social and
economic rank, "from the hewer of your wood to the drawer of water." What
begins with an address to "the heads of the tribes, your elders and your officers,"
includes everyone else, "your small children, your women, and your proselyte."
The entire family of Israel is to be included. This does not include only those
who are present, however, but also those who have already been and those of
future generations. This responsibility is not merely general but applies to the
way in which each person is expected to act as a guarantor for every other
person. Primary attention is to be paid to public conduct with respect to the
mitzvot, including prohibited and required conduct. This kind of responsibility is also somewhat asymmetrical from a social point of view. Children for
example, do not have the same kind of responsibility as adults (*Or HaChaim*
1999, vol. 5, 1969).

How do we explain how we are responsible for the future of people who
do not yet exist? And how can we be responsible to and for our predecessors,
to whom we are bound but who are no longer present? For Levinas, the key lies

in the effort to clarify what is meant by the time of others. Levinas challenges the traditional conceptualization of human time. He does so by first diagnosing the key concept of the passing of time as it is usually presented, disappearing into nothingness.

As we have explored, the very cornerstone of ethical life consists in the fact that the absent past and the absent future appear in the present, perhaps in different ways. The past of others appears by exerting a claim upon me. This claim comes from what Levinas calls "time immemorial." Time immemorial refers to anachronic time, where the incompleteness of the past makes it possible for it to endure in the present. It is never completely "over and done with." The breezy idiom of "moving on" is limited in advance by a covenantal sense of time in which the past time of others is taken up within my own. This is not simply a matter of memory, for as we learn from phenomenology, memory must be memory of something—that is, "the memorable." Anachronic time, the incompleteness of time past, as well as its possible reversibility in the moral realm, establishes a condition for the continuity of justice. As such, it can be tempered or altered by pardon, forgiveness, and reconciliation. Such movement permits time to pass into the future as a "diachrony refractory to all synchronization, a transcending diachrony" (OBBE 1991, 9).

The question that exceeds the bounds of our commentary while at the same time presupposing it is this: "[H]ow is time temporalized such that the diachrony of transcendence, of the other than Being, is signaled?" (Ibid., 10). Levinas makes this more concrete by linking this phenomenon to gratitude and prayer, although he does so in a very condensed form. Why is it necessary that the past be described as recoverable and bound to the present? "Men have been able to be thankful for the very fact of finding themselves able to thank; the present gratitude is grafted onto itself as onto an already antecedent gratitude. In a prayer in which the worshipper asks that his prayer be heard, the prayer as it were precedes or follows itself" (Ibid.). Levinas argues that we cannot see time simply as a simple succession of present moments. If we were to do that, then not only gratitude and prayer, but friendship, love, community, and filiality would not be understandable or meaningful.

We can see the counterargument, advanced by R. Yitzchak Arama. He states, "It is logical that a person cannot impose on untold numbers of future generations obligations that he himself had only assumed by a voluntary vow. Such a vow could obligate those descendants who agree to continue to honor it. Although, biologically speaking the son is of the flesh and blood of the father, such bonds tend to grow weaker from generation to generation" (*Akeydat*

Yitzchak, vol. 2, 894). While the claim made by Yitzchak Arama undoubtedly has empirical support, nonetheless it cannot explain why any vow should be taken seriously, voluntary or otherwise.

Yitzchak Arama suggests that time is, in fact, a succession of present moments. There is, therefore, no conceptual difference between past, present, and future, except so far as we speak of different faculties of the soul: memory, perception, and anticipation. The capacity to think of a time not yet, or of a time that will still be, is an integral part of binding word to deed and therefore making the phenomenon of a promise intelligible. This is also very much relevant to the statement in Nitzavim that affirms, regarding the covenant: "Not only with you alone, but both with those who are present here today as well as with those who are not here today" (Deut. 29:13).

In other words, this covenant has also been made with future generations. This implies two interrelated perspectives of Levinas. The first is that responsibility is not a limitation upon human freedom, but rather enables us to understand freedom altogether. Just as my generation is obligated to bequeath a habitable environment to the next, so, too, my spontaneity is limited in advance by the faces and claims of others. In this sense, I am also obligated to see that my children and their children are taught the Torah so that they might keep the words of its covenant (*Or HaChaim* 1999, vol. 5, 1971).

There is, however, a distinction between the proximate future, the one that I can stand in direct relation to, and the distant future that I cannot foresee. Even with respect to this distant future, I am not relieved of my obligation. This is why the following Torah portion *Vayeilech* announces two distinct but related mitzvot. These include the assembling of all the people together in the first year after the sabbatical year, and the commandment that each person write for him-or herself a scroll of the Torah. Even within the discontinuity necessary for new generations to emerge, there is a continuity achieved in coming together and for every person to be thoroughly versed in the words and obligations of the Torah.

"For this commandment that I command you today—it is not hidden from you, and it is not distant.... Rather the matter is very near to you—in your mouth and in your heart—to perform it" (Deut. 30:11–14). There is a certain democracy promised in the realm of action, even if there are differences in the level of understanding. The words spoken, their multiple meanings, may register differently with different people at different times. Nevertheless, as the text says, the key thing is "to perform it." There is no difference here between Moses and the water carrier. Each is obligated to perform the mitzvot. As Levinas says, the laws of the Torah stand in effect "as a fence of sanity around the madness of the contact with the Sacred that is unmediated by reason" (DF 1990, 144).

GOING FORWARD

Vayeilech: Went
(Deuteronomy 31:1–30)

Moses went and spoke these words to all of Israel. He said to them, I am a hundred and twenty years old today; I can no longer go out and come in.

—Deuteronomy 31-1

The question asked by most of the commentators is, where did Moses go when, as it says, "Moses went"? There is general agreement that he went to speak with the individual tribes of Israel to offer them words of encouragement and comfort. The encouragement was necessary for the encouragement implied that the Israelites could go forward, even without his presence. Even on his last day, Moses went out of himself to see the people in their own encampments; he did not ask them to come to him. This act of generosity is also accompanied by a sense of radical humility. Just as his whole life had been dedicated to the people, Israel, so too would this be true to the very last day of his life. He put the concerns, anxieties, hopes, and fears of all, and each of the Israelites before his own. The encouragement was meant for them to recognize that they could and must assume the responsibility for one another by carrying out the covenant, even in his absence. In this way, he further assured the transition to Joshua.

At the same time, Moses announced the mitzvah of *Hahkel*, which occurs as a gathering after the sabbatical year. This assembly was to include all of the men, women, and children as well as "the strangers who are within your gates" (Deut. 31:10–13). At a later time, the king in Israel would read out certain portions of the Book of Deuteronomy, in the presence of all the people of Israel. The emphasis upon each person of whatever rank, age, or background suggests that, in the language of Levinas, "a totality was brought together but not as a static or closed assembly or system." The timing of the reading on *Hahkel* was during the festival of Sukkot. The trace of the journey out of Egypt, where the people dwell in huts or "clouds of glory" for the better part of forty years, signifies the tension between the impermanence of human life and the permanence of what made the lives of all meaningful—that is, the devoted attachment to a certain way of life that remains promising despite the fact that life comes to an end. This is also to be accompanied by joy.

How can there be a sense of rejoicing when human existence is transient? As Ibn Ezra says, it was at this time that Moses gave each of the twelve tribes the blessing that appears only in the last portion of the Torah. More explicitly, "*S'forno* holds that after the covenant had been made, Moshe wanted the people to accept the covenant joyously, and not in mourning for his death. He therefore went to the tents of Israel, so as to inspire the people and to comfort them" (Nachshoni, vol. 5, 1387).

According to another view, immediately after the sabbatical year all class distinctions between rich and poor were suspended. Therefore, according to the *Kli Yakar*, "[T]here can be a true *Hahkel* (assembly), and unity among the people" (Ibid., 1390). Still, the mission of Israel, its purpose and promise, remains to be completely internalized.

The most striking and severe of all of the various conditions that can befall Israel is also announced at this time. "If the people forsake me, and annul my covenant, I will surely have concealed My face on that day" (Deut. 31:18). Why is this considered such an abysmal thought? The notion of the concealing or turning away of the divine countenance directly implies that the life of Israel will then continue according to the laws of nature, including human nature, alone. The medievals referred to this phenomenon as *Deus Absconditus*, or in Hebrew, *Hester Panim*. This is understood as a privative form of absence. The turning away of the face signifies the expression of indifference. Existentially, it means a return to the time of the state of nature, which is that of all against all. Yet, even in the absence of the divine face, we are not to understand ourselves as lost and directionless forever. The way back is understood to be through the adherence to the precepts of the Torah. This is what is meant by the sobering words of the Midrash Eicha: "You should love Me but better that you should love My Torah even more" (Sugarman 1979, 216n1).

Is this not why the last of the 613 mitzvot is that each person is required to write or participate in the writing of a Torah scroll? The teaching or way back to the path of the infinite or divine realism is not withdrawn. Therefore, the concept of return or *Teshuva* remains open. This represents a higher level of the phenomenon of absence. Even in our darkest hours, when we appear abandoned to our fate and the Teacher appears absent, we have before us a way of conducting ourselves that remains preeminently human. This is what Levinas refers to in his celebrated essay "To Love the Torah More than G'd." The apparent absence of G'd increases rather than diminishes my sense of responsibility for what I have already learned.

In his last lecture given at the Sorbonne, Levinas refers to this kind of absence as "transcendence to the point of absence." Levinas puts it this way in speaking of what he calls "illeity": "This way that the infinite has of referring, in the midst of its own desirability, to the nondesirable nearness, is denoted by the term illeity." In other words, I am called upon to remain faithful to a teaching that includes my standing guard for the other person even in the absence of a G'd who would superintend all of the outcomes of time and history. It is in this way, as the Talmud says, that "I must act as though the world depended on me alone" (GDT 2000, 224). This makes it possible, as Levinas says, for G'd to be different from every neighbor, or in other words, from everyone who is near. For in this way, G'd remains transcendently other to all concrete others, and therefore, to history as well.

Absence is experienced more frequently and more directly than transcendence. A transposition of Levinas's formula may be required. In this case, the phenomenon that would emerge would be transcendence to the point of absence. We would then recognize more clearly the difference between the momentary inversion of justice and what would appear to be the abandonment of just institutions. The hope would be for the return of just institutions and justice.

THE SONG OF THE TORAH

Haazinu: Listen
(Deuteronomy 31:1–52)

So now write the song for yourselves.

—Deuteronomy 31:19

The sages interpret the song as referring to the scroll of the Torah. The king of Israel, as Rav Soloveitchik, following Maimonides notes, is required to write two *sifre Torot* (DDY, 464). He writes one for himself as a common person, and he writes another, which never departs from him, in his role as leader and king. If the common person, or even the king cannot write his or her own sefer Torah, then it may be done by a surrogate. Nonetheless, what is most important here is the constancy of the Torah and the fidelity that it commands.

From a Levinasian perspective, it makes sense that the king should have his own copy of the Torah always with him. For, above all, the Torah commands responsible conduct, informed, interpreted, and applied by the tradition. The king, then, has added responsibility, not only for his personal conduct, or for the laws that are specifically directed at limiting his power, but also for the well-being of the whole of the nation. The Torah, then, comes to testify, not to kingly privilege, but to the added burden of responsibility. In its name, the king will not only be guided, but reproved. In this respect, the kings of Israel could never legitimately become absolute monarchs, since they in turn were always subservient to the law.

The modern division of powers has its antecedents in the specific roles of "checks and balances" that apply to the king, to the Kohen, to the prophet, and to the people. The case of the king who is chastened by the prophet is perhaps best exemplified by King David, who was told by the Prophet Nathan that he must atone and repent for his moral transgression with Batsheva (2 Sam. 12:7).

There is the counter example with Ahab, king over the Northern Kingdom of Israel, who refuses the reproof of Elijah the prophet for the seizing of Naboth's vineyard (1 Kings 21:2).

It is King David who is most visibly associated with music and song, thus carrying this responsibility out further. He used the lyre to soothe his predecessor, King Saul (1 Sam. 16:14). When he became king, according to the *aggadic* legend, a lyre was suspended above his bed, so that he would wake halfway through the night to learn Torah. The psalms composed by David are also referred to as songs (*tehilim*). To paraphrase Marcus Aurelius, Nothing human is alien to David's Book of Psalms.

In the house of study, ancient and modern, the Talmud is often learned out loud in what is referred to with slight derision as "sing-song." Looked at another way, it is not meant to be mesmerizing as is the case with a single mantra, but rather, as an expansive way of saying again, or reciting what has been said before. Such lyricism does not replace the content of what the Talmudic page announces. Rather, it reinvests the said with the possibility of a meaning that spills beyond the words in the saying.

In a similar way, the margins of the Torah scroll become part of the scroll itself. While the breakup of the Pentateuch into chapters and verses is a much later addition, drawn from printing conventions, the spaces between the *sedras*, the fifty-four Torah portions, denominated by the *Mesorah*, remain an integral part of the Torah itself. So, too, are the spaces that separate the words. While we are accustomed to think of these phenomena as peripheral, this is clearly not the case.

The margins of a Torah scroll, the spaces between words, reflect an absence, but not necessarily an absence that is easily filled in. If there were no absences or pauses or silences, we would have only one long sentence, spoken or written from the beginning of time. Perhaps this is hinted at by the mystical view that *Haazinu* contains the whole of the Torah and of Jewish history in condensed form (Ramban, Stone 1101n7). Still, for those of us with lesser imaginations, there is still much to be learned from what is left blank or remains unsaid.

Does not this absence also signify a kind of openness? And does not this openness, in turn, invite every new reader to become an interpreter, as Levinas indicates? He puts it this way:

> The multiplicity of people, each one of them indispensable, is necessary
> to produce all the dimensions of meaning: The multiplicity of meanings
> is due to the multiplicity of people. We can now appreciate in its full

weight, the reference made by the Revelation to exegesis, to the freedom
attaching to this exegesis and to the participation of the person listening
to the word, which makes itself heard now, but can also pass down the
ages to announce the same truth in different times. (LR 1989, 195)

All Talmudic learning, like all explanation, effects a movement of same to
other. This brings with it a kind of transcendence that belongs to the expression
of the meanings of words without devaluing the very words spoken or interpreted. Because the best kind of learning occurs with other people, it is always
accompanied by an ethics of transcendence.

The study, interpretation, and transmission of the Torah anticipate and
go beyond all contemporary notions of deconstructionism. The oral tradition
is already announced within the spaces and margins of the written Torah,
including the way in which the Torah scroll is to be written down. And is this
not why even in the eclipse of the divine face, we proceed, in a phrase that
Levinas likes to cite—"the four cubits of halakah?" (Berachos 8a).

THE BLESSING

Vazos Haberachah: Blessing
(Deuteronomy 33:1–34:12)

In the last portion of the Pentateuch, Moses gives his blessings to each of the tribes of Israel, ascends to Mount Nebo, and passes away in full vigor: "His eye had not dimmed and his vigor had not diminished." (Deut. 34: 7). He is succeeded by Joshua in accordance with the preparation for entry into the land of Promise. Is not the image of Moses ascending to a mountain to glimpse the land of Promise that he cannot enter, a depiction of the human situation as such? The midrash tells us that G'd listened to the pleading of Moses and offered him a proposition he could not accept. Moses could go into the land without the Israelites. Conversely, and decisively, the Israelites could enter the land that Moses would only glimpse.

Moses cannot enter the land of Promise and, in this way, Moses continues. Place, however important, is taken up by the realm of time, for "time bears a promise." Moses assumes what might be called a "generational responsibility" for Israel. While he is instructed to appoint Joshua as his successor, he does so unstintingly and without resentment. In this sense, he recognizes that all of time does not begin and end with him. In this way, the greatness of Moses is confirmed in his humility. His own divinely appointed tasks will be completed by and for others. Time then is more precious than eternity. It conserves not only the beginning but also the end, and provides for perpetually new beginnings, which have significance for me as well.

If we examine the last word of each of the first four books of the Torah, we see an allusion to a pattern that is revealing. The Book of Genesis ends with the word for Egypt in Hebrew, *Mitzraim*. *Mitzraim* is from the root word *tzar*, which means "limitation." The last word of the Book of the Exodus is "journeys," or *ma saihem*. We might then say that the limitations experienced in Egypt, are exceeded by the journeys of the Israelites to Mount Sinai, the last word of the book of Leviticus (*HarSinai*). To recapitulate, the journeys are for the sake of receiving the Torah at Sinai. The last word of the Book of Numbers is "Jericho," deriving from the root word of *yareach*, to smell. There is a strong view, expressed in the Talmud and the Zohar, that the messianic era will first be detected by the sense of smell (Berachos 57b). The last word of Torah found in Deuteronomy is "Israel," *Yisrael*. The Book of Deuteronomy reiterates some of the most salient themes that have come before, as well as prepares for entrance into the land of promise. Since the last letter of the Torah is a *lamed*, the last letter in the word "Israel," and the first letter of Genesis is *beis*, meaning *bereshesis* (beginning), then perhaps all of this can be read as a reminder of what has been taught and what remains to be studied and enacted. Together, if *lamed* is put before the *beis*, this spells the word *lev*, for "heart." That which is learned must be internalized. That which is studied must begin anew. Hence, the Torah remains the constant companion of the people, Israel.

Epilogue

The phenomenological approach to the Torah has helped to initiate conversation on the Bible and Levinas. It is hoped that some of his major contributions are now somewhat clearer by showing the relation between the Bible and his religious philosophy. At the same time, some portions of our book should make it easier for students interested in Levinas to be strengthened in their understanding of the Torah. To use the words of the title of a book of Maurice Blanchot, Levinas's close intellectual companion, *An Infinite Conversation* has been opened.

This book is most definitely not the last word on the subject. Every section of the Bible can be revisited in terms of his approach and categories. Here there is much work that remains to be done. In this way, the original aim of Levinas will be served, which require finding an alternative to reading the text dogmatically or merely psychologically. We have also tried to place the reflections of Levinas in conversation with some of the great thinkers and commentators on the Jewish Bible, past and present. Here, much more work remains to be done.

An entire book remains to be written on Levinas's expansion of the commentary of Rashi. Both approaches are radically descriptive, but those of Levinas, while not embedded entirely in the view of the tradition, have a philosophic originality that makes sense to modern ears. The reflections on Levinas and Soloveitchik in *The Fence and the Neighbor: Emmanuel Levinas, Yeshayahu Leibowitz, and Israel among the Nations* is perceptive, yet partial. Both thinkers begin with our existential situation to which they repeatedly refer. The phenomenological approach of Levinas does not concern itself with the kind of theological positions raised by the Rav. Surely, such similarities and differences can be elucidated in detail. This would perhaps give a new vibrancy to the movement widely and elastically known as "modern orthodoxy."

Since our own employment of Levinas's reflections on Talmud are partial and fragmentary at best, these discourses can be elaborated in such a way that the contents of both the Talmud and the biblical material are more clearly delineated. Another project whose opening can be glimpsed here is the comparison of the writings of R' Samson Raphael Hirsch to those of Levinas. Both thinkers highlight the ethical dimensions of the Torah. Hirsch does a superior job of showing how Jewish Law expresses this morality. But Levinas's metaphysical positions, phenomenologically grounded, are in my view much more adequate than those of Hirsch, without the neo-Kantian or Hegelian baggage.

Levinas is mostly taken at his word that his thinking arises from a Lithuanian tradition, a specifically non-Hasidic rationalist position (misnagid). Levinas appears to differentiate himself emphatically from Martin Buber, the first modern European popularizer of the Hasidic movement, thought, and literature. It should be kept in mind, however, that unlike Buber's philosophy, Hasidic thought from its inception is certainly within the framework of the Jewish legal tradition. Levinas's refusal to distinguish the philosophy of Buber from the thought and practices of the Hasidic movement is, in my view, a serious omission. The Hasidic notion that one person can engage in a kind of radical empathy for another (mislavish in yiddish) is a theme of many Hasidic teachings. For example, there is a sense of communal responsibility advocated by the founder of Hasidism, Israel ben Eliezer (the Ba'al Shem Tov), with various emphases until the present. Levinas expands the notion of responsibility, from all Israel is responsible for one another to all people are responsible for one another. Among Hassidim perhaps, only the most recent Lubavitcher Rebbe took a similar position. In any event, this area deserves further research.

One of the most dynamic and controversial figures in the contemporary Jewish scene is the French thinker Bernard Henri-Levy. Because Levy is such a public figure and, at times, quite flashy, does not mean that we should take his thought and life without serious regard. Levy considers himself to be deeply indebted to the philosophy of Levinas. His political and moral activism is accompanied by significant personal risk. See, for example, his book *Who Killed Daniel Pearl?* where he follows the footstep of the *Wall Street* journalist through Pakistan and discloses how close Daniel Pearl was to unravelling the nuclear secret advanced by the Pakistani scientist, A.Q. Khan. Recently, Levy published a book that merits more attention than it has received, *The Genius of Judaism* (Random House, 2016). In this work, Levy might have accomplished more if he had explicated Levinas's own version of chosenness, rather than by diluting it in Levy's own expansive interpretation. For Levinas, the idea of the Jews as chosen, means simply responsibility for others, even to the extent of taking responsibility for the responsibility of others.

What Levinas has already accomplished is a concrete, phenomenological reading of the text that is not a matter of theology or apologetics. We may not be much further along in understanding the mysteries of death, human love relations that have fallen short, or generating a new way of viewing the crises that confront humanity at the present. Nonetheless, the nature of the conversation has been elevated by careful attention to the thought of Levinas, which better prepares us to wrestle with the existential problems that we confront.

Levinas has shown how the Hebraic tradition has much to say, not only to the first of the Abrahamic traditions, but to all of humanity. By beginning with the other rather than the self, he shows us how the meaning of existence can endure beyond our own lives; how human beings can respond to a message of brotherhood for one another. He also shows that the humanity of human beings is inscribed with a resilience that permits us to find a way that technology can aid us while still maintaining that each person is irreplaceable. We would do well to remember that his magnum opus was called *Totality 'and' Infinity*. Totality is not left behind; otherwise, it would be impossible to explain the human role in relation to the rest of creation. Still for the humanity of the human to reach its full expression, infinity must first be glimpsed in the sphere of the interpersonal.

As Derrida has reminded us, it will take generations of readings until we begin to grasp the full reach of the Oeuvre of Levinas (*Adieu to Emmanuel Levinas*). In working through the elements of his phenomenological philosophy, it is especially vital to keep this in mind. Let us remember, in closing, that Edmund Husserl, the founder of phenomenology, understood that this could make important advances through collaborative work, while always returning to its beginnings anew.

Appendix One

Aggadah: Portions of the Talmud and the Torah dealing with the nonlegal sections of the text. The emphasis is upon the moral and ethical teachings.

D'rosh: Refers to the moral or what is sometimes called the "homiletical" dimension of the text. In other words, what lessons can be learned from the text. The emphasis is usually on the ethical dimension of the text.

Gemara: The gemara is the commentary on the mishhah, written down between the second and fifth centuries by the *Amoraim*—that is, "the masters of the gemara living in Babylonia or in Israel between the first and fifth centuries CE" (*The Burnt Book,* 309). "The Babylonian Talmud was completed on 37 of the 63 tracts of the Mishnah. Its main purpose was to clarify the Mishnah, establish which opinions are binding, provide derivations of the laws … and provide … stories to enhance the discussions.… All subsequent codifications of Torah laws are binding only in so far as they are based on the (Babylonian tradition) also referred to as Talmud Bavli" (Kaplan *The Handbook of Jewish Thought,* 191).

Halakah: The legal portions of the text of the Talmud and the Torah. The halakah is more restrictive and therefore less open to interpretation than the *aggadah*. Such laws involve the practical application of the biblical commandments, or *mitzvot.*

Jewish Bible: As used in the book, *Levinas and the Torah,* refers to the Pentateuch. What I am calling the Jewish Bible, or what is more often referred to as the Hebrew Scriptures refers here to the Pentateuch as understood by the oral tradition, or rabbinic commentary tradition, subsequently written down in the Mishnah, Talmud, and Midrash.

Mesorah: Commonly and idiomatically used to refer to the rabbinic transmission of the biblical-Talmudic tradition. It can also be used interchangeably with the word "tradition." Technically, it refers to notes that were written down by scribes from the seventh to the tenth centuries.

Midrash: A dimension of the biblical text that focuses on the moral or philosophic meaning. As such, it is one of the four major levels of reading the biblical text and/or the Talmud. It may be further subdivided into midrash aggadah, which deals with the nonlegal or "narrative" portion of the text, and midrash halakah, which elucidates the legal aspects of Scripture and/or Talmud.

Midrash Tanchuma: "Genre of Rabbinical literature, selections from *Halachic* and/or *Aggadic* teachings of the *Tannaim* and *Amoraim* arranged according to the verses of the Torah (Stone 1300)....An aggadic midrash on the Pentateuch" (Stone, 1302).

Midrash Rabbah: (MR) First printed in 1512 in Constantinople. Subsequently, emendations were interpolated in the Cracow 1587 edition, upon which all further editions of the text were based.

Mishnah: The codification of Jewish law written down and redacted at the end of the second century CE. The Mishnah contains six volumes dealing with every legal facet of Jewish life.

Mitzvot: Refers to the 613 commandments that according to the Talmud are found in the first five books of the Hebraic Bible. Of these, 248 are affirmative—do this do that—365 are prohibited—don't do this don't do that. According to the *Chafetz Chaim* in *The Concise Book of the Mitvot,* there are seventy-seven positive mitzvot and 194 prohibitive mitvot that presently pertain to the realm of action in the contemporary world. In addition, there are twenty-six mitzvot that are contingent upon the land of Israel. An alternative view is that 369 apply today, of these 126 affirmative and 243 are prohibitive (Kaplan *The Handbook of Jewish Thought,* vol. 1, 360).

PaRDes: From the Hebrew for "orchard," an acronym that pertains to the four levels of the reading of the Torah. The four levels are usually understood to be the plain meaning of the text—that is, its surface or apparent meaning—not its so-called literal meaning, which is thought, by the rabbinic common tradition, to be impossible; in other words, there is no literal meaning. The plain meaning of the text in Hebrew is referred to as the *P'shat.* These four levels often interpenetrate one another.

P'shat: Refers to the plain meaning of the text. The major commentator dealing with the plain meaning of the text, its language, and the reference is Rashi. *Remez* pertains to the allusive or allegorical meaning of the text.

Remez: Refers to the elusive or allegorical portion of the text. The *remez* helps give the reader insight into intimations of events, figures and passages in the text.

Drosh: Refers to moral and philosophic meaning of the text.

Sod: Refers to the "mysterium" of the text. The mystery is discussed and often found in the Zohar, the main work of the Kabbalah.

Tanakh: Refers to the Hebrew Bible in its entirety, including the Pentateuch, the prophets, and the writings.

Torah: In its most restricted sense, the term "Torah" (derived from the Hebrew *Ho'orah*—meaning teaching or way) refers to the Pentateuch, or first five books of the Hebrew bible.

Appendix Two

A-Dieu: "Bad Conscience and the Inexorable." Literally "to-God." As used by Levinas, it may mean "God Bless" as well as the more common unhyphenated "adieu" in the sense of leave-taking.

Conatus Essendi: *Otherwise than Being*. Term borrowed from Spinoza, indicating the way that the self arises and maintains itself in order to preserve itself. The term, for Levinas, represents the Hobbesian view of each struggling against each for its life and identity. This term encapsulates a train of thinking that reappears in various guises in Hegel, Nietzsche, and Heidegger. Levinas contrasts the *Conatus Essendi* with each for-the-other expressed as responsibility and "substitution." See below.

Desire: *Totality and Infinity*. Contrasted with need. While need fills a lack within totality, desire is bestirred by its relation to the Infinite, and is, therefore, inherently metaphysical.

Diachrony: *Time and the Other*, *Otherwise than Being*. The phenomenon of "lived-time" (temporality) arising in relation to the other. Time and alterity are described in relation to each other. For Levinas, the diachronic character of temporality is irreducible.

Egology: *Time and the Other*. Egology refers everything subject back to itself. This is an encrypted term employed by Levinas for philosophy and its inability to escape existential autobiography. This is close to what Levinas diagnoses as the collective colloquy of the soul with itself, beginning in Plato and continuing to dominate Western philosophy to the present.

The Face: (*le visage*) "Is Ontology Fundamental?" *Totality and Infinity*. The countenance that serves as the origin of expression. For Levinas, the face of the other is the inviolable limit imposing restraint on my spontaneity in advance of its being exercised. The mobility of the countenance of the other calls forth continuing response from the "I." The face reveals itself through expression, as much through absence as through presence, and its visibility is glimpsed in turning toward someone rather than in the state of being gazed at. Prior to thermatizing, it is a necessary condition for making expression meaningful.

Here I Am: (me voici) *Otherwise than Being.* Corresponds to the Hebrew, *Heneini* (i.e., "Here I am to answer, Here I am ready to respond"). This is phenomenology, assuming not a simple spatial location (as in the natural attitude), but a sense of readiness to respond to what is demanded of me. (See Genesis 22.)

Illeity: *Otherwise than Being.* A Latinism, coined by Levinas, to refer to the radical alterity of the absolutely other, which is "transcendent to the point of absence."

Il y a: *Existence and Existents.* Literally "there is"—impersonal being, raw existence. The il y a unfolds as separate instants temporally, without orientation, direction, or purpose. Biblically, it corresponds to *tohu v'vohu,* the chaos and void prior to creation.

Ipseity: *Totality and Infinity.* Levinas describes this as "a passive folding back on onself." This term denotes the self-sameness of personal identity.

Maieutics: *Totality and Infinity.* An encoded term used by Levinas for Plato's model of knowledge as recollection (anamnesis). Refers specifically to midwivery employed by the philosopher as teacher to deliver the interlocutor, as student, of the ideas with which he or she is already pregnant. Levinas positions maieutics within egology.

Obsession: *Otherwise than Being.* Obsession indicates a complete passivity, rendering the subject into the mode of the accusative. Obsession renders the subject responsible, beyond its own intentions, even for what it does not will. In the concrete sense, this means, for Levinas, a responsibility for what others do, even against me in the persecution I am forced to undergo. In its recurring character, obsession breaks open the limits of identity and opens the subject to responsibility for the other.

Ontology: "Is Ontology Fundamental?" A study of Being. In Heidegger, ontology means that which is common to all beings, or Being in general. Levinas associates ontology with an absence of transcendence. For Levinas, "[O]ntology" is a coded term that begins with Parmenides and culminates in Heidegger. Fundamental ontology ends, for Levinas, in a totality.

Otherwise than Greek: *Otherwise than Being* (i.e., the Hebraic tradition containing prephilosophical experiences and subjects that Levinas elevates to the level of the philosophical).

Proximity: *Otherwise than Being.* Levinas describes proximity as "extending the subject in its very subjectivity, which is both a relationship and a term of that relationship" (86). Proximity, beyond simple location, makes the approach to the neighbor or third person possible by orienting subjectivity toward the other.

Responsibility: *Otherwise than Being*. A meta-ethical category endowed with a significance, centrality, and irreducibility not previously known in the history of philosophy. For Levinas, it is the very orientation of consciousness towards the other, for the other. In this way responsibility is prior to consciousness, which it founds. Levinas affirms, "It is this responsibility for the creature that constitutes 'the self.'"

Said: (*le dit*). *Otherwise than Being*. In its simplest sense, the said involves the contents of language. This includes propositions, statements, and the syntax of ordered discourse. The said belongs to the realm of totality and ontology. Grammatically, it appears in the declarative mode.

Saying: (*le dire*) The saying involves what is intended or expressed prior to the said. It aims to and beyond the other to the third person. It belongs to the domain of ethics and infinity. Grammatically, it may appear in the imperative or interrogative, evocative modes.

Substitution: "*Otherwise than Being: Beyond Essence*." In substitution, the "I" becomes non-interchangeable in relation to the other. In this way, the "I" can substitute for the other. The phenomenon of substitution thus inverts the ontological "essence" of being. By this Levinas means that inverts the *conatus essendi*.

Trace: "Meaning and Sense." Levinas characterizes the trace in the following way: "[T]he trace is the insertion of space in time." The trace is analogous to the "fingerprints," which make it possible to identify the event after it has passed. Levinas indicates that it is not a sign like any other, although it can be taken for one. It helps to form an absolute past that unites all times. In this sense, it is what makes memory possible.

Biblical Translations and Commentaries

HEBREW BIBLE

Berlin, Adele, and Marc Zvi Brettler. 2004. *The Jewish Study Bible: Featuring the Jewish Publication Society Tanakh Translation*. New York: Oxford University Press.

Cohen, A., ed. 1983. *The Soncino Chumash*. London: Soncino Press.

Davis, Menachem, ed. 2010. *The Interlinear Chumash* (Pentateuch). Schottenstein Edition. Brooklyn: Mesorah Publications.

Kaplan, Aryeh (MeAm Lo'ez), ed. and trans. 1981. *The Living Torah*. Brooklyn: Moznaim Publishing.

———. ed. 1990. *The Torah Anthology*. Vols. 1–5. Brooklyn: Moznaim Publishing.

———. 1992. *Handbook of Jewish Thought*. Vols. 1 and 2. Brooklyn, Moznaim Publishing.

Scherman, Rabbi Nosson, ed. 1993. *The Chumash*. Stone Ed. Brooklyn: Mesorah Publications.

GLOSSARY OF COMMENTATORS CITED OR CONSULTED

1. **Midrash Rabbah (MR)**: Hebrew English edition. Mesorah Publications, Brooklyn, November, 2014.

2. **Metsudah Midrash Tanchuma (MT)**: 8 vols., edited by Avraham Davis, Brooklyn: Eastern Book Press, 2007. A magnificent edition of one of the oldest midrashim. It is a beautifully presented, exquisitely edited text.

3. **Rashi (R)**: Acronym for R. Shlomo Yitzchaki, 1040–1105. Standard commentator on the Pentateuch against which subsequent commentaries are measured. Rashi is known for commenting on the plain meaning of the text (*P'shat*).

4. **Metsudah Rashi (MR)**: 5 vols., translated by Avraham Davis, Metsudah Publications, 2002. The advantage of this version is that that it has a line-by-line, phrase-by-phrase translation.

5. **Akeydat Yitzchak (AY)**: A philosophical commentary on the Pentateuch by R. Yitzchak Arama, 1420–1494. This commentary is known for its

hyper-rationality and its frequent citations of Aristotle. *Akeydat Yitzchak: Commentary of Rabbi Yitzchak Arama on the Torah*, vols. 1–2, second ed., translated and condensed by Eliyahu Munk, Lambda Publishers, Inc, Jerusalem, Israel, 1990.

6. **Alshich (A)**: R. Moshe Alshich. A two-volume commentary on the *Tanach* by R. Moshe Alshich of sixteenth-century *Safed*. Commentary is known for its parables and its illustrative power. Translated by Eliyahu Munk. Brooklyn: Urim Publications, 2000.

7. **Hirsch**: R. Samson Raphael Hirsch, 1808–1888. Author of a six-volume commentary on the Pentateuch. This work is of extraordinary philosophic and hermeneutical value to contemporary readers. The focus is on the moral, rational, and linguistic dimensions of the text. Hirsch has been called a "modern version of the Targum Onkelos" because of his penetrating grasp of philology. First edition in English, 6 vols., translated by Isaac Levy, Gateshead, England: Judaica Press, 1989. This work was originally translated from German into Hebrew, and from Hebrew into English. Second edition, 5 vols., translated by Daniel Haberman, Nanuet, NY: Feldheim Publishers, 2014. The second edition was translated directly from German into English and reads somewhat more fluently.

8. **Ibn Ezra** (E): R. Abraham, 1089–1164. Author of a rationalist commentary on the entire *Tanach,* with ethical implications that approaches the text through grammatical analysis. In English. Many insights of the Ibn Ezra are expounded in the commentary in English by the Ramban from Messorah Publications. See below.

9. **Maharal**: Acronym for Yehuda Loewe, 1526–1606. Author of massive commentaries, including one on the Pentateuch. Combines rational and mystical dimensions. Only small selections translated into English.

10. **Maharasha**: Shlomo Eidls, 1555–1632. This text is commonly referred to by Levinas. His commentaries on the Aggadic sections of the Babylonian Talmud especially provide a background for many of Levinas's Talmudic discourses.

11. **Me'am Loez (MeL)**: Often referred to as the "Rashi of the Sephardic World." Originally begun in Ladino (Spanish-Hebrew) and subsequently translated into Hebrew then English. The project was initiated by R. Yaakov Culi and completed by his disciples. Translation of the initial volumes into English by R. Aryeh Kaplan and completed by others. A compendium of commentary, customs, and laws that reads like a single narrative on each subsection of the Torah.

12. **Yehuda Nachshoni (YN)**: *Studies in the Weekly Parashah*, vols. 1–5, are a five-volume compendium of classical, modern, and contemporary interpretations of major themes in the Torah.

13. **Rebbe Nachman of Breslov (B)**: The great-grandson of the Baal Shem Tov, founder of Chassidism, 1772–1810. One of the most original of the Chassidic masters. Author of many works. Cited in the text, *Rebbe Nachman's Torah*, vols. 1, 2, and 3, Genesis, Exodus/Leviticus, and Numbers/Dueteronomy.

14. **Noam Elimelech**: Of Lizhensk, 1717–1787. Arguably the best-known work of discourses in the Polish Hassidic tradition on the Pentateuch.

15. **Or HaChaim (OH)**: R. Chaim ben Attar, 1696–1743. Multivolume commentary. Inspired rationalist and Kabbalistic multivolume commentary on the Pentateuch. The Or HaChaim is especially illuminating in the way that moral considerations govern economic transactions.

16. **Ralbag**: Acronym for R. Levi ben Gershom, 1288–1344 (Gersonides). He explains the text rationally, particularly the moral lessons of each section, and he offers a summary of philosophical ideas.

17. **Ramban**: Maimonides. Acronym for R. Moshe ben Maimon, 1135–1204, *Guide for the Perplexed (Moreh Nevukim)*. The first chapter of the *Guide for the Perplexed* deals with the use of language in the Torah. It is helpful for all contemporary readers to read this chapter to gain a better understanding of what the Talmud means when it states that "the Torah speaks in the language of human beings." Maimonides comments on many passages within Scripture that are easily accessed by consulting the index of Scriptural passages appended to the M. Friedlander edition to the *Guide for the Perplexed*: Moses Maimonides, *Guide for the Perplexed* (GFP), translated by M. Friedlander, New York: Dover Publications, 1956; *Pearls of the Rambam: Maimonides' Commentary on the Torah*, 2 vols., selected from the *Mishnah Torah* by Rabbi Menachem Mendel Monsohn, English language version prepared by Avraham Berkovitz, Jerusalem: Mosad Harav Kook, 2008. Extremely useful in understanding Maimonides's elucidation of the biblical mitzvot classified by each of the fifty-four portions in the Pentateuch.

18. **Ramban**: R. Moshe ben Nachman (Nachmonides). A classic, balanced, penetrating analysis of the Pentateuch. Ramban is frequently at odds with Rashi on his interpretations. *Ramban Commentary on the Torah*, translated and annotated by Charles B. Chavel, Brooklyn: Judaica Press, 2005. See also, Hebrew/English version, *The Torah with Raban's Commentary Translated, Annotated, and Elucidated*, Brooklyn: Messorah Publications, 2008.

19. **Saadia Gaon**: *The Book of Beliefs and Opinions*, translated by Samuel Rosenblatt, New Haven, CT: Yale University Press, 1989.

20. **Rabbi Jonathan Sacks**: *Torah Studies: A Parsha Anthology*, Brooklyn: Kehot Publication Society, 2012.

21. **Sforno**: Ovaidia Sforno, 1475–1550. *Sforno Commentary on the Torah*, translated by Raphael Pelcovitz, Brooklyn: Messorah Publications, 2009. Sforno

deals with the plain meaning of the text as well as the ethical dimension in a very direct and incisive way.

22. **Sh'lah**: R. Isaiah Horwitz, 1560–1630. Acronym for *Shnie Luchos Habris* (the Two Tablets of the Covenant). A magnificent commentary on the Pentateuch combining rationalist and Kabbalistic approaches.

23. **Schneerson, Menachaem Mendel**: 1902–1994. *Likutei Sichot,* Kehot Publications, Brooklyn, NY, 1980.

24. **Soloveitchik**: R. Yosef Dov, 1903–1993. Also referred to in modern orthodox Jewish circles as "The Rav." Brilliant existential and philosophical analyses, many of which are still on tape. They have extraordinary explanatory power for the contemporary student of Tanach. *Darosh Darash Yosef: Discourses of Rav Yosef Dov Halevi Soloveitchik on the Weekly Parashah*, edited by Rabbi Avishai C. David, Brooklyn: Urim Publications, 2011.

25. **Talmud Bavli (BT)**: Babylonian Talmud. Completed between 499 CE and 505 CE. According to R. Aryeh Kaplan, "[T]he Gemara developed orally for several hundred years following the redaction of Mishnah" (*Handbook of Jewish Thought*). It combines both *Halakah* and *Aggadah* in some seventy-three volumes. It begins with a commentary on the *Mishnah* consisting of six orders and sixty-three tracts compiled from R. Yehuda HaNasi toward the close of the second century of the Common Era. The Mishnah deals almost exclusively with matters of Jewish law, while the Gemara is much more expansive and often goes off in directions that are not visibly connected with the Mishnah under discussion. The Babylonian Talmud includes numerous major commentaries. While the Mishnah is written in Hebrew, the Babylonian Talmud is written in Aramaic.

26. **Talmud Yerushalmi**: The Jerusalem Talmud was composed between the second and fourth centuries in Israel, particularly in the Galilee. It is much more concise than the Babylonian Talmud, but in certain instances, such as the law of the sabbatical year, it is necessary to have recourse to the Jerusalem Talmud. In matters of law it is universally agreed upon that the Babylonian Talmud takes precedence because of its greater scope, later date, and familiarity with the Jerusalem Talmud.

27. **Targum Onkelos**: Written by Onkelos, the Roman proselyte, considered the authoritative Aramaic translation of the Pentateuch. Virtually every published version of the Pentateuch in Hebrew is accompanied by the Targum Onkelos.

28. **Torah Temimah**: Vol. 3. Harav Baruch Halevi Epstein, 1860–1941. A line-by-line exposition of the *Chumash* by an esteemed modern commentator who focuses on the moral dimension of the text in the tradition of the yeshivot of

Lithuania. This commentary is particularly helpful in illuminating the Book of Leviticus.

29. **Chaim Volozhin**: 1749–1821. The primary disciple of the Vilna Gaon. *Nefesh Hachaim* (the Soul of Life) has an introduction to the French edition written by Emmanuel Levinas.

Works Cited

LEVINAS

*Note that some works are abbreviated in text

Levinas, Emmanuel. 1969/1988. *Totality and Infinity* (TI). Translated by Alphonso Lingis. Pittsburgh, PA: Duquesne University Press.

———. 1985. *Ethics and Infinity*. Translated by Richard Cohen. Pittsburgh: Duquesne University Press.

———. 1987. *Collected Philosophical Papers*. Translated by Alphonso Lingis. Dordrecht: Martinus Nijhoff Publishers.

———. 1987. *Time and the Other* (TO). Translated by Richard A. Cohen. Pittsburgh: Duquesne University Press.

———. 1989. *The Levinas Reader* (LR). Edited by Sean Hand. Oxford: Blackwell Publishers.

———. 1990. *Difficult Freedom*. Translated by Sean Hand. Baltimore, MD: Johns Hopkins University Press.

———. 1990. *Nine Talmudic Readings* (NTR). Translation and introduction by Annette Aronowicz. Indianapolis: Indiana University Press.

———. 1991. *Otherwise than Being or Beyond Essence* (OBBE). Translated by Alphonso Lingis. Dordrecht: Kluwer Academic Publishers.

———. 1993. *Outside the Subject* (OTS). Translated by Michael B. Smith. Stanford, CA: Stanford University Press.

———. 1994. *Levinas: Beyond the Verse*. Translated by Gary D. Mole. Indianapolis: Indiana University Press. Alternative: 2007. *Levinas: Beyond the Verse*. Translated by Gary D. Mole. London: Continuum.

———. 1996. *Basic Philosophical Writings*. Bloomington: Indiana University Press.

———. 1996. *Proper Names* (PN). Translated by Michael B. Smith. Stanford, CA: Stanford University Press.

———. 1998. *Of G'd Who Comes to Mind*. Translated by Bettina Bergo. Stanford, CA: Stanford University Press.

———. 1998. *Entre Nous*. Translated by Michael B. Smith and Barbara Harshav. New York: Columbia University Press.

——. 1999. *Alterity & Transcendence*. Translated by Michael B. Smith. New York: Columbia University Press.

——. 1999. *New Talmudic Readings* (NwTR). Translated by Richard A. Cohen. Pittsburgh: Duquesne University Press.

——. 2000. *God, Death, and Time*. Translated by Bettina Bergo. Stanford, CA: Stanford University Press.

——. 2001. *Existence and Existents*. Translated by Alphonso Lingis. Pittsburgh: Duquesne University Press.

——. 2001. *Is It Righteous to Be? Interviews with Emmanuel Levinas*. Edited by Jill Robbins. Stanford, CA: Stanford University Press.

——. 2003. *On Escape* (OE). Translated by Bettina Bergo. Stanford, CA: Stanford University Press.

——. 2004. *Unforeseen History* (UH). Translated by Nidra Poller. Chicago: University of Illinois Press.

——. 2006. *The Promise of Phenomenology: Posthumous Papers of John Wild* (POP). Edited by Richard Sugarman and Roger Duncan. Lanham: Lexington Books.

——. 2007. *In the Time of the Nations*. Translated by Michael Smith. London: Continuum. Alternative: 1994. *In the Time of Nations*. Translated by Michael Smith. Indianapolis: Indiana University Press.

COMMENTATORS AND RABBINIC TEXTS

2012. *Babylonian Talmud* (*Talmud Bavli*) (BT). Schottenstein edition. Brooklyn: Mesorah.

Culi, Rabbi Yaakov. 1977. *The Torah Anthology: Me'am Loez Series* (MeL). Translated by Rabbi Aryeh Kaplan. Brooklyn: Moznaim.

David, Rabbi Avishai C., ed. 2011. *Darosh Darash Yosef: Discourses of Rav Yosef Dov Halevi Soloveitchik on the Weekly Parashah* (DDY). Jerusalem: Urim Publications.

Kleinman, ed. 2013. *Midrash Rabbah* (MR). Hebrew English ed. Brooklyn: Mesorah.

Maimonides, Moses. 1956. *Guide for the Perplexed* (GFP). Translated by M. Friedlander. New York: Dover Publications.

Torah Temimah, Vol. 3. 1989. Translated by Rav Shraga Silverstein. Spring Valley, NY: Feldhein Publishers.

NOT ABBREVIATED IN TEXT

Ajzenstat, Oona. 2001. *Driven Back to the Text: The Premodern Sources of Levinas's Postmodernism.* Pittsburgh: Duquesne University Press.

Akedas Yitzchak. 1997. *Akeydas Yitzchak: Commentary on the Torah.* Vols. 1–2. Brooklyn: Mesorah.

Akeydat Yitzchak: Commentary of Rabbi Yitzchak Arama on the Torah. 1990. Vols. 1–2, second edition. Translated and condensed by Eliyahu Munk. Jerusalem, Israel. Urim Publications.

Aristotle. 1999. *Nichomachean Ethics.* Translated by Terrance Irwin. Indianapolis: Hackett Publishing.

Aronowicz, Annette. 2003. "The Little Man with the Burned Thighs: Levinas's Biblical Hermeneutic." In *Levinas and Biblical Studies,* edited by Tamara Cohn Eskenazi, Gary A. Phillips, and David Jobling. Atlanta, GA: Society of Biblical Literature.

Attar, Rabbi Chayim Ben. 1999. *Or HaChayim: Commentary on the Torah.* Vols. 1–5. Translated and annotated by Eliyahu Munk. Jerusalem: Lambda Publishers.

Bamidbar. 2005. *Midrash Tanchuma.* Translated by Rabbi Menachem Davis. Brooklyn: Eastern Book Press.

Buber, Martin. 2014. *Between Man and Man.* New York: Macmillan.

Chofetz Chaim (Rabbi Yisrael Meir Kagan haKohen). 1990. *The Concise Book of Mitzvoth: The Commandments Which Can Be Observed Today.* Jerusalem: Feldheim Publishers.

Cohen, Richard. 2000. "Biblical Humanism and Its Relevance to the Humanities." *Phenomenological Inquiry,* 65–79. Vol 24. Belmont, MA: The World Institute for Advanced Phenomenological Research and Learning.

——. 2010. *Levinasian Meditations: Ethics, Philosophy, and Religion.* Pittsburgh: Duquesne University Press.

Eisenmann, Moshe. 2002. *Beginnings.* Baltimore, 104–10.

Epstein, Harav Baruch Halevi. 1989. *Torah Temimiah.* Vol. 3. Spring Valley, NY: Feldheim Publishers.

Gaon, Saadia. 1989. *The Book of Beliefs and Opinions* (Emunah V'daas). Translated by Samuel Rosenblatt. New Haven, CT: Yale University Press.

Hansel, Georges. 2012. "The Bible, the Talmud, and Sacrifice." Originally based upon a lecture that he gave at a conference in Paris, Winter Session.

Hirsch, Samson Raphael. 1981/1962. (Horeb) *Horeb: A Philosophy of Jewish Laws and Observances.* Translated by Dayan I. Grunfeld. New York: The Soncino Press.

Kahan, Rabbi A.Y. 1987. *The Taryag Mitzvos*. Brooklyn: Keser Torah Publications.

Kaplan, Aryeh. 1992. *Handbook of Jewish Thought*. Vol. 1, 2. Brooklyn: Moznaim Publishing.

Kimchi and Abarbanel. 1994. *The Twelve Prophets*, Revised 2nd Edition. New York: Soncino Books.

Kramer, Chaim, ed. 2011. *Rebbe Nachman's Torah*. Lakewood, NJ: Breslov Research Institute.

Levinas, Emmanuel. 2003. *Humanism of the Other*. Translated by Nidra Poller. Chicago: University of Illinois Press.

Maimonides, Hilchos Melachim. 1997. *Mishneh Torah: Hilchos De'os*. Translated and annotated by Eliyahu Touger. Brooklyn: Moiznaim Publishing.

Maimonides, Hilchos Melachim. 2005. *Mishneh Torah*. Brooklyn: Mozniam Publishing Corporation.

Maimonides, Moses (Rambam). 2008. *Pearls of the Rambam*. Vols. 1–2. Translated by Avraham Berkovitz. Jerusalem: Mosad Harav Kook.

Malka, Solomon. 2006. *Emmanuel Levinas: His Life and Legacy*. Pittsburgh: Duquesne University Press.

Nachshoni, Yehuda. 1988. *Studies in the Weekly Parashah*. Vols. 1–5. Brooklyn: Mesorah Publications.

Ouaknin, Marc-Alain. 1998. *The Burnt Book: Reading the Talmud*. Princeton, NJ: Princeton University Press.

Peperzak, Adriaan Theodoor. 1997. "The Platonism of Emmanuel Levinas." In *Platonic Transformations*. Lanham: Roman & Littlefield.

Rashi (Solomon ben Isaac). 1995. *The Metsudah Chumash/Rashi: Bamidbar*. Vol. 4. Translation by Rabbi Avrohom Davis. Hoboken. NJ: KTAV Publishing House.

——. 1994. *The Torah: With Rashi's Commentary Translated, Annotated, and Elucidated*. Vol 3: *Vayikra/Leviticus*. Saperstein ed. Edited by Rabbi Yisrael Isser Zvi Herczeg. Brooklyn: Mesorah Publications.

Scherman, Rabbi Nosson, ed. 1993. *The Chumash*. Stone Edition. Brooklyn: Mesorah Publications.

Straus, Erwin Walter. 1980. *Phenomenological Psychology*. New York: Garland Publishing.

Sugarman, Richard. 1980. *Rancor against Time: The Phenomenology of "Ressentiment."* Hamburg: Felix Meiner Verlag.

——. 2002. "Emmanuel Levinas: The Ethics of the Face to Face/the Religious Turn." In *Phenomenology World-Wide: A Guide for Research and Study*, edited by Anna-Teresa Tymieniecka. Dordrecht, Netherlands: Kluwer Academic Publishers.

——. Commentary on "To Love the Torah More than God," by Emmanuel Levinas. *Judaism* 28, no. 110 (spring 1979): 216–23.

Telushkin, Joseph. 1991. *Jewish Literacy*. New York: William Morrow/Harper Collins.

Wygoda, Shmuel. 2006. "The Phenomenology of Time in the Philosophy of Levinas: Temporality and Otherness in the Hebraic Tradition." In *Analecta Husserliana*, edited by Anna-Theresa Tymieniecka. Dordrecht, Netherlands: Springer.

Zornberg, Avivah Gottlieb. 1995/2011. *The Beginning of Desire: Reflections on Genesis*. New York: Knopf Doubleday Publishing Group.

SECONDARY SOURCES ON LEVINAS

Ajzenstat, Oona. 2001. *Driven Back to the Text: The Premodern Sources of Levinas's Postmodernism*. Pittsburgh: Duquesne University Press.

Burggreave, Roger, et al. 2012. *Levinas Autrement*. Series Bibliotheque Philosophique de Louvain. Leueven, Belgium: Peeters Publishers.

——, Joelle Hansel, et al. 2012. *Recherches Levinassiennes*. Series Bibliotheque Philosophique de Louvain. Leuven, Belgium: Peeters Publishers.

——. 2002. *The Wisdom of Love in the Service of Love*. Milwaukee, WI: Marquette University Press.

Cohen, Richard A. 1986. *Face to Face with Levinas*. Albany: State University of New York Press.

——. 1994. *Elevations*. Chicago: University of Chicago Press.

——. 2001. *Ethics, Exegesis and Philosophy: Interpretation After Levinas*. Cambridge, UK: Cambridge University Press.

——. 2010. *Levinasian Meditations: Ethics, Philosophy, and Religion*. Pittsburgh: Duquesne University Press.

De Boer, Theo. 1997. *The Rationality of Transcendence: Studies in the Philosophy of Emmanuel Levinas*. Amsterdam, Netherlands: C.G. Geiben.

Hansel, Georges, and Cristian Ciocan. 2005. *Levinas Concordance*. Dordrecht, Netherlands: Springer.

——. 2010. *Israel's Singularity and Ethical Universality*. Toulouse, France: Summer.

Hansel, Joelle. 2006. *Levinas de l'être a l'Autre*. Paris: Presses Universitaires de France.

Katz, Claire Elise. 2003. *Levinas, Judaism, and the Feminine*. Bloomington: Indiana University Press.

Newton, Adam Zachary. 2001. *The Fence and the Neighbor*. Albany: State University of New York Press.

Paden, William E. 2016. *New Patterns of Comparative Religion: Passages to an Evolutionary Perspective*. London: Bloomsbury Academic.

Peperzak, Adriaan Theodoor. 1997. *Beyond: The Philosophy of Emmanuel Levinas*. Evanston, IL: Northwestern University Press.

Peperzak, Adriaan. 1993. *To the Other: An Introduction to the Philosophy of Emmanuel Levinas*. West Lafayette, IN: Purdue University Press.

Tymieniecka, Anna-Teresa, ed. 2002. "Emmanuel Levinas: The Ethics of 'Face to Face'/The Religious Turn." *Phenomenology World-Wide: A Guide for Research and Study*. Dordrecht, Netherlands: Kluwer Academic Publishers.

Index

Printed in Great Britain
by Amazon

44347629R00253